The Second Fifty Years

Promoting Health and Preventing Disability

Robert L. Berg and Joseph S. Cassells, Editors

INSTITUTE OF MEDICINE
Division of Health Promotion and Disease Prevention

National Academy Press
Washington, D.C. 1990

National Academy Press • 2101 Constitution Avenue, N.W. • Washington, DC 20418

NOTICE: The project that is the subject of this report was approved by the Governing Board of the National Research Council, whose members are drawn from the councils of the National Academy of Sciences, the National Academy of Engineering, and the Institute of Medicine. The members of the committee responsible for the report were chosen for their special competencies and with regard for appropriate balance.

This report has been reviewed by a group other than the authors according to procedures approved by a Report Review Committee consisting of members of the National Academy of Sciences, the National Academy of Engineering, and the Institute of Medicine.

The Institute of Medicine was chartered in 1970 by the National Academy of Sciences to enlist distinguished members of the appropriate professions in the examination of policy matters pertaining to the health of the public. In this, the Institute acts under both the Academy's 1863 congressional charter responsibility to be an adviser to the federal government and its own initiative in identifying issues of medical care, research, and education.

This project was supported by funds from the National Institute on Aging, the National Institute for Dental Research, the Food and Drug Administration, the Alliance on Aging, the Charles A. Dana Foundation, and the Pew Charitable Trusts.

Library of Congress Cataloging-in-Publication Data

Institute of Medicine (U.S.). Division of Health Promotion and
    Disease Prevention.
        The second fifty years : promoting health and preventing
    disability / Division of Health Promotion and Disease Prevention,
    Institue of Medicine.
            p. cm.
        Report of a study undertaken by the Committee on Health Promotion
    and Disability Prevention for the Second Fifty.
        Includes bibliographical references.
        Includes index.
        ISBN 0-309-04339-5
        1. Aged—Health and hygiene—United States. 2. Health promotion—
    United States. 3. Aged—Diseases—United States. 4. Aged—
    Services for—United States. 5. Primary Prevention—in old age.
    I. Institute of Medicine (U.S.). Committee on Health Promotion and
    Disability Prevention for the Second Fifty. II. Title.
        [DNLM: 1. Health Promotion—United States. 2. Health Services for
    the Aged—trends—United States.   WT 30 I5915]
    RA564.8I57   1991
    613'.0438' 0973—dc20
    DNLM/DLC
    for Library of Congress   90-13385
                                                                    CIP

Cover photograph: SUPERSTOCK, Inc.

Acknowledgment
Joseph Stokes III, M.D.
1924-1989

———

The Committee on Health Promotion and Disability Prevention for the Second Fifty would like to make special mention of the contribution of Joseph Stokes III, M.D. Dr. Stokes was instrumental in organizing and outlining the risk factors to be researched for this project, and his passing provided personal inspiration to the committee for further research in the area of cancer screening. This report was created to provide effective preventive and intervention procedures for physicians, the public, long-term care facilities, colleges, and universities. It is the committee's wish that this information will help raise the consciousness of the American public regarding healthy life practices and aging.

Committee on Health Promotion and Disability Prevention for the Second Fifty

ROBERT BERG (*Chairman*), Professor and Chairman, Department of Preventive, Family/Rehabilitation Medicine, Strong Memorial Hospital, Rochester, New York

ELIZABETH T. ANDERSON, Professor and Chair, Community Health and Gerontology Department, University of Texas Medical Branch, School of Nursing, Galveston

WILLIAM APPLEGATE, Chief, Division of Geriatric Medicine, University of Tennessee, Memphis

JEROME AVORN, Director, Program for Analysis of Clinical Strategies, Harvard Medical School, Boston, Massachusetts

BEN D. BARKER, Professor and Dean, School of Dentistry, University of North Carolina, Chapel Hill

JOHANNA T. DWYER, Director, Frances Stern Nutrition Center, New England Medical Center Hospital, and Professor of Medicine and Community Health, Tufts University Medical School, Boston, Massachusetts

A. ALAN FISCHER, Professor and Chairman, Department of Family Medicine, Indiana University School of Medicine, Indianapolis

PEARL S. GERMAN, Professor, Department of Health Policy and Management, School of Hygiene and Public Health, Johns Hopkins University, Baltimore, Maryland

L. JOSEPH MELTON III, Professor and Head, Section of Clinical Epidemiology, Mayo Clinic, Rochester, Minnesota

RISA LAVIZZO-MOUREY, Acting Director, Program in Geriatric Medicine, University of Pennsylvania, Philadelphia

GEORGE C. ROUSH, Director of Research, Cancer Prevention Research Institute, New York, New York

FREDERICK L. RUBEN, Professor of Medicine, University of Pittsburgh School of Medicine, Pittsburgh, Pennsylvania

ANNE R. SOMERS, Adjunct Professor, Robert Wood Johnson Medical School, University of Medicine and Dentistry of New Jersey, Haverford, Pennsylvania

JOSEPH STOKES III,* Boston University Medical Center, Boston, Massachusetts

ALBERT J. STUNKARD, Professor of Psychiatry and Psychology, University of Pennsylvania School of Medicine, Philadelphia

Liaison Members

LEOPOLD G. SELKER, Associate Dean for Academic Affairs, College of Associated Health Professions, University of Illinois at Chicago, Chicago

R. KNIGHT STEEL, West Newton, Massachusetts

Commissioned Writers

ARTHUR L. CAPLAN, University of Minnesota Center for Biomedical Ethics, Minneapolis (Appendix A)

MICHAEL NEVITT, Clinical Epidemiology Program, San Francisco General Hospital, University of California, San Francisco (Chapter 15)

Consultants

HELEN C. GIFT, Chief, Health Promotion Section, National Institute of Dental Research, Bethesda, Maryland

SHIRLEY P. BAGLEY, Assistant Director for Special Programs, National Institute on Aging, Bethesda, Maryland

Institute of Medicine Staff

GARY B. ELLIS, *Division Director*

JOSEPH S. CASSELLS, *Study Director*

TED MILLER, *Research Assistant*

CRISTELLYN D. BANKS, *Special Project Assistant/Sr. Secretary*

---

*Deceased May 1989.

Preface

———

Although the advances of recent years in the field of public health and acute care have been unprecedented, we are having trouble coping with success. People live longer, but their lives are not necessarily better. To accommodate the changing needs of an increasingly older society, we must broaden the traditional goals of health—curing disease and preventing its occurrence—to include preventing the ill from becoming disabled and helping the disabled cope with and prevent further disability. Dealing with disease must include dealing with the consequences of disease.

This report of the study undertaken by the Committee on Health Promotion and Disability Prevention for the Second Fifty was written to assist the health care community in achieving this crucial transition. It is also the product of the Institute of Medicine's (IOM) long-standing interest in examining the aging population. A number of recent IOM publications (*Health in an Older Society, Aging in Today's Environment, The Social and Built Environment in an Aging Society,* and *Improving the Quality of Care of Nursing Homes*) have addressed the effects of ever-increasing numbers of elderly citizens on public attitudes, public behavior, and public policies. This report extends that interest to specific health issues and risk factor modification.

The dynamism of American health care demands an equally dynamic report. In the past several years, the number and scope of health promotion and disease and disability prevention programs have expanded significantly. This expansion can be attributed to a wide range of sources that include not only recent scientific findings but also new philosophies of health care. In the future, some of these new approaches may prove extremely beneficial to the health of older Americans. Nevertheless, the purpose of this report is not to provide an updated list of everything that is new. Rather, it was written primarily as an analysis of those approaches to health promotion and disability prevention for which there are adequate data from which to draw intelligent conclusions that may benefit the nation's older population.

The committee believes that the innovative drive that animates U.S. health care today is a positive force, but it also believes that the course of American health care must be guided by a careful balance of optimism and prudence. The report therefore measures the effectiveness of new techniques designed to achieve old but worthy goals—such as improving nutrition and oral health and reducing hypertension and osteoporosis—and analyzes the current debate concerning new goals. Although no report is likely to satisfy every need, readers of this volume will find a wide variety of topics, ranging from the controversial techniques of intervention to the philosophical assumptions that inform broad health care goals. They will also find specific recommendations for the service, research, and education communities. In short, it is our hope that every reader will find something of interest—and something useful as well.

Robert L. Berg, Chairman
Joseph S. Cassells, Study Director

Contents

————

Appendixes

The Second Fifty Years

Summary

─────

Americans are growing older. People over age 65 make up about 12 percent of the population now, and their proportion is predicted to reach 23 percent by the year 2040. The implications of an aging population for health care are being widely discussed but seldom with the understanding that health promotion and disability prevention are workable concepts for people in the "second 50" years of life.

Toward that end, an assortment of diseases, causes of injury, and risk factors was selected for examination in this study. All play a significant role in disability in older people. They are misuse of medications, social isolation, physical inactivity, osteoporosis, falls, sensory loss, depression, oral health, screening for cancer, nutrition, smoking, high blood pressure, and infectious diseases. In the broadest sense they all are risk factors; each may function as the initial or early stage of a train of events leading to disability. High blood pressure (or hypertension) is a useful example of these relationships. It is a disease, but it is also a powerful causative factor for strokes and coronary artery disease, disorders that involve impairments of organ function; these may be followed in turn by losses of everyday personal functions and, ultimately, limitations in social roles. The World Health Organization has built a classification system around the transition from physical impairments on the organ level, to losses of personal function such as hygiene and feeding, to limitations in more social settings—conditions of impairment, disability, and

1

handicap, respectively. This system is discussed and recommended by the committee as a framework for the consequences of disease in Chapter 2.

Besides a causal role in the process of disablement, each of the 13 issues selected met two other criteria. They had to affect appreciable numbers of older people, and interventions to modify them had to be available, although not necessarily fully developed. Although arthritis and Alzheimer's disease are not included in this report, their absence here should not be taken as a signal that they are undeserving of national attention.

The report covers a wide range of health policies. Each chapter provides a definition of the health risks related to the central topic, a discussion of incidence and prevalence, costs and measures of cost, remediability, and a set of recommendations to the research, education, and service communities. These chapters address fields with varying degrees of maturity. Some issues such as high blood pressure, osteoporosis, and smoking are familiar to health care professionals, and so these chapters have been written to inform policymakers and the public about the latest findings and their relevance for health policy. Other issues such as physical inactivity, depression, nutrition, and sensory loss are familiar topics but still in the early stages of development in terms of research, service standards, and procedures to address the functional difficulties of older people. These chapters discuss the available evidence and suggest ways in which these fields should be broadened in light of the aging population. Of this latter group, perhaps social isolation is the youngest of all. This chapter therefore discusses strategies for laying theoretical groundwork.

GENERAL ISSUES OF HEALTH PROMOTION AND DISABILITY PREVENTION

Unfortunately, American culture clings to some very pessimistic assumptions about aging. Growing old is often associated with frailty, sickness, and a loss of vitality. We frequently assume that older individuals are a burden to the state, their families, or even to themselves. In fact, many older individuals lead satisfying lives and maintain their health well beyond society's expectations.

"Quality of life": we are called upon as health professionals to improve it, yet it is an elusive goal. Certainly one reason is that no one individual or institution has proposed a definition that all can agree with. The committee will not attempt a definition in this report but would simply like to put forth the observation that health professionals who do not believe that there is a "quality life" for older people will not strive to assist older individuals to achieve it. The same could be said of society in general. Our misplaced pessimism gives rise to the particularly troubling consequence that many more individuals who could experience a fulfilling maturity are denied the chance by these stereotypes.

This pessimistic attitude toward aging is carried over into our nation's health policies. Health research, education, and service policies are often written as though our older generations are beyond help. Although there is sufficient evidence of the benefits of health promotion and disability prevention among older individuals, many of them are not advised to stop smoking, to begin exercising, to be screened for various forms of cancer, or to be immunized against infectious diseases. Research with older people can be challenging methodologically and ethically, but the future centrality of health in old age means that these difficulties should be addressed now.

Obviously, older people encounter more health problems than the general population, but there ought to be a distinction between pessimism and realism. Realistically, we can expect that an aging population will mean a significant increase in the number of individuals seeking care for chronic illnesses, disabilities, and acute conditions. Nevertheless, we should not let pessimism become an obstacle to the introduction of new research on interventions to restore and maintain function among physically or mentally impaired older people. There are ways to help individuals keep their physical limitations from becoming major limitations in society, and these ought to be pursued through a combination of research, health services policy, education, and legislation.

The foremost reason for expanding health and social services to the elderly ought to be the benefits provided to individuals, but there are also societal benefits involved in health promotion and disability prevention. When older individuals are denied the opportunity to participate in constructive roles, it is not simply they who are cheated. The most obvious example occurs when we deny someone who is capable, but there is also the hidden discrimination of denying opportunities to regain these capabilities.

An essential part of a new outlook on the health needs of the aging population is to recognize our responsibility to improve the quality of life for those who have already become ill or are disabled. Two goals have been at the core of health care: to cure disease and to prevent its occurrence. To accommodate the changing needs of an increasingly older society we must add several imperatives: we must promote health throughout life, and we must also prevent the ill from becoming disabled and help the disabled to prevent further disability.

The central message of all the chapters of this report is intended for a broad audience, but it can be most clearly articulated when addressed directly to practicing health professionals, especially physicians. That message is: the responsibility neither begins nor ends with acute care. Individuals who come to physicians should be encouraged to adopt healthier lifestyles and avail themselves of preventive services. Patients with successfully treated acute conditions may need rehabilitation and assistance in learning to cope with long-term residual physical impairments. Moreover, a majority of older individuals are likely to have chronic conditions that greatly increase the chances for some kind of functional limitation. Older individuals do experience some diminution of function, but many of today's health professionals dismiss virtually all functional limitations as the natural consequences of aging. A major purpose of this report is to dissuade health professionals from the belief that growing old necessarily means growing frail.

CONCLUSIONS AND RECOMMENDATIONS

The committee recognizes that the risks associated with disease and disability in later life are linked to unhealthy behavior in earlier years. However, a full review of all health promotion activities is beyond the scope of this report. The full report, therefore, includes recommendations for new services, research, and professional and public education largely devoted to the later half of life. This section of the summary provides a brief description of the major points asserted in each of the chapters. The committee's major conclusion can be summarized as follows: *The long-term consequences of disease are too important to ignore. The health professional's responsibility cannot begin or end with cure.*

High Blood Pressure

• Medicare and private insurance should reimburse for physician visits to evaluate blood pressure.

• Public education and public health strategies need to be developed to promote detection and treatment of high blood pressure, especially among black males, isolated older persons, and other people unlikely to have access to periodic health care.

• Research should be performed to determine the cost-effectiveness of treating mild diastolic high blood pressure in older people, with emphasis on quality-adjusted life years.

• The efficacy of nonpharmacologic intervention in treating diastolic or isolated systolic high blood pressure in older people should be tested further.

• More sophisticated measures of risk in mild hypertensives over age 50 are needed.

Medications

• The proper medication can have a significant therapeutic effect; improper medication can be disabling and deadly.

• Age must be taken into account when testing drugs for efficacy, side effects, and dosage. Very few drugs now undergo testing in the elderly.

• Health professionals must learn more about the drugs their older patients are taking, both prescribed and unprescribed, and the multiple manifestations of the adverse reactions associated with their use.

• Older people must learn more about the medicines they take, the signals that prompt a consultation with their physician, and the enhanced danger of taking multiple medications.

Infectious Diseases

• Pneumonia and influenza are among the leading causes of death and morbidity from infection among older people.

• Safe and effective vaccines to prevent pneumonia and influenza are available and should be universally used in persons over age 50.

• Nosocomial (institutionally acquired) infections have a major deleterious impact on persons over 50 and require good infection control practices in hospitals and nursing homes.

Osteoporosis

• Osteoporosis progresses silently until fractures occur; therapy cannot then replace lost bone. Additional research is needed to design cost-effective screening programs so that those at high risk of osteoporosis can be identified and treated early.

• The number of osteoporotic fractures that will occur each year is large and will continue to increase in the foreseeable future.

New efforts are needed to identify the determinants of poor outcomes following these fractures and to develop optimal patient management programs that reduce disability to the extent possible.

- Older persons would be wise to ensure adequate calcium and vitamin D intake, reduce tobacco and excessive alcohol use, and increase physical activity although data about the efficacy of these measures to prevent age-related fractures are limited.
- Postmenopausal women, especially those who experienced an early menopause, should discuss with their physicians the desirability of estrogen replacement therapy.

Sensory Loss

- Standardized definitions of sensory loss in vision and hearing need to be established.
- The availability and accessibility of services or devices to prevent sensory losses from becoming personal and social disadvantages need to be improved. Public and private insurers should consider covering the cost of these items.
- Further research including longitudinal studies is needed to gain a greater understanding of single and multiple sensory losses.

Oral Health

- Dental and oral disabilities are unnecessary and preventable in adults.
- Attaining oral health goals requires appropriate patterns of self care, access to appropriate professional services, and fluoridation of community water supplies.
- Greater efforts should be made to determine the incidence, prevalence, and natural history of dental and oral disabilities as well as the cost-effectiveness of interventions for their prevention and control.

Cancer Screening

- Existing studies indicate that screening for cancer will be at least as effective in persons aged 50 to 80 as in younger persons.
- Cancers in older persons are at least as biologically aggressive as cancers in younger persons.
- *Nonetheless*, data indicate that several populations of women over age 50 have 12 to 17 percent less screening for cancers of the breast and cervix as compared with younger populations.

Nutrition

- Diet and nutrition are as important in the promotion and maintenance of the health of older people as in younger people; they are critical in the causation and control of many health problems.
- Functionally related assessments and screening of nutritional status should be routine among older individuals, especially those in nursing homes.
- Because nutrition plays an important role in health before, during, and after illness, interventions should be comprehensive. In particular, consideration should be given to interventions that recognize the essential contribution of nutrition to the quality of life and independent function.
- We know very little about the minimal daily nutrient and energy requirements for older people; further research is needed.

Smoking

- It is never too late to stop smoking. People of all ages should be advised against smoking.
- All advertising of tobacco products should be banned.
- Policymakers should continue to promote smoke-free environments.

Depression

- Support for research on depression in the elderly, including estimates of its prevalence, should be increased.
- Physician training to detect and treat depression in older persons must be improved and expanded.
- Discriminatory limitations of reimbursement for psychiatric care by Medicare and other insurers must be removed.

Physical Inactivity

- A sedentary lifestyle creates unnecessary health risks. Older individuals can avoid these risks, maintain self control, and gain a sense of empowerment by becoming physically active.
- Physical activity can be promoted through social support in the community and home, through improving perceptions of health and self, and by creating access to safe, convenient, and inexpensive places to exercise.
- Health care professionals should collaborate with exercise

specialists in developing programs in exercise counseling, promotion, and instruction.

- Research should focus on behavioral change and should attempt to make exercise a routine practice for older adults.

Social Isolation

- A lack of family and community supports plays an important role in the development and exacerbation of disease. An absence of social support reduces compliance with medical care regimes and weakens the body's defenses through psychological stress.
- Isolated individuals must be identified, and strategies for increasing social contact and diminishing feelings of loneness must be developed.
- Clinicians, family, friends, and social institutions bear a responsibility for diminishing social isolation.
- Clinics and various types of community organizations may offer solutions to social isolation by increasing their contact with older people.

Falls

- Falls among the elderly are a major cause of mortality, morbidity, and disability. Hip fracture is the most devastating consequence of falls, but other fractures, severe soft tissue injury, fear of falling, and loss of mobility and independence are frequent and often serious consequences. Effective prevention of falls could substantially reduce disability among the elderly.
- Most falls in the elderly are multifactorial, resulting from the convergence of health-related, pharmacologic, environmental, behavioral, and activity-related causes. The interaction of these risk factors for falling is poorly understood. Studies are needed to increase understanding of the causal role of these antecedents to falls.
- Prevention of falls must not unnecessarily compromise quality of life and independence of the elderly. Controlled trials are needed to determine which treatable risk factors are causal and to guide prevention efforts. In particular, randomized trials of exercise and strength training, conservative use of psychotropic medications, and targeted treatment of selected chronic and acute medical conditions are needed.

• Studies of the biomechanical and other determinants of fall injuries, particularly the understanding of impact responses and tolerances, should be emphasized as a potential means of preventing fall injuries through the environmental control of mechanical energy. This might lead to the design of energy-absorbing surfaces or unobtrusive protective clothing for high-risk older persons.

1

Introduction

Living is not the good, but living well.
The wise man therefore lives as long as he should,
not as long as he can. He will observe where
he is to live, with whom, how, and what he is to do.
He will always think of life in terms of
quality, not quantity.

— Seneca

T he United States is an aging society. The elderly (aged 65 and older) constituted 12.4 percent of the population in 1988, and this proportion is projected to rise to approximately 14 percent in 2010, accelerating to nearly 22 percent by 2030.[49] Today, this age group comprises some 30 million people; it is expected to grow to 39 million in 2010 and 66 million in 2030. Paralleling this growth is an overall increase in the median age of the U.S. population. From the present all-time high of 32.1 years the median age is projected to rise to 36 years in the year 2000 and to 42 years in 2030. The bolus effect of the baby boom cohort is less influential after 2030, and the median age rises more slowly thereafter. Nevertheless, it continues to rise.

Although the human life span has not changed, human life expectancy has changed dramatically. Life expectancy at birth is now 74.8 years—78.3 for females and 71.3 for males.[39] Moreover, the elderly population itself is becoming older. Of those over the age of 65, 9.6 percent are aged 85 or older, and that percentage will reach 15.5 percent in 2010.

The implications of these demographics for health care in a society with finite resources are enormous, involving medical, social, and economic dilemmas that cannot be ignored. Already the nation's annual expenditures for health approach a half trillion dollars, and the public portion of that figure, reflected in Medicare and Medicaid expenditures, is more than 50 percent and rising. More telling, 30 percent of Medicare costs are for care in the last year of life. Should we continue to devote these resources to the provision of acute care, or should we allocate more of them to prolong independent functioning in a community setting? A major factor in whether prolonged well-being can be achieved will be the success of programs for health promotion and disease and disability prevention.

Typically, such programs have been targeted at the young and the middle-aged, but there is increasing evidence to suggest that they are useful to older individuals as well.[24,35,40] In particular, these programs bring a valuable perspective to chronic illness in the over-50 population. Older individuals are more likely than younger persons to experience such illness, which often triggers processes that begin with physical impairment but that may progress into a myriad of limitations: the loss of independent function, emotional difficulties, and impediments to daily, work-related, and social activities. Many older persons can be spared all or part of this progression to dependency and diminished function, but reversing such a course requires attention by health professionals not only to the disease itself but also to its consequences.

Health promotion and disability prevention supports and encourages healthful behavior and the prevention of chronic and acute conditions through risk reduction. This approach also makes room for broader notions of disability care and prevention, departing from traditional disease model frameworks in the care of the elderly in a number of ways. With this new perspective, prevention is more comprehensive; that is, points of prevention for chronic illness and disability are defined throughout life, including periods after the onset of these difficulties. Rehabilitation and social supports that recognize the heterogeneity of the older population are also an important part of this approach.

Chronic illness and disability are constant companions of the elderly today and are likely to remain so, at least for the near term. Whatever progress is made in the prolongation of functional independence will come slowly and will depend heavily on research in the basic biology of aging and the genetic determinants of age and predisposition to disease. With that reality in mind, common sense dictates moving from the traditional primary prevention/"cure" model to a framework that incorporates the reduction of morbidity and the maintenance of maximal functioning as its goal. Intuitively, such a shift makes economic sense as well. But are there interventions that will produce these outcomes?

This report attempts to address some of these issues. It has been prepared by the Committee on Health Promotion and Disability Prevention for the Second Fifty. Why the "second fifty?" The human life span is about 100 years, and there is evidence that around the 50th birthday, people begin to consider their mortality and pay more attention to their health.[34]

Improvements in methods of health promotion and disability prevention for people over the age of 50—including improvements in the care and advice given by health professionals—could yield major dividends in the form of physical, mental, and social well-being with reduced functional disability, a shortened term of expensive medical services, and a postponement of long-term care. It is only within recent years that older populations have been the focus of research in the field of health promotion and disease and disability prevention.[7,20,25,35,38] Indeed, there is little agreement about what health promotion and disability prevention means for the health of persons over the age of 50. Even when related data have been available, there have been few analyses that draw inferences for older populations, little effort to quantify the benefits of such programs, and no consensus on what the evidence might mean for research and clinical practice among those aged 50 and older.[9,13,48] In addition, there has been no systematic consolidation of the literature on rehabilitation practices in older populations with that on health promotion and disability prevention. As a result, there is little information on a number of difficult questions for the over-50 age group.[6,21,45] For example, what age groupings or functional categories should be developed for this group to target health promotion and disability prevention interventions more effectively? What is known about the effects of such risk factors as smoking, high blood pressure, oral diseases, poor nutrition, and inactivity on different age segments of this population? What are the mechanisms and intervening processes that result in undesirable health effects or losses of functional ability?

Prevention of premature disability and mortality for older individuals requires greater understanding of the changes in risk factors for these groups. Thus, one of the most significant problems facing those who would design interventions for the older population is the lack of an updated risk factor knowledge base. Most risk factor research has involved either the general population, the young, or the middle-aged.[7,38,56] There have been few systematic studies of special risks, high or low, among those aged 50 and older.[9,12] In addition, there are serious shortcomings in knowledge about the mutability of behaviors already classified as risks.[10,32]

The relative lack of knowledge on risk factors for those over 50 has led to several major efforts to acquire more longitudinal cohort data. The ongoing Framingham studies[33] and the longitudinal research known as the Alameda County studies are being used to address some of the questions about risk factors for older persons. Ongoing work at the National Cancer Institute (NCI) exploring the risk of occurrence and reoccurrence of malignancy in those over the age of 50 will further strengthen this knowledge base.[32] Findings from the Centers for Disease Control (CDC) risk factor update project and statewide risk factor surveys[14] and the National Health and Nutrition Examination Survey (NHANES) follow-up studies[15] are other important additions to understanding.

Over the past decade the Public Health Service (PHS) has begun to identify priorities in health promotion and disease prevention for the general population.[1,52,53,54] In addition, the recently released U.S. Preventive Services Task Force report on clinical preventive services[18] and the Carter Center Health Policy Project[2] have developed listings of priority health conditions. Of the two earlier noteworthy attempts to set health priorities for older populations, one dates from 1981,[19] and the other covers chronic conditions only.[40] The Health Objectives for the Year 2000 project will be particularly helpful in updating these priorities. A forthcoming Institute of Medicine report on a national research agenda on aging will add substantially to the knowledge base as well.

Information is still lacking on a number of important aspects of risk for older persons. Research designs for examining the effects of risk factors on older persons should include social epidemiological as well as medical factors.[5,8,11,29,32,37,42,47,56] Questions such as the specific impacts of social isolation and socioeconomic status, as well as the effects of other social epidemiologic variables, on the health status[28] of older persons warrant careful attention. Answers to such questions may be found in part through review and classification of the evidence on both the physiological correlates of psychosocial changes[44] and the interaction between biological and behavioral risk factors.

Another area that requires greater understanding is the severity or strength of particular risk factors for older individuals. Although much is known, for example, about a number of factors of coronary heart disease risk (e.g., cigarette smoking, high blood pressure, high blood cholesterol[17], the strength of other such factors (e.g., high dietary sodium,[27,43] obesity[3,17]) is currently under challenge. A key task involves determining which methods are most valid for revealing the strength of risk factors for the over-50 population.

In short, an integrated, coherent synthesis of existing findings, in the form of an updated knowledge base, must be developed to enable the required advances in research and clinical practice. Although the National Institutes of Health consensus development conferences[17] and the U.S. Preventive Services Task Force[18] offer models for assessing what is known, these approaches have not yet systematically focused on currently available information on risk factors among older persons. Merely assembling the risk factor literature poses formidable problems because the information is scattered and lacks any consensus on key terms. Although researchers typically keep abreast of the literature on risk factors in the realm of their disciplinary interests, the limited scope of their work often fails to take account of the interactive nature of multiple risk factor problems in older persons. More important, there seems to be little agreement on the form of informational structures such as key word indices.

Just as more integrated, coherent knowledge of risk factors is basic to continuing reassessment of their effects on the over-50 population, so evidence from health promotion and disability prevention research is important in assessing the effectiveness and benefits of approaches currently in use (both those that target the highest risk groups and those that reflect a more integrated strategy) to guide the development of future interventions. This body of knowledge, however, suffers from some of the same problems that characterize risk factor research for the elderly—for example, the lack of agreement about what health promotion and disability prevention means for those aged 50 and older.[23] That lack reflects a relatively undeveloped conceptual base for such programs, a problem that impedes efforts to develop a systematic framework for understanding. Even the traditional classifications of prevention are difficult to apply to older people.[32] The distinctions between primary, secondary, and tertiary prevention fit so poorly into the language of chronic disease that numerous efforts have been launched to develop uniform classifications of functional status. Prevention in rehabilitation terms is focused on preventing, maintaining, and modifying the loss of function as a result of physical, mental, or social impairments. Rather than disease prevention, the focus becomes disability prevention, an emphasis that seems a particularly important conceptual approach to studies of older people.

The heterogeneity of the over-50 population is another issue that must be addressed for both risk factor and intervention research and implementation. All individuals over the age of 50 cannot be grouped into a single category. Development of a conceptual basis and a classification system for health promotion and disability prevention must take into account where older individuals are in the life course.

Two major problems currently impede the delivery of preventive services for older persons. First, Medicare reimbursement primarily covers acute care and prohibits payment for preventive services except immunizations against pneumococcal pneumonia and hepatitis B and short-term rehabilitation.[46,52] Second, and perhaps more critical, there is a lack of agreement about what kinds of interventions really work because there have been few rigorous evaluations of prevention strategies. (The debate over whether to intervene to control moderate high blood pressure is an example of the prevailing uncertainties regarding the use of certain high-risk versus integrated strategies.[16,22,31,50]) Consensus regarding the effectiveness of particular interventions is needed to target resources efficiently and to support the development of reimbursement policies for preventive services. Evaluation research is also necessary to assess the value of public and private experiments in prepayment arrangements that provide incentives for health promotion and disability prevention, such as Health Care Financing Administration (HCFA) and CDC demonstrations,[26] and the INSURE[30] and On Lok[4] projects. Congressional interest in such questions[51] appears to be growing as legislators seek solutions to budget problems.

The absence of widely accepted criteria for determining the type and strength of the scientific evidence necessary for formulating preventive interventions is a serious barrier to progress in this arena, as is the inadequate assimilation into practice and action of comprehensive "state-of-the-art" reviews.

Two related questions also apply: What evidence is appropriate for the decision to implement one or another intervention, and what measures of outcome may be accepted as surrogates for the traditional measures? The second question usually evokes suggestions of randomized clinical trials and other cumbersome and expensive experimental methods. The first may eventually be answered by the U.S. Preventive Services Task Force,[18] building on the work of the Canadian Task Force on the Periodic Health Exam.[13] Currently, however, the growth of the number of interventions and the mix of preventive health services continues to outpace the translation of firm research evidence into sound prevention recommendations.

This report addresses some of these issues as they relate to a selected group of specific risk factors. As part of their preparation for the study the committee members received the list of priorities prepared by the Division of Health Promotion and Disease Prevention of the Institute of Medicine and the Committee of Prevention Coordinators of the National Institutes of Health as well as others.[19,40] The committee agreed that the following matters should receive specific attention.

- An integrated, coherent synthesis of new material and findings about risk factors and interventions should be prepared and made available to policymakers, the public, and practitioners on a periodic basis.
- The elderly themselves need to be the focus of a separate, targeted educational program concerning risk factors and interventions.
- Research should be conducted to find better ways to measure the strength of risk factors and less cumbersome and costly methods for measuring and comparing the benefits of interventions.
- The impact and effectiveness of intervention strategies should be measured and the results compared to identify the best approach, one that targets the highest or higher risk group(s) or one applied to the entire population.
- A better conceptual base should be developed and a more uniform system of classification should be defined and implemented for describing the body of knowledge on risk factors and interventions in the population aged 50 and older.
- Intervention outcomes should be examined not only in terms of lives prolonged but also of morbidities and disabilities slowed or reversed and quality of lives enhanced. Progress should be gauged both by advancements in promoting health and by improvements in managing chronic illness, particularly in the patient's capacity to cope with illness and disability. There is a need for more sensitive measures of quality of life in the years saved and new methods to assess the outcomes of health promotion and disability prevention programs.
- Several policy issues clamor for resolution. What type of health promotion benefit should be considered under Medicare and other payment mechanisms? What are the overall benefits of health promotion and disability prevention for persons aged 50 and older? What definitions, measures of impact, or terms should be used to support policy analysis in this area?

Early in its work the committee recognized the large number of risk or causative factors that could be explored and decided to use three criteria to prioritize those it would address: prevalence, burden, and measurable mutability through the use of possible interventions. Thus, Chapters 3 through 15 examine the knowledge base of each of the following risk factors: high blood pressure, medication use, specific infectious diseases, osteoporosis, sensory deprivation, oral health problems, screening for cancer, nutrition, smoking, depression, physical inactivity, social isolation, and falls. The chapters review the prevalence of each factor in the over-50 population and its burden in terms of mortality, morbidity, and functional disability. Interventions to prevent, detect, treat, or modify the effect of these risk factors on the health and functional independence of older people are discussed, and the effectiveness of these interventions is examined both for the entire population above age 50, and for specific subgroups of that population. Based on these reviews, specific recommendations are proposed—for individuals, providers, advocacy groups, policymakers, and third-party payers.

In addition, recognizing the gap between what is known and what needs to be known, the committee where appropriate proposes a research agenda to bridge that gap. These research recommendations complement the work of another Institute of Medicine committee that is developing a national research agenda on aging in all its aspects.

Despite the burden of chronic illness and associated disabilities experienced by the aging in this society, the committee recognizes the great heterogeneity of this population and emphasizes that healthy aging is not an oxymoron. More important, the committee urges an expansion of elder care that looks beyond the primary prevention and cure model toward the maintenance or restoration of maximal functioning in the face of chronic illness.

REFERENCES

1. Abdellah, F. G., and Moore, S. R. (eds.). Proceedings of the Surgeon General's Workshop: Health Promotion and Aging. Washington, D.C.: Department of Health and Human Services, Public Health Service, 1988.
2. Amler, R. W., White, C. C., et al. Closing the Gap: Cross-Sectional Analysis of Unnecessary Morbidity and Mortality in the United States. The Carter Center of Emory University, Health Policy Consultation, Nov. 26-28, 1984, Atlanta, Ga.
3. Andres, R. Presentation at the conference, Aging in the 21st Century, Montefiore Centennial Series, Rockefeller University, New York City, October 12, 1984.
4. Ansak, M. L., and Lindhein, R. On Lok: Housing and Adult Day Health Care for the Frail Elderly. Berkeley: Center for Environmental Design Research, College of Environmental Design, University of California at Berkeley, 1983.
5. Badura, B. Lifestyles and health: Some remarks on different viewpoints. Social Science and Medicine 1984; 19:341-347.
6. Berg, R. L. The prevention of disability in the aged. In: John M. Last (ed.), Public Health and Preventive Medicine. New York: Appleton-Century-Crofts, 1980, pp. 1283-1299.
7. Berkman, L., and Breslow, L. Health and Ways of Living: The Alameda County Study. New York: Oxford University Press, 1983.
8. Berkman, L. F., and Syme, S. L. Social networks, host resistance and mortal-

ity: A 9-year follow-up study of Alameda County residents. American Journal of Epidemiology 1979; 109:186-204.

9. Besdine, R. W. The database of geriatric medicine. In: J. W. Rowe and R. W. Besdine (eds.), Health and Disease in Old Age. Boston: Little, Brown, 1982, pp. 1-15.

10. Black, J. S., and Kapoor, W. Health promotion and disease prevention in older people: Our current state of ignorance. Journal of the American Geriatrics Society 1990; 38(2):168-172.

11. Blazer, D. Social support and mortality in an elderly community population. American Journal of Epidemiology 1982; 115:684-694.

12. Branch, L. G., and Jette, A. M. Personal health practices and mortality among the elderly. American Journal of Public Health 1984; 74(10):1126-1129.

13. Canadian Task Force on the Periodic Health Examination. The periodic health examination. Canadian Medical Association Journal 1979; 121:1193-1254.

14. Centers for Disease Control. Risk Factor Update Project: Final Report (under Contract USPHS 200-80-0527). Atlanta, Ga., February 1982.

15. Cornoni-Huntley, J., Barbano, H. E., Brody, J. A., et al. National Health and Nutrition Examination I—Epidemiologic follow-up survey. Public Health Reports 1983; 98:245-252.

16. Curb, J. D., Bohani, N. O., Schnaper, H., et al. Detection and treatment of hypertension in older individuals. American Journal of Epidemiology 1985; 121(3):371-376.

17. Department of Health and Human Services, National Institutes of Health. OMAR, Consensus Development Conference Statement, Vol. 5, No. 7, 1984.

18. Department of Health and Human Services, Public Health Service. Guide to Clinical Preventive Services: Report of the U. S. Preventive Services Task Force. Washington, D.C., 1989.

19. Department of Health and Human Services, Public Health Service. Strategies for Promoting Health for Specific Populations. Publ. No. 81-50169. Washington, D.C., 1981.

20. Donahue, R. P., Abbott, R. D., Reed, D. M., and K. Yano. Physical activity and coronary heart disease in middle-aged and elderly men: The Honolulu heart program. American Journal of Public Health 1988; 78:683-685.

21. Dychtwald, K. (ed.) Health promotion and disease prevention for elders. Generations 1983; 7(3):5-7.

22. Fries, E. D. Should mild hypertension be treated? New England Journal of Medicine 1982; 307:306-309.

23. Fries, J. F., Green, L. W., and S. Levine. Health promotion and the compression of morbidity. Lancet 1989; 1(8636):481-483.

24. German, P. S., and Fried, L. P. Prevention and the elderly: Public health issues and strategies. Annual Review of Public Health (United States) 1989; 10:319-332.

25. Green, L. W., and Gottlieb, N. H. Health promotion for the aging population: Approaches to extending active life expectancy. In: J. R. Hogress (ed.), Health care for an aging society. New York: Churchill Livingstone, 1989, pp. 139-154.

26. Greenlick, M., Lamb, S., Carpenter, T., et al. A successful Medicare prospective payment demonstration. Health Care Financing Review 1983; 4(4):85-97.

27. Gruchow, H. W., Sobscinski, K. A., and Barboriak, J. J. Alcohol, nutrient

intake and hypertension in U.S. adults. Journal of the American Medical Association 1985; 253(11):1567-1570.

28. Hamburg, D. A., Elliott, G. R., and Parron, D. L. (eds.) Health and Behavior. Washington, D.C.: National Academy Press, 1982.

29. Hodgson, J. L., and Buskird, E. R. Effects of environmental factors and life patterns on life span. In: D. Danon, N. W. Shock, and M. Marois (eds.), Aging: A Challenge to Science and Society. Vol. 1: Biology. Oxford: Oxford University Press, 1981.

30. The INSURE Project on Lifecycle Preventive Health Services. Industrywide Network for Social, Urban and Rural Efforts. Washington, D.C., 1980.

31. Joint National Committee on Detection, Evaluation, and Treatment of High Blood Pressure. The 1980 report of the treatment of high blood pressure. Archives of Internal Medicine 1980; 140:1280-1285.

32. Kane, R. L., Kane, R. A., and Arnold, S. B. Prevention in the Elderly: Risk Factors. Paper prepared for the Conference on Health Promotion and Disease Prevention for Children and the Elderly, Foundation for Health Services Research, September 16, 1983.

33. Kannel, W. B., and Gordon, T. Cardiovascular risk factors in the aged: The Framingham study. In: S. G. Haynes and M. Feinlieb (eds.), Second Conference in the Epidemiology of Aging. Publ. No. 80-969. Bethesda: National Institutes of Health, 1980.

34. Karp, D. A. A decade of reminders: Changing age consciousness between fifty and sixty years old. The Gerontologist 1988; 28(6):727-738.

35. Larson, E. B. Health promotion and disease prevention in the older adult. Geriatrics 1988; 43(Suppl.):31-39.

36. McCormick, J., and Skrabanek, P. Coronary heart disease is not preventable by population interventions. Lancet 1988; 2:839-841.

37. McCoy, J. L., and Edwards, B. E. Contextual and sociodemographic antecedents of institutionalization among aged welfare recipients. Medical Care 1981; 19:907-921.

38. Multiple Risk Factor Intervention Trial Research Group. Multiple risk factor intervention trial: Risk factor changes and mortality results. Journal of the American Medical Association 1984; 248(2):1465-1477.

39. National Center for Health Statistics. Health, United States, 1988. Department of Health and Human Services Publ. No. (PHS)87-1232. Washington, D.C.: Department of Health and Human Services, December 1988.

40. Office of Technology Assessment. Technology and Aging in America. Washington, D.C., June 1985.

41. Oliver, M. F. Reducing cholesterol does not reduce mortality. Journal of the American College of Cardiology 1988; 12:814-817.

42. Paffenberger, R. S. Early predictors of chronic disease. In: R. C. Jackson, J. Morton, and M. Sierra-Franco (eds.), Social Factors in Prevention. Berkeley: University of California Public Health Social Work Program, 1979.

43. Phillips, K., Holm, K., and Wu, A. Contemporary table salt practices and blood pressure. American Journal of Public Health 1985; 75:405-406.

44. Riley, M. W., and Bond, K. Beyond ageism: Postponing the onset of disability. In: M. W. Riley, B. B. Bess, and K. Bond (eds.), Aging in Society: Selected Reviews of Recent Research. Hillsdale, N.J.: Lawrence Erlbaum Associates, 1983.

45. Rowe, J. W. Health care for the elderly. New England Journal of Medicine 1985; 312(13):827-835.

46. Smith, S. A. Patient education: Financing under Medicare. Patient Education and Counseling 1986; 8:299-309.

47. Solomon, K. The depressed patient: Social antecedents of psychologic changes in the elderly. Journal of the American Geriatrics Society 1981; 29:14-18.

48. Somers, A. R., Kleinmen, L., and Clark, W. D. Preventive health services for the elderly: The Rutgers Medical School project. Inquiry 1982; 19:190-198.

49. Spencer, G. (U.S. Bureau of the Census). Projections of the population of the United States, by age, sex, and race: 1988 to 2080. Current Population Reports Series P-25, No. 1018. Washington, D.C., January 1989.

50. Stegman, M. R., and Williams, G. O. The elderly hypertensive: A neglected patient. Journal of Family Practice 1983; 16:259-262.

51. U.S. Congressional Record. January 31, 1985:S919-922. Washington, D.C.: U.S. Government Printing Office.

52. U.S. Department of Health, Education and Welfare, Public Health Service. Promoting Health, Preventing Disease: Objectives for the Nation. Washington, D.C.: U.S. Government Printing Office, 1980.

53. U.S. Department of Health, Education and Welfare, Public Health Service. Healthy People. Washington, D.C.: U.S. Government Printing Office, 1979.

54. U.S. Department of Health, Education and Welfare, Public Health Service. Implementation plans for attaining objectives for the nation. Public Health Reports 1983; 98(5—Suppl.):2-177.

55. Wingard, D., Berkman, L., and Brand, R. A multivariate analysis of health related practices. American Journal of Epidemiology 1982; 116:765-775.

56. Zuckerman, D. M., Kasl, S. V., and Ostfeld, A. M. Psychosocial predictors of mortality among elderly poor. The role of religion, well-being, and social contacts. American Journal of Epidemiology 1984; 119:(3):410-423.

2

Disability Classification

Although disabilities have been the subject of health care research and services for many years, the field remains in conceptual disarray. Even today, health professionals share neither a common means of defining disabilities nor a common sense of the health care industry's role with regard to people with disabilities. This chapter addresses some of the difficulties and trade-offs involved in selecting a disability classification system to solve these problems and explains the committee's reasons for advocating the World Health Organization's *International Classification of Impairments, Disabilities, and Handicaps.*[18]

Why pursue a new means of classifying disability? Issues of disability classification have often revolved around the politically sensitive task of deciding whether particular individuals are eligible for social insurance programs, a process that in many circumstances provokes significant controversy. Many health professionals have, therefore, attempted to avoid these controversies by avoiding disability.[7] With the prospect of providing care for an ever-larger aging population, however, the problems of disability classification deserve fresh attention. Older people are more likely to experience chronic illness that, over time, may contribute to disability, and the current lack of organization of disability concepts may leave American health care unprepared to deal with the growing future needs of this population. The committee's efforts, therefore, have been directed toward the identification of a disability classification system that offers a framework sensitive to the long-term needs of people with disabilities and that is likely to lead to a more unified understanding of these concepts among health professionals.

Even without many of the political pressures that accompany efforts to certify individuals for government benefits, the task of disability classification remains deeply complicated. There are major incompatibilities between the thinking that currently dominates American health care and the service needs of people with disabilities. The following sections give an account of these difficulties, discuss the current state of affairs in disability classification and its effects on disability research, and explain the committee's decision to advocate the World Health Organization's system.

DISABILITY AND THE DISEASE MODEL

The dominant framework for understanding the majority of health problems in the United States is that of the acute care community, that is, the disease model. Yet more and more health professionals are beginning to question the wisdom of using this approach to meet the needs of people with disabilities and those at risk for disability[2,8,19]—in particular, the elderly, the fastest growing group at high risk for disabilities.[16,17] An acute care framework provides a poor view of disability for a number of reasons. Acute care perspectives are primarily restricted to somatic conditions, yet contemporary concepts of disability include phenomena that go well beyond this sphere. Disability may limit an individual's capacity to live independently or care for him- or herself; it may interfere with maintaining or initiating relationships, pursuing career goals, or enjoying leisure activities. Disability may also erect barriers to personal autonomy (e.g., the inaccessibility of public accommodations) and political empowerment (e.g., through prejudice or discrimination) in American culture.

The acute care perspective on health is also problematic for understanding and meeting the needs of people with disabilities and those who are at risk for disability. In the acute care framework, health is most often associated with cure, a linkage that is too limiting in the disability arena. (Some of the problems inherent in the health-equals-cure perspective are apparent when one considers that there is a cure for tuberculosis but no counterpart in treatments for missing or dysfunctional legs.) Health care that reduces its ultimate goal to that of the strictly curative is also likely to make the implicit assumption that health and the absence of disease are essentially synonymous. This assumption makes room for primary prevention, but it neglects the prevention of disabilities after a disease has been cured or measures to address the needs of individuals with chronic conditions.

Moving from the level of organ or cell function to a consideration of the social effects of disability exposes further incompatibilities between disease-centered thinking and broad notions of disablement. The effects of disease are located in well-defined spaces—the organs and tissues of the human body. By contrast, the spaces disabilities affect are not well defined. Unlike human organs, an individual's life in society cannot be neatly divided into separate parts or components; when such divisions are attempted, the enormous variety of human existence guarantees small likelihood of consensus regarding either the divisions themselves or what constitutes "normal functioning" within them.

These incompatibilities are evident in the structure of acute care thinking. Each disease constitutes a paradigmatic set of signs and symptoms. Medical diagnosis is the categorical assignment of the patient's concrete and particular health problems to one or several universal disease types. Diagnosis therefore incorporates a shift in which a particular individual's sickness is assimilated into an established and consistent category that is (often) recognized universally within the health care system and associated with specific methods of treatment. Disease classification systems are designed to classify concepts that remain static and abstract.[4] By contrast, the social manifestations of disabilities must be understood relative to the particular abilities an individual hopes to maintain or achieve. These abilities vary among individuals—they are often matters of individual preference, culture, and social expectations. Attempts to "diagnose" disability according to easily recognized physical abnormalities or by general standards of behavior and social performance may cause the personal aspects of disablement to be overlooked. For example, is it right—or, more important, will the necessary kind of care be delivered— if two wheelchair-bound individuals are classified as having the same disability if one is a mason and the other a writer? In this case, an apparently similar problem assumes quite different proportions and dimensions. Thus, social life not only resists well-defined divisions, but the uniqueness of an individual life makes it highly resistant to universal and abstract categories, which are an essential part of the logic of modern clinical methods. (It should be noted that the uncategorical nature of disabilities is not simply a problem for acute care thinking but for any and all methods that attempt to box a disabled person's difficulties into predetermined categories of ill health.)

Despite these complications, there have been continuing attempts to define universal and abstract standards for describing and treating disabilities. Although these systems are often criticized for being inequitable, unjust, and inadequate, they serve a necessary purpose. The health care system in this country has been built on the understanding that illnesses can be categorized and are likely to follow a predictable course. These systems, therefore, provide the structure essential to integrate disabilities into the U.S. social insurance and health care systems. This means that the imperative is to find a system suited to the nation's needs but to remain sensitive to its inherent problems and open-minded about alternatives.

The alternative to the acute care approach to disabilities explored in this report is the array of new methods and goals known as health promotion and disability prevention. This new approach makes room for broader notions of disability care and treatment, departing from the traditional disease model framework. Healthy behavior and the prevention of chronic and acute conditions through risk reduction are stressed, as in health promotion and disease prevention. However, in this approach, prevention is more comprehensive; that is, points of prevention for chronic illness and disability are defined throughout life, including periods after the onset of these difficulties. Rehabilitation and social supports tailored to the diverse needs of the over-50 population are also an important part of health promotion and disability prevention.

Although the health promotion and disability prevention approach escapes many of the constraints of traditional acute care frameworks, the majority of its services are not delivered independently of existing health care systems. It therefore requires a common set of definitions, shared concepts to guide health policies and permit the dialogue necessary to advance disability treatment and prevention among health care providers. The following section discusses two of the recent efforts to classify disabilities and presents the committee's recommendations for the future development of this field.

CLASSIFYING DISABILITIES

As noted above, defining standards for disability in its broader manifestations is exceedingly difficult. There have been numerous attempts to devise disability classification systems in the United States, in part because of the rise of social insurance programs such as workmen's compensation, veterans' benefits, and social security programs.[7,10] Another important source of disability classifications has been health interview surveys. From the time of their introduction to the United States, these surveys have grown increasingly sophisticated, and by the 1950s Katz and Lawton had developed short sets of survey questions based on behavioral theories of human function. These indexes are known as the Activities of Daily Living (ADLs), which measure abilities in six functions (bathing, dressing, toileting, transfer, continence, and feeding), and the Instrumental Activities of Daily Living (IADLs), which are concerned with more complex tasks (e.g., shopping, cooking, housekeeping, laundry, use of transportation, managing money, managing medications, use of telephones).[9] Another measure, limitations in major activities, asks respondents about their ability to work, attend school, or perform housework.[5] (A list of many of the major surveys, including those with questions on disability, can be found in the National Research Council publication, *The Aging Population in the Twenty-first Century: Statistics for Health Policy*.[15]) Each of these measures has been widely used—or retooled for use—in surveys and functional assessment inventories.

Despite their widespread use, however, each of the classification systems that have come into use in this country suffers from limitations of one kind or another. From a research perspective, the use of self-reported measures raises questions concerning the standardization of the participant's answers. Disability measures have also been problematic as public policy-making tools. The eligibility criteria of the nation's social security insurance programs have been criticized for relying on the narrowly defined criteria of the disease model to determine disability.[7,10] In health policy, the ADLs and IADLs have similar constraints. Although not dependent on the disease model, they do not have a systematic means of defining psychological difficulties, and they do not provide insight into certain social contributions to disability, such as discrimination. The systems measuring limitations in major activities, on the other hand, may indicate the presence of some social contributions to disability but do not provide sufficient information to inform health interventions. These limitations have been recognized and other forms of classification, including attempts to combine these measures, have been attempted, but there has been no consensus on a system that could provide a sufficiently broad understanding of disability. These and other specific measures provide insights into the way disabilities affect important parts of most people's lives, but their scope is too narrow. Moreover, health care measures are now called on to assess the quality of life, but without a fuller perspective on the effects of disability, such classification and measurement systems do not have a convincing claim to make such assessments.

In the search for solutions, epidemiologists, demographers, physicians, insurers, and other health-related professionals have looked to classification systems that attempt to provide a comprehensive framework for understanding and acting on both the physical and social dimensions of disabilities. Several attempts have been made to classify a broad range of disability phenomena into categories organized according to various "levels," from the pathological to the individual to the social, on which disabling conditions exist. The World Health Organization's[18] (WHO) *International Classification of Impairments, Disabilities, and Handicaps* (ICIDH) and the Nagi system[11,12,13,14] are widely used and frequently discussed examples of this type of system. They both address somatic, cognitive, economic, and psychosocial dynamics; however, although they share common names for some of their categories, the criteria for determining category boundaries differ.

The Nagi system is intended to provide general categories and a common conceptual model of disability processes for use in the multidisciplinary setting of disability research. The system draws a careful framework for understanding disabilities built around four basic concepts: pathology, impairment, functional limitation, and disability. The subdivisions for these concepts are, in part, based on concepts introduced previously by other systems for classification and assessment.

The Nagi system is designed to correspond to the findings of empirical research. The demarcations between categories are said to mirror a set of "natural" divisions* suggested by survey research. For example, categories to identify the severity of functional limitations in "physical performance" and "emotional performance" (two subcategories of the more general functional limitation category) were determined by analyzing survey data that indicated natural clusterings of individuals with similar severity scores.[12,13]

These and other strict epistemological standards limit the number of categories in the system. It therefore remains at a more abstract and less inclusive level of organization, eschewing highly detailed categories that may not fit neatly into the overall structure of the system or that are not backed by empirical evidence.[14] By contrast, the organization of the WHO system reflects a desire to change

---

*Nagi distinguishes the "natural" approach from more artificial methods that might, for example, have divided a 0-8 rating scale into such categories as 0-1.9, 2.0-3.9, and so forth, or that might set the boundaries of categories so as to achieve an equal distribution of individuals between them, rather than making divisions on the basis of clusters of individuals.[13]

Classification Level	Disease (or injuries or congenital abnormality)	Impairment	Disability	Handicap
Planes of Experience		Exteriorized	Objectified	Socialized
$\rightarrow$ General Progression of the Consequences of Disease $\rightarrow$				
Example:	Osteoporosis with hip fracture	Hip impairment	Climbing staircases, steps, walking	Mobility and independence handicaps

FIGURE 2-1   The World Health Organization's *International Classification of Impairments, Disabilities, and Handicaps.*

the landscape of health services by introducing measures of disability designed to direct system users to new health care goals.

The WHO system categorizes a wide range of disease consequences and suggests points of intervention (to prevent further development) and forms of assistance to help individuals cope with their difficulties. The form and organization of the system are similar to WHO's *International Classification of Diseases* (ICD-9) especially in many of its subcategories; the overall structure , however, is informed by a theory of "planes of experience" in the development of illness and disability. This gives rise to four main categories: disease/disorder, impairment, disability, and handicap (Figure 2-1). The WHO manual describes these planes of experience (pp. 24-25) as follows:[18]

1. Something abnormal occurs within the individual; this may be present at birth or acquired later. A chain of causal circumstances, the "etiology," gives rise to changes in the structure or functioning of the body, the "pathology." Pathological changes may or may not make themselves evident; when they do they are described as "manifestations," which, in medical parlance, are usually distinguished as "symptoms and signs." These features are the components of the medical model of disease.

2. Someone becomes aware of such an occurrence; in other words, the pathological state is *exteriorized.* Most often the individual himself becomes aware of disease manifestations, usually referred to as "clinical disease." In behavioral terms, the individual has become or been made aware that he is unhealthy. His illness heralds

recognition of impairments, abnormalities of body structure and appearance, and of organ or system function, resulting from any cause. Impairments represent disturbances at the organ level.

3. The performance or behavior of the individual may be altered as a result of this awareness, either consequentially or cognitively. Common activities may become restricted, and in this way the experience is *objectified*. Also relevant are psychological responses to the presence of disease, part of so-called illness behavior, and sickness phenomena, the patterning of illness manifested as behavior by the individual in response to the expectations others have of him when he is ill. These experiences represent disabilities, which reflect the consequences of impairments in terms of functional performance and activity by the individual. Disabilities represent disturbances at the level of the person.

4. Either the awareness itself, or the altered behavior or performance to which this gives rise, may place the individual at a disadvantage relative to others, thus *socializing* the experience. This plane reflects the response of society to the individual's experience, be this expressed in attitudes, such as the engendering of stigma, or in behavior, which may include specific instruments such as legislation. These experiences represent handicap, the disadvantages resulting from impairment and disability. The explicit concern with the value attached to an individual's performance or status obviously makes this the most problematical plane of the disease consequences.

Because the WHO system was designed as a classification manual for the consequences of disease, it does not elaborate the particular conditions that fall under the disease/disorder level. Impairments, the first WHO level with detailed subcategories, include "any loss or abnormality of psychological, physiological, or anatomical structure or function." As noted in the description above, these changes occur, in principle, at an organ level and begin with the development of pathological processes (although the impairment may outlast the pathological activity or may be of genetic origin). The next level, disabilities, describes restrictions or inabilities measured against social expectations of what "normal" humans can perform in managing the "essential components of everyday living" (e.g. personal care, locomotor activities, behaviors commonly expected of individuals). The last category in the WHO system is handicaps, which are disadvantages for a given individual, resulting from an impairment or disability, that limit or prevent "the fulfillment of a role that is normal for that individual." The handicap level is used to assess the impact of an impairment or disability in relation to the roles chosen by an individual and the social expectations that accompany that role. The assessment criteria of this level, however, are largely limited to "survival roles," or "six key dimensions of experience in which competence is expected of an individual": orientation, physical independence, mobility, occupation, social integration, and economic self-sufficiency.

The potential effects of osteoporosis provide a convenient example of the WHO classification system (see Figure 2-1). Any resulting mechanical or motor dysfunction, for example, as a consequence of fracture would be classified as an impairment. The system provides detailed subcategories specifying functional limitations of particular limbs and major skeletal components such as hip and thigh impairments. Resulting difficulties in walking on flat terrain, traversing discontinuities (e.g., occasional steps between levels or the gap between platform and train), or climbing staircases are separate subcategories under the disabilities classification level. General mobility limitations or the resulting diminution of physical independence are classified as handicaps. The system provides general guidelines for assessing their severity.

More widespread use of the WHO classification system offers several advantages, although like any such system it is not perfect. There is an urgent need to bring the concepts of disability and its prevention to the attention of physicians, and the familiar form of the WHO system is a suitable mechanism for their introduction. The system also provides a highly comprehensive perspective on disabling consequences of disease and the available interventions. It also holds promise as a means of achieving a common vocabulary for research and the systematic organization of concepts to facilitate data collection and assessment. In addition, the WHO system has already begun to achieve worldwide acceptance. Although some of the subcategories assert an order of disability phenomena that is neither empirically corroborated nor intuitively obvious, this disadvantage will be outweighed if the system encourages large numbers of health professionals to adopt this format as a regular means of recording data on disabilities.

Much of the appeal of the WHO classification system lies in the new health care goals made explicit in its subcategories. It is in this context that the Committee on Health Promotion and Disability Prevention for the Second Fifty encourages physicians to shift their attention—and with it their frame of reference—toward providing comprehensive help for their elderly disabled patients. As a first step toward this goal the committee supports the use of the WHO system, the *International Classification of Impairments, Disabilities, and*

Handicaps, as a descriptive framework for the disabling conditions associated with risk factors for older populations, including the conditions discussed in the remaining chapters of this report. The committee notes that health care for older individuals is currently in transition. Thus, methods that appear relevant and useful today may become outmoded as the discussion of disability classification continues. It is the committee's hope that widespread use of the WHO system will bring health professionals into this arena to contribute their views and insights to the development of alternative approaches. The committee also urges careful attention to the views of members of the disabled community, as well as bioethicists (see Appendixes A and B of this report), whose unique perspectives often reveal overlooked distinctions between disability in the abstract and in the "real" world.

REFERENCES

1. Berkowitz, E., and D. Fox. The politics of social security expansion: Social security disability insurance, 1935-1986. Journal of Policy History 1989; 1(3):233-260.
2. Caplan, A. L. Is medical care the right prescription for chronic illness? In: S. Sullivan and M. E. Lewin (eds.), The Economics and Ethics of Long-Term Care and Disability. Lanham, Md.: University Press of America, 1988, pp. 73-89.
3. Engelhardt, H. T. The concepts of health and disease. In: A. L. Caplan, H. T. Engelhardt, and J. J. McCartney (eds.), Concepts of Health and Disease. Reading, Mass.: Addison-Wesley, 1981, pp. 31-45.
4. Foucault, M. The Birth of the Clinic, A. M. S. Smith, trans. New York: Random House, 1973.
5. Haber, L. D. Issues in the Definition of Disability and the Use of Disability Survey Data. Presentation at the Workshop on Disability Statistics of the Committee on National Statistics, National Research Council, Washington, D.C., 1989.
6. Institute of Medicine. National Agenda for the Prevention of Disability. Washington, D.C.: National Academy Press, forthcoming.
7. Institute of Medicine. Pain and Disability: Clinical, Behavioral, and Public Policy Perspectives, M. Osterweis, A. Kleinman, and D. Mechanic (eds.). Washington, D.C.: National Academy Press, 1987.
8. Jennings, B., D. Callahan, and A. L. Caplan. Ethical challenges of chronic illness. Hastings Center Report 1988; 2(Suppl.):1-16.
9. Katz, S. Assessing self-maintenance: Activities of daily living, mobility, and instrumental activities of daily living. Journal of the American Geriatrics Society 1983; 31(12):721-727.
10. Markowitz, G., and Rosner, D. The illusion of medical certainty: Silicosis and the politics of industrial disability, 1930-1960. Milbank Quarterly 1989; 67(2, Part 1):228-253.
11. Nagi, S. Z. Some conceptual issues in disability and rehabilitation. In: M.

B. Sussman (ed.), Sociology and Rehabilitation. Washington, D.C.: American Sociological Society, 1965.

12. Nagi, S. Z. Disability Concepts and Prevalence. Presented at the Mary Switzer Memorial Seminar, Cleveland, Ohio, 1975.

13. Nagi, S. Z. An epidemiology of disability among adults in the United States. Milbank Quarterly 1976; Fall:439-467.

14. Nagi, S. Z. Appendix A. In: Institute of Medicine, Report on a National Agenda for the Prevention of Disabilities. Washington, D.C.: National Academy Press, forthcoming.

15. National Research Council, Panel on Statistics for an Aging Population. The Aging Population in the Twenty-first Century, D. Gilford (ed.). Washington, D.C.: National Academy Press, 1988.

16. Rice, D. P., and M. P. LaPlante. Chronic illness, disability, and increasing longevity. In: S. Sullivan and M. E. Lewin (eds.). The Economics and Ethics of Long-Term Care and Disability. Lanham, Md.: University Press of America, 1988, pp. 9-55.

17. U.S. Congress, Office of Technology Assessment. Health promotion/disease prevention and nutrition in the elderly. In: Technology and Aging in America, Publ. No. OTA-BA-264. Washington, D.C., June 1985.

18. World Health Organization. International Classification of Impairments, Disabilities, and Handicaps. Geneva: World Health Organization, 1980.

19. Zola, I. K. Policies and programs concerning aging and disabilities: Towards a unifying agenda. In: S. Sullivan and M. E. Lewin (eds.). The Economics and Ethics of Long-Term Care and Disability. Lanham, Md.: University Press of America, 1988.

3

High Blood Pressure

R eports on the prevalence of high blood pressure in the elderly indicate that between 30 and 50 percent of persons over the age of 50 may have chronic hypertension.[7,25] Elevated levels of both diastolic blood pressure (DBP) and systolic blood pressure (SBP) are strong predictors of subsequent cardiovascular disease in the elderly.[38] In the past two years there has been an explosion of new knowledge on the epidemiology, pathophysiology, and treatment of high blood pressure in older individuals.[7]

Because the risk of future cardiovascular morbid and mortal events rises in a continuous fashion as either systolic blood pressure or diastolic blood pressure rises, there is no threshold of either systolic or diastolic pressure that can be described definitively as hypertensive.[40] Nonetheless, for operational purposes, this chapter will use the following definitions based on clinical conventions and on recommendations issued in 1985 by a National Heart, Lung and Blood Institute advisory committee (the Subcommittee on Hypertension Definition and Prevalence). Isolated systolic hypertension is defined as a systolic blood pressure greater than or equal to 160 millimeters of mercury (mmHg) and a diastolic pressure of less than 90 mmHg. Systolic/diastolic hypertension is defined as a diastolic blood pressure greater than or equal to 90 mmHg. This chapter focuses on the risk associated with high blood pressure, the efficacy and cost-effectiveness of detection and treatment (for the prevention of future complications), and recommendations regarding high blood pressure and its management directed toward elderly persons, health care professionals, and policymakers. The chapter does not discuss details of clinical diagnosis or treatment because these issues have been recently reviewed elsewhere.[7]

BURDEN

Several epidemiologic studies have indicated that, in most countries, average systolic blood pressure increases throughout the life span whereas average diastolic blood pressure rises until ages 55 to 60 and then levels off.[38] This increase in blood pressure occurs in persons who have previously been classified as hypertensive and those classified as normotensive. However, data from the Framingham longitudinal research and other studies indicate that not all individuals experience an aging-related increase in blood pressure.[38] In addition, population studies from nonindustrialized societies indicate that average blood pressure among such groups does not tend to rise with age.[51]

Estimates of the true prevalence of high blood pressure vary greatly depending on the age and race of the population, the blood pressure level used to define hypertension, and the number of measurements made.[15] The prevalence of both systolic/diastolic high blood pressure and isolated systolic high blood pressure is considerable in persons over the age of 50. Because levels of diastolic blood pressure tend to level off around age 55, the prevalence of systolic/diastolic high blood pressure tends to be constant for persons aged 50 and older.[25] Therefore, although some authors speak in general terms of the rise in prevalence of high blood pressure with age, the prevalence of systolic/diastolic high blood pressure rises little with age.[50] Actually, it is the rise in isolated systolic high blood pressure that accounts for most of the overall increase; the prevalence of systolic/diastolic high blood pressure in persons over the age of 50 is about 15 percent in whites and 25 percent in blacks.[33] The prevalence of isolated systolic high blood pressure varies with increasing age from 1 or 2 percent at age 50 to greater than 20 percent over age 80[32,50,57] and does not appear to differ according to race. Therefore, the total prevalence of high blood pressure in the elderly is not quite as high as the 50 to 60 percent figure that is frequently reported.[63]

Unfortunately, there are only limited data to estimate the rate of onset of new incidence cases of high blood pressure in the elderly. Follow-up analyses of the National Health and Nutrition Examination Survey 1 (NHANES1) data indicate that the incidence of high blood pressure (defined as SBP > 160 mmHg and/or DBP > 95 mmHg, based on one blood pressure measurement) increases by about 5 percent for each 10-year interval after age 18 and peaks between 55 to 64 years of age. The reported incidence rates from the NHANES data over an average of 9.5 years of follow-up were approximately 20 percent for white men and women over the age of 55 and 30 and 40 percent for black males and females, respectively. Based on the definition used, these rates would include both systolic/diastolic high blood pressure and isolated systolic high blood pressure. The estimates are inflated, however, because they are based on only one blood pressure reading per study (the original survey and the follow-up) taken more than 9 years apart. Analysis of Framingham data (also based on one reading but measured biennially) indicates that the cumulative incidence of isolated systolic blood pressure is about 418 per 1,000 in men and 533 per 1,000 in women.[77] Because of differences in definition and in the frequency of and intervals between measurements, these data are difficult to interpret. Nonetheless, it appears that the number of new incidence cases of isolated systolic high blood pressure continues to increase in persons over age 55.

Although the clinical treatment of high blood pressure has classically focused on diastolic blood pressure levels, epidemiologic data indicate that, for middle-aged and older adults, the systolic blood pressure level is more predictive of future cardiovascular morbidity and mortality.[13,37] Both systolic pressure and diastolic pressure, however, remain independently predictive of future vascular events. Analyses of Framingham data indicate that 42 percent of strokes in elderly men and 70 percent of strokes in elderly women are directly attributable to hypertension.[37] Again, systolic blood pressure appears to be slightly more predictive of strokes than diastolic blood pressure, and the risk gradients for systolic blood pressure do not wane with advancing age.

When all cardiovascular risk factors in the elderly are taken into account, it is clear that increased systolic blood pressure levels are the single greatest risk (other than age itself) for increased cardiovascular disease in persons over the age of 50.[38] It is also clear that increased blood pressure interacts with other cardiovascular risk factors to compound the risks. For instance, although total serum cholesterol lessens somewhat as a cardiovascular risk factor in the elderly, it still confers some element of risk (especially when fractionated into the low-density lipoprotein/high-density lipoprotein [LDL/HDL] ratio) and compounds the risk for hypertensives.[38] In addition, recent reports from the Framingham study indicate that left ventricular hypertrophy is more prevalent in older persons and highly correlated with increased systolic blood pressure.[59] It has been known for some years that the development of left ventricular hypertrophy is itself an independent cardiovascular risk factor.[36]   It is also becoming clear that left ventricular hypertrophy in hypertensives confers increased risk of ventricular arrhythmias.[43]

Finally, data from the National Center for Health Statistics indicate that coronary heart disease is the most common cause and cerebrovascular disease the third most common cause of mortality and morbidity in persons over the age of 50. Even as age advances into the seventies and eighties, coronary heart disease and cerebrovascular disease continue to be among the three most common causes of both mortality and morbidity. Further data from the National Center for Health Statistics indicate that coronary heart disease and cerebrovascular disease account for a majority of the disability seen in the population between the ages of 50 and 75. After the age of 75, degenerative processes such as arthritis and dementia began to account for approximately an equivalent amount of disability. In terms of disease-related disability and health care expenditures for persons over the age of 50, cardiac and circulatory disorders are responsible for more than 50 percent of such expenses.

PATHOPHYSIOLOGY

The pathophysiology of both systolic/diastolic high blood pressure and isolated systolic high blood pressure in the elderly involves an increase in peripheral vascular resistance.[7,45] Certainly, as humans age, structural changes in the blood vessels account for some of the change in peripheral resistance.[30] It is also possible that functional changes in the vascular smooth muscle are a contributory factor.[1,7] Actually, the overall pathophysiology of high blood pressure in black and elderly persons exhibits a similar profile.[7,44,73] Both black and elderly hypertensives tend to be sodium sensitive and have low renin levels, as well as increased vascular resistance. It has been suggested that black hypertensives are particularly likely to conserve sodium with expansion in extracellular volume and consequent development of high blood pressure.[44,73]

UTILITY OF SCREENING

Several studies have shown that the casual office blood pressure measurement is strongly predictive of subsequent cardiovascular and cerebrovascular events.[37] Yet recent analyses of data collected in a national multicenter clinical trial (the Hypertension Detection and Follow-up Program) indicate that the average of multiple measures of blood pressure over several different visits is more likely to approximate a person's true individual blood pressure.[55] In addition, studies have indicated that, at times, the office measurement of blood pressure consistently overestimates blood pressure in certain persons known to have "white coat hypertension."[53] According to some recent research, values for ambulatory blood pressure measurement in middle-aged persons may be more predictive of end organ damage than are casual measures of office blood pressure.[75] Questions remain, however, as to how prevalent pseudohypertension is in elderly persons, and this topic is an important area for continued investigation. Currently, it would appear that multiple office blood pressure measurements or, in selected situations, ambulatory blood pressure measurements are highly predictive of subsequent cardiovascular risk. Therefore, office or ambulatory blood pressure monitoring is sufficiently sensitive and specific as a screening test for true high blood pressure. Furthermore, although some investigators have recently determined that indirect assessment of blood pressure with a mercury sphygmomanometer may cause spuriously high readings of blood pressure in older persons with calcified arteries (as compared with direct intra-arterial measurement),[60,71] experience with mass screening programs indicates that mercury sphygmomanometer blood pressure measurement is an acceptable screening test for a large majority of the population.[56]

EVIDENCE THAT TREATMENT IS BENEFICIAL

The discussion in this section emphasizes data obtained from large, properly conducted randomized controlled trials. In instances in which such data are not available, data from cohort or case-control studies are reported. For the purposes of this analysis, studies of the efficacy of treating diastolic high blood pressure in the elderly are limited to randomized trials whose design and sample size are adequate to generate sufficient statistical power—specifically, to have greater than a 50/50 chance of detecting a 25 percent reduction in mortality or morbidity endpoints.

In reviewing the studies discussed below, the reader should be aware that there is great variability among clinical trials in the way endpoints are classified. Because of the different ways events are categorized and because of limited sample sizes that do not allow for subgroup comparisons, it is often difficult to distinguish the impact of treatment on rates of specific endpoints such as stroke, congestive heart failure, or myocardial infarction.

Evidence That Treatment of Systolic/Diastolic
High Blood Pressure Is Beneficial

There is ample evidence from large multicenter controlled trials that the treatment of systolic/diastolic high blood pressure in individuals between the ages of 50 and 69 years of age is beneficial.[33,49,72] The results of these trials are summarized in Table 3-1. For persons over the age of 50, the Veterans Administration (VA) study reported a reduction (nonsignificant) in aggregate cardiovascular morbidity, the Hypertensive Detection and Follow-up Program (HDFP) reported a reduction in total mortality, and the Australian Trial on Mild Hypertension reported a trend toward reduced stroke and aggregate ischemic heart disease. The only subgroup data available on the effects of treatment analyzed by race and sex come from the HDFP and do not indicate that race and sex significantly affect the benefits of treatment.

Because most major high blood pressure trials had studied only selected groups of "young old" persons, the European Working Party on Hypertension in the Elderly was designed to study whether medication treatment of diastolic high blood pressure in older subjects reduced morbidity or mortality. This trial enrolled persons over the age of 60 (mean age, 72 years) into treatment or placebo groups.[3] After an eight-year follow-up, analysis revealed no effects of medication on mortality from all causes but did show a significant (27 percent) reduction in the cardiovascular mortality rate. There was also a statistically significant (38 percent) reduction in cardiac mortality and a nonsignificant ($P = .12$) but impressive 32 percent reduction in cerebrovascular mortality. Treatment appeared to be effective for persons with entry systolic blood pressure from 160 to 239 mmHg, but the treatment did not appear to have an impact on participants with entry diastolic blood pressure in the range 90 to 95 mmHg.[4] The reduction in endpoints seen in the intervention group disappeared in persons over the age of 80, suggesting that treatment might not be effective in persons of advanced age. However, the number of participants aged 80 and older was small, and these subgroup data thus are not definitive. Persons over the age of 80 with diastolic high blood pressure who are relatively biologically "young" could be treated; the rationale for treating biologically frail persons aged 80 or older (particularly those with substantial noncardiovascular comorbid problems) may be less compelling.

In general, as shown in Table 3-2, treated patients over 60 years of age have relative reductions in cardiovascular morbidity or mortality similar to the reductions that occur in patients under 50 years of

TABLE 3-1 Randomized Trials of the Treatment of Diastolic High Blood Pressure in the Elderly: Summary of Design and Outcome

Study[a]	Type	Age (yrs.)	Blood Pressure (mmHg)[b]	Medication[c]	Outcome
VA	Randomized, double-blind, placebo-controlled	60–69	DBP 90–114	HCTZ/ Reserpine	A 32% decrease in cardiovascular morbidity, did not reach significance. Magnitude of difference consistent with overall study.
HDFP	Randomized, special care vs. referred care	60–69	DBP 90–115	CTLD/ Reserpine or alpha-methyldopa	Statistically significant 16.4% reduction in total mortality for special care group.
Austr.	Randomized, double-blind, placebo-controlled	60–69	DBP 95–109	CTZ/ various second step	A 39% reduction in trial endpoints for this treatment subgroup; did not reach statistical significance but reduction similar to overall study group.
EWPHE	Randomized, double-blind, placebo-controlled	60–97	DBP 90–119 SBP 160–239	HCTZ-triamterene/ alpha-methyldopa	Significant 38% reduction in cardiac mortality; 32% reduction in cerebrovascular mortality did not quite reach significance.
Coope	Randomized, single-blind, no placebo for controls	60–79	DBP ≥ 05 SBP ≥ 1 70	Beta blocker/ BNFZD	A 30% reduction in fatal strokes; no effect on myocardial infarction.

[a]VA = Veterans Administration Cooperative Study (see reference no. 73); HDFP = Hypertension Detection and Follow-up Program (see reference nos. 32 and 33); Austr = Australian Trial on Mild Hypertension (see reference no. 50); EWPHE = European Working Party on Hypertension in the Elderly (see reference nos. 2 and 3); Coope = Coope and Warrender study (see reference no. 16).

[b]DBP = diastolic blood pressure; SBP = systolic blood pressure.

[c]HCTZ = hydrochlorothiazide; CTZ = chlorothiazide; BNFZD = benfluorothiazide; CTLD = chlorthalidone.

TABLE 3-2 Impact of Antihypertensive Therapy on Cardiovascular Morbidity and Mortality by Age Group

Study	Relative Reduction[a] (percentage)		Absolute Reduction[b] (per 1,000 person-years)	
	< 50 Years	>60 Years	< 50 Years	>60 Years
Veterans Administration Cooperative (morbidity)	55	59	21	100
Hypertension Detection and Follow-up Program (mortality)	6	16	2	25
Australian Trial on Mild Hypertension (cardiovascular trial endpoints)	20	26	5	10

[a] Relative reduction = the percentage of decline in the event rate in the intervention group compared with the placebo group.

[b] Absolute reduction = the total number of events prevented in the treatment group versus the comparison group per 1,000 person-years of treatment.

age.[7] Yet when these data are analyzed by the absolute number of events prevented per 1,000 person-years of treatment, it is also clear that more total events are prevented in participants over age 60.[7] Elderly persons have higher rates of cardiovascular events; if they experience the same percentage of benefit as younger persons from drug treatment for diastolic high blood pressure, then the reduction in total number of events is greater in the older persons. Therefore, the benefit attributable to the treatment of diastolic high blood pressure increases with age and with the severity of the diastolic high blood pressure. The absolute benefit from drug treatment of diastolic high blood pressure in persons over the age of 60 varies from 10 events prevented per 1,000 person-years for individuals with mild diastolic high blood pressure (90 to 104 mmHg) to 100 events per 1,000 person-years for individuals with moderate diastolic high blood pressure (105 to 115 mmHg).

Evidence That Treatment of Isolated Systolic High Blood Pressure Is Beneficial

To date there are no data from randomized controlled trials to demonstrate that treatment of isolated systolic high blood pressure lowers subsequent rates of cardiovascular morbidity or mortality. In addition to the epidemiologic data reviewed above, however, there are data from one large cohort study indicating that, over a seven-year follow-up period, control of systolic pressure in treated hypertensives tended to result in more beneficial cardiovascular morbidity and mortality.[6] Moreover, data from the Systolic Hypertension in the Elderly Program pilot study suggest that isolated systolic hypertension can be treated easily with minimum side effects.[31]

Impact of Treatment on Cerebrovascular Versus Coronary Heart Disease

Clinical trials of the treatment of diastolic high blood pressure have shown that treatment reduces the rate of strokes and heart failure but has little effect on coronary heart disease rates.[23] Possible explanations for this lack of benefit include the following: (1) the study cited may have had too short a duration to demonstrate a benefit in terms of the natural history of coronary heart disease; (2) some of the subjects in the studies may have experienced too vigorous a lowering of diastolic blood pressure, which may have adversely affected coronary artery blood flow, particularly to the subendocardial layer during diastole;[20] or (3) it is possible that diuretics (which increase lipids and glucose and lower potassium) may have had adverse effects.[40] Currently, the dilemma remains regarding the effect on coronary heart disease of treatment of high blood pressure.

Target goals for blood pressure lowering should be modest. Three recent descriptive studies have shown that there may be a J-shaped relationship between treated levels of diastolic blood pressure and mortality from myocardial infarction; that is, those patients with the greatest lowering of diastolic pressure actually had higher rates of fatal myocardial infarction than did patients with more modest lowering. Two recent studies in middle-aged hypertensives[20,67] and one in elderly hypertensives[6] have also shown this effect. Therefore, a modest lowering of DBP to about 85 to 88 mmHg appears most appropriate for the elderly.

Impact of the Treatment of High Blood Pressure on Total Mortality

With the exception of the Hypertension Detection and Follow-up Program, none of the large multicenter trials shown in Table 3-2 have demonstrated that treatment of high blood pressure has an impact on total mortality. Some have viewed this finding as a rationale for not recommending treatment for high blood pressure; it should be noted, however, that the size of the samples used in these clinical trials were inadequate to test a hypothesis with regard to effects of treatment on total mortality. When the results of all randomized trials of the treatment of diastolic high blood pressure were recently pooled in a meta-analysis, it appeared that a small but significant reduction in total mortality may have occurred across all age groups.[42] The data are inadequate, however, to draw conclusions about the impact of the treatment of high blood pressure on total mortality in persons over the age of 50.

Adverse Effects of Antihypertensive Therapy

Concerns about toxicity resulting from antihypertensive therapy in the elderly have led many authors to advise restraint or even therapeutic nihilism with respect to the treatment of high blood pressure in this group.[76] Theoretically, there are several reasons why the risk/benefit ratio for the treatment of high blood pressure might increase with age. It is believed that the elderly are particularly susceptible to many of the side effects of antihypertensive medication.[34,76] For instance, elderly patients are more likely to develop hyponatremia and hypokalemia when treated with standard doses of diuretics.[27,34] It is also thought that older patients are more likely to develop side effects such as depression and confusion when treated with antihypertensive medications that affect the central nervous system (e.g., beta blockers or drugs that affect the alpha adrenergic nervous system).[9] There is good evidence to indicate that the baroreceptor reflex becomes less sensitive with age.[28,41] As a result, the elderly could be more sensitive to the postural hypotensive effects of antihypertensive medications, with a consequent increased propensity for falls and fractures.[14]

Although some have argued that elderly persons with high blood pressure actually need higher blood pressure for adequate perfusion of vital organs (e.g., the brain and kidney),[35] most studies have not shown that judicious use of antihypertensive medications in the elderly has a significant adverse effect on either renal or cerebral perfusion.[12,55,68] It is clear from the work of Strandgaard that in middle-aged patients with chronic essential hypertension the pressure-flow curve for cerebral autoregulation is reset to the right. The chronic hypertensive thus would be more susceptible to cerebral hypoperfusion if mean arterial pressure were lowered substantially and acutely.[66] It is quite possible that a similar situation might exist in an elderly patient who had high blood pressure for a number of years. Further work indicates that cautious, slow lowering of blood pressure to normal levels in the chronic hypertensive together with continued control results in a resetting of the cerebral pressure-flow autoregulation curve to the left —the more normal configuration.[10,63] A few studies in middle-aged hypertensives suggest that acute initiation of antihypertensive drugs can lower cerebral perfusion modestly,[12] but chronic administration of appropriate doses of antihypertensive medications does not adversely affect cerebral blood flow.[12,66,67]

It is surprising that there are few data from large-scale clinical trials regarding the toxicity of antihypertensive medication in the elderly. A group of investigators from the Hypertension Detection and Follow-up Program reported that the total rate of adverse effects from the treatment of mild to moderate systolic/diastolic high blood pressure was less for the subgroup aged 60 to 69 at entry than for those under the age of 50.[22] These data are helpful but should be viewed with caution: persons in the 60-69 age range are classified as the "young old" and may not be as susceptible to side effects as the "old old" (aged 75 and older). In addition, such trials tend to select "well" subjects and are not necessarily representative of elderly patients who have one or more serious comorbid diseases.

The largest available data set on the toxicity of antihypertensive therapy in the elderly comes from the European Working Party on Hypertension in the Elderly and its randomized study of the efficacy of the treatment of systolic/diastolic high blood pressure in a cohort of patients with a mean age at entry of 72 years.[4] Early reports from this trial indicate that treatment with a thiazide-triamterene combination (followed by alphamethyldopa as a second-step agent when needed) resulted in mild increases in glucose intolerance, serum creatinine, and uric acid and a mild decrease in serum potassium in the treatment group.[2] Treatment does not appear to have had a significant long-term effect on serum cholesterol levels.[5] To date, only limited data on side effects have been reported, but there was no significant difference between the treatment and control groups in the rate at which patients were dropped from the study because of presumed drug-related side effects. The biochemical side effects listed above were not thought to outweigh the benefits of treatment.

Questions still remain about possible negative impacts of antihypertensive therapy on the quality of life for elderly patients. Only a few trials of antihypertensive drug therapy (in any population, young or old) have adequately quantified the impact of reported adverse effects on subjects' quality of life.[19,70] Most trials have simply counted the total number of reported adverse effects without attempting to describe either qualitatively or quantitatively their impact on physical, emotional, or cognitive function or overall perceptions of quality of life.[67] Quality of life issues that are important to the elderly and that may be influenced by antihypertensive therapy (but that have not been well studied) include emotional state (depression, life satisfaction, anxiety), cognitive or intellectual processing (memory, psychomotor speed, problem solving), physical functioning (ability to perform self-care tasks, upper and lower extremity speed, gait and balance), and social interaction (social activities, contacts).[75] The adage, "in the elderly it is as important to add life to years as years to life," is relevant here.

NONPHARMACOLOGIC THERAPY

Nonpharmacologic therapy, including weight loss, sodium restriction, moderate consistent aerobic exercise, and relaxation therapy all may be helpful in individual patients, particularly those with borderline elevations of blood pressure.[40] Unfortunately, the only available studies of the efficacy of these measures have been conducted in young to middle-aged patients.[61] Currently, data indicate that, if the patient is overweight, moderate weight loss is the most effective nonpharmacologic treatment for high blood pressure, although questions remain regarding the efficacy of weight loss because many patients regain the lost weight over an extended period of time.[11] Studies of sodium restriction indicate that approximately one-third of hypertensive patients respond to sodium restriction, especially if sodium intake can be decreased below 80 milliequivalents per day.[69] There is some evidence that elderly hypertensives are more sodium sensitive than younger hypertensives, particularly among blacks.[68,78] Because the diet of many elderly persons includes substantial quantities of prepackaged or canned foods that are high in sodium, clinicians frequently find that their elderly patients would rather take a diuretic than severely restrict their salt intake. The limited data currently available on the impact of exercise and relaxation therapy on high blood pressure indicate that both interventions can have modest, short-term beneficial effects on blood pressure.

SUMMARY OF INTERVENTION DATA

In summary, it appears that treatment of diastolic high blood pressure in elderly persons is warranted but that the magnitude of benefit may be marginal in persons of advanced age or persons with very mild high blood pressure. In those cases, it is important to consider other parameters such as quality of life or economic status.

The goal for treatment should be a modest lowering of blood pressure, as noted above. Currently, there are insufficient data to draw conclusions regarding the treatment of isolated systolic high blood pressure.

COST-EFFECTIVENESS OF TREATMENT FOR HIGH BLOOD PRESSURE IN PERSONS OVER 50

There have been few adequate cost-effectiveness analyses of the treatment of high blood pressure in persons over the age of 50. An early cost-benefit analysis conducted by Stason and Weinstein[63] showed that the cost-benefit ratio for the treatment of diastolic high blood pressure appeared to improve as the severity of diastolic high blood pressure increased. Their analyses indicated that the cost of treatment to provide an additional year of quality-adjusted life could vary from $5,000 to more than $20,000 per year, depending on the age of the patient and compliance with treatment. In addition, their analyses indicated that the impact of treatment on quality-adjusted life years might be negligible after age 60. However, analyses of results of the European Working Party on Hypertension in the Elderly[4] plus new information from recent trials indicate that the treatment of moderate and severe diastolic high blood pressure (DBP > 100 mmHg) in persons over the age of 50 is probably cost-effective when compared with other standard preventive therapies. No definitive statement is possible regarding the cost-effectiveness of treating mild diastolic high blood pressure (DBP of 90 to 99 mmHg) in the elderly. In discussing cost-effectiveness, it should be pointed out that the individual benefit may be small, but the population benefit may be great. In an analysis of its treatment trial for mild hypertension, the British Medical Research Council determined that in order to prevent one stroke, 850 persons had to be treated for one year. Further analysis showed that, in the population treated, there was a 45 percent reduction in stroke incidence.[80]

SUMMARY

In conclusion, systolic/diastolic high blood pressure and isolated systolic high blood pressure are sufficiently prevalent to be considered important risk factors in persons over the age of 50. In addition, epidemiologic studies indicate that both systolic blood pressure elevations and diastolic blood pressure elevations are significant independent risk factors for subsequent cardiovascular and cerebrovascular morbidity and mortality; however, elevation of systolic blood pressure is the single most powerful cardiovascular risk factor in persons over the age of 50. Because cerebrovascular and cardiovascular morbidity and mortality impose a substantial burden on the elderly, treatment of high blood pressure should be considered. Current data from randomized controlled clinical trials indicate that the treatment of moderate to severe diastolic high blood pressure in the elderly is, indeed, warranted; treatment of mild diastolic high blood pressure in the elderly should be left to the judgment of individual clinicians and patients. The data are too limited at present to make a definitive statement about the treatment of isolated systolic hypertension.

RECOMMENDATIONS

Services

1.   Persons aged 50 and older without known cardiovascular disease should have their blood pressure checked:

A.   once every two years if their pressure has been normal previously and they have no family history or risk factors for cardiovascular disease (see also the clinical recommendations below);
B.   at least once per year if they have a family history or other risk factors for cardiovascular disease; or
C.   at least every six months if they have a past diagnosis of high blood pressure.

2.   Persons aged 50 and older with known cardiovascular disease should have their blood pressure checked at every physician visit and at least once per year if pressure previously was normal or every six months if the individual was previously thought to be hypertensive.

Clinical

Note: Patient blood pressures for assessment of hypertension should be based on the average of three measures taken during three visits.

1.   Patients with diastolic blood pressure greater than 100 mmHg should be treated pharmacologically.
2.   For patients with diastolic blood pressure of 90 to 100 mmHg,

nonpharmacologic therapy is recommended. If after three to six months, diastolic pressure is greater than 95 mmHg, a pharmacologic therapy regimen should be initiated.*

3. For patients with systolic blood pressure greater than 160 mmHg and diastolic pressure less than 90 mmHg, physician discretion should be used regarding therapy. However, in no case should therapy be aggressively pursued in the face of continued disabling side effects.

4. Patients should be informed of the actual expected magnitude of reduction in morbidity and mortality for pharmacologic treatment of their level of blood pressure as some may rationally prefer no treatment.

Research

1. The elderly should be included in studies of the efficacy and adverse effects of newer antihypertensive agents, treatments for mild diastolic high blood pressure, and nonpharmacologic interventions.

2. Methods for better risk stratification of elderly hypertensives should be developed to improve the accuracy of predictions of risk and contribute to more informed treatment of mild hypertensives in high-risk strata.

3. Studies should be conducted to examine the impact of the treatment of high blood pressure on cognitive function, mood, physical function, and quality of life.

4. The prevalence of false-positive diagnoses of high blood pressure in the elderly should be studied.

Policy

1. Medicare and private insurance should offer reimbursement for blood pressure screening.

2. Strategies should be devised to promote the detection and treatment of high blood pressure in those sectors of the over-50 population that are likely to have access only to periodic medical care—especially black males and isolated elderly persons.

---

*When pharmacologic therapy is chosen, the clinician should begin with one-half the usual dose and proceed slowly. Whenever possible, adjuvant nonpharmacologic therapy should be used.

REFERENCES

1. Abrass, I. B. Catecholamine levels and vascular responsiveness in aging. In: M. J. Horan, J. B. Dunbar, and E. C. Hadley (eds.), Blood Pressure Regulation and Aging: Proceedings of a National Institutes of Health Symposium. New York: Biomedical Information Corporation, 1986, pp. 123-130.
2. Amery, A., Berthauz, P., Birkenhager, W., et al. Antihypertensive therapy in patients above 60: Third interim report of the European Working Party on High Blood Pressure in the Elderly. Acta Cardiologica 1978; 33:113-134.
3. Amery, A., Birkenhager, W., Brixko, P., and Bulpitt, C. Mortality and morbidity results from the European Working Party on High Blood Pressure in the Elderly Trial. Lancet 1985; 2:1349-1354.
4. Amery, A., Birkenhager, W., Brixko, P., Bulpitt, C., et al. Efficacy of antihypertensive drug treatment according to age, sex, blood pressure, and previous cardiovascular disease in patients over the age of 60. Lancet 1986; 1:589-592.
5. Amery, A., Birkenhager, W., and Bulpitt, C. Influence of antihypertensive therapy on serum cholesterol in elderly hypertensive patients. Acta Cardiologica 1982; 37:235-244.
6. Applegate, W. B., Vander Zwaag, R., Dismuke, S. E., et al. Control of systolic blood pressure in elderly black patients. Journal of the American Geriatric Society 1982; 30:391-396.
7. Applegate, W. B. Hypertension in elderly patients. Annals of Internal Medicine 1989; 110:901-915.
8. Aquyagi, M., Deshmukh, V. D., Meyer, J. S., et al. Effect of beta-adrenergic blockade with propranolol on cerebral blood flow, auto-regulation, and CO_2 responsiveness. Stroke 1976; 7:219-295.
9. Avorn, J., Everitt, D. E., and Weiss, S. Increased antidepressant use in patients prescribed beta-blockers. Journal of the American Medical Association 1986; 255:357-360.
10. Barry, I., Sevendson, U. G., Vorsurp, S., et al. The effect of chronic hypertension and antihypertensive drugs on the cerebral circulation space. Acta Medica Scandinavica (Suppl.) 1982; 678:37-42.
11. Berchtold, P. Epidemiology of obesity and hypertension. International Journal of Obesity 1981; 5(Suppl. 1):1-7.
12. Bertel, O., and Marx, B. E., Effects of antihypertensive treatment on cerebral perfusion. American Journal of Medicine 1987; 82(Suppl. 3B):29-36.
13. Build and Blood Pressure Study. Chicago: Society of Actuaries, 1959.
14. Caird, F. L., Andrews, G. R., and Kennedy, R. D. Effect of posture on blood pressure in the elderly. British Heart Journal 1973; 35:527-530.
15. Colleandrea, M. A., Friedman, G. D., Nickman, M. Z., and Lynd, D. N. Systolic hypertension in the elderly. Circulation 1970; 41:239-245.
16. Coope, J., and Warrender, T. S. Lowering blood pressure. Lancet 1987; 1:1380.
17. Coope, J., and Warrender, T. S. Randomized trial of treatment of hypertension in elderly patients in primary care. British Medical Journal 1986; 293:145-114.
18. Cornoni-Huntley, J., LaCroix, A. Z., and Havlik, R. J. Race and sex differentials in the impact of hypertension in the United States: The National Health and Nutrition Examination Survey 1 Epidemiologic Follow-up Study. Archives of Internal Medicine 1989; 149:780-788.

19. Croog, S. H., Levin, S., Testa, M. A., et al. The effects of antihypertensive therapy on the quality of life. New England Journal of Medicine 1986; 314:1657-1664.
20. Cruickshank, J. M., Thorp, J. M., and Zacharias, F. J. Benefits and potential harm of lowering high blood pressure. Lancet 1987; 1:581-584.
21. Curb, J. D., Borhani, N. O., Blaszkowski, T. P., et al. Long-term surveillance for adverse effects of antihypertensive drugs. Journal of the American Medical Association 1985; 253:3263-3268.
22. Curb, J. D., Borhani, N. O., Entwisle, G., et al. Isolated systolic hypertension in 14 communities. American Journal of Epidemiology 1985; 121:362-369.
23. Cutler, J. A., and Furberg, C. D. Drug treatment trials in hypertension: A review. Preventive Medicine 1985; 14:499-518.
24. Dawson, D., Hendershot, G., and Fulton, J. Aging in the eighties: Functional limitations of individuals 65 and over. National Center for Health Statistics, Advance Data No. 133, June 1987.
25. Drizd, T., Dannenberg, A., and Engel, A. Blood pressure levels in persons 18-74 years of age in 1976-80 and trends in blood pressure from 1960-1980 in the United States. Department of Health and Human Services, Publ. No. (PHS) 86-1684. Vital Health Statistics, Series 11, 1986.
26. Final report of the Subcommittee on Nonpharmacological Therapy of the 1984 Joint National Committee on Detection, Evaluation, and Treatment of High Blood Pressure. Nonpharmacological approaches to the control of high blood pressure. Hypertension 1986; 8:444-467.
27. Flanenbaun, W. Diuretic use in the elderly; potential for diuretic-induced hypokalemia. American Journal of Cardiology 1986; 57:38A-43A.
28. Gribbin, B., Pickering, T. G., Sleigh, P., and Peto, R. Effect of age and high blood pressure on baroreflex sensitivity in man. Cardiovascular Research 1971; 29:424-431.
29. Griffith, D. N. W., James, I. M., Newbura, P. A., and Wollard, M. L. The effect of beta adrenergic receptor blocking drugs on cerebral blood flow. British Journal of Clinical Pharmacology 1979; 7:491-494.
30. Hallock, P., and Benson, I. C. Studies of the elastic properties of human isolated aorta. Journal of Clinical Investigation 1937; 16:595-602.
31. Hulley, S. B., Furberg, C. D., Gurland, B., McDonald, R., Perry, H. M., Schnaper, H. W., Schoenberger, J. A., Smith, W. M., and Vogt, T. M. Systolic hypertension in the elderly program: Antihypertensive efficacy of chlorthalidone. American Journal of Cardiology 1985; 56:913-920.
32. Hypertension Detection and Follow-up Program Cooperative Group. Blood pressure studies in 14 communities. Journal of the American Medical Association 1977; 237:2385-2391.
33. Hypertension Detection and Follow-up Cooperative Group. Five year findings of the Hypertension Detection and Follow-up Program. Journal of the American Medical Association 1979; 242:2562-2577.
34. Jackson, G., Piersoianouski, T. A., Mohon, W., et al. Inappropriate antihypertensive therapy in the elderly. Lancet 1976; 2:1317-1318.
35. Jones, J. V., and Graham, D. I. Hypertension and the cerebral circulation— its relevance to the elderly. American Heart Journal 1978; 96:270-271.
36. Kannel, W. B., Gordon, T., Castelli, W. B., and Margolis, J. R. Electrocardiographic left ventricular hypertrophy and risk of coronary heart disease. Annals of Internal Medicine 1970; 72:813-822.
37. Kannel, W. B., Gordon, T., and Schwartz, M. J. Systolic vs. diastolic blood

pressure and risk of coronary heart disease. American Journal of Cardiology 1971; 27:335-346.

38. Kannel, W. B., and Gordon, T. Evaluation of cardiovascular risk in the elderly: The Framingham Study. Bulletin of the New York Academy of Medicine 1978; 54:573-591.

39. Kannel, W. B. Some lessons in cardiovascular epidemiology from Framingham. American Journal of Cardiology 1976; 37:269-282.

40. Kaplan, N. M. Non-drug treatment of hypertension. Annals of Internal Medicine 1985; 102:359-373.

41. Langford, H. G., Blanfox, D., Oberman, A., et al. Dietary therapy slows the return of hypertension after stopping prolonged medication. Journal of the American Medical Association 1985; 253:657-664.

42. Lipsitz, L. A. Abnormalities in blood pressure hemostasis associated with aging and hypertension. In: M. J. Horan, M. Steinberg, J. B. Dunbar, and E. C. Hadley (eds.), Blood Pressure Regulation and Aging: Proceedings of a National Institutes of Health Symposium. New York: Biomedical Information Corporation, 1986.

43. MacMahon, S. W., Cutler, J. A., Furgerg, C. D., and Payne, G. H. The effects of drug treatment for hypertension on morbidity and mortality from cardio-vascular disease: A review of randomized trials. Progress in Cardiovascular Disease 1986; 29:99-118.

44. McLenachan, J. M., Henderson, E., Morris, K. I., and Dargie, H. J. Ventricular arrhythmia in patients with hypertensive left ventricular hypertrophy. New England Journal of Medicine 1987; 317:787-792.

45. Messerli, F. H. The age factor in hypertension. Hospital Practice 1986; 75:103-112.

46. Messerli, F. H., Sundgaard-Riise, K., Ventura, H. O., et al. Essential hypertension in the elderly: Hemodynamics. Lancet 1983; 2:983-986.

47. Meyer, J. S., Okamato, S., Sari, A., Koto, A., et al. Effects of beta-adrenergic blockade on cerebral auto-regulation and chemical vasomotor control in patients with stroke. Stroke 1974; 5:167-179.

48. National Center for Health Statistics. Annual summary of births, marriages, divorces, and deaths, U.S., 1985. Monthly and Vital Statistics, Series 34, 1986.

49. National Center for Health Statistics. National Ambulatory Medical Care Survey, U.S., 1979, Summary. Vital and Health Statistics, Series 13, No. 66, 1982.

50. National Heart Foundation of Australia. Treatment of mild hypertension in the elderly. Medical Journal of Australia 1981; 247:633-638.

51. Ostfeld, A. M. Epidemiologic overview. In: M. J. Horan, G. M. Steinberg, J. B. Dunbar, and E. C. Hadley (eds.), Blood Pressure Regulation and Aging: Proceedings of a National Institutes of Health Symposium. New York: Biomedical Information Corporation, 1986.

52. Page, L. B., and Friedlander, J. Blood pressure, age, and cultural change. In: M. J. Horan, G. M. Steinberg, J. B. Dunbar, and E. C. Hadley (eds.), Blood Pressure Regulation and Aging: Proceedings from a National Institutes of Health Symposium. New York: Biomedical Information Corporation, 1986.

53. Panel on Statistics for an Aging Population. The Aging Population in the Twenty-first Century: Statistics for Health Policy. Washington, D.C.: National Academy Press, 1988.

54. Pickering, T. G., James, G. D., Boddie, C., Harshfield, G. A., Blank, S., and

Laragh, J. H. How common is white coat hypertension? Journal of the American Medical Association 1988; 259:225-228.

55. Ram, C. B. S., Meese, R., Kaplan, N. M., Debous, M. D., Bonte, F. J., Forland, S.C., and Cutler, R. E. Antihypertensive therapy of the elderly: Effects on blood pressure and cerebral blood flow. American Journal of Medicine 1987; 82(Suppl. 1A):53-57.

56. Rosner, B., and Polk, B. F. Predictive values of routine blood pressure measurements in screening for hypertension. American Journal of Epidemiology 1983; 117:429-442.

57. Runyan, J. W. The Memphis Chronic Disease Program: Some comparisons in outcome and the nurse in the extended role. Journal of the American Medical Association 1975; 231:264-267.

58. Rutan, G., Kuller, L. H., Neaton, J. D., Wentworth, D. N., McDonald, R. H., and Smith, W. M. Mortality associated with diastolic hypertension and isolated systolic hypertension among men screened for the Multiple Risk Factor Intervention Trial. Circulation 1988; 77:504-514.

59. Samuelsson, O., Wilhelmsen, L., Anderson, O. K., Pennert, K., and Berglund, G. Cardiovascular morbidity in relation to change in blood pressure and serum cholesterol levels and treated hypertension. Journal of the American Medical Association 1987; 258:1768-1776.

60. Savage, D. D., Garrison, R. J., Kannel, W. B., Levy, D., Anderson, S. J., Stokes, J., Feinleib, M., and Castelli, W. P. The spectrum of left ventricular hypertrophy in a general population sample: The Framingham study. Circulation 1987; 75(Suppl. 1):126-133.

61. Spence, J. D., Sibbald, W. J., and Cape, R. D. Pseudohypertension in the elderly. Clinical Science and Molecular Medicine 1978; 55:399-402.

62. Spencer, G. Projections of the population by age, race, and sex: 1983-2080. Current Population Reports, U.S. Bureau of the Census, Series P-25, No. 952, 1984.

63. Stason, W. B., and Weinstein, M. C. Allocation of resources to manage hypertension. New England Journal of Medicine 1977; 296:732-739.

64. Statement on Hypertension in the Elderly: Report of the Working Group on Hypertension in the Elderly. Journal of the American Medical Association 1986; 256:70-74.

65. Stamler, R., Stamler, J., Grimm, R., et al. Nutritional therapy for high blood pressure. Journal of the American Medical Association 1987; 257:1484-1491.

66. Strandgaard, S., Olesen, J., Skinhoj, E., and Lassen, N. A. Auto-regulation of brain circulation and severe arterial hypertension. British Medical Journal 1973; 3:507-510.

67. Strandgaard, S. Auto-regulation of cerebral blood flow in hypertensive patients. Circulation 1976; 53:720-727.

68. Strandgaard, S. Cerebral blood flow and antihypertensive drugs in the elderly. Acta Medica Scandinavica 1983; 676(Suppl.):103-109.

69. Sullivan, J. M., Prewitt, R. L., and Ratts, T. E. Sodium sensitivity in normotensives and borderline hypertensive humans. American Journal of the Medical Sciences 1988; 295:370-377.

70. The Final Report of the Sub-Committee on Hypertension Definition and Prevalence of the 1984 Joint National Committee. Hypertension prevalence and status of awareness, treatment and control in the United States. Hypertension 1985; 7:457-468.

71. Toth, P. J., and Horwitz, R. I. Conflicting clinical trials and the uncertainty

of treating mild hypertension. American Journal of Medicine 1983; 75:482-488.

72. Vardan, S., Mookherjee, S., Warner, R., and Smulyan, H. Systolic hypertension: Direct and indirect blood pressure measurements. Archives of Internal Medicine 1983; 143:935-938.

73. Veterans Administration Cooperative Study Group. Effects of treatment in hypertension: Results in patients with diastolic blood pressure 90/114. Journal of the American Medical Association 1970; 1213:1143-1152.

74. Watkins, L. O. Racial differences in the management of hypertension. Journal of the National Medical Association 1989; 81(Suppl.):17-24.

75. Wenger, N. K., Matteson, M. E., Furberg, C. D, and Elinson, J. Assessment of Quality of Life in Clinical Trials and Cardiovascular Therapies. New York: LeJacq Publishing, Inc., 1984.

76. White, W. B., Schulman, P., McCabe, E. J., and Dey, H. M. Average daily blood pressure, not office pressure, determines cardiac function in patients with hypertension. Journal of the American Medical Association 1989; 261:873-877.

77. Williamson, J., and Chopin, J. M. Adverse reactions to prescribed drugs in the elderly: A multicenter investigation. Aging 1980; 9:73-80.

78. Wilking, S. V. B., Belanger, A., Kannel, W. B., D'Agostino, R. B., and Steel, K. Determinants of isolated systolic hypertension. Journal of the American Medical Association 1988; 260:3451-3455.

79. Zemel, M. B. and Sowers, J. R. Salt sensitivity and systemic hypertension in the elderly. American Journal of Cardiology 1988; 61:7h-12h.

80. Medical Research Council Working Group (MRC). MRC trial of treatment of mild hypertension: Principal results. British Medical Journal 1985; 291:97-104.

4
Medications

———

M edications play a unique role among the elderly because they can be major contributors to both increased functional capacity and increased disability. When used correctly, medications can be the single most important element of the therapeutic encounter. When used inappropriately, however, medications can generate considerable morbidity and even mortality. Striking changes, among the most dramatic seen in geriatric medicine, can occur in clinical status if needed drugs are provided to a patient who has not been receiving them or if medications with toxic side effects are removed.

The definition of disability related to medication (its presence or absence) presents several methodological problems. It is fairly easy to define some of the more straightforward complications of medication use (e.g., an acute allergic reaction), but these reactions are low on the list of drug side effects in the elderly, in terms of both frequency and clinical importance. Far more challenging is the definition and quantification of more relevant kinds of drug-induced morbidity, including falls and fractures, mental status changes, or, at the extreme end of the continuum, the broad category of functional, cognitive, and affective states that together are known as quality of life outcomes. Defining the disability-preventing actions of medications is equally difficult, which may tend to deter the consideration of these aspects. Both methodologically and conceptually, it is difficult to consider an event that did not occur—for example, a stroke in an older patient whose high blood pressure has been adequately controlled over several decades. Nevertheless, a balanced look at the role medications play in the health of the elderly requires consideration of such events, even though they may be identifiable only by the traces they leave in morbidity and mortality rates, rather than as observable entities in their own right.

There are important physiologic reasons why the role of medication increases (as does its potential for good or ill effect) throughout the second 50 years of life. First, in this part of the life cycle, illness occurs with increasing frequency, and such illness is often amenable to drug therapy. Less well understood are the ways in which the effects of medications are magnified by the physiology of even normal aging. There is a well-documented decrease in renal function with advancing age, which increases the effect of medications (e.g., digoxin, cimetidine, aminoglycosides) that are excreted primarily through the kidney.[39] Although there is a clear age-related decline *on average* as people age, more recent research has made it clear that there is great interindividual variability in the pace with which such declines occur.[28] This finding has important implications for the effect of medications on individual elderly patients: the older the patient, the less able the physician will be to predict the optimal dose of a medication on the basis of clinical judgment and routine laboratory tests alone. An even greater controversy surrounds the role of aging in the impairment of hepatic function, the other major route of elimination of drugs. Certain hepatic metabolic functions appear to diminish with age; they certainly do so in the face of illnesses that are more common in the elderly than in younger patients (e.g., congestive heart failure), thus decreasing the margin of safety for many medications.[48]

Other changes that occur in the second half of life also have profound implications for drug effects in the elderly. There is an age-related increase in the proportion of body weight that is fat as opposed to muscle, which tends to increase the half-life and steady-state concentration of lipophilic medications (such as the benzodiazepines) but has the reverse effect on polar drugs (such as lithium). There is also an inverse relationship between age and weight in the current American population. However, data indicate that physicians do not correct for such changes in determining the dose of several commonly used medications in the elderly, which results in the prescription of more milligrams per kilogram in elderly patients than in younger ones.[15]

Furthermore, research on changes in receptor physiology with age suggests that receptors for many commonly used medications may actually become more sensitive with advancing age, thus intensifying drug effects in the elderly at the very time that, because of the factors described above, the concentration of available drug is higher.[42]

BURDEN

Prevalence

A large number of studies, comprising thousands of patients in several countries, have shown that adverse drug reactions are an important cause of hospital admissions, accounting for between 3 and 8 percent of all admissions.[16,27] The frequency of adverse effects certainly rises with the coming of old age, but there is some question as to how much of this increase is explained by the increasing prevalence of disease in this age group as opposed to the independent contribution of age-related changes in pharmacokinetics and pharmacodynamics.[30] Nonetheless, from clinical, public health, and economic perspectives, it is certainly true that adverse effects of medications are an increasingly important contribution to hospitalization in the elderly, and debate has begun to focus on the preventability of such drug-related admissions. Are drug-induced illnesses more common in the elderly because they are inevitable consequences of the use of powerful therapeutic agents in an age group that needs them, or could more judicious use of therapies result in a reduction in the rates of adverse drug reactions? The latter possibility is addressed in a study of several hundred emergency admissions to a teaching hospital, in which preadmission outpatient records were reviewed to determine whether the admission could have been prevented. Investigators determined that, for drug-related admissions, fully 50 percent could have been prevented by more judicious prescribing from patients' ambulatory care physicians.[12]

Costs

The economic burden of drug-induced disability is difficult to measure with precision. Estimates can be made by considering the proportion of hospital days associated with adverse drug reactions (including those causing admission as well as additional days of hospitalization required by inpatient drug reactions) and adjusting this figure to reflect hospital days used by those over the age of 50. Using this method, which considers only hospital-related drug reactions, the cost of drug-induced illness is high.[23,49] The cost would need to be reduced substantially (perhaps as much as by half) if one were to include only *preventable* drug toxicity.

Another important aspect of the economic burden of medication-related disability is the cost of care for illnesses that could have been prevented or ameliorated by the rational use of drug therapy. This expense is even more difficult to calculate, but it can be roughly estimated by considering, for example, the reduction in the rate of stroke that can be achieved with the management of high blood pressure in this age group and then estimating the prevalence of nontreatment of hypertensive patients aged 50 and older. The costs of "preventable strokes that were not prevented" are substantial, bringing into perspective the contribution to total health care expenditures of medication under- as well as overuse.[1,45]

The Impairment/Disability/Handicap Sequence

Even in the most basic studies of drug effects, the elderly have been systematically neglected. For example, early studies of the treatment of essential hypertension contained few subjects over the age of 65, either because of perceived problems of accessibility or outright exclusion of such patients by the study design. It is only in the last few years that clinical trials specifically designed to address high blood pressure in the elderly have begun to appear.[2] Data from these studies indicate that it is, indeed, advantageous to treat high blood pressure in older patients, at least up to age 80, and that, applied widely, this practice could prevent considerable morbidity, especially from stroke. These findings, however, have not yet begun to permeate the consciousness of many practicing physicians (see Chapter 3 for a more detailed discussion of high blood pressure).

Evidence on the efficacy/risk profile of most new drugs is gathered in premarketing testing that generally includes only modest numbers of truly elderly subjects, most of whom are in better health than the typical geriatric patient who receives such medications once they have been marketed. Elderly patients are often excluded from trials because they are more likely to experience complications from therapy (or from underlying diseases). The result of their underrepresentation in new drug trials is that the scientific basis used by physicians (or patients) to make rational assessments of benefit and risk is deficient for many of the medications used most commonly in the older age group.[50] This problem is illustrated by the case of nonsteroidal anti-inflammatory drugs (NSAIDs) in the treatment of osteoarthritis. Degenerative joint disease is a major cause of disability in the second 50 years of life, and its medical management represents one of the most important ways in which drugs can enhance functional capacity in this age group. Yet even for this common class of medications, major questions remain concerning risks and benefits as a function of age. First, not enough is known about the differences between the newer NSAIDs and aspirin in this regard, despite the enormous difference in cost. Tinnitus can serve as a sign of salicylate toxicity in the young, but age-associated loss of high-frequency hearing may blunt its occurrence in the old. What are the implications of this understanding for drug choice in the management of arthritis? Similarly, it is possible that the important age-related difference in NSAID toxicity may not be the frequency with which gastrointestinal bleeding occurs but the frequency with which it is fatal, which may be higher in the elderly.[22] There is some provocative evidence on this point, but clearly, more data are needed.

Lipid-lowering therapy is another area of practice that lacks risk-benefit information in relation to the older patient. The reduction of serum cholesterol is seen by most authorities as an efficacious approach to the prevention of cardiac disease; yet there has been little study of the contributions of the new lipid-lowering drugs, particularly in the second half of life and despite the fact that the elderly are among the most prominent consumers of such agents. (Ironically, the old may be a cohort for whom such medication may be of considerably less importance.[46]) In addition to the methodological challenge of quantifying the relative benefit of prolonging life in older versus younger patients, there is also the thorny issue of quantifying the "good" derived from postponing or preventing cardiovascular disability in the two age groups. These difficulties are by no means unique to the evaluation of drug therapies and apply with equal vexation to such interventions as smoking cessation and dietary change. But intervention in the form of medication adds another level of complexity because of the higher frequency of "dis-benefits" that can occur with drugs, whether as adverse effects or greater costs. Considering only the former, even if benefits were relatively constant but the risk of adverse effects increased with age, there would probably be a point at which *on average* the medication would be as likely to do harm as good. Running in a completely opposite direction are speculations that the new class of lipid-lowering agents may prevent numerous forms of debility associated with the aging process, potentially turning the risk-benefit relationship around. Clearly, much more research is needed on the actual contribution of this important new class of drugs to health promotion and disability prevention in older patients.

Too few studies have considered the impact of drugs on functional capacity (its improvement or deterioration) in the second half of life. Typically, clinical endpoints reflect much more narrow therapeutic goals (e.g., the reduction of blood pressure) instead of focusing on the ways in which functional status (e.g., cognition, affect, or sexual potency) is affected by antihypertensive therapy. Recently, a larger view has been taken of drug effects in the elderly, which are frequently described as quality of life endpoints.[18] Within this framework, medications that initially appear to have comparable therapeutic efficacy in terms of a narrowly defined outcome may have vastly different effects on more broadly defined measures of health status. Specifically, antihypertensive therapies have different effects on cognition and mood, independent of their impact on blood pressure. Alternatively, quality of life outcomes may be the direct result of a drug's intended therapeutic effect, as when the successful treatment of incontinence has a positive impact on self-image and life satisfaction.[37]

Efforts to describe the outcomes of drug therapy in terms of a quantitative expression of such measures (such as the quality-adjusted life year, or QALY) have been few and far between. Considering the major methodologic and conceptual problems associated with this approach, it is not surprising and may in fact be beneficial. In the hands of some authors, the calculation of QALYs systematically devalues interventions that benefit the old because an intervention in the second half of life is likely to yield fewer "years saved." Each year of life may be further devalued by the presence of common conditions of old age, such as arthritis, or, in the schemes of some authors, by old age itself.[3]

Research on drug effects in the elderly suggests the complex ways in which aging and therapeutics can interact to affect health status. The frequency of adverse drug reactions (ADRs) increases with age,[30] although it is less than clear whether this increase is an effect of senescence itself or of the higher frequency of co-existing illness and polypharmacy in the elderly—an important distinction. Also unclear at times is the relationship between the prescribing event and the ADR, which may be temporally and clinically separated. For example, there is considerable uncertainty regarding the increase in hip fractures associated with psychoactive drug use in the elderly,[34] especially as other evidence suggests that medications can have a protective effect against this most disabling geriatric illness. (The use of estrogens or thiazides can reduce the frequency and severity of osteoporosis;[32,38] likewise, estrogens may prevent some cardiovascular disability in postmenopausal women.[14]) Nonetheless, ADRs are clearly an important cause of hospitalization and disability, much of which may be prevented through more judicious prescribing.[12]

An often overlooked contributing factor to ADRs is the interaction of self-prescribed over-the-counter medications with prescribed medications. In addition to being the largest consumers of prescription drugs, the elderly also are the largest consumers of over-the-counter drugs. As more of these over-the-counter medications become available, the potential adverse interactions will also increase. Moreover, the direct adverse effects of these drugs themselves need further study.[51]

Mental impairment resulting from the use of psychoactive drugs, in both institutionalized elderly and younger patients past the age of 50, is an issue of some controversy. Clearly, some reduction in cognitive capacity can result from chronic use of benzodiazepines and neuroleptics in some patients, but more needs to be learned about the nature and magnitude of such changes.[26,40] In one area of the mental health realm, however, age may provide protection from drug-induced disability. The depression associated with beta-blocker use appears to occur with less frequency in the old than in those who are younger, a phenomenon that may be related to the reduced sensitivity of adrenergic receptors with aging.[6]

PREVENTABILITY OF BURDEN

A large body of data indicate that there is considerable room for improvement in the way medications are used in the over-50 age group. Physicians are not as proficient as they might be in optimal prescribing for the elderly, a deficit reflected in actual prescribing practices[11, 33] and in surveys of physician knowledge.[4,20] In addition, physician-patient communication is often problematic, both in the areas of history taking for therapeutic decision making and communication about drug effects, precautions, and compliance.[17,19]

Fortunately, a number of interventions have been developed to address these problems; some have even been field-tested in randomized controlled trials. Traditional educational methods using group lectures and mailed informational material appear to be of limited efficacy in changing prescribing practices;[7,24,44] however, consistent, reproducible data indicate that in-person, face-to-face education provided by clinical educators (either pharmacists or other physicians) has proven effective in making physicians' prescribing decisions more precise. In several studies that track physician prescribing across six states, such interventions have resulted in a reduction in inappropriate prescribing that was both statistically and economically significant.[9,41] A formal benefit-cost analysis of the largest of these studies has further shown that the dollars saved by a third-party reimbursement program (Medicaid) actually exceeded the cost of running the program by a factor of 2 to 1.[43] This approach has now been extended to nursing homes, in which an educational outreach effort (also known as "public interest detailing") resulted in a significant reduction in the excessive use of psychoactive medication in the six long-term care facilities studied.[5] The intervention, which consisted of separate educational sessions with physicians, nurses, and aides, also resulted in an improvement in the cognitive status of residents in the experimental homes as measured by a detailed battery of neuropsychiatric and functional status tests.

RECOMMENDATIONS

Services

1. Physicians should review, with their elderly patients, all medications being taken, prescription and non-prescription, for appropriateness, potential adverse interactions, and continued need at least every six months.

2. Periodic medication review should be reimbursed as a non-procedural activity.

Research

1. Risk versus benefit: For many drug groups, it may not be appropriate to translate the risk and benefit properties of medications as determined in younger populations into care of the elderly. For example, although the efficacy of a drug may not diminish with age, the frequency and severity of the adverse effects it causes may well increase. Therefore, these drug characteristics should be reassessed in elderly patients de novo and not extrapolated from younger populations.

2. Impact on functional capacity: It is not enough to measure drug effects in older patients merely in relation to one immediate therapeutic goal (e.g., cessation of ventricular arrhythmias, decrease in intra-ocular pressure). Rather, the effects of drugs should be measured in relation to functional status and other less obvious endpoints, including central nervous system function, gait stability, and functional capacity of other organ systems.

Education

1. Virtually all health professional education (including that of most physicians, nurses, and pharmacists) is inadequate in its treat-

ment of therapeutics, as well as in its presentation of materials in geriatrics.[8] Considerably more information on the proper use of medications in the elderly should be systematically integrated into the curricula of health education programs, even as the knowledge base itself is extended in the manner described above.

2. Elderly patients themselves would benefit from additional education concerning their use of medications. Although some programs have been developed, more are needed, particularly to alert elderly patients and their families to the possibility of drug side effects (instead of emphasizing only patient responsibility for total compliance with prescribed regimens).[29]

Policymakers

1. There continues to be substantial controversy concerning drug testing in the elderly. Some fault the Food and Drug Administration for a lack of guidelines, which have been discussed since 1983 but never enacted as law; the agency and many in the pharmaceutical industry claim that discussion of these guidelines has resulted in voluntary compliance with their principles, making further regulatory action unnecessary.[47] At a minimum, data are needed to clarify whether this is, indeed, the case. In addition, distinctions must be made between the needs of patients labeled as "old" because they are 60 or older (many of whom are 61 or 62) versus truly geriatric patients in their eighties or more, with at least some coexisting illness. If voluntary compliance appears to be inadequate, stronger regulatory measures may be necessary.

2. New drugs to be used primarily among the elderly should be studied prior to marketing to determine their effects on important geriatric endpoints (e.g., intellectual functioning and other aspects of functional capacity), as well as the impact on their labeled indication.

3. Given the inadequate training of most physicians in the optimal use of medications in the elderly, it is not surprising that evidence of poor prescribing abounds, ranging from the improper choice of a dose or of agents within a class, to failure to prescribe an indicated therapy (e.g., an antihypertensive) for a patient who needs it.[31,36] In the coming decades, the increasing role of government and other payers in shaping clinical decision making will make it more acceptable to require demonstrations of competence in various areas of practice, including prescribing for the elderly, to maintain credentials or receive payment for services.[10]

4. Several groups have demonstrated that educational outreach by medical schools ("public interest detailing") can improve the prescribing of drugs, even in long-term care facilities,[5,9,41] and saves

more than it costs.[43] This approach should now be tested in large-scale demonstration studies.

5. The use of existing, claims-based data sets of prescription information to study drug effects in the elderly should be increased.[13,35] With such data sets, drug epidemiologists can provide surveillance to track adverse drug effects in key subpopulations. However, adequate funding has yet to be provided.

6. As developments in pharmacology and molecular biology produce ever more powerful (and costly) new additions to the therapeutic armamentarium, it will become increasingly important for the health care system to gain a more sophisticated understanding of drug effects defined broadly in the aging population. Consideration should be given to how drugs are tested for efficacy and risk, who participates in trials, what outcomes are studied, and how surveillance of drug effects on large populations is carried out, once the drugs are in widespread use.

REFERENCES

1. Amery, A., Birkenhauger, W., Brixko, R., et al. Efficacy of antihypertensive drug treatment in patients over 60. Lancet 1986; 1:589.
2. Applegate, W. B. Hypertension in elderly patients. Annals of Internal Medicine 1989; 110:901.
3. Avorn, J. Benefit and cost analysis in geriatric care: Turning age discrimination into health policy. New England Journal of Medicine 1984; 310:1294-1301.
4. Avorn, J., Chen, M., and Hartley, R. Scientific versus commercial sources of influence on the prescribing behavior of physicians. American Journal of Medicine 1982; 73:4-8.
5. Avorn, J., Soumerai, S. B., et al. Clinical consequences of a reduction in psychoactive drug use in nursing homes. The Gerontologist, in press.
6. Avorn, J., Everitt, D. E., Weiss, S., et al. Increased antidepressant use in patients prescribed beta-blockers. Journal of the American Medical Association 1986; 255:357-360.
7. Avorn, J., Olins, N. J., and Trotter, M. Efficacy of printed medication information for the elderly: A randomized controlled trial. Harvard Medical School, unpublished manuscript.
8. Avorn, J. Pharmacology and geriatric practice: A case study in technology nontransfer. Clinical Pharmacology and Therapeutics 1987; 42:674-676.
9. Avorn, J., and Soumerai, S. B. Improving drug-therapy decisions through educational outreach. New England Journal of Medicine 1983; 308:1457-1463.
10. Avorn, J. Testimony before a joint hearing of the U.S. Senate and House of Representatives. U.S. Congressional Record, S. Hrg. 98-392. Washington, D.C.: U.S. Government Printing Office.
11. Beers, M., Avorn, J., Soumerai, S. B., et al. Medication use in nursing home residents. Journal of the American Medical Association 1988; 260:3016-3020.
12. Bigby, J., Dunn, J., Goldman, L., Adams, J. B., Jen, P., Landefeld, C. S., and Komaroff, A. L. Assessing the preventability of emergency hospital admissions. A method for evaluating the quality of medical care in a primary care facility. American Journal of Medicine 1987; 83(6):1031-1036.

13. Bright, R. A., Avorn, J., and Everitt, D. E. Medicaid database development for epidemiologic research. Journal of Clinical Epidemiology, in press.
14. Bush, T. L., Barrett-Connor, E., et al. Cardiovascular mortality and non-contraceptive use of estrogen. Circulation 1987; 75:1102.
15. Campion, E. W., deLabry, L. O., and Glynn, R. J. The effect of age on serum albumin in healthy males: Report from the Normative Aging Study. Journal of Gerontology 1988; 43:M18-M20.
16. Caranosos, C. J., Stewart, R. B., and Cluff, L. E. Drug-induced illness leading to hospitalization. Journal of the American Medical Association 1974; 228:713.
17. Carty, M., Avorn, J., Everitt, D. E., and Bright, R. A. Physician-patient communication and geriatric medication use. The Gerontologist 1985; 25:33.
18. Croog, S. H., Levine, S., Testa, M. A., et al. The effects of hypertensive therapy on the quality of life. New England Journal of Medicine 1986; 314:1657-1664.
19. Everitt, D., Avorn, J., and Baker, M. The prescribing of hypnotics: Therapeutic decisions based on inadequate history. The American Journal of Medicine, in press.
20. Ferry, M. E., Lamy, P. P., Becker, L. A., et al. Physicians' knowledge of prescribing for the elderly. Journal of the American Geriatrics Society 1985; 33:616.
21. Greenblatt, D., Seller, E., and Shader, R. Drug disposition in old age. New England Journal of Medicine 1982; 306:1081-1087.
22. Griffin, M. R., Ray, W. A., and Schaffner, W. Nonsteroidal anti-inflammatory drug use and death from peptic ulcer in elderly persons. Annals of Internal Medicine 1988; 109:359-363.
23. Grymonpre, R. E., Mitenko, P. A., Sitar, D. S., Aoki, F. Y., and Montgomery, P. R. Drug-associated hospital admissions in older medical patients. Journal of the American Geriatrics Society 1988; 36:1092-1098.
24. Haynes, R. B., Davis, D. A., McKibbon, A., and Tugwell, P. A critical appraisal of the efficacy of continuing medical education. Journal of the American Medical Association 1984; 251:61-64.
25. Jaffe, M. E. The clinical investigation of drugs for use by the elderly: Industry initiatives. Clinical Pharmacology and Therapeutics 1987; 42:677-680.
26. Larson, E. B., Kukull, W. A., Buchner, D., et al. Adverse drug reactions associated with global cognitive impairment in elderly persons. Annals of Internal Medicine 1987; 107:169-173.
27. Levy, M., Kewitz, H., Altwein, W., et al. Hospital admissions due to drug reactions: A comparative study from Jerusalem and Berlin. European Journal of Clinical Pharmacology 1980; 17:25.
28. Lindeman, R. D., Tobin, J. D., and Shock, N. W. Longitudinal studies on the rate of decline in renal function with age. Journal of the American Geriatrics Society 1985; 33(4):278-285.
29. Morrow, D., Leirer, V., and Sheikh, J. Adherence and medication instructions: Review and recommendations. Journal of the American Geriatrics Society 1988; 36:1147-1160.
30. Nolan, L., and O'Malley, K. Prescribing for the elderly. Part I. Sensitivity of the elderly to adverse drug reactions. Journal of the American Geriatrics Society 1988; 36:142-149.
31. Nolan, L., and O'Malley, K. Prescribing for the elderly. Part II. Prescribing patterns: Differences due to age. Journal of the American Geriatrics Society 1988; 36:245-254.
32. Quigley, M. E., Martin, P. L., Burnier, A. M., and Brooks, P. Estrogen therapy arrests bone loss in elderly women. American Journal of Obstetrics and Gynecology 1987; 156:1516-1523.

33. Ray, W. A., Federspiel, C. F., and Schaffner, W. A study of antipsychotic drug use in nursing homes: Epidemiologic evidence suggesting misuse. American Journal of Public Health 1980; 70:485-491.

34. Ray, W. A., Griffin, M. R., Schaffner, W., Baugh, D. K., and Melton, L. J. III. Psychotropic drug use and the risk of hip fracture. New England Journal of Medicine 1987; 316:363-369.

35. Ray, W. A., and Griffin, M. R. Use of Medicaid data for pharmacoepidemiology. American Journal of Epidemiology 1989; 129:837-849.

36. Reidenberg, M. M. Drug therapy in the elderly: The problem from the point of view of a clinical pharmacologist. Clinical Pharmacology and Therapeutics 1987; 42:677-680.

37. Resnick, N. M., and Yalla, S. V. Management of urinary incontinence in the elderly. New England Journal of Medicine 1985; 313(13):800-805.

38. Riggs, B. L., and Melton, L. J. (eds.) Osteoporosis. New York: Raven Press, 1988.

39. Rowe, J. Aging, renal function, and response to drugs. In: L. Jarvik (ed.), Clinical Pharmacology and the Aged Patient. New York: Raven Press, 1981.

40. Salzman, C. Clinical Geriatric Psychopharmacology. New York: McGraw-Hill, 1984.

41. Schaffner, W., Ray, W. A., Federspiel, C. F., and Miller, W. D. Improving antibiotic prescribing in office practice. Journal of the American Medical Association 1983; 250:1728.

42. Scott, J. C., and Stankski, D. R. Decreased fentanyl and alfentanil dose requirements with age: A simultaneous pharmacokinetic and pharmacodynamic evaluation. Journal of Pharmacological and Experimental Therapeutics 1987; 204:159-166.

43. Soumerai, S. B., and Avorn, J. Economic and policy analysis of university-based drug "detailing." Medical Care 1986; 24:313-331.

44. Soumerai, S. B., and Avorn, J. Efficacy and cost-containment in hospital pharmacotherapy: State of the art and future directions. Milbank Memorial Fund Quarterly 1984; 62(3):447-474.

45. Strandgaard, S., and Haunso, S. Why does anti-hypertensive treatment prevent stroke but not myocardial infarction? Lancet 1987; 2:658.

46. Taylor, W. C., Pass, T. M., Shepard, D. S., and Komaroff, A. L. Cholesterol reduction and life expectancy. A model incorporating multiple risk factors. Annals of Internal Medicine 1987; 106(4):605-614.

47. Temple, R. FDA discussion paper on testing of drugs in the elderly. Department of Health and Human Services, Public Health Service, Food and Drug Administration, Washington, D.C., September 1983.

48. Vestal, R., Norris, A., Tobin, J., Cohen, B., Shock, N., and Andres, R. Antipyrine metabolism in man: Influence of age, alcohol, caffeine, and smoking. Clinical Pharmacology and Therapeutics 1975; 18:425-432.

49. Williamson, J., and Chopin, J. M. Adverse reactions to prescribed drugs in the elderly: A multicentre investigation. Age and Ageing 1980; 9:73.

50. Wolfe, S. M., et al. Worst Pills, Best Pills. Washington, D.C.: Public Citizen, 1988.

51. Abrams, R. C., and Alexopoulous, G. S. Substance abuse in the elderly: Over the counter illegal drugs. Hospital and Community Psychiatry 1988; 39(8):822-823.

5

Risk Factors for Infection in the Elderly

There appears to be a direct relationship between increasing age and susceptibility to infections, although the documentation is weak for many specific infectious diseases.[18,47,55] Factors that may contribute to the predisposition of the elderly to infections include impaired immune function,[47,55] anatomic and functional changes,[8] and degree of exposure to infections. Certain infections are important risk factors for the elderly because the illnesses they cause reduced quality of life during the infection and are at times fatal. The environment of an elderly individual can also influence his or her exposure to infections, with long-term care facilities[28] and hospitals[47] bringing greater risk than living at home. Data on community-acquired infections (i.e., acquired in "the community" rather than in institutions) are more limited than data from institutional settings.[47]

The range of infections that present serious risks for the elderly is great and includes the following: respiratory infections including pneumonia,[17] influenza,[47] and tuberculosis;[18] bacteremia;[18] and nosocomial (hospital-acquired) infections.[47] Other types of infections also have been cited as particular problems for the elderly including urinary tract infections, salmonellosis, and hepatitis.[18] Undoubtedly, there are other infectious diseases that present risks for the elderly, but limited data preclude their identification at this time.

Given existing knowledge of the burdens caused by infections and the limited range of current preventive measures, only a few of the infection categories mentioned above can be given priority for prevention at the present time. Thus, in this chapter, the committee has chosen to highlight pneumococcal infections, influenza, and nosocomial infections. Each deserves high priority for prevention because each is a serious risk factor for the elderly and can be prevented to a great extent with existing interventions.

PNEUMOCOCCAL DISEASE

Pneumococcal disease has long been recognized as an important risk factor for the elderly. This category includes pneumonia, bronchitis, bacteremia, and meningitis caused by any one of the 83 serotypes of *Streptococcus pneumoniae*. Pneumococcal pneumonia is the most common form of community-acquired pneumonia in the elderly, accounting for up to 60 percent of cases[14,34,35,36,37,52] and for up to 20 percent of nosocomial pneumonias.[10,52] Pneumococcal bacteremia, which is more easily proven than pneumococcal pneumonia, occurs in up to one-quarter of cases of pneumococcal pneumonia. Population-based studies have shown that the elderly sustain the highest pneumococcal bacteremia rates of any population group—50 per 100,000 persons over the age of 65,[36,37] which is more than three times greater than the rates for younger persons.

The costs of pneumococcal diseases are great because the elderly require hospitalization and the illnesses often cause complications.[26,32] Although pneumococcal pneumonia does not result in permanent lung damage, complications from bacteremia and meningitis are common and can damage other organ systems. Death rates from pneumococcal bacteremia range from 20 to 80 percent, increasing with age and complications.[10,26,36,37]

Although antibiotics are considered to be effective in the treatment of pneumococcal diseases, deaths and complications often occur despite the prompt use of effective antibiotics. Further reductions in morbidity and mortality from pneumococcal diseases require that preventive measures be used. Pneumococcal polysaccharide vaccine is the only currently available preventive measure. This vaccine was first developed in the 1940s but was temporarily abandoned with the advent of antibiotics. With growing recognition of the limitations of antibiotics, the vaccine was again introduced in the late 1970s. Some of the controlled studies of the vaccine have not demonstrated a protective effect;[16,48] other research, including case-control studies, have shown pneumococcal vaccine to be both immunogenic[43,44] and safe,[15] and to provide up to 70 percent efficacy in the elderly.[50,51] A vaccine works by providing protective levels of type-specific antibodies. Confidence in the effectiveness of the current 23-valent pneumococcal polysaccharide vaccine—that is, the assurance factor for its efficacy—is high. This vaccine has also been judged most useful for the elderly in terms of cost-effectiveness and has been recommended for all elderly persons by the Centers for Disease Control as well as the American College of Physicians.[11,40,42,53]

The committee thus recommends that 23-valent vaccine be given to all elderly persons, particularly those 65 years of age or older. Because antibodies resulting from vaccine are long-lasting, the vaccine will only need to be given once to most persons. It should be strongly considered for anyone 50 years of age or older with underlying disease (e.g., a heart condition). Revaccination should be considered for elderly persons who received only 14-valent vaccine. Medicare Part B currently pays for the vaccine and the costs of administration, but there has been little promotion of this benefit and many are unaware of its existence.

Because pneumococcal vaccine is less effective in immunosuppressed persons, the committee urges that more immunogenic vaccines be developed. (The conjugated H. influenza vaccine currently available could be used as the prototype.) There is also a great need for more education of physicians, public health agencies, and the elderly themselves regarding the benefits of pneumococcal vaccine. Medicare should promote the vaccine more actively (an individual's Medicare card could indicate whether he or she had received the vaccine), and industry and government should promote or conduct research aimed at improving the existing versions. There should also be incentives provided by third-party payers for persons to be immunized. Giving vaccine on entry to long-term care or at the time of discharge from a hospital are other ways to increase the vaccine's use.

INFLUENZA

Influenza, a respiratory infection caused by any of the strains of the antigenically variable influenza A and B viruses, is one of the major risk factors for the elderly. Influenza epidemics occur every year, usually during the winter months. Estimates of the costs of such epidemics cite staggering figures derived from medical costs, hospitalizations, loss of productivity, and mortality.[30,31,54] Household survey data suggest that influenza leads all other illness categories in terms of restricted activity and bed days,[1] whereas viral surveys have demonstrated that the elderly consistently have the highest hospitalization and death rates from influenza of any population group.[3,5,6,7,13,20,33,41] Even in winters with "limited" influenza activity, there are more than 20,000 excess deaths from influenza in the United States, 80 to 90 percent of which occur among the elderly. Influenza can lead to such complications as pneumonia, both viral and bacterial, and cardiac respiratory failure. It can also aggravate preexisting conditions such as diabetes or asthma. Lengthy periods are needed to recover from influenza.

Morbidity and mortality from influenza are largely unnecessary because effective preventive measures in the form of safe, effective vaccines became available in the late 1960s. Modern vaccines are trivalent, with two type A and one type B strains, and contain egg-grown viruses. (Vaccines are contraindicated in persons allergic to eggs.) All current influenza vaccines contain only inactivated (killed) viruses and must be given every year because of changing viruses and declining antibody levels. In field studies, vaccines have proven to be approximately 70 percent effective in preventing influenza illness, with the remaining 30 percent of vaccinees suffering a milder illness than that acquired by unvaccinated persons. Vaccines are effective in elderly persons living in the community[24,27] as well as those in long-term care,[38,39] although they are less immunogenic in the immunosuppressed elderly. For immunized immunosuppressed persons and for persons unable to take vaccines, antiviral prophylaxis or treatment (or both) with amantadine is effective against influenza A strains.[2] However, vaccines are the only protection against type B influenza viruses. Influenza vaccine can be effectively given even during an epidemic if the vaccinee is also given prophylactic doses of amantadine for the 14 days required for vaccine-induced antibodies to develop. The assurance factor for influenza vaccines and the antiviral amantadine is high.

The costs and benefits of influenza vaccine have been estimated.[30,31,54] Because vaccines, although safe and relatively inexpensive, must be given to millions of high-risk elderly each year, it was concluded that influenza vaccines were not cost-saving. They were considered cost-effective, nevertheless, because they produced substantial health benefits for low unit costs.[30,31,54]

The committee strongly endorses the use of influenza vaccine and, where indicated, amantadine for the elderly. Amantadine should be used as prophylaxis during epidemics for persons allergic to eggs. The committee also considers the recent Health Care Financing Administration (HCFA) initiative (to conduct pilot studies for determining whether Medicare should fund influenza immunization) to be a positive step. (Presumably, if the pilot studies can demonstrate cost reductions for Medicare claims, HCFA will deem influenza vaccine to be beneficial and affordable.) Furthermore, the committee urges increased education for the elderly, for physicians and other health care workers, and for persons having close contact with the elderly regarding the safety and benefits of influenza vaccine. In short, the committee believes health policymakers should recognize the severe impact of influenza and its preventability.

Much research is needed to improve existing means of controlling influenza. There are currently several candidate live virus vaccines that are safe, easy to administer, and capable of longer-lasting protection. However, resources are required to conduct the necessary large-scale trials prior to licensure. In addition, better antiviral drugs are needed. Rimantadine,[38] a derivative of amantadine that is safer for the elderly and easier to use, should be made available. An antiviral agent effective against influenza B virus is also needed.

Innovative means are required to make delivery of the current vaccines easier. Regardless of the delivery means or vehicle used, however, influenza vaccines should be required for all nursing home residents and personnel and should be given to any elderly person discharged from the hospital during the fall or winter.* Influenza and pneumococcal vaccines should be promoted together because unlike some combinations they are still safe and effective when given simultaneously. The promotion and marketing of such vaccines by the pharmaceutical industry would be helpful.

NOSOCOMIAL INFECTIONS

Nosocomial infections are infections of any type that are not present on admission to a hospital but develop after the third hospital day. They are unlike the previous risk factors discussed in this chapter in that they are not one specific infection; nevertheless, they constitute an important risk for the elderly. The incidence of nosocomial infections is greater in the elderly than in any other population groups; the elderly have the highest rates of nosocomial urinary tract infections, infected surgical wounds, and nosocomial pneumonia and bacteremia.[17,23,25,46] In addition, the incidence rates for these infections increase with each day in the hospital.[45] The costs resulting from nosocomial infections are also great because they prolong hospital stays and often require separate treatment.[9,51] These infections cause severe morbidity and may result in death.[21,22]

Much progress has been made in preventing nosocomial infec-

---

*For elderly individuals living at home, vaccines also should be administered to their contacts (e.g., children, grandchildren, or household contacts who could expose the elderly person to influenza).

tions, which contributes not only to the health of patients but also to cost-effective health care provision. Rigorous infection control practice emphasizes infection surveillance, isolation practices, handwashing, sterile techniques, and other procedures, all of which can reduce the occurrence and spread of nosocomial infections.[29] Many of these practices are appropriate for long-term care facilities as well. The trend toward shortened hospital stays and outpatient alternatives to hospitalization has reduced the opportunity for nosocomial infections to occur. In addition, the assurance factor for good infection control practice is very high.

INFECTIONS IN LONG-TERM FACILITIES

Preventing nosocomial infections in long-term care facilities is a challenge, in large part because discharging patients is not an option for control. The vaccines mentioned above for influenza and pneumococcal disease, as well as good infection control practice, are crucial for the prevention of infection in nursing homes. Other preventive measures in long-term care include ongoing surveillance to identify problems, monitored hygienic practices in the kitchen to avoid salmonella and other diarrheas, skin care to avoid decubitus ulcers, and proper use of Foley catheters. Proper protective isolation is needed for anyone with infectious diarrhea. In instances in which tuberculosis has been recognized, tuberculin skin testing of residents and staff is needed to identify the spread of infection; in addition, isoniazid prophylaxis should be considered for infected persons.* The two-step tuberculin test is needed for most persons over age 50. The administration of tetanus vaccine should be considered for injury-prone residents as most elderly individuals have not been previously immunized.†

The committee recommends that accrediting agencies require the institution of proper infection control practices as part of nursing home licensure standards. In addition, efforts should continue to avoid unnecessary hospitalizations and to encourage shorter hospital stays. Research into ways to reduce infection in long-term care facilities is also needed, as are standards for infection control.

---

*Tuberculosis can present as a pneumonia; therefore, any pneumonia in the long-term care setting should be considered potentially as a case of tuberculosis. Skin testing should utilize the two-step technique if negative on the original test. Employees in long-term care should be screened for tuberculosis.

†Methicillin-resistant *Staphylococcus aureus* infections are becoming more common in nursing home patients, requiring vancomycin treatment when these infections cause disease. Unfortunately, prevention of these infections has been an elusive goal and remains problematic.

OTHER INFECTIONS

The infections discussed thus far—pneumococcal disease, influenza, and nosocomial infections—deserve priority among prevention efforts for the elderly because they are risk factors with known prevalence and with severe impacts; moreover, they have well-understood prevention methods with high assurance factors. Other high-risk infections also deserve some mention, however.[12,19] For example, tuberculosis remains a problem for elderly individuals. Detecting cases in the older population is difficult; in addition, isoniazid prophylaxis has greater risks for the elderly than for younger persons. Safer preventive therapy and better early case detection is particularly needed for older individuals. Fever of unknown origin is not unusual for the elderly and often results in lengthy and costly evaluations. More expedient and less expensive methods of diagnosing the causes of such fevers are needed. Infectious diarrhea, endocarditis, meningitis, urosepsis, and pressure sores are other examples of infections in the elderly for which better methods of prevention are needed. Any elderly person with valvular heart conditions known to predispose an individual to endocarditis should receive antibiotic prophylaxis for any procedure known to cause bacteremia. All elderly individuals with a known risk factor for the acquired immune deficiency syndrome (AIDS) (e.g., homosexuality, intravenous drug abuse, prior blood transfusions, or hemophilia) should be screened and counseled about human immunodeficiency virus infection.

RECOMMENDATIONS

Services

1. All elderly persons, particularly those aged 65 and older, should receive 23-valent pneumococcal polysaccharide vaccines.

2. Revaccination of elderly persons should be considered for those who have received only 14-valent pneumococcal vaccine.

3. All persons aged 65 and over should receive influenza vaccination annually. Consideration should be given to using amantadine as prophylaxis for those individuals with an allergy to eggs.

4. Pneumococcal and influenza vaccines should be given to all nursing home residents. Vaccination should be considered for all elderly persons discharged from hospitals during the fall and winter.

5. Good infection control practices should be implemented in all institutions but especially in long-term care facilities to combat nosocomial infections. Accrediting agencies should demand proper infection control practices for nursing home licensure.

Research

1. Industry and government should promote or conduct research to improve existing pneumococcal and influenza vaccines. Because these vaccines are less effective in immunosuppressed persons, special attention should be given to improving their immunogenicity.

2. More research is needed to develop better antiviral drugs.

Education

1. Medicare should promote the use of pneumococcal and influenza vaccines more actively. Because these vaccines can be administered safely and effectively at the same time, they should be promoted jointly.

2. Programs should be developed to educate physicians, public health agencies, and the elderly themselves regarding the benefits of the vaccines.

REFERENCES

1. Adams, P. F. Acute conditions and restricted activity during the 1985-86 influenza season. National Center for Health Statistics, Advance Data No. 132, pp. 1-4, 1987.

2. Arden, N. H., Patriarca, P. A., Fasano, M. B., Liu, K. J., Harmon, M. W., Kendal, A. P., and Rimland, D. The roles of vaccination and amantadine prophylaxis in controlling an outbreak of influenza A(H3N2) in a nursing home. Archives of Internal Medicine 1988; 148:865-868.

3. Barker, W. H., and Mullooly, J. P. Influenza vaccination of elderly persons: Reduction in pneumonia and influenza hospitalizations and deaths. Journal of the American Medical Association 1980; 244:2547-2549.

4. Barker, W. H., and Mullooly, J. P. Impact of epidemic Type A influenza in a defined adult population. American Journal of Epidemiology 1980; 112:798-813.

5. Barker, W. H., and Mullooly, J. P. Underestimation of the role of pneumonia and influenza in causing excess mortality. American Journal of Public Health 1981; 71:643-645.

6. Barker, W. H., and Mullooly, J. P. Pneumonia and influenza deaths during epidemics. Implications for prevention. Archives of Internal Medicine 1982; 142:85-89.

7. Barker, W. H. Excess pneumonia and influenza associated hospitalization during influenza epidemics in the United States, 1970-78. American Journal of Public Health 1986; 76:761-765.

8. Beeson, P. B. Alleged susceptibility of the elderly to infection. Yale Journal of Biology and Medicine 1985; 58:71-77.

9. Brachman, P. S., Dan, B. B., Haley, R. W., Hooton, T. M., Garner, J. S., and Allen, J. R. Nosocomial surgical infections: Incidence and cost. Surgical Clinics of North America 1980; 60:15-25.

10. Chang, J. I., and Mylotte, J. M. Pneumococcal bacteremia: Update from an

adult hospital with a high rate of nosocomial cases. Journal of the American Geriatrics Society 1987; 35:747-754.

11. Committee on Immunization. Guide for Adult Immunization. Philadelphia: American College of Physicians, Council of Medical Societies, 1985.

12. Cunha, B. A. (ed.) Infectious Diseases in the Elderly. Littleton, Mass.: PSG Publishing Company, 1988.

13. Eickhoff, T. C., Sherman, I. L., and Serfling, R. E. Observations on excess mortality associated with epidemic influenza. Journal of the American Medical Association 1961; 176:104-110.

14. Filice, G. A., Darby, C. P., and Fraser, D. W. Pneumococcal bacteremia in Charleston County, South Carolina. American Journal of Epidemiology 1980; 112:828-835.

15. Fiumara, N. J., and Waterman, G. E. Statewide geriatric immunization program with polyvalent pneumococcal vaccine. Current Therapeutic Research 1979; 25:185-192.

16. Forrester, H. L., Jahnigen, D. W., and LaForce, F. M. The efficacy of pneumococcal vaccine in a high-risk population. American Journal of Medicine 1987; 83:425-430.

17. Freeman, J., and McGowan, J. E. Risk factors for nosocomial infections. Journal of Infectious Diseases 1978; 138:811-819.

18. Gardner, I. D. The effect of aging on susceptibility to infection. Reviews of Infectious Disease 1980; 2:801-810.

19. Gleckman, R. A., and Gantz, N. M. (eds.) Infections in the Elderly. Boston: Little, Brown and Company, 1983.

20. Glezen, W. P. Serious morbidity and mortality associated with influenza epidemics. Epidemiologic Reviews 1982; 4:25-44.

21. Gross, P. A., Neu, H. C., Aswapokee, P., Antwerpen, C. V., and Aswapokee, B. Deaths from nosocomial infections: Experience in a university hospital and a community hospital. American Journal of Medicine 1980; 68:219-223.

22. Gross, P. A., and Antwerpen, C. V. Nosocomial infections and hospital deaths. A case-control study. American Journal of Medicine 1983; 75:658-662.

23. Gross, P. A., Rapuano, C., Adrignolo, A., and Shaw, B. Nosocomial infection: Decade-specific risk. Infection Control 1983; 4:145-147.

24. Gross, P. A., Quinnan, G. V., Rodstein, M., LaMontagne, J. R., Kaslow, R. A., Saah, A. J., Wallenstein, S., Neufeld, R., Denning, C., and Gaerlan, P. Association of influenza immunization with reduction in mortality in an elderly population. Archives of Internal Medicine 1988; 148:562-565.

25. Haley, R. W., Hooton, T. M., Culver, D. H., Stanley, R. C., Emori, T. G., Hardison, C. D., Quade, D., Shachtman, R. H., Schaberg, D. R., Shah, B. V., and Schatz, G. D. Nosocomial infections in U.S. hospitals, 1975-1976. Estimated frequency by selected characteristics of patients. American Journal of Medicine 1981; 70:947-959.

26. Hook, E. W., Horton, C. A., and Schaberg, D. R. Failure of intensive care unit support to influence mortality from pneumococcal bacteremia. Journal of the American Medical Association 1983; 249:1055-1057.

27. Howells, C. H. L., Vesselinova-Jenkins, C. K., Evans, A. D., and James, J. Influenza vaccination and mortality from bronchopneumonia in the elderly. Lancet 1985; 1:381-383.

28. Jackson, M. M., and Fierer, J. Infections and infection risk in residents of long-term care facilities: A review of the literature, 1970-1984. American Journal of Infection Control 1985; 13:63-77.

29. Joint Commission on the Accreditation of Hospitals. Infection control. In: AMH/84 Accreditation Manual for Hospitals. Chicago: Joint Commission on the Accreditation of Hospitals, 1983, p. 69.

30. Kavet, J. Influenza and public policy. Doctoral dissertation, Harvard School of Public Health, 1972.

31. Klarman, H. E., and Guzick, D. Economics of influenza. In: P. Selby (ed.), Influenza: Virus, Vaccines, and Strategy. New York: Academic Press, 1976, pp. 255-270.

32. Lipsky, B. A., Boyko, E. J., Inui, T. S., and Koepsell, T. D. Risk factors for acquiring pneumococcal infections. Archives of Internal Medicine 1986; 146:2179-2185.

33. Liu, K. J., and Kendal, A. P. Impact of influenza epidemics on mortality in the United States from October 1972 to May 1985. American Journal of Public Health 1987; 77:712-716.

34. MacFarlane, J. T., Finch, R. G., Ward, M. J., and MacRae, A. D. Hospital study of adult community-acquired pneumonia. Lancet 1982; 2:255-258.

35. Marrie, T. J., Haldane, E. V., Faulkner, R. S., Durant, H., and Kwan, C. Community-acquired pneumonia requiring hospitalization. Is it different in the elderly? Journal of the American Geriatrics Society 1985; 33:671-680.

36. Mufson, M. A. Pneumococcal infections. Journal of the American Medical Association 1981; 246:1942-1948.

37. Mufson, M. A., Oley, G., and Hughey, D. Pneumococcal disease in a medium-sized community in the United States. Journal of the American Medical Association 1982; 248:1486-1489.

38. Patriarca, P. A., Kater, N. A., Kendal, A. P., Bregman, D. J., Smith, J. D., and Sikes, R. K. Safety of prolonged administration of rimantadine hydrochloride in the prophylaxis of influenza A virus infections in nursing homes. Antimicrobial Agents and Chemotherapy 1984; 26:101-103.

39. Patriarca, P. A., Weber, J. A., Parker, R. A., Hall, W. N., Kendal, A. P., Bregman, D. J., and Schonberger, L. B. Efficacy of influenza vaccine in nursing homes. Reduction in illness and complications during an influenza A(H3N2) epidemic. Journal of the American Medical Association 1985; 253:1136-1139.

40. Patrick, K. M., and Woolley, F. R. A cost-benefit analysis of immunization for pneumococcal pneumonia. Journal of the American Medical Association 1981; 245:473-477.

41. Perrotta, D. M., Decker, M., and Glezen, W. P. Acute respiratory disease hospitalizations as a measure of impact of epidemic influenza. American Journal of Epidemiology 1985; 122:468-476.

42. Recommendations of the Immunization Practices Advisory Committee. Pneumococcal polysaccharide vaccine. Morbidity and Mortality Weekly Report 1989; 38:64-76.

43. Roghmann, K. J., Tabloski, P. A., Bentley, D. W., and Schiffman, G. Immune response of elderly adults to pneumococcus: Variation by age, sex, and functional impairment. Journal of Gerontology 1987; 42:265-270.

44. Ruben, F. L., and Uhrin, M. Specific immunoglobulin-class antibody response in the elderly before and after 14-valent pneumococcal vaccine. Journal of Infectious Diseases 1985; 151:845-849.

45. Saviteer, S. M., Samsa, G. P., and Rutala, W. A. Nosocomial infections in the elderly. Increased risk per hospital day. American Journal of Medicine 1988; 84:661-666.

46. Scheckler, W. E., and Peterson, P. J. Nosocomial infections in 15 rural

Wisconsin hospitals: Results and conclusions from 6 months of comprehensive surveillance. Infection Control 1986; 7:397-402.

47. Schneider, E. L. Infectious diseases in the elderly. Annals of Internal Medicine 1983; 98:395-400.

48. Simberkoff, M. S., Cross, A. P., Al-Ibraham, M., Baltch, A. L., Geiseler, P. J., Nadler, J., Richmond, S., Smith, R. P., Schiffman, G., Shepard, D. S., and Van Eeckhout, J. P. Efficacy of pneumococcal vaccine in high-risk patients. Results of a Veterans Administration cooperative study. New England Journal of Medicine 1986; 315:1318-1327.

49. Shapiro, E. D., and Clemens, J. D. A controlled evaluation of the protective efficacy of pneumococcal vaccine for patients at high risk of serious pneumococcal infections. Annals of Internal Medicine 1984; 101:325-330.

50. Sims, R. V., Steinman, W. C., McConville, J. H., King, L. R., Zwick, W. C., and Schwartz, J. S. The clinical effectiveness of pneumococcal vaccine in the elderly. Annals of Internal Medicine 1988; 108:653-657.

51. Spengler, R. F., and Greenough, W. B. Hospital costs and mortality attributed to nosocomial bacteremias. Journal of the American Medical Association 1978; 240:2455-2458.

52. Verghese, A., and Berk, S. L. Bacterial pneumonia in the elderly. Medicine 1983; 62:271-285.

53. Willems, J. S., Sanders, C. R., Riddiough, M. A., and Bell, J. C. Cost effectiveness of vaccination against pneumococcal pneumonia. New England Journal of Medicine 1980; 303:553-559.

54. Willems, J. S., and Sanders, C. R. Cost-effectiveness and cost-benefit analysis of vaccines. Journal of Infectious Diseases 1981; 144:486-493.

55. Yoshikawa, T. T., Norman, D. C., and Grahn, D. Infections in the aging population. Journal of the American Geriatrics Society 1985; 33:496-503.

6

Osteoporosis

—————

O steoporosis involves bone loss from the skeleton that leads to reduced bone strength and an increased likelihood of fractures. A variety of processes cause bone loss, which may progress silently for decades until fractures occur late in life. Strictly speaking, osteoporosis ("porous bone") is a histological diagnosis wherein the bone tissue is relatively normal but there is too little of it. Clinically, osteoporosis is heralded by the occurrence of characteristic fractures or, prior to the onset of fractures, by reduced bone mineral density as assessed by noninvasive techniques. Although some confusion results from the use of these different definitions, the condition is indisputably a common one. An estimated 20 to 25 million Americans are at increased risk for fracture by virtue of low bone density, and more than a million fractures in the United States each year are attributable to osteoporosis. Many of these fractures result in disability or death; together, they cost the nation an estimated $7 to $10 billion annually, costs that will rise in the future as the population ages. Some of these fractures can be prevented by reducing bone loss, but methods for accomplishing such reductions have not been systematically applied. This chapter summarizes present knowledge concerning the pathophysiology of osteoporosis and reviews evidence regarding the efficacy of potential interventions. On the basis of this information, recommendations are made that should lead to a reduction in the disability produced by this important disorder of older Americans.

BURDEN OF OSTEOPOROSIS AND FRACTURES

Osteoporosis may affect the entire skeleton but, with the exception of tooth loss and ill-fitting dentures related to bone loss in the oral cavity,[20] fractures constitute the only important adverse health consequence of this disorder. However, the medical and social consequences of these age-related fractures make osteoporosis a significant public health problem. Table 6-1 indicates some of the dimensions of this problem.

Morbidity

The fractures linked to osteoporosis occur at many skeletal sites because bone loss is widespread, but proximal femur (hip) fractures, distal forearm (wrist or Colles') fractures, and vertebral (spine) fractures are the most important types. Each year in the United States there may be up to a quarter of a million each of hip fractures and wrist fractures and perhaps twice that number of vertebral fractures.[27] More precise figures are difficult to obtain—hip fracture victims are generally hospitalized, but hospital discharge data also count readmissions for additional care. Most other fractures, including the majority of wrist and spine fractures, are treated on an outpatient basis, but outpatient data are not routinely collected. This lack of accurate data on fracture occurrence nationally is an impediment to the design and implementation of an effective control program. Some steps to improve this situation were outlined in a 1985 National Research Council/Institute of Medicine report entitled *Injury in America;*

TABLE 6-1 Impact of Fractures in the United States

Consequence	Hip Fracture	Wrist Fracture	Spine Fracture
Excess mortality	12%	None	None
Morbidity			
Lifetime risk			
Males	5%	2%	?
Females	15%	15%	35%
Cases per year			
(approximate)	250,000	240,000	500,000
Disability	+++[a]	+	++

Cost (1984) All fracture sites combined = $18 billion

[a]Indicates relative impact.

they include the establishment of an injury surveillance system with more accurate identification of specific injuries and their causes.

Nevertheless, it is clear that fractures are quite common and that osteoporosis is responsible for a substantial portion of them, a figure currently estimated at more than 1.3 million fractures annually.[35] The significance of these numbers is better grasped by noting that the lifetime risk of a hip fracture, 15 percent in white women and 5 percent in men,[5] is equivalent to the combined lifetime risk of developing breast, uterine, or ovarian cancer in women and about the same as the lifetime risk of prostate cancer in men. These fractures increase dramatically in incidence with aging, and, at any age, rates are greater for women than for men (Figure 6-1). Based on the few data available, the same general pattern applies to nonwhite populations, but rates for these groups are lower.[27]

Mortality

The fractures associated with osteoporosis may, in turn, lead to substantial disability and, in the case of hip fractures, even death. Hip fractures lead to an overall 5 to 20 percent reduction in expected survival.[5] The excess mortality may be seen for up to six months following the fracture and varies with age and sex (there appear to be no detailed data concerning the influence of race). For example, about 90 percent of hip fracture victims under 75 years of age are still alive one year later (92 percent of those expected to be alive), compared with only 73 percent (83 percent of expected) of those aged 75 years and older at the time of their fracture.[27] Despite their greater average age when fractures occur, survival is better among women, 83 percent of whom are still alive one year after the fracture, compared with only 63 percent of men. Survival is mediated primarily by coexisting serious illnesses[24] but, after the first six months, is about as expected for persons of comparable age and sex in the general population. Still, hip fractures are associated with many deaths and are partly responsible for the fact that falls are the leading cause of accidental death among men and women aged 75 years or older in the United States and the second leading cause among those aged 45 to 74 years. In contrast, wrist fractures and osteoporotic spine fractures cause no increase in mortality.[27]

Disability

A substantial minority of hip fracture patients are nonambulatory or dependent even before the fracture. However, the devastating

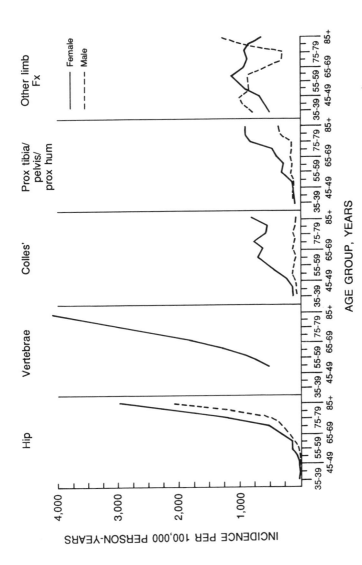

FIGURE 6-1 Age- and sex-specific incidence rates for various fractures among Rochester, Minnesota, residents. Source: L. J. Melton III and S. R. Cummings, "Heterogeneity of Age-related Fractures: Implication for Epidemiology," *Bone and Mineral*, Vol. 2, pp. 321-331, 1987. Elsevier Science Publishers, used with permission.

impact of this injury on the remainder cannot be denied. Of those able to walk before sustaining a hip fracture, for example, half cannot walk independently afterward.[30] The ability of such patients to get about and care for themselves is obviously compromised and their quality of life considerably reduced. Indeed, poor ambulation is one of the strongest predictors of nursing home admission,[4,10] along with the absence of caretakers in the home.[4] In addition to their preexisting medical problems, hip fracture survivors often develop other complications such as pressure sores, pneumonia, urinary tract infections, and arrhythmias, which add to the problems of rehabilitation posed by the fracture itself. Also, depression, common in these individuals, may be exacerbated by the fracture and subsequent hospitalization.[31] Ultimately, up to one-third of hip fracture victims may be totally dependent.[16] As a result of these factors, the risk of institutionalization is great. More than 60,000 nursing home admissions have been attributed to hip fractures annually,[36] along with more than 7 million restricted activity days (62.5 days per episode) among noninstitutionalized individuals in the United States each year.[14] As many as 8 percent of all nursing home residents have had a hip fracture.[14]

Functional recovery after a hip fracture is predicted by prefracture independence (in terms of mobility and performing the activities of daily living), mental impairment (dementia and psychosis as well as confusion during hospitalization), depression, and surgical result, among others.[4,31,33] There is indirect evidence, however, that these factors can be manipulated to alter recovery outcomes. When, as a result of introducing the prospective payment system, the average duration of hospitalization for hip fracture in one large community hospital fell from 21.9 to 12.6 days, the proportion of patients who remained in nursing homes one year later rose from 9 percent to 33 percent.[10] This change was accompanied by a decline in the number of physical therapy sessions and a reduction in the distance patients could walk prior to discharge. Health maintenance organization (HMO) enrollees in the same system, however, performed even less well by these measures yet were only half as likely to be in a nursing home at the end of the year. Moreover, early discharge has been associated with a high level of return to pre-injury independence in selected patients when a program of home rehabilitation is employed.[38] There are several uncontrolled studies such as this that provide tantalizing evidence that an organized program of rehabilitation might yield impressive gains in functioning following a hip fracture. Delineation of an optimal program and its test by clinical trial is an urgent priority.

Despite the fact that only one-fifth of patients with wrist fractures are hospitalized, they account for 48,000 hospital admissions and a further 422,000 physician office visits by persons 45 years of age or older in the United States each year.[14] Distal forearm fractures also lead to more than 6 million restricted activity days annually but have generally been considered free of long-term disability. Yet more recent reviews show that persistent pain, loss of function (diminished range of motion or strength), neuropathies, and posttraumatic arthritis are quite common.[8,9] One-fifth to one-third of wrist fracture patients have a fair to poor functional result,[8] but it is not known whether this leads to any particular handicap. The main risk factors for poor outcome are the severity of the original injury and the adequacy of fracture reduction.

Patients with collapse fractures of the vertebrae often present in considerable pain, but the more common types of spine fractures (anterior wedging and vertebral endplate fractures) may occur gradually and be diagnosed only incidentally on a chest x-ray taken for another purpose.[27] Because atraumatic vertebral fractures do not require reduction and almost never lead to spinal cord injury, only a minority of patients are medically attended. Still, vertebral fractures in patients aged 45 years or older account for 52,000 hospital admissions and 161,000 physician office visits each year, as well as more than 5 million restricted activity days.[14] Although it is generally understood that these fractures may lead to progressive loss of height, kyphosis, posture changes, and persistent pain that interferes with activities of daily living,[46] neither acute nor chronic disabilities associated with vertebral fractures have ever been assessed in a systematic way. This unsatisfactory situation should be corrected as soon as possible.

Costs

The total cost of fractures may be as much as $18 billion per year, and osteoporosis accounts for at least a third of this total,[14] estimated most recently at $7 to $10 billion annually.[35] Because most of these fractures occur in elderly individuals, wages foregone or years of life lost are not the primary determinants of cost. Rather, the important expenses are for inpatient and outpatient medical services and for nursing home care. In 1986 these direct costs included an estimated 322,000 hospitalizations and almost 4 million hospital days for women aged 45 and older for whom osteoporosis-related conditions were the primary cause of admission; more than half of the total was for hip fractures.[36] Osteoporosis was a contributing cause of admission in an additional 170,000 hospitalizations for an extra 290,000 hospital days. In women of this age, there were 2.3 million physician visits for osteoporosis in 1986. At each visit, one-third of the women needed an x-ray, one-fourth required physiotherapy, and most received a prescribed medication for the condition. There were also an estimated 83,000 nursing home stays for osteoporosis-related causes in 1986, with an average duration of stay of one year. Altogether, these direct costs of osteoporosis totaled $5.2 billion for women alone, of which $2.8 billion were for inpatient services and $2.1 billion were for nursing home care.[36]

Such costs can only rise in the future because the elderly population is growing rapidly. Between 1988 and 2050, the actual number of individuals aged 65 and older will increase from 30 to 67 million in the United States.[5] Because the incidence of osteoporosis-related fractures rises with age, this growth in the elderly population will eventually result in a doubling or tripling of the number of hip fractures seen each year, with increases for the other fracture sites as well. It is projected that in only 30 years' time, there could be almost 350,000 hip fractures each year in the United States at an annual cost estimated to be between $31 and $62 billion.[7] This alarming situation can be at least partially avoided if methods to preserve bone mass can be refined and exploited for the entire population, young and old.

DETERMINANTS OF FRACTURES

The risk of fracture in any given situation depends on the degree of trauma experienced and the ability of the skeleton to resist such forces. Bone density in the skeleton can decline to such a point that fractures occur spontaneously, and violent accidents can impose loads capable of breaking any bone. Usually, however, both skeletal integrity and trauma are important. For example, the risk of falling (and particularly of falling heavily) generally increases with age, whereas bone strength diminishes. As a consequence, fracture incidence rises dramatically (especially for hip fractures for which the age-related increase is exponential), and the amount of trauma required to produce a fracture declines.[27] Although the occurrence of a fracture is a complex event (Figure 6-2), interventions are usually directed either at bone mass or trauma, and risk factors should be considered in that light.

Bone Mass

The skeleton is constantly being renewed through a linked process of bone resorption and bone formation.[34] In young adults,

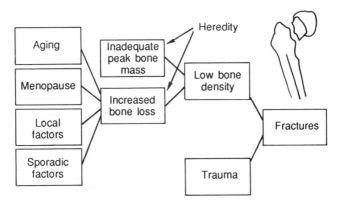

FIGURE 6-2 Conceptual model of the pathogenesis of fractures related to osteoporosis. Source: Modified from B. L. Riggs, "Osteoporosis" in *Cecil Textbook of Medicine,* J. B. Wyngaarden and L. H. Smith, eds., 18th ed., W. B. Saunders, Philadelphia, Pa., 1988, pp. 1510-1515. Reprinted with permission.

the two processes are closely coupled so that bone mass remains stable until the early to middle thirties. With aging, however, bone formation does not keep pace with resorption, and bone mass gradually diminishes. Over the course of their life, women may lose a third of their original cortical (or compact) bone, which forms the shafts of limb bones and constitutes up to 80 percent of the skeleton.[43] They may lose half of their trabecular (or cancellous) bone, which accounts for the remaining 20 percent and makes up the ends of the limb bones and most of the spine, pelvis, and other flat bones of the skeleton. Men lose about two-thirds of these amounts. This bone loss is the result of (1) age-related endogenous factors that occur universally in the population and account for the slow bone loss that occurs over life in both sexes; (2) an accelerated phase of bone loss associated with menopause in women and hypogonadism in a small number of men; and (3) factors that occur sporadically in the population and, when present, increase the rate of bone loss (e.g., certain medical and surgical diseases that produce "secondary" osteoporosis).[43]

This decline in bone mineral density (a pathogenic trait) leads to a disproportionately greater decrease in bone strength (asymptomatic disease) and to an increase in symptomatic disease (i.e., fractures). Because there are no symptoms until fractures occur, relatively few people are diagnosed in time for effective therapy to be administered, even though bone mineral density can be accurately assessed in vivo as a measure of fracture risk (see the appendix to this chapter). Population-based studies demonstrate a gradient of continuously increasing hip fracture incidence associated with declining bone mineral density in the proximal femur, rising wrist fracture incidence with decreasing bone mass in the radius, and increasing vertebral fracture incidence and prevalence with falling bone density in the spine.[17] Several prospective studies show, in addition, that bone mass measurements predict the risk of fractures generally.[15,49] Altogether, roughly 20 to 25 million individuals in the United States have sufficiently low bone density that they are at increased risk of fracture.[35]

Although bone mineral density accounts for most of the ultimate strength of bone tissue,[26] other skeletal factors may be important as well. Biomechanically, the body compensates for age-related bone loss by an increase in the diameter of limb bones, which raises their resistance to bending and twisting. However, this compensatory process is less marked at the ends of limb bones or in the vertebrae, sites at which the fractures associated with osteoporosis typically occur. Strength may also be compromised by age-related increases in the fragility of bone tissue.[26] Although bone architecture and bone quality are important determinants of bone strength, neither can be accurately assessed by noninvasive means for use in risk prediction, and neither can be intentionally altered by a specific therapy. Consequently, they are not considered further.

Trauma

Some fractures are spontaneous, whereas others (especially vertebral fractures) result from everyday activities. Most of the fractures related to osteoporosis, however, occur in conjunction with falls. Falling increases the chance of fracture at any given level of bone mass, as does the inability to dissipate the kinetic energy produced by a fall.[26] The annual risk of falling rises with age, from about one of five women aged 60 to 64 to one in three aged 80 to 84,[6] but only about 5 to 6 percent of falls lead to a fracture of any kind, and only 1 percent lead to a hip fracture.[11]

The pathophysiology of falling is not well understood, and many of the risk factors that have been recognized, such as gait and balance disorders, diminished reflexes and strength, or reduced vision,[48] are difficult to correct. Once bone mass has fallen to such a point that fractures begin to occur, however, there are few other therapeutic options than to try to prevent falls. Among elderly women, for example, who have lost most of the bone they will lose over life and who may have bone density so low that they are at high risk of fracture, the emphasis in prevention has to be on falling. Therefore, programs to reduce the fractures associated with osteoporosis must also include attempts to lower the frequency and severity of falls (see Chapter 15).

PREVENTABILITY OF OSTEOPOROSIS

The bone mass a person has in later life is determined by the peak bone mass achieved in young adulthood and by the subsequent rate of bone loss. Peak bone mass has a strong genetic component because skeletal size is heritable; it would not be surprising if bone loss had a similar genetic element, but this has not been described. Neither peak bone mass nor subsequent bone loss are obviously affected by traditional environmental factors like sanitation or pollution, although fractures are influenced by environmental hazards that induce falls. Instead, host factors are predominant. Endogenous factors such as age, sex, and the effects of specific diseases are considered to be important, and attention has also focused on certain behaviors, including diet, exercise, and smoking. Present knowledge relates these factors mostly to bone mass or fracture risk. How they might influence rehabilitation and health outcomes has been little studied.

Peak Bone Mass

The factors that influence peak adult bone mass are not well described. In general, however, white women have lighter skeletons than white men or black women, whereas black men have the heaviest skeletons.[43] The skeletons of Asians appear to be intermediate between those of blacks and whites. In all three races, women have lower peak bone mass than men. Because initial bone mass is an important determinant of bone mass later in life, these differences may partially explain observed racial and sexual differences in the incidence of osteoporosis and fractures. However, such generalizations should not obscure the fact that some whites have high bone mass, whereas individual nonwhites may have low bone mass and fractures. Moreover, there seem to be exceptions to the general pattern: Hispanics appear to have hip fracture rates that are even lower than American blacks,[45] whereas the Bantu people of South Africa have extremely low fracture rates but also low bone mass.[27] These observations highlight the need to delineate the factors that determine peak bone mass and to better quantify the effect of peak bone mass on fracture risk at older ages. Because no intervention regarding peak bone mass is possible at age 50, however, emphasis in this report must be placed on the risk factors for bone loss.

Hypogonadal Bone Loss

Estrogen deficiency at menopause is an important cause of bone loss and subsequent fractures. Perimenopausal women experience an accelerated phase of bone loss lasting five years or more that accounts for a substantial proportion of their lifetime bone loss.[43] This accelerated phase is associated with a high rate of bone turnover (there is an increase in bone formation but an even greater increase in bone resorption) that can be prevented by estrogen replacement therapy (ERT). Men do not undergo the equivalent of menopause, but gonadal function does decrease in some elderly men, and overt male hypogonadism often is associated with vertebral fractures.[28]

A large number of trials have compared estrogens with placebos and other treatments to determine their effect on bone mass, and nearly all indicate that estrogens are more effective in maintaining bone mass.[17] For example, in one randomized controlled trial of three groups of women followed from six weeks, three years, or six years after oophorectomy, estrogen significantly retarded bone loss for as long as prescribed but at least ten years.[22] Recent data suggest that ERT may be effective in slowing bone loss up to the age of 70.[39] Because the effect of treatment is to reduce bone resorption, however, postmenopausal ERT can slow bone loss, but it cannot restore the biomechanical competence of the skeleton to normal once a substantial amount of bone has been lost.[34] Because lost bone is essentially irreplaceable, emphasis in women 50 to 69 years of age must be on preserving existing bone mass. Greater benefits are achieved with earlier treatment because bone mass is maintained at a higher level.

Estrogens also appear to be effective in preventing fractures. One randomized controlled trial showed that only 4 percent of oophorectomized women on ERT lost height compared with 38 percent of women who were not being treated; almost 90 percent of the latter group with height loss had evidence of vertebral fractures.[23] Although randomized trials of ERT for prevention of hip fracture are less feasible owing to the long delay between menopause and the typical age at which these fractures occur, case-control studies consistently show about a 50 percent reduction in hip and Colles' fractures with long-term ERT.[17]

To intervene by preserving bone density before irreversible bone loss has occurred, patients must be stratified on the basis of fracture risk so that high-risk individuals can be identified. The bone density of any specific individual cannot be determined without direct measurement.[17] A variety of noninvasive bone mass measurement techniques can be used (Table 6-2), including single-photon absorpti-

TABLE 6-2 Comparison of Bone Densitometry Techniques

Technique[a]	Site	Relative Sensitivity (%)	Precision (%)	Accuracy (%)	Duration of Examination (minutes)	Absorbed Dose (millirems)	Cost ($)
Standard technique							
SPA	Proximal radius	1X	2-3	5	15	10	75
DPA	Spine, hip	2X	2-4	4-10	20-40	5	100-150
QCT	Spine	3-4X	2-5	5-20	10-20	100-1,000	100-200
Newer developments							
SPA-R	Distal radius, calcaneus	2X	1-2	5	10-20	5-10	50[b]
DEX-A	Spine, hip	2X	1-2	3-5	5	1-3	75[b]
QCT-A	Spine, hip	3-4X	1-2	5-10	10	100-300	100[b]

[a] SPA = single-photon absorptiometry; SPA-R = rectilinear SPA; DPA = dual-photon absorptiometry, DEXA = DPA with a dual-energy x-ray source; QCT = quantitative computed tomography; QCT-A = QCT with advanced software and hardware capabilities.
[b] Projected cost.

Source: H. K. Genant, J. E. Block, P. Steiger, C. C. Glueer, B. Ettinger, and S. T. Harris, "Appropriate Use of Bone Densitometry," Radiology, Vol. 170, pp. 817-822, 1989.

ometry (SPA), dual-photon absorptiometry (DPA), dual-energy x-ray absorptiometry (DEXA), and quantitative computed tomography (QCT), which are outlined in the appendix to this chapter. Because the range of bone mass at each age is great relative to the small accuracy error of measurement by any of these techniques, women with low, average, or high bone mass can be easily identified. These noninvasive tests are safe and well accepted by patients. Moreover, the accuracy of bone mass measurement compares favorably with that of many accepted clinical tests, including such screening tests as those for serum cholesterol.[17] However, the efficacy of osteoporosis screening for preventing fractures has not been demonstrated directly, and no program has been endorsed.[40]

The level of bone mineral density at which treatment should be initiated for fracture prevention is another criterion that has not yet been determined.[17] At present, this decision is made by individual physicians and patients; the absence of generally accepted guidelines for patient management further hinders the implementation of a population-wide mass screening program for osteoporosis. Nonetheless, Ross and colleagues[44] modeled the savings that might result from treating 50-year-old white women with a regimen that slowed bone loss by 50 percent. They estimated that osteoporotic fractures could be reduced by one-third if the women in the lowest half of the bone mass distribution were all treated. Similarly, Cummings and colleagues[7] calculated a 25 percent reduction in hip fractures in white women by the year 2020 if half of them accepted long-term estrogen use beginning at age 50; they estimated that the overall reduction in hip fractures would be less (18 percent) because men and nonwhite women would be unaffected by this strategy. Indeed, there is no current strategy for preventing osteoporosis in men and nonwhite women, even though they constitute a substantial proportion of all fracture victims.

Previous cost-effectiveness analyses showed little change in life expectancy but some improvement in quality-adjusted life with ERT in women aged 55 to 70 years with osteoporosis.[50] The cost for each quality-adjusted year of life gained was $5,460 to $15,100 for women with a uterus (depending on whether endometrial biopsies were done periodically) and $3,250 for women without a uterus. These figures were said to be comparable to the benefits of treating moderate to severe high blood pressure. However, osteoporosis was defined in that study on the basis of vertebral fractures alone; consequently, the benefits were understated. By considering the risks of hip, wrist, pelvis, humerus, and spine fractures, along with the possible adverse effects of ERT on cancer risk and its potential beneficial effects on cardiovascular disease, Hillner and colleagues[12] found that 15 years of ERT in 50-year-old women were associated with an additional 0.67 quality-adjusted years of life. This benefit increased by 0.17 quality-years for each 10 percent decrease in fracture rates.

Despite data that consistently show a beneficial effect of estrogen on bone mass and fracture risk, only about 5 percent of post-menopausal women are on long-term ERT.[17] The reluctance of physicians to prescribe and of women to comply with such therapy may be related to uncertainty regarding benefits and risks. Endometrial cancer is a concern[18] unless progesterone is used concomitantly, but progesterone may negate the cardioprotective effects of unopposed estrogen.[3] There is also the possibility of an increased incidence of breast cancer. Although such an increase appears to be small and has not been found in all studies, recent suggestions of a heightened risk of breast cancer following combined estrogen and progestin administration[1] indicate a need for additional research to resolve this important question. On the other hand, almost all studies have found a decreased risk for cardiovascular disease in unopposed estrogen users,[2,47] although no controlled clinical trials have been completed. Although the potential cardiovascular benefits of estrogen are likely to be greater than the benefits of fracture reduction, prevention of heart disease is not an approved indication for ERT. In short, many unanswered questions remain.

The other approved therapy for osteoporosis, calcitonin, has not been used extensively for preventing bone loss because of its expense and the need for parenteral administration of present formulations.[35] Calcitonin, and investigational drugs like the bisphosphonates, also act by reducing bone loss. Sodium fluoride, an investigational drug known to increase bone mass in the spine and believed to reduce vertebral fracture rates, has little effect on bone mass in the limbs. Because hip fracture risk is not reduced and may actually be increased somewhat, fluoride has no role in osteoporosis prophylaxis.[29] As is obvious from these observations, improved therapeutic approaches are needed, especially approaches that preserve bone without introducing unpleasant side effects or worrisome complications.

Age-related Bone Loss

This slow form of bone loss continues throughout life and is the major source of bone loss in both sexes. The determinants of age-related bone loss are not precisely known but may include impaired regulation of osteoblasts (the cells that make bone), deficiencies of calcium or vitamin D, and decreased muscle mass associated with inactivity. Bone cell function and regulation is the subject of intensive research at present,[35] but it is not yet possible to intervene to improve osteoblast function. Consequently, attention is directed to the role that calcium, vitamin D, and exercise play in bone loss.

The dietary requirement for calcium is relatively high because of the obligatory fecal and urinary losses of 150 to 250 milligrams per day (mg/day).[41] When the amount of calcium absorbed from the diet is insufficient to offset these losses, calcium must be withdrawn from bone, which contains 99 percent of the total body stores. Moreover, active intestinal absorption of calcium decreases with aging, particularly after age 70, in response to a decrease in biologically active vitamin D.[41] This phenomenon, in turn, may be due to age-related loss of kidney tissue with its enzyme that converts vitamin D to the active form or to a decrease in vitamin D receptors in intestinal cells.

The level of calcium intake required to overcome these problems is controversial, and population studies generally have not demonstrated a strong relationship between calcium intake and bone loss.[19] The recommended daily allowance (RDA) for calcium has not been rigorously established but is currently set at 800 mg/day for adults.[35] The efficacy of this recommendation is uncertain, however. Recent trials have generally found that calcium supplementation shortly after the menopause has little effect on spinal bone loss and only a modest effect on bone loss from the limbs.[41] It is conceivable that calcium would be more effective after the estrogen-dependent phase of accelerated bone loss has ended, but data regarding this hypothesis are conflicting as well. A prospective study that measured rates of bone loss from the vertebrae and radius by serial bone density measurements found no relationship between calcium intake and bone loss.[42] In contrast, a cohort study of elderly men and women living in a retirement community in California showed that those who had hip fractures within 14 years after initial evaluation had had a lower calcium intake at the baseline examination. [13] There are no randomized controlled clinical trials that show directly that calcium supplementation prevents fractures. Nonetheless, the mean dietary calcium intake reported for the general population barely approximates the RDA for calcium in American men and is only 550 mg/day in middle-aged and elderly women.[35] Consequently, it seems prudent to ensure at least the minimum recommended levels of calcium intake at all ages. Detailed guidelines are available.[32]

Similarly, it is reasonable to ensure an adequate vitamin D intake. Such assurance is important because there is an age-related decrease in the ability of the skin to synthesize vitamin D and in the ability of the intestine to absorb it.[41] Thus, although most people get enough vitamin D through sunlight exposure and their normal diet, housebound elderly persons are prone to vitamin D deficiency,[32] particularly when they do not take supplementary vitamins and are consuming a diet marginal in vitamin D. The full extent of this problem is unknown; however, it is correctable with appropriate vitamin D supplementation.

Finally, it has been suggested that age-related bone loss could result, in part, from a decline in activity and fitness.[37] Certainly it is true that bone responds to changes in loading: activity may cause an increase in bone mass, whereas disuse can result in dramatic bone loss.[46] One study[21] of hospitalized adults who required therapeutic bed rest showed that the bone mineral content in the lumbar spine decreased about 0.9 percent per week (equivalent to one year's worth at normal rates), although the rate of loss usually declines over time until a new steady state is reached. The exact pathophysiology of disuse osteoporosis is not known, nor are there specific approaches to remedy the situation except through restored activity. Nonetheless, this type of osteoporosis is a particular concern with regard to the rehabilitation of elderly people after an injury or other serious insult.

On a more positive note, it is thought that increased activity might help to retard bone loss and prevent osteoporosis.[35] A number of short-term trials, mostly uncontrolled, indicate that exercise programs may augment bone mass,[25] but it is not known whether these gains are maintained or whether they lead to a reduction in fractures. Increased activity throughout life appears to be generally beneficial, however, and should be encouraged.[32] Specific recommendations regarding increased activity for older individuals are provided in Chapter 13.

Secondary Osteoporosis

Bone loss may be exacerbated by certain medical diseases, surgical procedures, and medications (Figure 6-3). Although such conditions may be a major cause of osteoporosis in some individuals, in general the bone loss from these factors is additive to the age-related slow bone loss that occurs universally and to the accelerated bone loss that occurs postmenopausally in women.[43] Relatively common causes of this additional bone loss are corticosteroid and anticonvulsant use, gastrectomy, hyperthyroidism, and chronic obstructive lung disease. Less common are such conditions as Cushing's disease, acromegaly, hypopituitarism, and multiple myeloma. Altogether, one or more of these factors may be present in as many as 20 percent

Uncommon Conditions that Contribute Little to Osteoporosis

Acromegaly	Hyperparathyroidism	Osteogenesis imperfecta
Cushing's disease	Hypopituitarism	Multiple myeloma

Important Risk Factors

Cigarette smoking	Gonadal hypofunction	Leanness
Dilantin therapy	Hemiplegia	Obstructive lung disease
Ethanol consumption	Hyperthyroidism	Phenobarbital therapy
Gastrectomy	Inactivity	Thyroidectomy

Common Conditions with No Increased Risk for Osteoporosis

Diabetes mellitus	Parkinsonism	Peripheral vascular disease
Diverticulitis	Peptic ulcer disease	Stroke (without paralysis)
Inguinal hernia	(without gastrectomy)	Thyroid adenoma
Osteoarthritis	Rheumatoid arthritis	Urolithiasis
	(without disability)	

FIGURE 6-3 Relative impact in the community of various purported causes of "secondary" osteoporosis. Source: L. J. Melton III and B. L. Riggs, "Clinical Spectrum," Chapter 6 in B. L. Riggs and L. J. Melton III, eds., *Osteoporosis: Etiology, Diagnosis, and Management,* Raven Press, New York, 1988, pp. 155-179.

of women and 40 percent of men with vertebral or hip fractures.[28] The greater proportion of men affected by secondary osteoporosis is due to their lower background level of the condition—men start with greater bone mass, lose bone less rapidly over life, and do not live as long as women. Consequently, men with fractures are more likely to have a specific cause of excessive bone loss; thus, identification and management of secondary osteoporosis should be a primary consideration for them.

The actual importance, however, of many of the putative causes of "secondary" osteoporosis (along with a host of other conditions not listed here) is uncertain. For example, population-based studies have shown that non-insulin-dependent diabetes mellitus was not associated with any increased risk of fracture or bone loss (in contrast to results of less rigorous clinical studies); recent work raises similar questions about the impact of asymptomatic hyperparathyroidism,[28] which is the form increasingly being diagnosed. Other conditions, like rheumatoid arthritis and stroke, are only indirectly linked to bone loss and fractures as a result of disease-induced disability and consequent disuse osteoporosis.[28] An important research priority, therefore, is to assess the practical impact of the myriad conditions associated with secondary osteoporosis to identify those with a significant influence on fracture risk in the population.

Smoking is also associated with reduced bone mass, as well as with hip and vertebral fractures, and is correlated with another risk factor, ethanol use.[5] Ethanol may depress bone formation by a direct toxic effect on osteoblasts, and tobacco consumption may exert a similar effect on bone.[28] However, smoking is also associated with earlier menopause and with less obesity (which is protective for osteoporosis), whereas excess alcohol use has been linked with nutritional deficiencies and abnormal vitamin D metabolism.[28] Because smoking has other adverse effects (see Chapter 11), the habit should be discouraged. What impact a reduction in smoking would have on reducing osteoporotic fractures, however, is not known.

RECOMMENDATIONS

Services

1. A surveillance system should be developed to monitor osteoporosis prevention efforts. One element of such an effort should be the organization of national fracture data bases that capture outpatient fractures and fracture-related disability and institutionalization. In addition, "small area" analysis should be performed to identify populations at high risk for fracture.

2. As recommended in the report *Injury in America*, a national capacity should be developed for the quick identification and control of outbreaks of specific injuries, as well as a consistent, accurate system for coding the causes of injuries to be used by hospitals. In addition, more refined data on the specific types and causes of injuries are needed to develop effective interventions, and research is needed to determine the short- and long-term costs of injuries.

3. Osteoporosis prevention efforts should be integrated into national and local injury control programs. Adequate reimbursement (both public and private) should be sought for osteoporosis prevention efforts, including bone mass screening tests, drug prophylaxis for bone loss, and rehabilitation after fracture, once these strategies have demonstrated efficacy in reducing adverse health outcomes.

4. To increase the likelihood of rehabilitation after any disabling illness or injury, better methods should be developed to integrate the activities of medical care providers of various disciplines along with community and family resources.

Research

1. Specific bone mass screening and treatment recommendations should be developed, in particular the delineation of guidelines for standardized bone mass measurements and consensus on an overall treatment approach to osteoporosis prophylaxis. In addition,

the U.S. Preventive Services Task Force guidelines on osteoporosis screening should be reassessed. Related efforts should include quantification of the costs and benefits of estrogen replacement therapy (ERT), especially those relating to its controversial effects on the risk of coronary heart disease and breast cancer, and an investigation of the potential role of screening for men and nonwhite women.

2. Better therapies are needed to prevent postmenopausal bone loss. New drugs for osteoporosis prophylaxis should be developed and tested that do not have ERT side effects or complications (bisphosphonates, etc.).

3. The pathophysiology of age-related bone loss should be characterized to help identify new leads for therapy. In particular, the use of ERT for bone loss in the elderly should be evaluated. Controlled clinical trials should also be conducted to investigate the effects of calcium supplements and more realistic exercise programs for preventing bone loss in the elderly.

4. The prevalence and importance of risk factors for osteoporosis should be determined, including estimations of the national population at risk of fracture by virtue of low bone mass (men as well as women and nonwhites as well as whites) and the prevalence of risk factors (for attributable risk). Any difference in risk factor prevalence among races, genders, regions, or other demographic variables should be identified. Such research should also seek an explanation for the lower fracture risk (as compared to whites) found among Hispanic, black, and Asian populations. In addition, the important causes of secondary osteoporosis should be determined.

5. An optimal, postfracture rehabilitation program should be developed. Related research should include efforts to generate better data about fracture-related disabilities (especially those resulting from spinal fractures), quantify the determinants of functional impairment after hip or other such fractures, and determine barriers to aggressive rehabilitation. Controlled clinical trials should be conducted to demonstrate the merits of promising rehabilitation activities.

6. Research should continue on identifying modifiable determinants of serious falls (see Chapter 15).

Education

Policymakers

Recent research findings that bear on governmental policy matters should be interpreted to encourage more informed decisions by policymakers. In addition, the effects of mid-life actions on subsequent medical costs to corporations for osteoporosis and fractures among their retirees should be documented and disseminated.

Providers

Treatment guidelines for osteoporosis screening and prophylaxis should be widely disseminated, and physicians, nurses, therapists, and other care providers should be educated regarding the need for and techniques of rehabilitation. Particular attention should be given to preventing vitamin D deficiency in the housebound elderly.

The Public

Women should be informed about the circumstances (risk factors, etc.) under which they should seek assessment for osteoporosis. Healthy lifestyles should be promoted (although there is no certainty that this will significantly reduce fracture occurrence), with an emphasis on good nutrition (including adequate intake of calcium and vitamin D), increased exercise, and decreased smoking and alcohol use. Practical information regarding calcium supplementation (preparation, dosages, etc.) should also be disseminated.

APPENDIX

SCREENING TESTS FOR OSTEOPOROSIS

Many different techniques have been used to assess bone mass. The most widely available, as well as the most accurate and precise, methods include single-photon absorptiometry, dual-photon absorptiometry, and quantitative computed tomography. These have been reviewed extensively (see P. L. Kimmel, "Radiologic Methods to Evaluate Bone Mineral Content, "*Annals of Internal Medicine*, Vol. 100, pp. 908-911, 1984); thus, only those aspects especially pertinent to screening are summarized here, along with features of the newest modality, dual-energy x-ray absorptiometry. Much of the information in the appendix is taken from two reports from the National Center for Health Services Research and Health Care Technology (M. Erlichman, *Dual Photon Absorptiometry for Measuring Bone Mineral Density and Single Photon Absorptiometry for Measuring Bone Mineral Density*, Health Technology Assessment Reports No. 6 and 7, respectively, U. S. Department of Health and Human Services, Rockville, Md., 1986).

SINGLE-PHOTON ABSORPTIOMETRY

Single-photon absorptiometry (SPA) is a widely used technique that involves passing a highly collimated monoenergetic beam of photons (using ^{125}I as the source) across a limb and monitoring the transmitted radiation with a sodium iodide scintillation detector. Differential photon absorption between bone and soft tissue allows calculation of the total bone mineral content in the path of the beam, measured as grams per centimeter. This technique is limited to peripheral sites such as the radius or os calcis; as a result, it cannot measure bone density in the hip or spine, nor can it discriminate between cortical and trabecular bone.

The accuracy error for SPA is generally said to be around 4 to 5 percent. The precision (reproducibility) of the latest SPA technology (rectilinear SPA) is good, in the range of 1 to 2 percent in clinical settings. Patient acceptability is also quite good, and scan times are relatively short—an examination requires that a person sit in a chair for approximately 10 to 20 minutes. The radiation dose is low (2 to 5 millirems [mR]), with a negligible whole-body dose. Charges per scan range from $35 to $120.

DUAL-PHOTON ABSORPTIOMETRY

This technique emits photons at two different energies (using [153]Gd as the source), which permits direct measurement of bone mineral density (area density in grams per square centimeter) in the proximal femur and lumbar spine. However, dual-photon absorptiometry (DPA) cannot distinguish between cortical and trabecular bone at those sites.

The accuracy error of DPA is about 3 to 6 percent for spine and 3 to 4 percent for the femoral neck; the estimated precision for measurements of the lumbar spine is about 2 to 4 percent and for the femoral neck, about 4 percent. Patient acceptability is good, but rectilinear scanning times are long, varying from 20 to 40 minutes for regional measurements and up to 40 to 60 minutes for total body measurement. A regional scan entails only 5- to 15-mR exposures, although the use of spine films to rule out fractured vertebrae increases the radiation dose substantially. Charges for DPA vary widely but usually exceed $125.

DUAL-ENERGY X-RAY ABSORPTIOMETRY

In this new absorptiometry technique, the dual-energy peaks are obtained by filtering x-rays or switching kilovoltage. The high count rate obtained from the x-ray source permits considerably faster scan times with improved precision, which should increase the utility of this modality for osteoporosis screening. Source size and columnation are also smaller, and spatial resolution is better as a result. The precision of this technique is on the order of 1 percent or less. Dual-energy x-ray absorptiometry, or DEXA, can assess the spine or proximal femur with radiation exposure of less than 5 mR.

QUANTITATIVE COMPUTED TOMOGRAPHY

Quantitative computer tomography (QCT) also depends on the differential absorption of ionizing radiation by calcified tissue. Measurements, usually from a single energy source, are compared with a standard mineral reference (such as K_2HPO_4 solution) to calculate the bone mineral equivalent, which is expressed in milligrams of K_2HPO_4 per cubic centimeter. Areas of interest can be selected, including cortical bone, trabecular bone, or an integral assessment of the entire bone. Usually, the lumbar spine is chosen for assessment, but the technique can be adapted to other skeletal sites.

The accuracy error for QCT in the clinical setting is about 5 to 10 percent, with reproducibility of 1 to 4 percent. Patient acceptance is good, and a scan of the spine can be performed in about 15 minutes. Charges range from $100 to $400. In the most modern scanners, the radiation dose for single-energy QCT of the vertebrae is as low as 100 to 300 mR, but the dose varies widely and, depending on the equipment, can range up to 1,250 or 1,500 mR with scout films of the spine.

REFERENCES

1. Bergkvist, L., Adami, H. O., Persson, I., Hoover, R., and Schairer, C. The risk of breast cancer after estrogen and estrogen-progestin replacement. New England Journal of Medicine 1989; 321:293-297.
2. Bush, T. L., Barrett-Connor, E., Cowan, L. D., Criqui, M. H., Wallace, R. B., Suchindran, C. M., Tyroler, H. A., and Rifkind, B. M. Cardiovascular mortality and noncontraceptive use of estrogen in women: Results from the Lipid Research Clinics Program follow-up study. Circulation 1987; 75:1102-1109.
3. Bush, T. L., and Barrett-Connor, E. Noncontraceptive estrogen use and cardiovascular disease. Epidemiology Reviews 1985; 7:80-104.
4. Ceder, L., Thorngren, K. G., and Walldén, B. Prognostic indicators and early home rehabilitation in elderly patients with hip fractures. Clinical Orthopaedics and Related Research 1980; 152:173-184.
5. Cummings, S. R., Kelsey, J. L., Nevitt, M. C., and O'Dowd, K. J. Epidemiology of osteoporosis and osteoporotic fractures. Epidemiology Reviews 1985; 7:178-208.
6. Cummings, S. R., and Nevitt, M. C. Epidemiology of hip fractures and falls.

In: M. Kleerekoper, and S. M. Krane (eds.), Clinical Disorders of Bone and Mineral Metabolism. New York: Mary Ann Liebert, Inc., Publishers, 1989, pp. 231-236.

7. Cummings, S. R., Rubin, S. M., and Black, D. The coming epidemic of hip fractures in the United States. Clinical Orthopaedics and Related Research, in press.

8. de Bruijn, H. P. The Colles fracture, review of literature (Chap. 3). Acta Orthopaedica Scandinavica 1987; 58(Suppl. 223):7-25.

9. Dobyns, J. H., and Linscheid, R. L. Fractures and dislocations of the wrist. In: C. A. Rockwood, Jr., and D. P. Green (eds.), Fractures, vol. 1. Philadelphia: J. B. Lippincott Company, 1975, pp. 345-440.

10. Fitzgerald, J. F., Moore, P. S., and Dittus, R. S. The care of elderly patients with hip fracture: Changes since implementation of the prospective payment system. New England Journal of Medicine 1988; 319:1392-1397.

11. Gibson, M. J. The prevention of falls in later life. Danish Medical Bulletin 1987; 34(Suppl. 4):1-24.

12. Hillner, B. E., Hollenberg, J. P., and Pauker, S. G. Postmenopausal estrogens in prevention of osteoporosis: Benefit virtually without risk if cardiovascular effects are considered. American Journal of Medicine 1986; 80:1115-1127.

13. Holbrook, T. L., Barrett-Connor, E., and Wingard, D. L. Dietary calcium and risk of hip fracture: 14-year prospective population study. Lancet 1988; 2:1046-1049.

14. Holbrook, T. L., Grazier, K., Kelsey, J. L., and Stauffer, R. N. The Frequency of Occurrence, Impact and Cost of Selected Musculoskeletal Conditions in the United States. Chicago: American Academy of Orthopedic Surgeons, 1984.

15. Hui, S. L., Slemenda, C. S., and Johnston, C. C., Jr. Age and bone mass as predictors of fracture in a prospective study. Journal of Clinical Investigation 1988; 81:1804-1809.

16. Jensen, J. S., and Bagger, J. Long-term social prognosis after hip fractures. Acta Orthopaedica Scandinavica 1982; 53:97-101.

17. Johnston, C. C., Melton, L. J. III, and Lindsay, R. Clinical indications for bone mass measurements. Report of the Scientific Advisory Committee of the National Osteoporosis Foundation. Journal of Bone and Mineral Research 1989; 4(Suppl. 2):1-28.

18. Judd, H. L., Meldrum, D. R., Defton, L. J., and Henderson, B. E. Estrogen replacement therapy: Indications and complications. Annals of Internal Medicine 1983; 98:195-205.

19. Kanis, J. A., and Passmore, R. Calcium supplementation of the diet. II. Not justified by present evidence. British Medical Journal 1989; 298:205-208.

20. Kribbs, P. J., Smith, D. E., and Chesnut, C. H. III. Oral findings in osteoporosis. Part II. Relationship between residual ridge and alveolar bone resorption and generalized skeletal osteopenia. Journal of Prosthetic Dentistry 1983; 50:719-724.

21. Krølner, B., and Toft, B. Vertebral bone loss: An unheeded side effect of therapeutic bed rest. Clinical Science 1983; 64:537-540.

22. Lindsay, R., Aitken, J. M., Anderson, J. B., Hart, D. M., McDonald, E. B., and Clark, A. C. Long-term prevention of postmenopausal osteoporosis by estrogen. Lancet 1976; 1:1038-1041.

23. Lindsay, R., Hart, D. M., Forrest, C., and Baird, C. Prevention of spinal osteoporosis in oophorectomized women. Lancet 1980; 2:1151-1154.

24. Magaziner, J., Simonsick, E. M., Kashner, T. M., Hebel, J. R., and Kenzora, J. E. Survival experience of aged hip fracture patients. American Journal of Public Health 1989; 79:274-278.

25. Marcus, R., and Carter, D. R. The role of physical activity in bone mass regulation. Advances in Sports Medicine and Fitness 1988; 1:63-82.

26. Melton, L. J. III, Chao, E. Y. S., and Lane, J. Biomechanical aspects of fractures. In: B. L. Riggs and L. J. Melton III (eds.), Osteoporosis: Etiology, Diagnosis, and Management. New York: Raven Press, 1988, pp. 111-131.

27. Melton, L. J. III. Epidemiology of fractures. In: B. L. Riggs and L. J. Melton III (eds.), Osteoporosis: Etiology, Diagnosis, and Management. New York, Raven Press, 1988; pp. 133-154.

28. Melton, L. J. III, and Riggs, B. L. Clinical spectrum. In: B. L. Riggs and L. J. Melton III (eds.), Osteoporosis: Etiology, Diagnosis, and Management. New York: Raven Press, 1988, pp. 155-179.

29. Melton, L. J. III. Fluoride in the prevention of osteoporosis and fractures. Journal of Bone and Mineral Research 1990; 5:S163-S167.

30. Miller, C. W. Survival and ambulation following hip fracture. Journal of Bone and Joint Surgery 1978; 60-A:930-934.

31. Mossey, J. M., Mutran, E., Knott, K., and Craik, R. Determinants of recovery 12 months after hip fracture: The importance of psychosocial factors. American Journal of Public Health 1989; 79:279-286.

32. National Institute of Arthritis and Musculoskeletal and Skin Diseases. Osteoporosis: Cause, Treatment, Prevention. NIH Publ. No. 86-2226. Bethesda, Md.: National Institutes of Health, 1984.

33. Nickens, H. W. A review of factors affecting the occurrence and outcome of hip fracture, with special reference to psychosocial issues. Journal of the American Geriatrics Society 1983; 31:166-170.

34. Parfitt, A. M. Bone remodeling: Relationship to the amount and structure of bone, and the pathogenesis and prevention of fractures. In: B. L. Riggs and L. J. Melton III (eds.), Osteoporosis: Etiology, Diagnosis, and Management. New York: Raven Press, 1988, pp. 45-93.

35. Peck, W. A., Riggs, B. L., Bell, N. H., Wallace, R. B., Johnston, C. C., Jr., Gordon, S. L., and Shulman, L. E. Research directions in osteoporosis. American Journal of Medicine 1988; 84:275-282.

36. Phillips, S., Fox, N., Jacobs, J., and Wright, W. E. The direct medical costs of osteoporosis for American women aged 45 and older, 1986. Bone 1988; 9:271-279.

37. Pocock, N., Eisman, J., Gwinn, T., Sambrook, P., Kelly, P., Freund, J., and Yeates, M. Muscle strength, physical fitness, and weight but not age predict femoral neck bone mass. Journal of Bone and Mineral Research 1989; 4:441-448.

38. Pryor, G. A., and Williams, D. R. R. Rehabilitation after hip fractures: Home and hospital management compared. Journal of Bone and Joint Surgery 1989; 71-B:471-474.

39. Quigley, M. E. T., Martin, P. L., Burnier, A. M., and Brooks, P. Estrogen therapy arrests bone loss in elderly women. American Journal of Obstetrics and Gynecology 1987; 156:1516-1523.

40. Report of the U.S. Preventive Services Task Force. Chapter 40. Screening for postmenopausal osteoporosis. In: Guide to Clinical Preventive Services. Washington, D.C., 1989.

41. Riggs, B. L., and Melton, L. J. III. Involutional osteoporosis. In: Oxford Textbook of Geriatric Medicine, in press.

42. Riggs, B. L., Wahner, H. W., Melton, L. J. III, Richelson, L. S., Judd, H. L., and O'Fallon, W. M. Dietary calcium intake and rates of bone loss in women. Journal of Clinical Investigation 1987; 80:979-982.

43. Riggs, B. L., and Melton, L. J. III. Medical Progress: Involutional osteoporosis. New England Journal of Medicine 1986; 314:1676-1684.

44. Ross, P. D., Wasnich, R. D., MacLean, C. J., Hagino, R., and Vogel, J. M. A model for estimating the potential costs and savings of osteoporosis prevention strategies. Bone 1988; 9:337-347.

45. Silverman, S. L., and Madison, R. E. Decreased incidence of hip fracture in Hispanics, Asians, and blacks: California hospital discharge data. American Journal of Public Health 1988; 78:1482-1483.

46. Sinaki, M. Exercise and physical therapy. In: Riggs, B. L., and Melton, L. J. III (eds.), Osteoporosis: Etiology, Diagnosis, and Management. New York: Raven Press, 1988, pp. 457-479.

47. Stampfer, M. J., Willett, W. C., Colditz, G. A., Rosner, B., Speizer, F. E., and Hennekens, C. H. A prospective study of postmenopausal estrogen therapy and coronary heart disease. New England Journal of Medicine 1985; 313:1044-1049.

48. Tinetti, M. E., Speechley, M., and Ginter, S. F. Risk factors for falls among elderly persons living in the community. New England Journal of Medicine 1988; 319:1701-1707.

49. Wasnich, R. D. Fracture prediction with bone mass measurements. In: H. K. Genant (ed.), Osteoporosis Update 1987. San Francisco: Radiology Research and Education Foundation, 1987, pp. 95-101.

50. Weinstein, M. C. Estrogen use in postmenopausal women—costs, risks, and benefits. New England Journal of Medicine 1980; 303:308-316.

7

Preventing Disability Related to Sensory Loss in the Older Adult

———

S enses link individuals to their environment. Sight and hearing allow for communication; taste, olfaction, proprioception, and temperature perception provide the information necessary not only to traverse safely but to enjoy the world. Diminution, to some degree, of any or all of these senses is a recognized consequence of aging in many people.[2,42] Although the loss of any of the senses is potentially disabling, vision and hearing will be the focus of this paper—for several reasons. Losses in these two areas are among the most prevalent conditions among elderly Americans.[35,38] In addition, decreased vision and hearing have been linked to limitations in physical, emotional, and social functioning,[8,12,42,49,53] which therefore makes the spectrum of potential disability and handicap very broad. From a practical point of view, impairments in these two areas are potentially preventable as are the associated disabilities and handicaps.[6,33] Limiting this chapter to sight and hearing also allows for development of an agenda for preventing sensory impairment and associated disability or handicap that reflects current knowledge. It is not intended to suggest that other sensory losses do not deserve careful attention.

DEFINITION AND PREVALENCE

Both visual and hearing impairments rank among the 15 most prevalent chronic conditions in Americans aged 65 and older.[37] Yet varying definitions of visual impairment affect the magnitude of its incidence and prevalence. The National Health Interview Survey defines visual impairment as the ability to read newsprint. According to this measure, preliminary data indicate that approximately 13 percent of noninstitutionalized Americans aged 65 and older have some form of visual impairment.[23] Of this group, 8 percent suffer with a severe impairment, which is defined as the inability to read newsprint even with glasses.[39] The severely impaired therefore also include those who are blind in both eyes.[39] The survey reports that 3.2 percent of respondents reported blindness in one eye, and 1 percent reported blindness in both eyes.[23] Legal blindness, on the other hand, is defined as 20/200 vision or worse. (An eye with 20/200 vision sees at 20 feet that which an eye with 20/20 vision can see at 200 feet.) Confident estimates of the prevalence of legal blindness, however, are not available.

If one defines poor visual acuity as anything equal to or worse than 20/50 vision, the incidence of visual loss increases by 13 percent between ages 60 and 69 and 32 percent among those 70 to 80 years old.[42] Using the same definition (20/50 or worse), 11 percent of persons aged 65 to 73 who wear glasses are impaired; 26 percent of this age group who do not wear glasses are also impaired.[38] By 80 years of age, only 10 to 20 percent of this group will have a visual acuity of 20/20.[42] Performance on tests of stereoscopic acuity decrease from nearly 100 percent at age 30 to approximately 60 percent at age 80.[42] Performance on red-green color match tests decrease from 60 percent at age 30 to less than 10 percent at age 70.[42]

Hearing loss is also measured using different definitions and therefore yields varying prevalence estimates as well. Using a threshold of 40 decibels (dB) (speech is generally at the 50-dB level—see Figure 7-1) for any two measured frequencies, the prevalence of hearing impairment is 45 per 100,000 for those 17 to 44 years of age, 119 per 100,000 for those 45 to 64 years of age, and 282 per 1,000 for those over 64 years of age.[6] Preliminary data from the National Health Interview Survey show a similar distribution in the population aged 64 and older; they also indicate that hearing impairment (defined as "the reported presence of deafness in one or both ears or any other trouble hearing"[23]) varies with age and sex. Twenty-three percent of individuals aged 65 to 74, 32.7 percent of those 75 to 84, and 48.4 percent of those 85 and older show hearing impairment. Men had a greater percentage of hearing impairments in each age range. For example, among those 65 to 74 years old, 30 percent of the men were impaired as compared with 17.5 percent of the women.[23] Other studies that focus on sensory loss among specific populations (e.g., nursing home residents) have found even higher prevalence rates.[3,19,47] For ex-

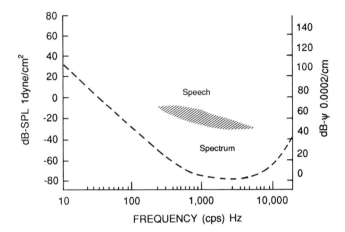

FIGURE 7-1 Human audiogram with absolute threshold of hearing expressed in reference to dB-SPL and the psychophysical thresholds dB-ψ, at various frequencies, with the minimum audible pressure (MAP) at the eardrum. Shaded area represents audible frequency spectrum for human speech. Source: J. M. Ordy and K. R. Brizee, *Sensory Systems and Communication in the Elderly*, Raven Press, New York, 1979.

ample, the Framingham Heart Study Cohort reported a prevalence of hearing impairments of 83 percent among men and women aged 57 to 89 years of age.[35] It should be noted, however, that this study used a threshold of 20 dB, which is considerably lower than the 40 dB used in many other studies.[6,35] When a higher threshold (40 dB) was used, the prevalence of hearing impairments was 48 percent. Two studies reporting hearing impairment prevalences among nursing home residents found rates of 94 percent and 82 percent.[3,47]

In some cases these prevalence data are drawn from population-based surveys, but the data are limited in ways that affect the ability to estimate the true burden of disease in all other adult populations. For example, the lack of detailed racial and ethnic identifiers limits an understanding of prevalence among Hispanic and other minority populations. Existing national survey data comparing blacks and whites suggest that there may be differences in hearing loss between these groups, particularly for the higher frequencies.

ETIOLOGIC BREAKDOWN

Visual Impairments

The leading causes of visual impairment among the elderly are cataracts, glaucoma, macular degeneration, and diabetic retinopathy.[6,16,42,50,53]   The incidence of cataracts increases steadily with age and is responsible for the largest number of new cases of blindness.[50] Between the ages of 50 and 80 there is a ninefold increase from 4 to 46 percent in the percentage of the population with visual acuity of less than 20/30 as a result of cataracts.[50] Although it is beyond the scope of this chapter to discuss the details of cataract pathology and pathophysiology, the type and location of the cataract have implications for the type of visual impairment and therefore the type of disability and handicap experienced. For example, nuclear cataracts result in poor distance acuity, whereas posterior cataracts result in poor near vision. In advanced stages, however, the visual impairment resulting from cataracts is usually global. Visual impairment from cataracts is frequently progressive, but the rate of visual impairment can vary considerably (occurring over a space of months to one of years).

Glaucoma is associated with progressive visual field defects that can eventually become extensive enough to cause serious visual impairment, even blindness.[22] Open-angle glaucoma is the second most common cause of blindness in the elderly. The congressional Office of Technology Assessment has estimated that approximately 4,600 elderly people go blind from glaucoma each year and that 0.5 percent of 65-year-olds and 1.1 percent of 75-year-olds will develop glaucoma within five years.[43] Blacks, diabetics, and people with a family history of glaucoma seem to be at increased risk.[31] Similarly, blindness is more likely to occur in blacks with glaucoma and to occur at an early age.[26] The most significant predictor of the development of glaucoma is elevated intraocular pressure, but it is by no means a perfect predictor, which complicates screening for glaucoma in the elderly. Thirty percent of those with very high intraocular pressures (>30 mmHg) will develop glaucoma over a 17- to 20-year period. Overall, people with significantly increased ocular pressure are seven times more likely to develop glaucoma than those with normal intraocular pressure.[43]

Accurate figures for the prevalence of macular degeneration (loss of central vision in both eyes, frequently characterized by spots of pigmentation and other abnormalities) as a cause of blindness are not available; however, data pooled from the National Health and Nutrition Examination Survey and the Framingham Eye Study indicate that it is a leading cause of blindness among older adults. The incidence of macular degeneration increases with age especially after the age of 50.[16] Prevalence estimates in the 65- to 75-year-old age group are 6.9 percent in white females, 11.4 percent in black females, 9.6 percent in white males, and 9.3 percent in black males. Data on other racial and ethnic groups are not readily available. Exudative matter (from blood vessels, often including serum, fibrin, and white blood cells) is the more common cause of blindness. Hyperopia (a condition in which images come into focus behind the retina) is the most frequently reported risk factor for macular degeneration; other factors including a family history of hyperopia, decreased handgrip, and systemic high blood pressure have been reported in case-control studies.[15] Generally, visual loss is caused by an ingrowth of choroidal neovascularization and the formation of round or oval macular scars. Unlike visual impairment that results from cataracts and glaucoma, visual impairment that results from macular degeneration usually occurs suddenly.

Diabetic retinopathy is the next most common cause of blindness among older adults. One-third of all diabetic patients have some retinopathy, which carries a high risk of sudden visual loss as a result of a vitreous hemorrhage or retinal detachment, or both.

There are two reasons why it is important to keep in mind the specific etiologies of visual loss. First, the natural history of each of these causes of visual impairment is very different; therefore, the extent and timing of the associated disabilities are likely to be very different in both individuals and populations.[22,43,50] Second, the availability and effectiveness of treatment for each of these conditions vary. Consequently, the ability to prevent not only the associated disability but the visual impairment itself will vary across conditions. Some of the committee's recommendations related to visual impairment will necessarily be linked to specific etiologies of visual impairment.

Hearing Impairments

The most common cause of bilateral hearing impairment among the elderly, presbycusis, is characterized by increased thresholds for high-frequency tones, recruitment, and difficulty with speech comprehension (see Figure 7-2).[17] There is a 25 percent reduction in speech comprehension that occurs between the ages of 50 and 80; the reduction is particularly noticeable with complex, rapid patterns of speech.[6,17]

Pathologically, there are four types of presbycusis: sensory, mechanical, strial, and neuronal.[17] The exact nature of the hearing impairment as recorded on an audiogram differs with each of these. The etiology of presbycusis is poorly understood, but the pattern of hearing loss is very similar to that associated with noise exposure.[17] Indeed, age-related hearing impairment is much less common among populations living in relatively noise-free environments.[27,45]

Although presbycusis is the most common cause of hearing

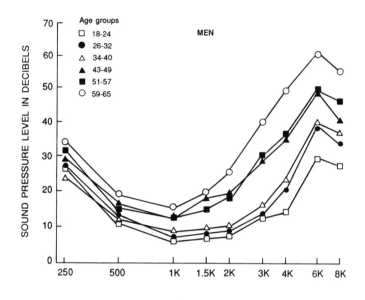

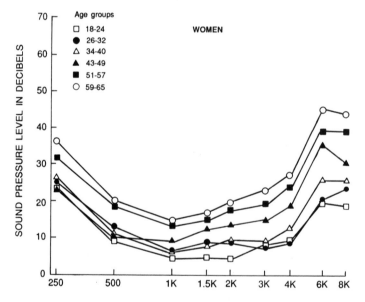

FIGURE 7-2 Mean threshold values for hearing pure tones as a function of frequency for men and women in six different age groups. The subjects in this study were carefully screened for excessive noise exposure and any history of diseases known to affect hearing. Age groups in years 18–24 (□-□); 26–32 (●-●); 34–40 (△-△); 43–49 (▲-▲); 51–57 (■-■); and 59–65(○-○). Source: J. M. Ordy and K. R. Brizee, *Sensory Systems and Communication in the Elderly*, Raven Press, New York, 1979.

impairment among the elderly, there are other causes of hearing loss in the older population as well. Today's cohort of older adults whose childhoods precede the antibiotic era may suffer the sequelae of untreated otitis media (an infection causing inflammation of the middle ear) to a greater extent than will future post-antibiotic era cohorts. Vascular disease, thyroid disease, and arthritis are other common causes of hearing impairment because of the relatively high prevalence of these conditions among older people. Thus, as with visual loss, the specific etiology of hearing loss is important in structuring preventive strategies.

DISABILITIES ASSOCIATED WITH SENSORY LOSS

The burden imposed on the elderly by the two specific sensory impairments discussed in this chapter has been inadequately studied. The prevalence of sensory impairment among various age groups is known, but nuances in prevalence among specific racial and ethnic subgroups are not. Sensory impairment is common among older adults because many common diseases and conditions can result in sensory impairment. A true understanding of this burden requires an understanding of the impact of sensory impairment. Unfortunately, in this area there are more questions than answers. As confusing as the data are for individual senses, they are still better than the virtually nonexistent data regarding the impact of multiple sensory impairments. More work is urgently needed to clarify the disabilities and handicaps associated with individual and multiple sensory impairments.

Although hearing and visual losses are each the result of a separate set of heterogeneous diseases, disabilities, or impairments,[6,16,17,36,42,43,50] both types of losses can substantially decrease an individual's ability to interact with the environment and communicate with others.[42] These sensory impairments, whose effects on an individual are seen as being similar, often lead to disability and handicaps. As a result, an exploration of the nature of the disabilities and handicaps associated with hearing and vision losses, and the evidence supporting their existence, seems the most logical place to begin. Social isolation, depression, cognitive loss, and psychoses, as well as common physical limitations, are often associated with hearing or vision deficits.[4,8,10,12,29,48,49,51,53,54,57,58] However, the scientific evidence supporting the relationship of these handicaps to hearing and visual impairments is not strong enough to be considered conclusive.

Social isolation has been described among older adults with

sensory impairments and disabilities,[58] but discerning the degree to which it can be attributed to either visual or hearing impairment is challenging. Because of the small sample sizes and variable definitions employed in studies of social isolation and sensory impairment, the strength and nature of their relationship are uncertain at best.[24,29,58] The determinants of social isolation are multifactorial and might include age, educational level, living situation, and external factors such as the availability of transportation, in addition to sensory impairment. Two studies that consider social isolation among elderly individuals with either visual or hearing impairments conclude that these sensory deficits play a role in such isolation.[24,58] The finding is strengthened by the observation that more severe hearing impairment is associated with greater degrees of social isolation.[58] (In this study social isolation was measured with the Subjective Isolation Scale and the Objective Isolation Scale of the Comprehensive Assessment and Referral Evaluation.[21] The measurement criteria for social isolation of the other study[24] are available in the text.) Neither study, however, measures social isolation in a control group, although both use multiple regression to control for potentially confounding variables such as age and type of activity. Both studies report on clinic-based populations with sample sizes of less than 100. Given the small samples, limited generalizability, and study designs of this research, the relationship between social isolation and visual or hearing impairment must still be considered questionable.

Much of the work linking sensory impairment to psychiatric illnesses, such as paranoid psychosis, depression, or other affective disorders, lacks adequate control groups or thorough statistical analysis. A. F. Cooper and colleagues have published several studies reporting a high prevalence of long-standing hearing impairment among elderly patients with paranoid psychoses and affective disorders.[7,8,9] (The mean age of paranoid patients studied was 67.3 years, and the mean age of those with affective disorders was 69 years.) In general, Cooper found that patients with paranoid psychoses had a higher prevalence of hearing impairment and disability than those with affective disorders. Patients with paranoid psychoses also tended to have more severe hearing impairment over all of the frequencies tested.[9] Cooper also reported an increased incidence of psychoses in elderly patients with decreased visual acuity.[10]

Whereas Cooper's early work lacked controls, other such studies have not. For example, a study conducted at Johns Hopkins' Hearing and Speech Clinic involving 174 outpatients found that 47 percent of those with some hearing impairment scored high on a screening test for psychiatric illness, as compared with 30 percent of those with normal hearing.[49] Similarly, a population-based study involving 365 patients over the age of 70 living in a London borough found a significant relationship between depression and deafness that persisted even after controlling for age and socioeconomic status.[18] There was no relationship, however, between the severity of the hearing impairment or disability and the severity of the depression.

In short, much of the work in this area is descriptive. The basic assumption made in all these studies—that poor hearing actually preceded the psychiatric disease—is not confirmed; this must be tested through a prospective study. A case-control study that controls for most potential confounders also has yet to be performed. Although later studies are suggestive, they are not definitive, and because many studies are done abroad, their results are not generalizable to all American populations. These issues are further obfuscated by a contradictory cohort study among elderly hospitalized psychiatric patients in England that did not show the expected association between paranoid and affective disorders and sensory deficits.[34] This study has methodological limitations, however, similar to those already mentioned. Thus, the relationship between sensory impairments and serious psychiatric illness is only suggestive at best. Furthermore, the small samples of most studies do not allow comment on the relationship of an additional variable—that is, age.

Until very recently, the relationship between sensory impairments and cognitive deficits has been fraught with similar methodologic problems. Several studies have concluded that a relationship exists between either visual or hearing impairment and dementia.[41,49,53,54,58] Other studies have not been able to document such a relationship.[18,51] The lack of adequate controls, limited sample sizes, and heterogeneous definitions of both sensory impairment and cognitive deficits that characterize most of these studies makes it difficult to interpret their findings and come to any definitive conclusions. Recently, Uhlman conducted a case-control study involving 100 cases of Alzheimer's type dementia and 100 nondemented controls matched by age, sex, and education.[54] This study reported a higher prevalence of significant hearing impairment (odds ratio, 2) among Alzheimer's cases. Even though the findings of the available studies do not allow definitive conclusions to be drawn with regard to the relationship between hearing impairment and cognitive decline, the Uhlman study adds weight to the suggestion that hearing loss *is* associated with cognitive dysfunction. A similar statement cannot as yet be made with regard to visual impairment and cognitive loss.[49]

Sensory loss disabilities have yet to be fully characterized, although the literature suggests several potential types. Surveys conducted by the National Center for Health Statistics indicate that older adults consider visual impairment but not hearing impairment to be among the six leading contributors to their perceived disability.[37] A recent article reported a correlation between visual impairment and hip fracture.[14]

When six categories of leisure activities were evaluated in a group of low-vision elderly, the participants reported a significant decrease in active and sedentary crafts, such as gardening and auto maintenance or sewing and knitting, respectively.[24] There were no significant changes in travel, sports, social activities, the use of radio, or television.[24] Data gathered in the second and third waves of the Massachusetts Health Care Panel Study indicate that older noninstitutionalized individuals who report visual decline are more likely to need assistance in the so-called instrumental activities of daily living* than those who report continuing excellent or good vision.   There were no significant differences, however, in the performance of the activities of daily living* or in bed days between the two groups. The Massachusetts study also indicated that older individuals with declining vision tended to have other disabilities (e.g., difficulties related to stair climbing or heavy housework) and handicaps in social function related to transportation. In addition, mental health and self-perceptions of health were likely to be problematic among the visually impaired.[4]

Finally, losing the ability to drive in the United States can be a serious handicap, particularly in areas where public transportation is limited. The clinical determinants of driving skills have yet to be established; however, evidence is mounting that age-associated loss of peripheral vision may be a significant factor in driving performance.[30,44] To ensure both the independence of older people and the public safety, driver retraining courses for older people should be directed toward improving some age-related declines in sensory function and in learning to compensate for others.

In summary, many of the associations postulated between sensory losses and various emotional or physical disabilities are potentially

---

*The Activities of Daily Living (ADLs) and Instrumental Activities of Daily Living (IADLs) are short lists of basic activities considered useful in measuring the progress of recovery or diminution of basic human function. The most basic are the ADLs, which in this study were used to assess the need for assistance in walking, transferring, dressing, bathing, eating, and grooming. The IADLs measure skills relating to the ability to adapt to one's environment. This study measured the need for assistance in the following IADLs: housekeeping, transportation, grocery shopping, food preparation, number of meals requiring assistance, and the ability to pay bills.

devastating and as such have tremendous implications for an older adult's quality of life. Yet the vast majority of the studies describing these associations have serious methodological limitations—for example, study designs that do not include control groups or a population-based sampling procedure. The lack of standards for determining which age groups to study and the lack of criteria to define sensory impairments and the nature and severity of the resulting disabilities make comparison across studies difficult. Therefore, although the relationship between sensory impairment and physical, emotional, or cognitive disabilities is intuitively obvious, it is impossible to make definitive statements regarding that relationship at this time.

APPROACHES TO PREVENTION

Preventing sensory loss logically involves interventions at primary, secondary, and tertiary points in the etiologic chain. Approaches that involve the actual prevention of sensory loss have yet to be developed. Such primary preventive strategies will necessarily be related to specific etiologies of sensory loss and are likely to involve screening for early sensory losses that create impairments and disability. This review uncovered no literature that addressed the potential benefits of primary prevention for sensory impairment in populations over the age of 50.

Most of the literature focuses on secondary preventive practices, in particular, screening, or the timing of therapeutic interventions to prevent disability. The recommendations for screening vary with the particular disease being addressed. Screening for visual impairment resulting from glaucoma, for example, requires a very different approach than screening for visual impairment from cataracts.

The issues related to glaucoma screening were recently reviewed by the Office of Technology Assessment.[43] Once a person is screened for glaucoma and found to have the disease, treatment aimed at reducing intraocular pressure is the standard of care, even though such treatment has not been shown definitively to prevent blindness. The data are strongly suggestive, and there are randomized controlled trials currently in progress, but conclusions regarding the utility of early detection and treatment of glaucoma in the prevention of blindness cannot be made at this time.[43] There is inconclusive evidence that early detection and treatment can prevent visual loss owing to macular degeneration.

There are several ways to screen for hearing impairment. For example, there are a number of physical measures and scales that seem to correlate reasonably well with pure tone audiometry, the current "gold standard."[32,52] Pure tone audiometry can be made more or less sensitive and specific depending on the frequencies tested and the decibel threshold used to define hearing loss. Third, there are hearing handicap scales.[11,25,55] Studies correlating perceived handicaps with pure tone audiometry indicate that the perception of a handicap correlates best with pure tone losses above 40 dB among the elderly. Perceived disability may be related to educational level, as well as economic status and participation in activities.[56] Preventing disability or handicap from sensory impairment in vision or hearing therefore cannot rely solely on screening strategies.[6,43]

Theoretically, disability can be prevented by restoring the lost sense, which is the guiding principle of the strategy in senile cataracts and presbycusis. However, restoring a sense does not always prevent disability or restore function. For example, in the absence of underlying retinal disease, cataract removal and lens implantation has been shown in most cases to be effective in restoring reasonable vision.[50] The crucial issue is the timing of the surgery and determining whether surgical intervention will improve the disability. Studies have shown that functional status improves in some patients following cataract surgery and that the improvement persists at least to the one-year follow-up point;[1,13] the aspects and extent of disability and handicap will vary according to the demands and expectations placed on individuals. Factors other than the technical outcome of surgery, however, are also important in improving functional status—for example, mental status, level of functioning, measured visual acuity, and age.[1]

Very little work has been done to evaluate the effectiveness of aural rehabilitation in diminishing disability arising from hearing impairment. A small study involving 18 subjects demonstrated that disability (as measured by the Hearing Handicap Inventory for the Elderly) decreased after treatment with a hearing aid.[46] However, this sample is too small to allow any generalization of its results to other populations. There have been no studies to demonstrate improvement in cognitive function, decreased depression, or greater social participation after aural rehabilitation.[40,46] Although the literature suggests that a hearing aid is only one component of a rehabilitation program, there has been no systematic evaluation of other possible components that might be appropriate for older adults (e.g., lip reading, telephone amplification).[40]

Evaluating the degree to which disability can be prevented by developing strategies to minimize specific functional deficits related to sensory impairment is impossible based on current knowledge. As the first section of this chapter notes, there is no literature that convincingly ascribes specific functional deficits, be they physical, emotional, or social, to sensory losses. For now, general conclusions about the ability to prevent disability and handicap by addressing sensory loss in older adults must await further study.

RECOMMENDATIONS

Policymakers and Government Agencies

In 1979 Robert Butler and Barbara Gastel presented a description of research challenges related to hearing and age to the National Institute on Aging.[5] Many of the same issues were raised in 1986 when an international work group of hearing experts gathered to discuss hearing problems in the elderly.[6] Unfortunately, most of the recommendations made in 1979 and 1986 are still applicable today. These two reports highlight a characteristic feature of the entire sensory impairment literature: an inadequate understanding of the nature of the disabilities and handicaps associated with sensory impairment and therefore an inadequate understanding of how to approach prevention. The specific recommendations presented below are designed to fill some of the gaps in information in these areas.

1. Services or devices that appear to help prevent disability or handicap owing to sensory impairment should be evaluated for availability and accessibility. Many of these services or devices are expensive, and their costs are not reimbursed by public or private insurance plans in this country. Comparisons with other nations that cover these services should be helpful.

2. Sensory impairment should remain a high priority for research. Projects designed to improve our understanding of the nature of the disabilities associated with sensory impairment are a crucial first step. It is important that individual sensory impairments be examined, but it is equally important to examine multiple sensory impairments to understand their interactive effects on disability and handicap.

3. The development of uniform criteria for the definition of individual sensory impairments (e.g., hearing impairment, visual impairment) should be encouraged.

4. Funding should be increased for programs aimed at educating older adults about sensory impairments and their prevention, treatment, and sequelae.

5. Researchers should be encouraged to incorporate investigations of sensory impairment into longitudinal studies. The natural

history of age-related sensory impairment is poorly understood, and longitudinal studies are the best way to address this deficit.

6. The sections of regularly conducted national surveys that address sensory impairment should be expanded.

7. Studies of sensory impairment in minority populations should be increased, especially in instances in which current data suggest there is increased risk among some populations.

Professional Societies

Professional societies and other such organizations are in the best position to coordinate efforts toward standardization, encourage cooperative study, establish guidelines, and educate their members as well as the public. Especially in the case of hearing impairment, there is a particular need to appreciate the problems faced by older adults.[20,28]

1. Uniform definitions of sensory impairment that can be used by all concerned disciplines should be developed and promoted.

2. Uniform measurements of disability as well as handicap related to individual and multiple sensory impairments should be developed. These efforts should build on well-validated measures of functional status (physical, mental, emotional, and social).

3. The implementation of multicenter, randomized controlled trials should be promoted to investigate screening and treatment practices.

4. Educational programs should be developed for the elderly person who may already be suffering from untreated or inadequately treated sensory losses. Programs should also be designed for the homebound or illiterate elderly.

5. Interdisciplinary bodies should be established to address the issues related to multiple sensory losses, including prevalence, interactions among sensory losses, and the impact of multiple sensory deficits.

6. Existing guidelines and regulations covering the dispensing of devices for the treatment of sensory losses, particularly hearing loss, should be reviewed.

7. Creative mechanisms should be developed to reduce the financial barriers that prevent older adults from receiving devices and services.

Clinicians

1. Sensory evaluations should always be included in routine, periodic evaluations. Although referrals may not always be neces-

sary, it is appropriate to question the patient regarding any sensory deficits or diminishment he or she may be experiencing.

2. Special attention should be given to medications and conditions that might contribute to sensory impairment.

3. Patients with perceived decreased hearing should be referred for screening by an audiologist.

4. Diabetic patients should be referred to an ophthalmologist annually.

5. Biannual screening should be recommended to all patients at high risk for glaucoma. Tonometry alone is not adequate screening for glaucoma.

6. Because many older patients are poorly informed about sensory loss, clinicians should develop a library of patient information on sensory impairment, its screening, disabilities, and treatments.

7. Patients should be taught the signs and symptoms of sensory impairment—particularly those related to hearing and visual impairment.

8. Patients should be taught how to minimize the safety risks associated with sensory impairment.

9. Clinicians should discuss the importance of adequate glare-free lighting with their visually impaired patients.

10. Magnifying glasses should be prescribed for patients with macular degeneration that is still at an early stage.

11. Clinicians should provide information on large-print books and newspapers to visually impaired patients.

12. All patients should be questioned routinely to uncover hearing impairment.

13. Elderly patients should be taught how to position themselves in a room to minimize visual and hearing deficits.

REFERENCES

1. Applegate, W. B., Miller, S. T., and Elam, J. T. Impact of cataract surgery with lens implantation on vision and physical function in elderly patients. Journal of the American Medical Association 1987; 257:1064-1066.

2. Bartoshuk, L. M., Rifkin, B., and Marks, L. E. Taste and aging. Journal of Gerontology 1986; 41:51-57.

3. Bingea, R. L., Raffin, M. J. M., Aune, K. J., et al. Incidence of hearing loss among geriatric nursing home residents. Journal of Auditory Research 1982; 22:275-283.

4. Branch, L. G., Horowitz, A., and Can, C. The implications for everyday life of incident self-reported visual decline among people over age 65 living in the community. The Gerontologist 1989; 29(3):359-365.

5. Butler, R. N., and Gastel, B. Hearing and Age: Research challenges and the National Institute on Aging. Annals of Otology 1979; 88:676-683.

6. Christiansen, J., Eric, J., Kennedy, T. E., et al. Hearing problems and the elderly. Danish Medical Bulletin 1986; 33:1-22.
7. Cooper, A. F. Deafness and psychiatric illness. British Journal of Psychiatry 1976; 129:216-226.
8. Cooper, A. F., and Curry, A. R. The pathology of deafness in the paranoid and affective psychoses. Journal of Psychosomatic Research 1976; 20(2):97-105.
9. Cooper, A. F., Curry, A. R., Kay, D. W. K., et al. Hearing loss in paranoid and affective psychoses of the elderly. Lancet 1974; 2(7885):851-854.
10. Cooper, A. F., and Porter, R. Visual acuity and ocular pathology in the paranoid and affective psychoses of later life. Journal of Psychosomatic Research 1976; 20:107-114.
11. Corbin, S., Reed, M., Nobbs, H., et al. Hearing assessment in homes for the aged: A comparison of audiometric and self-report methods. Journal of the American Geriatrics Society 1984; 32:396-400.
12. Eastwood, M. R., Corbin, S. L., Reed, M., et al. Acquired hearing loss and psychiatric illness: An estimate of prevalence and co-morbidity in a geriatric setting. British Journal of Psychiatry 1985; 147:552-556.
13. Elam, J. T., Graney, M. J., and Applegate, W. B. Functional outcome one year following cataract surgery in elderly persons. Journal of Gerontology 1988; 43:M122-M126.
14. Felson, D., Anderson, J., Hannan, M., et al. Impaired vision and hip fracture: The Framingham Study. Journal of the American Geriatrics Society 1989; 37:495-500.
15. Ferris, F. L. Senile macular degeneration: Review of epidemiologic features. American Journal of Epidemiology 1983; 118:132-149.
16. Ghafour, M. M., Allan, D., and Foulds, W. S. Common causes of blindness and visual handicap in the rest of Scotland. British Journal of Ophthalmology 1983; 67:209-213.
17. Gilad, O., and Glorig, A. Presbycusis: The aging ear, Part I. Journal of the American Auditory Society 1979; 4:195-217.
18. Gilhome-Herbst, K., and Humphrey, C. Hearing impairment and mental state in the elderly living at home. British Medical Journal 1980; 281:903-905.
19. Gilhome-Herbst, K., and Humphrey, C. Prevalence of hearing impairment in the elderly living at home. Journal of the Royal College of General Practitioners 1981; 31:155-160.
20. Gluck, M. E., Wagner, J. L., and Duffy, B. M. The Use of Preventive Services by the Elderly. Washington, D.C.: Health Program, Office of Technology Assessment, Congress of the United States, January 1989.
21. Gurland, B., Kuriansky, J., Sharpe, L., Simon, R., Stiller, P., and Birkett, P. The Comprehensive Assessment and Referral Evaluation (CARE)—Rationale, development and reliability. International Journal of Aging and Human Development 1977-1978; 8(1)9-42.
22. Hart, W. M., and Becker, B. The onset of evolution of glaucomatous visual field defects. Ophthalmology 1982; 89:268-279.
23. Havlik, R. J. Aging in the eighties: Impaired senses for sound and light in persons age 65 years and over. Preliminary data from the supplement on aging to the National Health Interview Survey: United States, January-June 1984. DHHS Publ. No. (PHS)86-1250. Advance data from Vital and Health Statistics of the National Center for Health Statistics, No. 125, September 19, 1986.

24. Heinemann, A. W., Colorez, A., Frank, S., et al. Leisure activity participation of elderly individuals with low vision. The Gerontologist 1988; 28:181-184.
25. High, W. S., Fairbanks, G., and Glorig, A. Scale for self-assessment of hearing handicap. Journal of Speech and Hearing Disorders 1964; 29:215-230.
26. Hiller, R., and Kahn, H. A. Blindness from glaucoma. American Journal of Ophthalmology 1975; 80:62-67.
27. Hinchcliffe, R. Hearing levels of elderly in Jamaica: A pilot survey. Annals of Otology, Rhinology and Laryngology 1964; 73:1012-1019.
28. Humphrey, C., Gilhome-Herbst, K., and Faurqi, S. Some characteristics of the hearing-impaired elderly who do not present themselves for rehabilitation. British Journal of Audiology 1981; 15:25-30.
29. Jones, D. A., Victor, C. R., and Vetter, N. J. Hearing difficulty and its psychological implications for the elderly. Journal of Epidemiology and Community Health 1984; 38:75-78.
30. Keltner, J. L., and Johnson, C. A. Visual function, driving safety, and the elderly. Ophthalmology 1987; 94(9):1180-1188.
31. Leske, M. C. The epidemiology of open-angle glaucoma: A review. American Journal of Epidemiology 1983; 118(2):166-191.
32. Lichtenstein, M. J., Bess, F. H., and Logan, S. A. Validity of screening tools for identifying hearing-impaired elderly in primary care. Journal of the American Medical Association 1988; 259:2875-2878.
33. Mitchell, P. Prevention of blindness in Australia. Australian Family Physician 1985; 14:757-765.
34. Moore, N. C. Is paranoid illness associated with sensory defects in the elderly? Journal of Psychosomatic Research 1981; 25:69-74.
35. Moscicki, E. K., Elkins, E. F., Baum, H. M., et al. Hearing loss in the elderly: An epidemiologic study of the Framingham Heart Study Cohort. Ear and Hearing 1985; 6:184-190.
36. Murphy, R. P. Age-related macular degeneration. Ophthalmology 1986; 93:969-971.
37. National Center for Health Statistics (Moss, A. J., and Parsons, V.). Estimates from the National Health Interview Survey, U.S., 1985. DHHS Publ. No. (PHS) 86-1588. Washington, D.C.: National Center for Health Statistics, 1986.
38. National Center for Health Statistics. Refraction status and motility defects of persons 4-74 years. United States 1971-1972. Publ. No. (PHS) 86-1250. Vital and Health Statistics, Series 11, No. 206, 1978, pp. 89-93.
39. Nelson, K. A. Visual impairment among elderly Americans: Statistics in transition. Journal of Visual Impairment and Blindness 1987; 81:331-334.
40. Newman, C. W., and Weinstein, B. E. The hearing handicap inventory for the elderly as a measure of hearing aid benefit. Ear and Hearing 1988; 9:81-85.
41. Ohta, R. J., Carlin, M. F., and Harmon, B. M. Auditory acuity and performance on the mental status questionnaire in the elderly. Journal of the American Geriatrics Society 1981; 29:476-478.
42. Ordy, J. M., and Brizee, K. R. Sensory Systems and Communication in the Elderly. New York: Raven Press, 1979.
43. Power, E. J., Wagner, J. L., and Duffy, B. M. Screening for Open-Angle Glaucoma in the Elderly. Washington, D.C.: Health Program, Office of Technology Assessment, Congress of the United States, October 1988.
44. Retchin, S. M., Cox J., and Fox, I. L. Performance based measurements

among elderly drivers and nondrivers. Journal of the American Geriatrics Society 1988; 36(9):813-819.

45. Rosen, S., Bergman, M., Plester, D., et al. Presbycusis study of a relatively noise-free population in the Sudan. Annals of Otology, Rhinology and Laryngology 1962; 71:727-743.

46. Rousseau, P. Hearing loss in the elderly. American Family Physician 1987; 36(3):107-113.

47. Schow, R. L., and Nerbonne, M. A. Hearing levels among elderly nursing home residents. Journal of Speech and Hearing Disorders 1980; 45:124-132.

48. Singerman, B., Riedner, E., and Folstein, M. Emotional disturbance in hearing clinic patients. British Journal of Psychiatry 1980; 137:58-62.

49. Snyder, L. H., Pyrek, J., and Smith, K. C. Vision and mental function of the elderly. The Gerontologist 1976; 16:491-495.

50. Straatsma, B. R., Foos, R. Y., and Horowitz, J. Aging-related cataract: Laboratory investigation and clinical management. Annals of Internal Medicine 1985; 102:82-92.

51. Thomas, P. D., Hunt, W. C., and Garry, P. J. Hearing acuity in a healthy elderly population: Effects on emotional, cognitive, and social status. Journal of Gerontology 1983; 38:321-325.

52. Uhlmann, R. F., Rees, T. S., Psaty, B. M., et al. Validity and reliability of auditory screening tests in demented and non-demented older adults. Journal of General Internal Medicine 1986; 4(2):90-96.

53. Uhlmann, R. F., Larson, E. B., and Koepsell, T. D. Hearing impairment and cognitive decline in senile dementia of the Alzheimer's type. Journal of the American Geriatrics Society 1989; 34:207-210.

54. Uhlmann, R. F., Larson, E. B., Rees, T. S., et al. Relationship of hearing impairment to dementia and cognitive dysfunction in older adults. Journal of the American Medical Association 1989; 261:1916-1919.

55. Ventry, I. M., and Weinstein, B. E. Identification of elderly people with hearing problems. ASHA 1983; 25(7):37-42.

56. Weinstein, B. E. Validity of a screening protocol for identifying elderly people with hearing problems. ASHA 1986; 28(5):41-45.

57. Weinstein, B. E., and Amsel, L. Hearing loss and senile dementia in the institutionalized elderly. Clinical Gerontologist 1986; 4:3-15.

58. Weinstein, B. E., and Ventry, I. M. Hearing impairment and social isolation in the elderly. Journal of Speech and Hearing Research 1982; 25:593-599.

8

Oral Health Problems in the "Second Fifty"

―――――

The relations between oral and general health are dynamic. When oral health is compromised, overall health and quality of life may be diminished.[16,33,45] On the other hand, the rewards of good oral health are not insignificant. The optimal function of the oral cavity depends on the integrity of the dentition and supporting structures. The five most serious oral functional impairments of the older adult are (1) perioral and oral mucosal tissue pathologies (cancers and precancerous formations); (2) severe, untreated caries and periodontal diseases; (3) tooth loss resulting from oral diseases and conditions;(4) oral expressions of systemic diseases and side effects from medications; and (5) orofacial pain (including dry mouth and pain of undiagnosed origin). Reduced oral function is usually associated with the occurrence of a combination of these impairments.

The health of the oral cavity—that is, the teeth, oral soft tissues, underlying bone, neurosensory apparatus, immune system, and glandular mechanisms—is critical to chewing, tasting, swallowing, and speech, as well as to adaptation to dentures, if worn. It also contributes to self-esteem, nutrition, facial esthetics, and protection from systemic infection and injury. Self-esteem and social function may be significantly diminished by chewing disorders, which are common among the elderly. Moreover, difficulties with chewing are most frequently associated with an urgent need for care but are rarely reported as morbidity.[13,16,45,46]

Fortunately, the oral health, oral hygiene practices, and dental service utilization of older age groups have improved over the past several decades. Moreover, continued improvements are projected as the cohorts that swell the ranks of the older generations include a greater number and larger proportion of better educated, more affluent dentate individuals than ever before.[7,15] An older individual who retains his or her own teeth, however, is at continued risk for oral diseases. An estimated 40 percent of older Americans during the next two decades will constitute an oral special needs category based on complex health problems and functional status.[41] The chronic and progressive nature of oral diseases may result in tooth loss and disability. Prevention and early intervention are therefore critical, and impairments that are not addressed early have a greater likelihood of becoming disabling.

There is no epidemiological evidence to suggest that tooth loss or specific oral diseases are a necessary concomitant of the aging process, nor do all persons over age 50 fall into a single descriptive group in terms of oral health.[7] Rather, it appears that there is a great deal of heterogeneity in the older population, depending on lifetime oral health experiences, related medical conditions, and social and economic status.

BURDEN

All adults enter their second 50 years at risk for multiple oral diseases and conditions. At age 50, 11 percent have lost their teeth, and the remainder have an average of only 22 teeth. Among those with teeth at age 50, 5 percent have untreated coronal caries, 42 percent have untreated root caries, 40 percent have gingivitis, and 17 percent have periodontitis.[43] Salivary dysfunction apparently begins to increase in prevalence at this age. Individuals beyond age 50 exhibit rising levels of dysfunction through increased tooth loss, root caries, periodontal diseases, pain, and oral complications of general systemic conditions.

Physical impairments of the oral cavity most often affect chewing, swallowing, phonetics, and social functions. The nature of an individual's impairment, combined with various other risk factors, determines whether the impairment will become disabling or handicapping. The transition to disability and handicap, however, is in large part dependent on appropriate self-care and professional preventive care for older adults.[32] Strategies must be developed to diminish oral diseases and injuries and to remove barriers to self-care and professional services. Descriptions of the major burdens faced by the older population, including prevalence data, are provided below.

Perioral Tissue and Oral Mucosal Tissue Pathologies and Oral Cancer

Numerous oral mucosal conditions are prevalent among older adults. Sometimes they are secondary to systemic disease; at other times they occur as a result of side effects of medication, ill-fitting dentures, and substance abuse (e.g., tobacco and alcohol).[10] In a series of screenings conducted between 1957 and 1972 among older white adults in Minnesota, 10 percent had at least one oral lesion that was unusual enough to be recorded. In this population the prevalence of leukoplakia, a precancerous condition, was 29.1 per 1,000, and the prevalence of oral cancer was 0.9 per 10,000.[11] Herpes virus, papilloma, and pemphigus are also common among older adults.

Oral cancers are life threatening and cause severe handicaps. In the United States each year, 9,400 persons die of oral cancer, and some 30,000 people develop the disease. Although oral cancers constitute only 3 to 4 percent of all cancers in the United States, only one-half of the affected population are alive five years after diagnosis.[1] Most survivors suffer serious functional impairment and have an exceptionally high risk of subsequent primary and secondary malignancies; thus, they are at great risk for further disabilities or handicaps. The prevalence of oral cancer is greater among men than women and increases with age, with the great majority of cases occurring after the age of 40.

The long-term impact of tobacco use and alcohol on the condition of teeth and the development of soft-tissue lesions—specifically, oral cancer—are more apparent in older individuals. It has been estimated that 75 percent of oral cancers can be attributed to using tobacco and drinking alcohol. The risk of oral cancer for tobacco users is 4 to 15 times greater than for nonusers, increasing with both duration and frequency of tobacco use. Individuals with lower educational levels or infrequent dental visits are also more likely to suffer from soft-tissue lesions.[10]

Caries

Dental caries contribute directly to impairments through pain and discomfort; they contribute indirectly through tooth loss. Severe and persistent caries can become disabling or handicapping. Dental caries in older adults are manifest primarily as (1) cervical caries associated with plaque accumulation at the gingival margin; (2) root caries associated with gingival recession; (3) secondary phenomena to medical conditions or pharmaceutical challenges; and (4) recurrent caries adjacent to restorations on coronal or root surfaces.[7,24] The etiology of root caries, which are essentially limited to adults, may involve physical and oral health as well as behavioral and social factors.[9]

It appears likely that the coronal caries process is the same regardless of age. Most older adults are at relatively low risk of developing caries. As with children, those who are susceptible usually exhibit high levels of the disease.[24] Once caries are present, the contribution to tooth loss is mainly a function of whether the lesion is treated and, if so, how many times the restoration requires replacement.

In 1985-1986, adults aged 65 and older who attended senior centers had an average of 20 decayed or filled coronal tooth surfaces, with about 92 percent of these surfaces being filled.[43] In working adults, aged 50-64, about 95 percent of the surfaces had been filled. Additionally, as individuals age, there is an increase in the prevalence of root surfaces caries.[5,9,24,43,47] In the 50-to-54 age group, about 42 percent of individuals have root surface caries. This prevalence increases steadily to 54 percent by ages 60 to 64 in the working population. Among dentate older adults at senior centers in 1985-1986 the prevalence of root caries increased from 64 percent in the 65-to-69 age group to 71 percent in the 75-to-79 group. Only about half (54 percent) of these root surfaces were filled.[43]

The caries process reflects the interaction of four basic risk factors: a susceptible tooth surface, the presence of a sufficient number of cariogenic microorganisms, inadequate fluoride exposure, and ingestion of a caries-conducive diet. Other factors conducive to dental caries include a history of high caries prevalence, reduced salivary flow, altered salivary composition, gingival recession, and poor oral hygiene. Certain systemic conditions, medications, psychiatric disorders, and social or personal conditions may potentiate some of these risk factors.

Periodontal Diseases

Periodontal diseases are a function of a selective microflora active in a conducive environment. The severity of periodontitis is measured by the magnitude of gingival inflammation, pocket depth, and loss of periodontal attachment. Loss of attachment, which is the main predictor of tooth loss from periodontal diseases, is of major concern if it is extensive and progresses more rapidly than expected.[44]

Severe periodontal diseases contribute to oral dysfunctional impairment directly through gingival bleeding, pain, and discomfort, and indirectly through tooth loss. Depending on the level of involvement, periodontal diseases can be disabling or handicapping. Less severe periodontal disease may lead to social dysfunction as a result of bad breath.

The prevalence and severity of periodontal diseases increase with age, yet most individuals have signs of destructive disease in only a few sites at periodic intervals.[7,43,44] The higher prevalence and severity of periodontal diseases among older persons may not be the result of enhanced susceptibility but rather may reflect the accumulation of disease over time.[44] These diseases are prevalent in otherwise healthy individuals, although certain systemic conditions (e.g., diabetes) appear to be associated with more severe types of periodontal diseases.

Ninety percent of individuals aged 65 and older need some type of periodontal treatment; 15 percent need complex treatment.[27] The periodontitis of persons who have retained their teeth to old age is often of the type that, at any given site, progresses slowly.

Other Oral Conditions

Trauma is a key factor in tooth loss, and although it is usually associated with activities of youth, it is not uncommon for older adults as a result of automobile accidents, falls, or biting into food. Traumatic injuries and jaw fractures have immediate and long-term consequences. Injured teeth may be loosened or displaced, or they may be broken (exposing dentine or pulp) or avulsed. Like injuries to other parts of the body, injury to the orofacial area can have social-psychological side effects. Unlike injuries to other parts of the body, injuries to teeth are unique in that healing does not follow the usual reparative processes.

Certain diseases of the salivary glands, including local inflammatory diseases and Sjogren's syndrome, are more common in older than in younger adults.[36] Acute suppurative sialoadenitis, as well as chronic recurrent sialoadenitis, is more common in older, seriously ill, debilitated patients. The prevalence of Sjogren's syndrome—lymphoepithelial lesions—is second in prevalence only to rheumatoid arthritis among the connective tissue diseases, with onset typically in women 40 to 60 years of age. There is some indication that submandibular saliva and possibly minor gland secretions may be affected by aging.[36]

Oral symptoms of hypofunctional or nonfunctional salivary glands are unpleasant and painful and affect speech, taste, chewing, and swallowing. Xerostomia (dry mouth), a frequent side effect of medications, may increase susceptibility to infections—both oral and systemic—and have an impact on nutrition.[5,36] It may also increase susceptibility to caries and periodontal diseases.

Oral conditions that were, in the past, considered stereotypical of aging are now beginning to be seen in a different light. Research does not support a consensus regarding the causes of diminution of stimulated parotid fluid output, structural changes in epithelium, atrophic change in oral mucosa, and generalized reductions in taste acuity and perception. Evidence suggests that other factors, such as polypharmacy, inadequate nutrition, or systemic diseases may be the precursors of these conditions and not age per se. Other age-related changes in taste, olfaction, and oral sensation, such as touch, temperature, and pressure sensibility, have been observed but have not been well described or documented.[34]

Tooth Loss

Because tooth loss is the sequela of caries, periodontitis, and trauma, it is a general indicator of the amount of severe oral diseases experienced by an individual or a population.[49] The relationship between tooth loss and oral diseases, however, is complicated. Tooth loss also reflects aspects of the dental delivery system that are not disease related—for example, the cost, access to, and utilization of dental services, limitations of existing technology, and variations among treatment options offered and chosen in the dentist/patient interaction. A population's level of tooth loss is therefore a reflection of cultural values as well as the availability, accessibility, cost, and appropriateness of preventive services and treatment.

Despite a steady decline in the rate of edentulousness (toothlessness) over the past several decades, 55 percent of individuals aged 85 or older were edentulous in 1986.[39] Edentulism decreases in the younger age groups of the "second 50": 44 percent of those aged 75 to 84, 30 percent of those aged 65 to 74, 22 percent of those aged 55 to 64, and 12 percent of those aged 45 to 54. There appears to be both a cohort and an aging effect in this trend. Thus, overall edentulousness will be considerably reduced, without any intervention, over the next few decades. Edentulism continues to be more prevalent among older persons below the poverty level, however, and among those with fewer years of education.[39]

Edentulous people often face severe psychological, social, and physical handicaps. Among older adults, loss of natural dentition can complicate systemic health problems and may interact adversely with certain behaviors. Even when missing teeth are replaced with well-constructed dentures, there are limitations in speech, chewing ability, and quality of life. As many as 60 percent of denture wearers have denture-related problems, including soft tissue lesions.[28]

Functional impairments are not limited to complete loss of teeth. Tooth loss increases after the age of 35 and increases considerably in the over-50 age groups.[37] Replacement of missing teeth is necessary to retain an adequately functioning dentition. Some prosthodontic treatment is needed by 27 percent of noninstitutionalized older adults, and the lack of replacement represents a considerable disability.[28] Prosthodontics treatment need is associated with socioeconomic status and race,[4,23,26] in part reflecting the expense of bridges, partial dentures, and other prosthetic services.

Oral Expressions of Medications, Systemic Conditions, and Diseases

Medications for age-related systemic conditions (e.g., congestive heart failure, diabetes, depression, sleep disturbances, chronic pain) have been shown to have direct and indirect effects on oral health status and dental treatments.[29] Approximately 120 physical or mental diseases manifest symptoms in the oral cavity or affect oral function. The prevalence and burden of most of these conditions increase with age.[29]

Studies of a rural Iowa population revealed that more than 75 percent of a population aged 65 and older took medications that could affect oral health or dental treatment. Commonly used drugs affect blood clotting and cause oral ulcerations or sloughing of soft tissue. Others interface with oral health care. About one-fourth of these older adults take muscle relaxants and medications for anxiety, which can interact adversely with drugs commonly used in dental surgery for sedation and pain relief. Drugs commonly used by older persons for cardiac conditions can interact adversely with local anesthetics containing epinephrine. In addition, broad-spectrum antibiotics, medications for diabetes, systemic corticosteroids, phenytoin for convulsions, nifedipine used for cardiovascular diseases, medications for angina and congestive heart failure, and antipsychotic medications may be associated with abnormal healing, predisposition to infection, overgrowth of gingival tissue, inability to tolerate long, stressful appointments, and abnormal oral-facial movements.[34]

Iatrogenic causes of salivary gland dysfunction are significant. About one-half of the older individuals in the Iowa study took drugs that may contribute to xerostomia (e.g., antihypertensives, antihistamines, decongestants, diuretics, painkillers, and tranquilizers). Moreover, ionizing radiation and chemotherapeutics, common therapies for cancer in older adults, can severely affect the salivary glands and the oral mucosa and may result in radiation caries.

Aging diabetic patients in particular are vulnerable to oral infections and impaired healing, which may lead to chronic destructive periodontal disease and other oral problems.[29] Psychoses, affective disorders, and sleep disturbances, on the other hand, may affect the patient's willingness or ability to perform appropriate oral hygiene or seek dental services, thus affecting oral health, speech, or swallowing.[29] Neurological problems, including stroke, Alzheimer's disease, and Parkinson's disease, can adversely affect oral functions.

Slower movements, reduced agility, arthritis, Alzheimer's disease, impaired vision and hearing, urinary dysfunction, and vascular insufficiency may all undermine the ability to follow recommendations for self-care. They may also make it impossible for an older individual to visit a dental office or to tolerate lengthy visits. Finally, diet, particularly fermentable carbohydrates, may have a considerable impact on oral conditions and root caries.

Orofacial Pain

Orofacial pain is a condition of great concern in that 20 to 25 percent of all chronic pain problems are localized in this region. Chronic and acute pain can adversely affect oral functions, which ultimately has a significant impact on general health and quality of life. These effects appear to be substantial for older adults; although the epidemiology of orofacial pain is not well documented, chronic and acute pain generally, and in the orofacial region specifically, appear to be more prevalent in the elderly. Within the oral region, pain related to "dry mouth," temporomandibular joint dysfunction syndrome, generalized orofacial pain, various arthroses, and oral cancers are known causes of chronic pain.

BURDEN PREVENTABILITY

Based on current projections, it is assumed that each succeeding cohort to enter the "second 50" will have more teeth and greater expectations regarding tooth retention. This dramatic change in the nature of oral health for aging individuals creates new challenges for research, education, and clinical care. In spite of major successes in dental research, treatment, and prevention over the past several decades, oral diseases of all kinds remain among the most costly of

U.S. health problems (the national bill for dental services in 1988 was $30+ billion).[40] With the projected increase in the number of dentate older adults, ability to pay may become an increasingly critical factor.[51] Dentate older adults are seeking and receiving complex, expensive dental services at a proportionately greater rate than younger adults.[19] Although preventive services are generally less expensive than restorative procedures, they nevertheless represent a basic cost in personal health care services. Considerable restorative work (secondary prevention) will be needed by upcoming cohorts to maintain a functional dentition; as a result, the total absence of insurance or prepayment mechanisms, and the failure of many reimbursement systems to acknowledge and support preventive services, may create significant barriers to regular use of dental services in the over-50 population.[15,19]

Many direct risk factors for common oral diseases of older adults are known. The reduction of those factors, or their actual elimination, is possible through appropriate preventive self-care, elimination of high-risk behaviors, professionally provided preventive, diagnostic, and therapeutic care, and a supportive environment.

Prevention of Oral Cancer

At present, there is no consensus regarding secondary prevention of oral cancer. Oral cancer screening procedures have yet to be tested for sensitivity and false-positive rates; there is also concern that a complete oral exam is too impractical for physicians to perform with every periodical visit.[48]

All high clinical suspicions of oral cancer indicate the need for biopsy, regardless of other diagnostic tools. Most oral lesions are detected when they are in an advanced state and are easily seen owing to their large size. Because the probability of developing oral cancers varies by location and behavior, early detection of oral cancers, when lesions are smaller, depends on an acute sense of the high-risk areas of the mouth and the connection between risk behaviors (e.g., smoking and drinking) and the locus of the lesions.

For high-risk groups, a stronger consensus exists regarding primary and secondary prevention. Good evidence suggests that an independent and synergistic risk exists for oral cancer as a result of smoking and excessive alcohol use. Tobacco chewing has also been linked to oral cancer. Patients who are at risk because of these behaviors should be counseled against them by their health care providers. These high-risk patients should be screened during periodical health exams and should be examined annually.

Prevention of Caries

The increased tooth retention of older individuals makes primary prevention and early (less invasive) treatment increasingly important for those over the age of 50.[15] Today's older adults have not benefited from a lifetime exposure to such preventive therapies as fluorides and dental sealants. The potential for disability and handicap can be effectively reduced, however, through low-invasive restorative approaches and fluorides. Much of what is known about preventing and controlling dental caries is based on children, although epidemiological data in young adults suggest that fluorides, which are proven to be efficacious in children, continue to work in adults.[47] Thus, for high-risk individuals, including those undergoing cancer treatment (chemotherapy and ionizing radiation), additional fluoride treatments are indicated to prevent oral sequelae.

Loss of salivary flow and changes in salivary composition are risk factors for caries. In some cases, medications may need to be altered. In other cases, agents to maintain a moist oral environment are used for patients at risk. Altering this risk requires interaction between dentists and physicians regarding medications and systemic diseases.

Prevention of Gingivitis and Periodontitis

Dental plaque retention is a major problem in older adults and is often exacerbated by existing restorations, rough root surface topology, and an inability to brush sufficiently. Diminished manual dexterity—in addition to more severe functional limitations associated with, for example, stroke, arthritis, or Parkinson's disease—may lead to a decreased ability to use a toothbrush and interdental devices.[29] For some, self-care may not be physically possible.[32] In addition, the motivation to prevent diseases and learn new techniques may be weaker in older individuals than for younger adults.

The prevention of gingivitis and periodontitis is directed toward altering the risk factors for these oral diseases. The most widely accepted methods are personal and professional mechanical oral hygiene measures (toothbrushing and interdental cleaning). If appropriately performed, these practices should substantially minimize the loss of teeth from periodontal diseases.

Prevention of Oral Pain

Reduction in oral dysfunction related to oral pain requires a better understanding of orofacial pain, appropriate interventions, and control of contributing diseases and conditions. In general, the selection of the mode of treatment for both acute and chronic pain will depend on the nature of the pain and various patient characteristics. Antidepressant medication has been useful for modulation of chronic pain. It should be noted, however, that dosages of antidepressants for chronic pain management are significantly lower than those needed for management of clinical depression. Premedication with nonsteroidal analgesics has been shown to be effective in modulating postoperative pain. A key challenge is the prevention and management of lesions in denture wearers and other related problems.

General Prevention

If the burdens of oral dysfunction in the older population are to be reduced, the barriers to self-care and professionally provided care must be removed. Of all the direct and indirect risk factors for oral dysfunction among older adults, the use of professionally provided services is the most affected by social, economic, environmental, and individual resources.[14] Social and economic factors, including lower levels of education, rural residence, and inability to pay, have been linked to the underutilization of services. Moreover, increased risk for candidiasis, denture ulcers, root caries, coronal caries, gingivitis, and periodontal disease has been linked to inadequate dental care in institutional settings.[8]

Besides factors such as the ability to pay and accessibility to care, the barriers to improved oral health often include a number of indirect factors that are correlated with oral functional impairments. For example, cultural and environmental conditions may predispose populations to oral health difficulties. Whether a community's water supplies are fluoridated, whether language barriers exist for individuals who seek preventive care—factors such as these should be taken into account in establishing methods for reducing the risks of oral diseases.

Attitudes, beliefs, and behaviors that predispose individuals to oral health problems can be modified through education. For example, fear, concerns for personal appearance, the value an individual places on oral health and dental care, and ignorance of oral health and prevention and treatment techniques can be overcome by educational efforts. Such information is especially important for older individuals who may never have learned appropriate dentally related behaviors or whose knowledge of prevention may be outdated.

Misinformation and confusion often discourage older persons from changing behaviors or seeking preventive services. In addition, the stereotypes of aging may undermine motives for maintaining oral health. These types of barriers can be eliminated in part by knowledgeable, caring providers whose attitudes, beliefs, and behavior are crucial to the oral health of a population. The dental health professional's knowledge of oral diseases, conditions, and preventive therapies, especially as related to older populations, substantially affects the prevention of oral health problems. Also of importance are the priority placed on oral health by physicians, nurses, and other non-dental health professionals and the information health care professionals can provide regarding financial assistance programs.

RECOMMENDATIONS

These general recommendations represent a broadly gauged approach to the complex oral health problems confronting older Americans, now and in the future. If they are undertaken with energy and resourcefulness, improved function, an enriched quality of life, and better overall health will result for these citizens.

Services

1. The proportion of the population who receive their water through optimally fluoridated public water systems should be increased.

2. The proportion of the population, as appropriate, who receive the benefits of fluoride through other means should also be increased.

3. Mechanisms should be developed to encourage interaction among dentists, pharmacists, physicians, and other health care providers to enhance the oral health of older adults.

Research

1. Studies should be conducted to examine the prevalence, incidence, cohort differences, and risk factors of oral dysfunction in older adults (e.g., tooth loss, oral cancer, oral mucosal conditions, oral sequelae of systemic diseases, chronic orofacial pain, trauma, salivary gland dysfunction, and aspects of caries and periodontal diseases).

2. The accuracy and feasibility of complete and abbreviated oral cancer screening procedures in primary care settings should be tested for both high-risk groups and the total adult population.

3. The pattern of developing oral functional disabilities and their underlying causation should be determined, and longitudinal studies of the natural history and microbiology of oral diseases should be conducted.

4. Investigations should continue to elucidate and characterize oral changes associated with "normal aging" and to assess their impact on oral function.

5. The relationship of systemic conditions, medications, and orofacial conditions in older adults should be explored.

6. Studies should be performed to investigate the lifelong effects of fluorides on dental caries in older adults.

7. The utilization of dental services by the elderly (both dentate and edentulous) should be assessed.

8. Methods/measures should be developed to identify older individuals at high risk for oral functional disabilities.

9. Acceptable definitions of quality of life outcome measures should be established, including a definition of functional dentition.

10. New methods of oral health care delivery for older adults should be developed, evaluated, and demonstrated. These innovations should include the delivery of services within the existing health care system or through alternate settings.

Public Policy

1. The use of preventive and early oral health diagnostic services should be encouraged through public- and private-sector incentives to expand and extend dental benefits to the retired population and through incentives for dental professionals to provide care to compromised older adults outside traditional dental care settings (e.g., long-term care facilities, mobile vans, portable equipment, institutions).

2. Within 30 days of entry into an institution, individuals should receive an oral examination and any required urgent care services. Annual oral examinations should be performed as needed.

3 Policies should be promoted to provide preventive services for currently underserved older adults.

Education

1. Educational efforts promoting cessation of tobacco and alcohol use should be increased.

2. Self-assessment instruments should be developed and tested to assist individual older adults and auxiliary health care professionals to learn the signs and symptoms of oral diseases.

3. The effectiveness of existing educational materials should be assessed.

4. Material should be developed specifically for dentate older adults and for particularly needy subpopulations (e.g., the homebound, the institutionalized), including information on self-care and the availability of services.

5. Institutional education programs for health professionals should be enhanced to improve knowledge, attitudes, and behaviors regarding primary prevention, diagnosis, and treatment for oral functional disabilities of older adults.

NOTE

This chapter is based, in part, on recent publications and meeting presentations and deliberations from workshops sponsored by the U.S. Public Health Service and the National Institutes of Health, addressing oral health promotion for adults and older Americans. These materials are not otherwise cited in the references and are thus listed below. Numbered references from the chapter follow.

Gift, H. C. Issues of aging and oral health promotion. Gerodontics 1988; 4:194-206.

National Institute of Dental Research. Challenges for the Eighties: National Institute of Dental Research Long-Range Plan. Washington, D.C., December 1983.

Oral Health Working Group, U.S. Surgeon General's Workshop on Health Promotion and Aging. Recommendations for oral health promotion activities with older adults. Gerodontics 1988; 4:207-208.

A Research Agenda for Health Promotion and Disease Prevention for Children and the Elderly. Health Services Research 1985; 19(6):Part 2.

A Research Agenda on Oral Health in the Elderly. Bethesda, Md.: National Institute on Aging, National Institute of Dental Research, and the Veterans Administration, 1986.

Corbin, S. B., Gift, H. C. and Singer, M. M. Draft National Oral Health Objectives for the Year 2000. Richmond, Va.: American Association of Public Health Dentistry, January 1990.

REFERENCES

1. American Cancer Society. Cancer Facts and Figures, 1987. New York: American Cancer Society, 1987.

2. Antczak, A. A., and Branch, L. G. Perceived barriers to the use of dental services by the elderly. Gerodontics 1985; 1:194-198.

3. Banting, D. W. Dental caries in the elderly. Gerondontology 1984; 3(1):55-61.

4. Baum, B. J. Characteristics of participants in the oral physiology component of the Baltimore Longitudinal Study of Aging. Community Dentistry and Oral Epidemiology 1981; 9:128-134.

5. Baum, B. J. Research on aging and oral health: An assessment of current status and future needs. Special Care in Dentistry 1981; 1(4):156-165.

6. Baum, B. J., and Bodner, L. Aging and oral motor function: Evidence for altered performance among older persons. Journal of Dental Research 1983; 62(1):2-6.

7. Beck, J. D. The epidemiology of dental diseases in the elderly. Gerondontology 1984; 3(1):5-15.

8. Beck, J. D., and Hunt, R. J. Oral health status in the United States: Problems of special patients. Journal of Dental Education 1985; 49:407-425.

9. Beck, J. D., Kohout, F. J., Hunt, R. J., and Heckert, D. A. Root caries: Physical, medical and psychosocial correlates in an elderly population. Gerodontics 1986; 3:242-247.

10. Blott, W. J., McLaughlin, J. K., Winn, D. M., et al. Smoking and drinking in relation to oral and pharyngeal cancer. Cancer Research 1988; 48:3282-3287.

11. Bouquot, J. E. Common oral lesions found during a mass screening examination. Journal of the American Dental Association 1986; 112:50-57.

12. Corbin, S. B., Maas, W. R., Klienman, D. V., and Backinger, C. L. 1985 National Health Interview Survey findings on public knowledge and attitudes. Public Health Reports 1987; 102:53-60.

13. Davies, A. M. Epidemiology and the challenge of aging. In: J. A. Brody, and G. L. Maddox (eds.), Epidemiology and Aging. New York: Springer Publishing Company, 1988, pp. 3-23.

14. Dolan, T. A., Corey, C. R., and Freeman, H. E. Older Americans' access to oral health care. Journal of Dental Education 1988; 52(11):637-642.

15. Douglass, C. W., and Gammon, M. D. Implications of oral disease trends for the treatment needs of older adults. Gerodontics 1985; 1(2):51-58.

16. Ettinger, R. L. Oral disease and its effect on the quality of life. Gerodontics 1987; 3:103-106.

17. Ettinger, R. L., and Miller-Eldridge, J. An evaluation of dental programs and delivery systems for elderly isolated populations. Gerodontics 1985; 1:91-97.

18. Evashwick, C., Rowe, G., Diehr, P., and Branch, L. Factors explaining the use of health care services by the elderly. Health Services Research 1984; 19(3):357-382.

19. Gambucci, J. R., Martens, L. V., Meskin, L. H., and Davidson, G. B. Dental care utilization patterns of older adults. Gerodontics 1986; 2:11-15.

20. Gift, H. C. Awareness and assessment of periodontal problems among dentists and the public. International Dental Journal 1988; 38:147-153.

21. Gift, H. C. Utilization of professional dental services. In: L. K. Cohen and P. S. Bryant (eds.), Social Sciences and Dentistry, vol. 2. London: Quintessence Publishing Company, 1984, pp. 202-266.

22. Greenlick, M. R., Sarvey, R., Lamb, S., et al. Prepaid dental care for the elderly in an HMO Medicare demonstration. Gerodontics 1986; 2:131-134.

23. Hand, J. S., and Hunt, R. J. The need for restoration and extractions in a non-institutionalized elderly population. Gerodontics 1986; 2:72-76.

24. Hand, J. S., Hunt, R. J., and Beck, J. D. Incidence of coronal and root caries in an older adult population. Journal of Public Health Dentistry 1988; 48(1):14-19.

25. Holtzman, J. M., and Berkey, D. B. Predicting utilization of dental services by the aged. Paper presented at the 40th Annual Scientific Meeting of the Gerontological Society of America, Washington, D.C., 1987.

26. Hughes, J. T., Rozier, R. G., and Ramsey, D. L. Natural History of Dental Diseases in North Carolina, 1976-1977. Durham, N.C.: Carolina Academic Press, 1988, pp. 250-254.

27. Hunt, R. J. Periodontal treatment needs in an elderly population in Iowa. Gerodontics 1986; 2:24-27.

28. Hunt, R. J., Srisilapanan, P., and Beck, J. D. Denture-related problems and prosthodontic treatment needs in the elderly. Gerodontics 1985; 1:226-230.

29. Irving, P. W. Diseases in the elderly with implications for oral status and dental therapy. In: P. Holm-Pedersen and H. Loe (eds.), Geriatric Dentistry, A Textbook of Oral Gerontology. Copenhagen: Munksgaard, 1986, pp. 179-186.

30. Kasper, J. A., Rossiter, L. F., and Wilson, R. A summary of expenditures and sources of payment for personal health services from the National Medical Care Expenditure Survey. NCHSR Data Preview No. 24. Washington, D.C.: U.S. Department of Health and Human Services, 1987.

31. Kiyak, H. A. An explanatory model of older persons' use of dental services: Implications for health policy. Medical Care 1987; 25(10):936-952.

32. Kiyak, H. A. Oral health promotion for the elderly. In: J. D. Matarazzo, S. M. Weiss, J. A. Hard, et al. (eds.), Behavioral Health: A Handbook of Health Enhancement and Disease Prevention. New York: J. Wiley, 1984, pp. 967-975.

33. Kiyak, H. A., and Mulligan, K. Studies of the relationship between oral health and psychological well-being. Gerodontics 1987; 3:109-112.

34. Levy, S. M., Baker, K. A., Semla, T. P., and Kohout, F. J. Use of medications with dental significance by a non-institutionalized elderly population. Gerodontics 1988; 43:119-125.

35. Loe, H., and Kleinman, D. (eds.) Dental Plaque Control Measures and Oral Hygiene Practices. Oxford: IRL Press Limited, 1986.

36. Mandel, I. D. Oral defenses and disease: Salivary gland function. Gerondontology 1984; 3(1):47-54.

36a. Mashberg, A., and Samit, A. M. Early detection, diagnosis, and management of oral and oropharyngeal cancer. CA: A Cancer Journal for Physicians 1989; 39(2):67-88.

37. Meskin, L. H., Brown, L. J., Brunelle, J. A., and Warren, G. B. Patterns of tooth loss and accumulated prosthetic treatment potential in U.S. employed adults and seniors, 1985-86. Gerodontics 1988; 4:126-135.

38. National Center for Health Statistics. Health promotion and disease prevention, United States, 1985. Vital and Health Statistics, Series 10, No. 163, 1988.

39. National Center for Health Statistics. Use of dental services and dental health, U.S., 1986. Vital and Health Statistics, Series 10, No. 165, 1988.

40. National Income and Product Account. Washington, D.C.: Bureau of Economic Analysis, U.S. Department of Commerce, 1986.

41. National Institute on Aging. Personnel for Health Needs of the Elderly through the Year 2000. Washington, D.C.: U.S. Public Health Service, September 1987.

42. National Study of Dental Health Outcomes Related to Prepayment: 1981. Rockville, Md.: Health Resources and Services Administration, 1987.

43. Oral Health of United States Adults: National Findings. NIH Publ. No. 87-2868. Washington, D.C.: National Institute of Dental Research, U.S. Department of Health and Human Services, 1987.

44. Page, R. C. Periodontal diseases in the elderly: A critical evaluation of current information. Gerontology 1984; 3(1):63-70.

45. Reisine, S. Defining social consequences in dentistry Paper presented at the 60th General Session of the International Association for Dental Research, New Orleans, La., March 1982. (Abstracts in the Journal of Dental Research, March 1982.)

46. Rosenberg, D., Kaplan, S., Senie, R., and Badner, V. Relationships among dental functional status, clinical dental measures, and generic health measures. Journal of Dental Education 1988; 52(11):653-657.

47. Stamm, J. W., and Banting, D. W. Comparison of root caries prevalence in adults with life-long residence in fluoridated and nonfluoridated communities. Journal of Dental Research 1980; 59:405.

48. U.S. Preventive Services Task Force. Guide to Clinical Preventive Services. Baltimore, Md.: Williams and Wilkins, 1989.

49. Weintraub, J. A., and Burt, B. A. Oral health status in the US: Tooth loss and edentulism. Journal of Dental Education 1985; 49(6):368-376.

50. Wilson, A. A., and Branch, L. G. Factors affecting dental utilization of elders aged 75 years or older. Journal of Dental Education 1986; 50(11):673-677.

51. Wolinsky, F. D., and Arnold, C. L. A birth cohort analysis of dental contact among elderly Americans. American Journal of Public Health 1989; 79(1):47-51.

9

Screening for Cancer

───────

S creening for cancer ranges from visual inspection to sophisticated radiologic or biochemical techniques.[2,10,26,34,70,81] It is generally associated with the subsequent verification of in situ or invasive
cancer and the surgical removal of all identifiable cancerous tissue.
A common example is mammography in an asymptomatic woman
over the age of 50. If the mammogram yields a suspicious finding,
such a screening may be followed by surgical removal of an invasive
but localized carcinoma of the breast. Cancer screening is a form of
secondary prevention and should be distinguished from primary
prevention (e.g., reductions in cigarette smoking to prevent the
occurrence of lung cancer) and treatment (e.g., lumpectomy and
lymphadenectomy or chemotherapy for breast cancer that is not
detected by screening).

In this chapter, the *incidence rate* refers to the proportion of a
population with cancer within a given limited time interval (e.g., 50
cases per 100,000 persons at risk per year), and *prevalence rate* refers
to the number of existing cases of cancer at a particular point in time
(e.g., 180 per 100,000 persons on January 1, 1982). Unless otherwise
designated, prevalence rates include those with previously diagnosed
cancer (whether or not they are free of cancer at the time of the
survey).

The prevention of death from cancer is often considered to be the
essential outcome for measuring the efficacy of cancer screening;[56,68]
unless otherwise noted, it is the definition of the efficacy of screen-

ing for cancer that is used here. One reason for this definition is the lack of epidemiologically based research using morbidity indicators. The advantages and disadvantages of this measure are discussed further in the section entitled "Preventability of Burden."

In this chapter, an ecologic study indicates the examination of population-based rates. Case-control studies involve rates of prior screening in cases (e.g., persons who have died from the cancer) as compared with such rates in controls (e.g., persons who have not died from the cancer and usually have not contracted it). Nested case-control studies refer to case-control studies conducted within a longitudinally defined cohort in which careful attempts are made to classify all members as to level of screening. This methodology limits the case-control comparisons to a fraction of the total cohort— for example, all cases who died from the cancer and five times as many age-stratified controls (the remaining controls are excluded).

Levels of assurance are based on whether evidence for efficacy involves the following: (1) different research designs, which may include ecologic and case-control studies, observational cohort studies, controlled nonrandomized studies, and randomized controlled trials; (2) the magnitude of the observed protective effect (e.g., an observed reduction in risk of 50 percent versus 10 percent); (3) the extent of care given to collecting data on the screening modality and on the outcome (e.g., death from the cancer), and the extent to which covariables such as socioeconomic status and race were considered; (4) the consistency in the results across different studies; (5) supporting data on sensitivity and specificity; and (6) the extent to which older age groups were studied.

BURDEN

Incidence, Mortality, Survival, and Prevalence

Age is the most consistent and strongest predictor of risk for cancer and for death from cancer. (The effect of age is so dramatic that incidence and mortality rates increase exponentially with age.)[21,71] Table 9-1 provides population-based incidence rates and incidence/mortality ratios from the Surveillance, Epidemiology, and End Results (SEER) program in the United States. The adult epithelial cancers are more common in persons over the age of 50 than in those under that age, and the rates of incidence and mortality increase with each decade of life after age 50. The incidence/mortality ratios imply that death rates for cancer generally increase with age more rapidly than incidence rates.

TABLE 9-1 Incidence (I) per 100,000 Persons and Incidence/Mortality (I/M) Ratios for Selected Cancer Sites, U.S. Surveillance, Epidemiology, and End Results Program, 1981–1985

Site	Age Groups												
	20–24	25–29	30–34	35–39	40–44	45–49	50–54	55–59	60–64	65–69	70–74	75–79	80–84
All Sites													
I	29	47	75	121	199	323	499	780	1,125	1,506	1,898	2,187	2,433
I/M	4.7	4.9	4.5	3.8	3.1	2.6	2.2	2.2	2.1	2.0	2.0	1.9	1.7
Rectum													
I	0.1	0.4	0.8	1.8	4.4	9.3	19.1	33.4	49.9	68.4	89.7	102.0	120.3
I/M	—	4.0	8.0	6.0	6.3	6.2	6.2	6.1	5.8	5.5	5.0	4.4	3.7
Lung													
I	0.2	0.5	1.6	5.8	19.1	44.2	88.5	156.0	221.8	287.0	329.0	313.2	274.0
I/M	2.0	1.7	1.6	1.4	1.4	1.3	1.3	1.3	1.3	1.2	1.2	1.1	1.1
Breast													
I	1.1	8.4	27.5	66.0	114.6	169.8	194.6	244.3	292.2	31.5	362.3	380.2	397.3
I/M	5.5	7.0	5.1	5.2	4.9	4.6	3.5	3.3	3.3	3.3	3.2	3.0	2.7
Cervix													
I	2.0	7.6	12.1	15.1	16.6	16.8	17.1	19.0	19.1	19.9	20.0	19.7	18.9
I/M	—	8.4	6.4	4.7	3.5	2.8	2.4	2.3	2.1	2.0	1.9	1.6	1.3
Melanoma													
I	2.7	5.6	8.7	12.1	13.8	15.6	17.5	20.2	21.5	22.0	23.3	24.6	26.8
I/M	9.0	8.0	6.7	7.1	5.5	5.0	4.5	4.2	4.0	3.5	3.0	2.9	2.6

SOURCE: Data abstracted from material provided by the Division of Cancer Prevention and Control, National Cancer Institute, 1988.

TABLE 9-2 Age-specific Prevalence Rates per 100,000 Persons for Selected Cancer Sites in Connecticut on January 1, 1982

Site	Age Group					
	0–29	30–49	50–59	60–69	70+	Total[a]
Men						
All sites	134.4	597.6	2,296.3	5,380.3	11,809.7	1,789.0
Pharynx	2.6	32.6	196.5	390.2	608.3	107.7
Colon	0.7	26.2	246.4	723.8	2,053.2	249.3
Rectum	0.3	13.4	161.1	477.3	1,123.2	144.7
Lung	0.8	27.7	238.6	564.5	757.6	134.8
Melanoma	5.6	74.5	200.7	238.3	261.3	80.6
Women						
All sites	142.7	1,169.8	4,538.0	7,530.7	10,635.0	2,221.6
Pharynx	2.8	24.1	96.3	165.1	198.8	45.5
Colon	1.7	31.8	251.2	662.8	1,887.7	224.1
Rectum	0.1	14.1	124.0	350.3	722.9	97.6
Lung	0.3	24.5	143.3	272.2	233.6	61.2
Melanoma	9.5	102.5	184.3	188.4	183.6	77.0
Breast	4.3	413.3	2,067.3	2,983.4	3,888.7	847.6
Cervix	8.1	120.8	286.6	447.4	528.0	138.4

[a]Age-adjusted to the 1980 U.S. population.

SOURCE: A. R. Feldman, L. Kessler, M. H. Myers, et al., "The Prevalence of Cancer: Estimates Based on the Connecticut Tumor Registry," *New England Journal of Medicine*, Vol. 315, pp. 1394-1397, 1986.

Table 9-2 presents prevalence data for selected cancers.[31] (Because the data come from a limited geographic region, the state of Connecticut, any given subgroup of the U.S. population may have a prevalence rate for a given cancer that is quite different from that shown in Table 9-2.) Incidence rates for colorectal cancer are about 5 to 10 percent higher in Connecticut than in remaining portions of the SEER areas; for breast cancer, they are somewhat higher in Connecticut as compared with other SEER areas. In general, however, these prevalence rates are probably not dramatically different from prevalence rates for the United States as a whole.[71]

As noted earlier, prevalence rates include those with previously diagnosed cancer who are free of the disease and also those who are not free of disease. For cancers with high incidence/mortality ratios, persons free of disease but with a prior diagnosis of cancer would generally represent the majority of prevalent cases. For example, persons aged 70 to 74 with rectal cancer have an incidence/mortality ratio of 5.0 compared with 1.2 in the same age group for lung cancer. For rectal cancer, the percentage of prevalent cases free of disease is much greater than that for lung cancer.

Impairment, Disability, Handicap, and Costs

A description of the aspects of cancer that pertain to impairment, disability, and handicap is difficult to derive from available published U.S. data, and in the absence of known prevalence rates for these cancer-related problems, a comprehensive description of the cost of cancer is not possible. Several morbidity and quality of life indices associated with specific cancers are listed below.[23,31,51,57,58,68,79]

Impairment

1. Psychological stress and fear associated with diagnosis of cancer at any site.
2. Bone pain (particularly with lung, breast, and prostate cancers).
3. Impairment of joint motion or joint discomfort (particularly at the shoulder in association with breast cancer).
4. Disfigurement, particularly with respect to surgery for head and neck cancer and breast cancer.
5. Generalized weakness associated with cachexia of cancer and with chemotherapy.

Disability

1. Behavioral difficulties, particularly those associated with embarrassment stemming from mastectomy or head and neck surgery.
2. Communication involving difficulties in phonation stemming from pharyngeal and laryngeal cancer and necessary surgery.

Handicap

1. Loss of employment (in association with loss of health insurance) or fear of loss of employment as a result of knowledge of an employer or insurer regarding the diagnosis of cancer in an employee.
2. All categories of handicap associated with progression of end-stage cancer.

PREVENTABILITY OF BURDEN

This section summarizes published data on the efficacy of screening for cancers in persons over the age of 50. The review focuses on those cancers that are generally accepted by most authoritative review groups as screenable without special reference to age: cancers of the female breast, uterine cervix, and colon and rectum; skin cancer (including melanoma); and oral cavity cancer.[2,10,26,44,81] Efficacy is defined as postponement or avoidance of death by the screening intervention.

Ecologic Considerations

The comparison of trends in population-based incidence and mortality rates for aggregate populations provides a useful background for considering the efficacy of screening. Long-term trends in incidence rates since around 1950 have a more positive slope than do corresponding long-term trends in mortality rates for invasive breast cancer, colorectal cancer, cancer of the uterine cervix, and melanoma skin cancer.[26,71] These patterns apply to the oldest age groups as well as to younger populations.[53,71] The differential patterns in incidence and mortality trends coincide with the introduction and increasing availability of breast physical exam and mammography, pap testing, physical exam of the skin, and increasing scrutiny of the large bowel using rigid sigmoidoscopy, fecal occult blood testing, and, since the 1970s, flexible sigmoidoscopy.

In these studies, however, the so-called ecologic fallacy may apply because the unit of analysis is an aggregate population. That is, undefined factors in these aggregate populations could also account for the observed patterns in time trends for incidence and mortality. The remaining portion of this chapter focuses on data in which the unit of analysis is the individual.

Female Breast Cancer

Table 9-3 summarizes four studies that examined screening efficacy in two or more age groups over the age of 50. Two other publications[4,64] provided information on two age groups only, but these studies were nevertheless consistent with the pattern in Table 9-3. (A seventh study in the United Kingdom has published a report indicating a modest protective effect.[81]) All six of the studies are consistent with a reduction in breast cancer mortality in age groups

TABLE 9-3 Results of Studies of Screening and Mortality from Breast Cancer in Persons Over the Age of 50[a]

Study	Results				
Health Insurance Plan of Greater New York[b]					
Age groups	40–44	45–49	50–54	55–59	60–64
Relative risk[c] of death from breast cancer	0.73	0.82	0.78	0.86	0.69
Number of deaths from breast cancer	(66)	(80)	(96)	(78)	(57)
Breast Cancer Detection and Demonstration Project[d]					
Age groups	35–49	50–59	60–74		
Observed/expected deaths from breast cancer	0.89	0.76	0.74		
Number of deaths from breast cancer	(49)	(51)	(25)		
Nijmegen, Netherlands[e]					
Age groups	35–49	50–64	65+		
Relative risk of death from breast cancer	1.23	0.26	0.81		
Number of deaths from breast cancer	(19)	(27)	(16)		
Utrecht, Netherlands[f]					
Approximate midpoint age group	54	59	64		
Relative risk of death from breast cancer	0.82	0.31	0.05		
Number of deaths from breast cancer	(12)	(14)	(20 over age 50)		

[a]Age groups for each study represent ages at entry into screening.

[b]This study recruited 60,000 women who were randomized to two groups: usual care or mammography plus a physical exam. The study was begun in 1963 and included a 16-year follow-up period. See the analyses by Habbema and colleagues (reference no. 37) and Schapiro and coworkers (reference no. 76).

[c]Defined as the probability of death from breast cancer in the screened divided by the probability of breast cancer in the unscreened.

[d]Fifty-five thousand self-referred women participated in this study, which involved two-view mammography as the screening modality. Begun in 1973, the study included a 9-year follow-up period and comparison with rates from the Surveillance, Epidemiology, and End Result (SEER) program areas. (See Morrison and colleagues, reference no. 56, for further analysis.)

[e]Female inhabitants of Nijmegen, Netherlands, were invited to participate in a nested study using single-view mammography as the screening modality. The study was begun in 1975. For further details, see reference nos. 82 and 83.

[f]This study was begun in 1974 and used a nested case-control design to study the effectiveness of xeromammography plus a clinical exam (see reference no. 20).

from 50 to 70 years by a factor of 1.2- to more than 3-fold as a result of the screening modalities. Furthermore, there is no overall indication of a decline in protective effect with increasing age; if anything, there is a suggestion that screening is more effective in postmenopausal women. Table 9-3 is consistent with a recent independent review.[28]

In fact, there may be some improvement in sensitivity or specificity of breast cancer screening with age, perhaps in part related to menopause, declining estrogen stimulation, and declining benign breast disease. Independent of this feature of the screening test, its predictive value would increase with age because positive predictive value is affected by the underlying prevalence of the cancer in the population subjected to the test, and Tables 9-1 and 9-2 demonstrate the increase in cancer incidence, mortality, and prevalence that occurs with age. Thus, for any given level of sensitivity and specificity, the positive predictive value of breast cancer screening will be much higher in older women. In other words, Table 9-1 suggests that, other factors being equal, the probability that a positive mammogram will, indeed, lead to a diagnosis of breast cancer is more likely in a 75-year-old woman than in a 45-year-old woman.

With respect to female breast cancer, the rate of advance of preclinical breast cancer may be somewhat longer in older persons than in younger persons.[22] However, this effect is probably not a large one (". . . for women over 50 the sojourn time increases slowly with age"[22]). In particular, the committee did not find evidence in published data that invasive breast cancers in the elderly were, as a group, less aggressive or less likely to kill the woman at any given stage at time of diagnosis. [1,6,14,35,39,55,76] (In particular, see the discussion with R. Peto noted in reference 70.) For example, in women who were 60 to 64 years old on entry into the study conducted by the Health Insurance Plan (HIP) of Greater New York (see Table 9-3), the number of incident cases of breast cancer after 16 years of follow-up were 68 and 69 in the screened versus unscreened groups, respectively, as compared with 425 and 443 over all women aged 40 to 64.[39] If breast cancer were relatively less lethal in this age group, more incident cases would have been identified in this group than in younger women.

In summary, with advancing age, there is a marked decline in the ratio of benign-to-malignant outcomes of biopsies in screened women and an improvement in the positive predictive value of mammography that can be in the range of 45 to 85 percent in women over the age of 65.[6,65]

Cancer of the Uterine Cervix

The efficacy of screening for cervical cancer is supported by time trends in incidence and mortality as noted above. In addition, a study by Hakama[40] provides differences in cervical cancer mortality trends by geographic region that correspond well with differing geographic trends in screening prevalence. Further supporting evidence comes from three case-control studies that have shown protective effects from pap testing by a factor of 2- to 3-fold or more.[8,16]

Clarke and Anderson demonstrated that the relative risk of death from cervical cancer was reduced in those who had undergone prior pap testing; the overall reduction in risk was similar to or greater in magnitude than that for invasive cancer.[16] The ability to use invasive cervical cancer as the case definition presumably stems from the sensitivity of pap testing to carcinoma in situ. Once the carcinoma had been removed, both invasive cervical cancer and death from cervical cancer would be prevented. The original study by Clarke and Anderson[16] provided some detail on the relative risk for invasive cervical cancer by age at diagnosis. Women in the sixth and seventh decades of life benefited from screening as much or more than younger women (see Table 9-4).

These results are consistent with other observations. In situ carcinoma of the cervix persists in its occurrence from ages 55 to 75

TABLE 9-4 Estimates of Relative Risk (Derived from Pap Testing) for Invasive Cervical Cancer by Age at Diagnosis from a Case-Control Study

Risk	Age Group			
	20–34	35–44	45–59	60+
Relative risk[a] for invasive cervical cancer	0.48	0.50	0.32	0.29
Number of cases	(16)	(36)	(102)	(58)[b]

[a]Defined as the probability of death from cervical cancer in the screened divided by the probability of cervical cancer in the unscreened.

[b]Overall prevalence of prior cervical cancer screening was 32 percent in cases and 56 percent in controls.

SOURCE: E. A. Clarke and T. W. Anderson, "Does Screening by 'Pap' Smears Help Prevent Cervical Cancer? A Case-Control Study," *Lancet,* Vol. 2, pp. 1-4, 1979.

and older.[4] Moreover, in a collaborative study of screening programs in eight countries involving 1.9 million women, there was no detectable decline in the sensitivity of cervical cancer screening up to the age of 65, the last age evaluated.[44]

Celentano and colleagues[13] have published data on the duration since the last screen of the protective effect derived from pap testing and have summarized data from several studies. Protection against invasive cervical cancer probably persists for four to six years after the last screen, although the magnitude of protection may decline by a factor of at least 2 after three years. Such information is relevant to determining whether arbitrary termination of cervical cancer screening in elderly persons is wise; this problem is discussed later in the chapter.

Cancer of the Colon and Rectum

Data on sigmoidoscopy[35,36,43,61,75] and fecal occult blood testing[5] demonstrate the potential of these procedures as effective screening tests for colorectal cancer. The predictive value of hemoccult testing improves as the age of the patient undergoing the screening increases.[60,84] Flexible sigmoidoscopy yields more data on the presence of cancer[62] and is better tolerated than rigid sigmoidoscopy. However, flexible sigmoidoscopy is limited to distal segments of the large bowel and may miss more than two-fifths of the cancers suspected by hemoccult.[60,63] Limitations in the overall sensitivity of hemoccult screening are being altered by newer, immunologically based tests;[41] these improvements could be particularly relevant to screening in the elderly, who may tolerate fecal occult blood testing much better than flexible sigmoidoscopy.

In studies of screening for colorectal cancer, there are few published data that adequately address problems of lead-time and length bias sampling (see the later "Discussion" section). A recently reported case-control study[62] (presented at meetings of the American Society for Oncology in 1989) found a 2- to 3-fold protective effect from screening sigmoidoscopy. Analyses by age of the results of this case-control study and other studies in progress[42,45,48] may clarify the protective potential of colorectal cancer screening in the elderly.

Skin Cancer (Including Malignant Melanoma)

The sensitivity and specificity of skin examinations for cutaneous malignant melanoma and for basal cell carcinoma appear to exceed 85 to 90 percent.[39,46,47,66,71] The efficacy of a thorough clinical examination of the skin is based primarily on the concept of a radial or horizontal growth phase of sufficient duration and extent so that gross anatomic recognition is feasible. If it is, the sensitivity and specificity noted above should lead to some reduction in mortality from skin cancer. To the committee's knowledge, there are only two sets of data that provide any evidence on this question. Greene and coworkers[37] found that, after implementation of surveillance for melanoma and dysplastic nevi, there was total elimination of mortality from melanomas in 14 families with the apparent autosomal dominant familial dysplastic nevus syndrome, a syndrome said to carry a virtually 100 percent risk for melanoma to the eighth decade of life in those with multiple large nevi. In a small set of pilot data that were gathered to prepare for a large field study of melanoma, an inverse association between prior examination of the skin and either late-stage or lethal melanoma was observed.[72]

To the committee's knowledge, there are no available data on the efficacy of screening for skin cancer in the elderly. It should be noted, however, that, with age, inspection of the skin becomes increasingly complex and may lead to greater difficulty in distinguishing neoplastic lesions.[72]

Screening for Other Cancers

Some attention has been given to screening for cancers of the mouth,[5,30,50] lungs,[27,73] and prostate.[15,30] For lung cancer, case-control data fail to show a protective effect from screening, and prospective data do not support a benefit from cytology as compared with chest x-rays among smokers.[73] Regarding prostate cancer, ultrasound screening of the prostate is probably a more sensitive measure than the digital rectal exam.[50] Whether use of the ultrasound procedure will lead to actual reductions in morbidity and mortality has not been fully evaluated.[50,70] Prostatic antigen assays do not appear to have sufficient specificity to allow their use in screening.[9] Controlled studies to account for lead-time and length bias sampling (see the next section) are particularly important in view of the high proportion of men over age 60 with changes of the prostate that are histologically malignant but biologically relatively benign. In summary, there are insufficient data at present to determine whether screening for this cancer produces benefits.

DISCUSSION

Table 9-5 summarizes evidence on the efficacy of screening in persons over the age of 50. The determination of efficacy in these

TABLE 9-5 Summary of Evidence for Efficacy of Screening for Cancer in Persons over the Age of 50

Cancer Site	Screening Intervention	Extent of Evidence and Limitations
Female breast	Mammography, with or without physical exam	Ecologic, case-control, and observational cohort studies; randomized controlled trial. None are contradictory; ages over 70 not extensively studied. Level of assurance:[a] A.
Uterine cervix	Pap smear	At least one case-control study showed more than a 3-fold reduction; multi-center ecologic study showed no evidence for decline in sensitivity to age 65. Level of assurance: A to B.
Large bowel	Hemoccult and flexible sigmoidoscopy	Efficacy in elderly not well studied (one case-control study and observational cohort studies tended to favor overall efficacy of screening). Increase in the use of medications in the elderly may affect sensitivity and specificity. Level of assurance: C.
Skin cancer, including melanoma	Skin exam	Efficacy in elderly not well studied (case-control study is in progress). Possible decline in accuracy of exam owing to changes in skin with age. Level of assurance: C.

[a]Levels of assurance ("A" being most confident) are based on whether (1) evidence comes from studies with different designs, which may include ecologic or case-control studies, observational cohort studies, controlled nonrandomized studies, and randomized controlled trials; (2) the extent of care given to collecting data on the screening modality and the occurrence of outcome and whether covariables were considered; (3) the consistency across different studies; and (4) the extent to which older age groups were studied.

studies is often based on prevention of death from the cancer. A disadvantage of the mortality measure is that it fails to address directly the question of quality of life and the impairments, disabilities, and handicaps that may be associated with the disease, prevention, or treatment. These deficiencies in the information these studies provide make it particularly difficult to develop cost-benefit analyses that have comprehensive implications. On the other hand, the use of mortality from cancer as an outcome measure has certain advantages in the context of a report on screening in the elderly. For example, one can conceive of a screening modality whose only effect is to advance the time of diagnosis prior to the eventual occurrence of death rather than to prevent death itself. In such an instance of lead-time bias, the elderly person is likely to be subjected to the negative effects that arise from being labeled as diagnosed with cancer, as well as the likelihood of additional uncomfortable or painful instrumentation or surgery; these effects occur in the absence of any real postponement of death from the cancer. Also, one could conceive of a screening modality whose effect was to identify tumors that are declared to be cancer but that in fact are without lethal potential or that, as a group, take many years to kill the individual and are much less aggressive in comparison to cancers that are identified on the basis of symptoms or routine clinical exams. In such an instance of length bias sampling, the social and medical consequences are the same as in the prior example: adverse interventions without material prolongation of life.

There are few available data on the efficacy of screening for breast cancer in those over the age of 75, but screening efficacy is well supported in the years from ages 50 through 65. Although data on screening for cervical cancer in women over age 50 are sparse, the Clarke and Anderson case-control study[16] and the ecologic studies noted earlier are consistent with a strong protective effect from cervical cancer screening through age 65. Taken together, the data on these two very different epithelial cancers support the conclusion that the predictive value of screening tests in the elderly is at least as good if not better than the positive predictive values characteristic of younger age groups.

From the standpoint of evidence of efficacy, it is difficult to support the notion of establishing an arbitrary age at which to terminate screening for cancer such as, for example, terminating screening for cancer of the cervix at age 65. Yet the committee notes that recent recommendations regarding cervical cancer are consistent with this practice.[32] This may well be counterproductive: if either sensitivity or specificity are, indeed, less in a given screening modality (which seems not to be the case in screening for cervical and breast cancer), this deficit may be partly or entirely offset by much greater predictive value at any given level of sensitivity and specificity owing to the more common occurrence of cancer (see Tables 9-1 and 9-2).

The issue of competing causes of death becomes increasingly important in the context of cancer screening and aging in the very elderly; for example, it is recognized[18] that average life expectancy is 6.9 years for an 85-year-old woman and that the average, untreated natural history between onset of detectable preclinical cancer and death from it may be nearly as long or longer. The importance of such an effect could be estimated with appropriately controlled studies.

Data from a 1987 survey and from other studies indicate that elderly populations have a lower prevalence of prior screening as compared with younger populations.[12,65] Table 9-6 summarizes the results for three screening modalities: pap smear, mammography, and fecal occult blood testing. In most instances, the prevalence of the never-screened was higher in those 70 years of age and older, with blacks over the age of 70 having the highest rates of never-screened persons. It is possible, however, that some of these effects might reflect the open-endedness of the oldest age group or failures to report prior screening in the elderly in this survey.

The above comments do not consider either factors reflecting quality of life, the discomfort of the screening procedures, or economic cost-benefit analyses. Eddy has developed estimates on the benefits and costs related to screening for breast cancer.[28] Increases in life expectancy in those aged 65 to 75 were approximately 60 to 90 percent of the increases in life expectancy that were achieved by screening women in age groups between the ages of 40 and 65; the cost of adding a year of life by screening for breast cancer was about 10 percent greater for women aged 65 to 74 as compared with women aged 55 to 65, but it was actually 31 percent lower than the cost for women in their forties.

Systemic biochemical screening tests[33] (for example, nuclear resonance spectroscopy of serum) are an interesting possibility, but they

TABLE 9-6 Percentage of Persons Reporting No Prior Screening Procedures

Age Group	Pap Smear	Mammography	Fecal Occult Blood Testing	
			Men	Women
White				
40–49	4.3	57.7	67.6	72.7
50–59	4.2	53.7	63.1	58.1
60–69	7.7	61.4	55.1	54.1
70+	22.6	71.8	61.4	60.4
Black				
40–49	2.7	64.0	78.6	77.3
50–59	10.7	69.9	72.7	69.9
60–69	21.9	71.7	62.2	69.2
70+	43.4	82.4	73.6	78.0

SOURCE: National Health Interview Survey, 1987.

are particularly problematic in the elderly because they might lead to extensive diagnostic evaluations without being able to focus on a particular organ site. However, there have been efforts to develop biochemical tests that would localize suspicion to a particular organ site such as the lung, breast, or prostate.[9,54,59]

RECOMMENDATIONS

Implementation of Screening

For persons over the age of 50, it is important to consider screening for cancer with the same inherent interest as for younger persons. Initially, at least, all elderly persons should be considered candidates for physical exam of the breast and mammography, pap testing, physical exam of the skin, fecal occult blood testing and flexible sigmoidoscopy to 35 centimeters, and oral exam.

The frequency of screening and the balancing of the limited screening options for this group (e.g., hemoccult versus flexible sigmoidoscopy) may be dramatically affected by such factors as the ability of the individual to undergo screening itself, the ability to tolerate surgery if a suspicious lesion is identified, the risk factors other than age that predispose the person to cancer, the incidence of the cancer, prior negative screening tests within the past 2 to 15 years, and the individual's life expectancy, which may change dramatically over a 5- to 10-year period among the very elderly.

Research

The committee recommends a systematic reanalysis of existing data sets, including those involving population-based rates, case-control data, and prospectively collected data, to evaluate the efficacy of screening in individual age groups over the age of 50. Furthermore, new data on screening should be collected, data that will address the relative importance of the several factors (e.g., tolerance to screening, life expectancy) noted in the previous paragraph.

Regarding colorectal cancer, the use of fecal occult blood testing, in comparison with flexible sigmoidoscopy, is particularly appealing for elderly individuals because it is noninvasive, and some of the recent modifications of this technique suggest improvements in specificity in comparison with prior occult blood testing. Studies should be conducted to evaluate these recent tests; their results could be particularly relevant to screening for colorectal cancer in the elderly. On the other hand, it would also be helpful to assess the degree to which elderly persons are capable of conducting fecal occult blood testing and to examine the tolerance of flexible sigmoidoscopy (to 35 and 60 centimeters) in subgroups of the elderly population. Also of interest and concern are the rates of complication of endoscopy, such as bowel perforation, in the age group over 50.

Prostate cancer is common in the elderly and is a potentially "screenable" cancer. Screening using ultrasound appears to have the potential to enhance screening sensitivity markedly; however, it will be impossible to evaluate the true efficacy of such screening without collecting data that take into account the problems of lead-time and length bias sampling.

Epidemiologically grounded methodologic research would be valuable in examining how to incorporate nonmortality measures of screening efficacy, including measures that would reflect impairment, disability, and handicap. This methodologic research should be statistical (e.g., the development of measures to estimate the prevalence of morbidity from existing incidence, mortality, and survival data); it should also consider ways to incorporate measures of cancer prevalence in routinely collected survey data (e.g., minimally, a self-report as to prior diagnosis and a self-report as to impairment associated with surgery on the skin, lymph nodes, or large bowel). Such research would then form the basis for studies of screening efficacy that would not have to be limited solely to measures of the avoidance of mortality from cancer but could also include quality of life. In addition, this research could address the costs of screening in the elderly, an area in which the reassuring findings of cost-benefit studies of cervical and breast cancer offer hopes of further favorable results.[11,44,52,77,85]

Education

The committee recommends educational programs primarily for the relatively noninvasive screening modalities: skin exams, breast physical exams, and mammography. Because of uncertainties regarding colorectal screening and the need to judge individually whether elderly persons should undergo fecal occult blood testing and endoscopy, education regarding screening for large bowel cancer is not recommended. It is difficult to recommend a vigorous educational campaign to convey specific information on two common cancers, colorectal cancer and prostate cancer, because of imprecision regarding estimates of efficacy and individual variations in tolerance to screening protocols. No educational effort is recommended for screening programs for lung cancer until there is better evidence regarding their efficacy.

REFERENCES

1. Adami, H. O., Malker, B., Holmberg, L., et al. The relation between survival and age at diagnosis in breast cancer. New England Journal of Medicine 1986; 315:559-563.

2. American Cancer Society. Cancer Facts and Figures. Atlanta, Ga.: American Cancer Society, 1988.

3. American Cancer Society. Summary of Current Guidelines of the Cancer-related Checkup: Recommendations. New York: American Cancer Society, 1988.

4. Anderson, I., Aspegren, K., Janzon, L., et al. Mammographic screening and mortality from breast cancer: The Malmo mammographic screening trial. British Medical Journal 1988; 297:943-948.

5. Baden, E. Prevention of cancer of the oral cavity and pharynx. CA 1987; 37:49-62.

6. Baden, J. P. Screening of colorectal cancer. Digestive Diseases and Sciences 1986; 31(Suppl. 9):43S-56S.

7. Baker, L. H. Breast cancer detection demonstration project: Five-year summary report. CA 1982; 32:4-35.

8. Berrino, F., Gatta, G., D'Alto, M., et al. Use of case-control studies in evaluation of screening programmes. In: P. C. Prorok and A. B. Miller (eds.), Screening for Cancer. 1. General Principles on Evaluation of Screening for Cancer and Screening for Lung, Bladder and Oral Cancer. Geneva: International Agency for Research on Cancer (IARC), 1984, pp. 29-43.

9. Brawer, M. K., and Lange, P. H. Prostate-specific antigen and premalignant change: Implications for early detection. CA 1989; 39:361-375.

10. Canadian Task Force on the Periodic Health Examination. The Periodic Health Examination. 2. 1985 Update. Canadian Medical Association Journal 1986; 134:724-729.

11. Carter, A. P., Thompson, R. S., Bourdeau, R. V., et al. A clinically effective breast cancer screening program can be cost-effective, too. Preventive Medicine 1987; 16(1):19-34.

12. Celentano, D. D., Shapiro, S., and Weisman, C. S. Cancer preventive screening behavior among elderly women. Preventive Medicine 1982; 11:454-463.

13. Celentano, D. D., Klassen, A. C., Weisman, C. S., et al. Duration of relative protective screening for cervical cancer. Preventive Medicine 1989; 18:411-422.

14. Charlson, M. E., and Feinstein, A. R. Rapid growth rate: A method of identifying node-negative breast cancer patients with a high risk of recurrence. Journal of Chronic Disease 1983; 36:847-853.

15. Chodak, G. W., Keller, P., and Schoenberg, H. Routine screening for prostate cancer using the digital rectal examination. Program Clinical Biology Research 1988; 269:87-98.

16. Clarke, E. A., and Anderson, T. W. Does screening by "pap" smears help prevent cervical cancer? A case-control study. Lancet 1979; 2:1-4.

17. Clarke, E. A. Re: "Case definition in case-control studies of the efficacy of screening" (letter). American Journal of Epidemiology 1982; 115:518-519.

18. Clinical Practice Committee, American Geriatrics Society Board of Directors. Screening for cervical carcinoma in elderly women. Journal of the American Geriatrics Society 1989; 37:885-887.

19. Clinical Practice Committee, American Geriatrics Society Board of Directors. Screening for breast cancer in elderly women. Journal of the American Geriatrics Society 1989; 37:883-884.

20. Collette, H. J. A., Day, N. E., Rombach, J. J., and deWaard, F. Evaluation of screening for breast cancer in a non-randomized study (the DOM project) by means of a case-control study. Lancet 1984; 1:1224-1226.

21. Cook, P. J., Doll, R., and Fellingham, S. A. A mathematical model for the age distribution of cancer in man. International Journal on Cancer 1969; 4:93-112.

22. Day, N. E., Bains, C. J., Chamberlain, J., et al. UICC project on screening for cancer: Report of the Workshop on Screening for Breast Cancer. International Journal on Cancer 1986; 38:303-308.

23. Dietz, J. H., Jr. Rehabilitation of the patient with cancer. In: P. Clabresi, P. S. Schein, and S. A. Rosenberg (eds.), Medical Oncology. New York: MacMillan, 1985, pp. 1501-1522.

24. Division of Cancer Prevention and Control, National Cancer Institute. 1987 Annual Cancers Statistics Review. NIH Publ. No. 88-2789. Bethesda, Md.: National Institutes of Health, 1988.

25. Drago, J. R. The role of new modalities in the early detection and diagnosis of prostate cancer. CA 1989; 39:326-336.

26. Early Detection Branch, Division of Cancer Prevention and Control, National Cancer Institute. Working Guidelines for Early Cancer Detection: Rationale and Supporting Evidence to Decrease Mortality. Bethesda, Md.: National Cancer Institute, 1987.

27. Ebeling, K., and Nischan, P. Screening for lung cancer—results from a case-control study. International Journal of Cancer 1987; 40:141-144.

28. Eddy, D. M. Screening for breast cancer. Annals of Internal Medicine 1989; 111:389-399.

29. Editorial. Diagnostic and therapeutic technology assessment (DATTA): Transrectal ultrasonography in prostatic cancer. Journal of the American Medical Association 1988; 259:2757-2759.

30. Elwood, J. M., and Gallagher, R. P. Dental surveillance produces earlier diagnosis of oral cavity cancers. Canadian Dental Association Journal 1986; 10:845-847.

31. Feldman, A. R., Kessler, L., Myers, M. H., et al. The prevalence of cancer. Estimates based on the Connecticut Tumor Registry. New England Journal of Medicine 1986; 315:1394-1397.

32. Fink, D. J. Change in American Cancer Society checkup guidelines for detection of cervical cancer. CA 1988; 38:127-128.

33. Fossel, E. T., Carr, J. M., and McDonagh, J. Detection of malignant tumors: Water-suppressed proton nuclear magnetic resonance spectroscopy of plasma. New England Journal of Medicine 1986; 315:1369-1376.

34. Frame, P. S. A critical review of adult health maintenance. Part 3. Prevention of cancer. Journal of Family Practitioners 1986; 22:511-520.

35. Friedman, G. D., Collen, M. F., and Fireman, B. H. Multiphasic health check-up evaluation: A 16-year follow-up. Journal of Chronic Disease 1986; 39:453-463.

36. Gilbertson, V. A. Proctosigmoidoscopy and polypectomy in reducing the incidence of rectal cancer. Cancer 1974; 34:936-939.

37. Green, M. H., Clark, W. H., Jr., Tucker, M. A., et al. High risk of malignant melanoma in melanoma-prone families with dysplastic nevi. Annals of Internal Medicine 1985; 102:458-465.

38. Green, A., Leslie, D., and Weedon, D. Diagnosis of skin cancer in the general population: Clinical accuracy in the Nambour survey. Medical Journal of Australia 1988; 148:447-450.

39. Habbema, J. D. F., van Dort Marssen, G. J., Van Putten, D. J., et al. Age-

specific reduction in breast cancer mortality by screening: An analysis of the results of the Health Insurance Plan of Greater New York Study. Journal of the National Cancer Institute 1986; 77:317-320.

40. Hakama, M. Trends in the incidence of cervical cancer in nordic countries. In: K. Magnus (ed.), Trends in Cancer Incidence: Causes and Practical Implications. Washington, D.C.: Hemisphere, 1982, pp. 279-292.

41. Hakkinen, I., Paasivup, R., and Partanen, P. Screening of colorectal tumours using an improved fecal occult blood test. Quantitative aspects. Gut 1988; 29:1194-1197.

42. Hardcastle, J. D., Armitage, N. C., Chamberlain, J., et al. Fecal occult blood screening for colorectal cancer in the general population: Results of a controlled trial. Cancer 1986; 58:397-403.

43. Hertz, R. E., Dedish, M. R., and Day, E. Value of periodic examinations in detecting cancer of the rectum and colon. Postgraduate Medicine 1960; 27:290.

44. International Agency for Research on Cancer (IARC) Working Group. Screening for squamous cervical cancer: Duration of low risk after negative results of cervical cytology and its implication for screening policies. British Medical Journal 1986; 293:659-664.

45. Kewenter, J., Bjork, S., Haglind, E., et al. Screening and rescreening for colorectal cancer: A controlled trial of fecal occult blood testing in 27,700 subjects. Cancer 1988; 62:645-651.

46. Koh, H. K., Lew, R. A., and Prout, M. N. Screening for melanoma skin cancer. Journal of the American Academy of Dermatology 1989; 20:159-172.

47. Kopf, A. W. Prevention and detection of skin cancer-melanoma. Cancer 1988; 62:1791-1795.

48. Kronborg, C., Fenger, O., Sondergaard, O., et al. Initial mass screening for colorectal cancer with fecal occult blood test. A prospective randomized study at Funen in Denmark. Scandinavica Journal of Gastroenterology 1987; 22:677-686.

49. Lee, F., Littrup, P. G., Torp-Pedersen, S., et al. Prostate cancer: Comparison of transrectal ultrasound and digital rectal examination for screening. Radiology 1988; 168:389-394.

50. Lee, F., Torp-Pedersen, S. T., and Siders, D. B. The role of transrectal ultrasound in the early detection of prostate cancer. CA 1989; 39:337-360.

51. Loescher, L. J., Welch-McCaffrey, D. W., Leigh, S. A., et al. Surviving adult cancers. Part 1. Physiologic effects. Annals of Internal Medicine 1989; 111:411-432.

52. Mandelblatt, J. S., and Fahs, M. C. The cost-effectiveness of cervical cancer screening for low-income elderly women. Journal of the American Medical Association 1988; 259:2409-2413.

53. McKay, F. W., Hanson, M. R., and Miller, R. W. Cancer Mortality in the United States: 1950-1977. National Cancer Institute Monograph No. 59. Washington, D.C.: U.S. Government Printing Office, 1982.

54. Moroz, C., Kahn, M., Ron, E., et al. The use of oncofetal ferritin-bearing lymphocytes as a marker for the screening, diagnosis and follow-up of patients with early breast malignancy: Screening of 34,000 women. Cancer 1989; 64:691-697.

55. Morrison, A. S. Screening in Chronic Disease. New York: Oxford University Press, 1985.

56. Morrison, A. S., Brisson, J., and Khalid, N. Breast cancer incidence and mortality in the breast cancer detection and demonstration project. Journal of the National Cancer Institute 1988; 80:1540-1547.

57. Mullan, F. Seasons of survival: Reflections of a physician with cancer. New England Journal of Medicine 1985; 313:270-273.

58. Mullan, F. Re-entry: The educational needs of the cancer survivor. Health Education Quarterly 1984; 10(Suppl.):88-94.

59. Mulshine, J. L., Tockman, M. S., and Smart, C. R. Considerations in the development of lung cancer screening tools. Journal of the National Cancer Institute 1989; 81:900-905.

60. Nelson, H., Pemberton J. H. Asymptomatic patients with positive stool guaiac (letter). Journal of the American Medical Association 1989; 261:1800.

61. Neugut, A. I., and Pita, S. Role of sigmoidoscopy in screening for colorectal cancer: A critical review. Gastroenterology 1988; 95:492-499.

62. Newcomb, P., Norfleet, R. G., Surewics, T. S., et al. Efficacy of fecal occult blood screening (abstract). Preventive Medicine, in press.

63. Nivatvongs, S., Gilbertsen, V. A., Goldberg, S. M., et al. Distribution of large bowel cancer detected by occult blood test in asymptomatic patients. Diseases of the Colon and Rectum 1982; 25:420-421.

64. Palli, D., Del Turco, M. R., Buiatti, E., et al. A case-control study of efficacy in a non-randomized breast cancer screening program in Florence, Italy. International Journal on Cancer 1986; 38:501-504.

65. Peters, R. K., Bear, M. B., and Thomas, D. Barriers to screening for cancer of the cervix. Preventive Medicine 1989; 18:133-146.

66. Presser, S. E., and Taylor, J. R. Clinical diagnostic accuracy of basal cell carcinoma. Journal of the American Academy of Dermatology 1987; 16:988-990.

67. Prorok, P. C., and Miller, A. B. (eds.) Screening for Cancer. 1. General Principles on Evaluation of Screening for Cancer and Screening for Lung, Bladder and Oral Cancer. Geneva: International Agency for Research on Cancer, 1984.

68. Rice, D. P., Hodgson, T. A., and Kopstein, A. N. The economic costs of illness: A replication and update. Health Care Finance Reviews 1985; 7:61-80.

69. Ries, L. G., Pollack, E. S., and Young, J. L., Jr. Cancer patient survival. Journal of the National Cancer Institute 1983; 70:693-707.

70. Robie, P. W. Cancer screening in the elderly. Journal of the American Geriatric Society 1989; 37:888-893.

71. Roush, G. C., Holford, T. R., Schymura, M. J., and White, C. Cancer Risk and Incidence Trends. Washington, D.C.: Hemisphere, 1987.

72. Roush, G. C., Nordlund, J. J., Forget, B., et al. Independence of dysplastic nevi from total nevi in determining risk for nonfamilial melanoma. Preventive Medicine 1988; 17:273-279.

73. Sanderson, D. R. Lung cancer screening: The Mayo study. Chest 1986; 89(Suppl.):324S-326S.

74. Seidman, H., Gelb, S. K., Silverberg, E., et al. Survival experience in the breast cancer detection demonstration project. CA 1987; 37:258-290.

75. Selby, J. V., Friedman, G. D., and Collen, M. F. Sigmoidoscopy and mortality from colorectal cancer: The Kaiser Permanente multiphasic evaluation study. Journal of Clinical Epidemiology 1988; 41:427-434.

76. Shapiro, S., Venet, W., Stract, P., et al. A randomized trial of breast cancer screening. In: Selection, Follow-up and Analysis in the Health Insurance Plan Study. National Cancer Institute Monograph No. 67. NIH Publ. No. 85-2713. Bethesda, Md.: National Cancer Institute, 1985.

77. Sickles, E. A., Weber, W. N., Glavin, H. B., et al. Mammographic screening: How to operate successfully at low cost. Radiology 1986; 160:95-97.

78. Sondek, E. J. Cancer Statistics Review, 1973-1986. NIH Publ. No. 89-2789. Washington, D.C.: U.S. Department of Health and Human Services, 1989.
79. Strauss, R. P. Psychosocial responses to oral and maxillofacial surgery for head and neck cancer. Journal of Oral Maxillofacial Surgery 1989; 47(4):343-348.
80. U.K. Trial of Early Detection of Breast Cancer Group. First results on mortality reduction in the U.K. Trial of Early Detection of Breast Cancer Group. Lancet 1988; 2:411-416.
81. U.S. Preventive Services Task Force. Guide to Clinical Preventive Services. Washington, D.C.: U.S. Department of Health and Human Services, 1989.
82. Verbeek, A. L., Hendriks, J. H., Holland, R., et al. Reduction of breast cancer mortality through mass screening with modern mammography: First results of the Nijmegen project, 1975-1981. Lancet 1984; 1:1222-1224.
83. Verbeek, A. L. M., Hendriks, J. H., Holland, R., et al. Mammographic screening and breast cancer mortality: Age-specific effects in the Nijmegen Project, 1975-82 (letter). Lancet 1985; 1:865-866.
84. Winawer, S. J., Andrews, M., Flehinger, B., et al. Progress report on controlled trial of fecal occult blood testing for the detection of colorectal neoplasia. Cancer 1980; 45:2959-2964.
85. Yu, S., Miller, A. B., and Sherman, G. J. Optimising the age, number of tests and test interval for cervical screening in Canada. Journal of Epidemiology and Community Health 1982; 36:1-20.

10
Nutrition

Dietary status and nutritional status are not synonymous. Dietary status is a measurement of what an individual is eating; nutritional status is the state of an individual's health as it is influenced by what is eaten. Diet is only one of many factors that may influence nutritional status. Thus, to provide an estimate of an individual's nutritional status, other measures are also used, including biochemical measurements of body fluids, anthropometric measurements, clinical findings, and medical history.

When diet alone is responsible for deficits in an individual's nutritional status, the person is said to be suffering from primary malnutrition. The forms of primary malnutrition that may arise simply as a result of deficits in dietary intake are undernutrition or starvation, protein calorie malnutrition, and various vitamin and mineral deficiency disorders such as iron deficiency anemia, scurvy (from a deficiency of ascorbic acid), and osteomalacia (from a deficiency of vitamin D). Excesses in some categories of dietary intake may give rise to obesity, hypervitaminoses, alcohol intoxication, and various dietary imbalances that all have adverse health effects. Deficits, imbalances, and excesses in nutrients may all be present simultaneously in some individuals.

Other factors may also give rise to malnutrition—for example, the presence of disease, special physiological states, or inborn errors of metabolism. Moreover, although the biomedical model tends to concentrate on biological variables, social and psychological factors can cause malnutrition as well. Food and eating have potent aesthetic and psychological attributes that are of great importance to maintaining the quality and enjoyment of everyday life. If a person's dietary intake is devoid of such characteristics owing to pathology arising from a physiological, psychological, or social cause, metabolism is deranged, appetites fall off, and eventually physical as well as emotional well-being may suffer. When malnutrition results from one or more of these causes, it is referred to as secondary malnutrition. Diet-drug or drug-drug interactions may also affect nutritional status adversely. Because this form of nutritional derangement is iatrogenic, it too is regarded as secondary malnutrition.

NUTRITION AND QUALITY OF LIFE

Favorable nutritional status throughout life can increase life expectancy. The increased expectation of life at birth that has taken place since 1900, as well as the growth in the expectation of life after 65 years of age, has been due in part to more favorable environmental conditions. Among these conditions has been an improvement in certain aspects of the food supply and dietary intakes, which have led to decreased prevalence of undernutrition and dietary deficiency diseases. Yet at the same time, other dietary factors have changed in the opposite direction—including several risk factors for chronic degenerative diseases (in particular, coronary artery heart disease, high blood pressure, and stroke) and certain cancers, which now account for at least 75 percent of all deaths and half of all bed confinement days among the elderly.[76]

Common chronic degenerative diseases with diet-related components as well as other diseases and cognitive impairments prevent functional independence. In 1985, more than 5 million people 65 years of age and older needed special care to remain independent; by the year 2000, more than 7 million people are likely to need such care. Many of these same individuals will need assistance with shopping, meal preparation, and eating.[34,87] The oldest old, that is, those over 85 years of age, are likely to be in special need of assistance in preparing food, eating, or planning their diets. Others, especially those with multiple, complex conditions, are also likely to require long-term care, either in or outside of institutions. Many residents of nursing homes and other long-term care facilities require therapeutic diets to deal with their health problems.[76] However, a lack of choice, limited variety, and poor quality of food may limit the enjoyment an individual derives from eating, even though minimal standards for nutrient intake are met in such facilities, in boarding homes, or even in the person's own home. Certain nutritional interventions among those aged 50 and older offer promise in helping meet national goals to reduce the number of days of restricted activity per year that result from acute or chronic conditions among the elderly.[22] And at all ages, attention to nutrition can increase the quality of life.

NUTRITION AND FUNCTION

The critical factor in a diminished quality of life for U.S. residents over 50 years of age is impairment in functional independence. Thus, a major concern of most elderly people is related to dependency. The average 68-year-old man today has a life expectancy of 13 years, which includes 4 years of progressive incapacity and increasing dependence. The segments of the population over 75 and over 85 years of age, the groups most likely to suffer functional impairments, are growing rapidly.[76] Therefore, the concerns of the elderly with respect to maintaining the activities of daily living, including those related to nutrition and foods, are likely to increase rather than decrease in the future.

FUNCTIONAL INDICES OF NUTRITIONAL STATUS

Functional assessments and indices in nutritional studies and in evaluations of service programs with a strong functional focus fell into disuse several decades ago, and renewed interest in them is only now beginning to surface. It is interesting to note that, in the earliest nutritional studies, a functional focus was often present. These early studies had a socioeconomic as well as a biological motivation and were usually concerned with the preservation or restoration of physical, psychological, social, or economic function by nutritional means. Many of the early justifications of the school milk, lunch, and breakfast programs for poor children were based on improvements in functionally related criteria (e.g., lowered absenteeism rates, greater alertness). The vitamin and mineral deficiencies that were common in the early part of this century were acute and could be clearly related to diet; if diet were altered, total cure could be expected. With certain other conditions, such as the associations between massive obesity, incidence of chronic diseases, and disabling conditions, functional indices of a crude sort (e.g., days of work lost, days of restricted activity) were used, and the effects of improved diet were also relatively easy to demonstrate.[27]

The range of available measures of physical, mental, and social function has expanded greatly.[42] Such measures include the Activities of Daily Living scale, as well as assessments of social competence (the Instrumental Activities of Daily Living scale) and mobility measures. In the field of nutrition, however, none of these measures or any other measures of disability have been used frequently, especially in studies in highly industrialized countries.[51] The effects of the diseases themselves and the treatments for the diseases (nutritional or other types) are rarely separated and measured. Thus, the effects of many nutritional therapies on function, quality of life, morbidity, and mortality are unavailable. Even more unfortunate, function in relation to eating is often not even considered in medical assessments. A recent survey revealed that the specifics of dietary history (either diet restrictions or details of food intake with respect to calories, the types of food actually eaten, and physical limitations on eating) and other functional measures were rarely found on standard history-taking forms used in hospitals and long-term care facilities.[60] These forms also neglected subjective comments by patients on the degree of their health, specifics of home living arrangements, the supporting services they received, and their dietary histories.[60]

Currently, the most common type of nutritional assessment used for older individuals comprises a clinical examination and one or more objective indices of functional impairment. The major advantage of a clinical examination, if it truly involves an assessment of functional status, is that it can incorporate observations of the individual actually performing the activities essential to preservation of independent function. When clinical assessments are combined with functional assessments of an objective nature, using such instruments as mental status measures, dietary intake and nutritional status measurements, measures of visual acuity and gait, and the Activities of Daily Living scale, more moderate cases of functional impairment are often revealed.[86] (A more typical clinical assessment that does not involve such functional assessments is useful in identifying severe impairments but may miss more moderate degrees of deficits in function.) Given the limited training most physicians, nurses, and dietitians receive in the specifics of functional assessment and, indeed, in many areas of care and assessment of the problems of the elderly, such care givers often find it difficult to assess the self-maintenance skills of elderly patients by clinical means. When fuller assessments of function or home visits to the elderly are conducted, however, they often reveal insights on function related to diet and eating.[88] Such a complete geriatric assessment is often helpful and should be mandatory when nonspecific failure to thrive with unexplained deterioration in nutritional status is evident.[7]

DIETARY INDICES

An assessment of dietary intake is another useful but often neglected tool for determining the nutritional status of the aging. Dietary status indices provide information that helps a clinician make the differential diagnosis between primary malnutrition owing to inadequate dietary intake and malnutrition resulting from other causes. They can also offer some estimate of the patient's habitual diet, foodways, and abilities to purchase, prepare, serve, and clean up after meals, as well as any special restrictions or food prohibitions. Once these data have been collected, dietary intake is then assessed against some standard for nutrition, which, in the United States, is most commonly the Recommended Dietary Allowances (RDAs). The RDAs are commonly agreed upon standards for planning and assessing nutrient intake at various ages that are published periodically by the National Research Council. At present, there are no separate recommendations for those over 55 years of age for most nutrients, owing to the absence of evidence on nutrient requirements among older individuals; however, there is some information on useful alterations in nutrient recommendations for older individuals, and these data have recently been summarized.[106] The most striking alteration in nutrient requirements for those over the age of 50 is the reduction in energy needs, which decreases by 6 percent from ages 51 to 75 and another 6 percent after 74 years of age. There are strong data to support the recommendations for decreased energy needs;[13,83,95,113] what is not so clear is whether the decreases in lean body mass that account for much of this decrease are inevitable with advancing age or simply an artifact of inactivity. Exercise programs and more physically active lives among those over 50 might preserve lean body mass and thereby increase resting metabolic rates (and consequent energy needs). Increasing physical activity also increases energy expenditures in discretionary physical activity, further increasing energy outputs.

Additional standards have been developed by a large number of expert bodies, including the National Research Council (NRC) for other substances in food such as cholesterol or dietary fiber that are not dealt with in the RDAs. One NRC committee recently published an authoritative report on diet and health that makes recommendations regarding a number of dietary constituents for which the RDAs do not provide quantitative guidance.[17] These recommendations were promulgated for all healthy adults, including the elderly.

ANTHROPOMETRY

Anthropometric indices of nutritional status such as weight, stature, and skinfolds, as well as changes in these indicators, correlate well with clinical and laboratory markers, at least in young and middle-aged adults. They pose difficult problems for use in the elderly, however, because there are no norms for body composition in older individuals. Some of the usual anthropometric measures (e.g., stature) may be difficult to obtain, especially in the very old; as a result, substitutes such as segmental measurements of the head to the knee may be more useful. Also, special equipment and extensive training in its use may be required for some of the more elaborate measurements. Yet despite these limitations, even simple, standardized measurements of weight can be helpful in monitoring nutritional status and are easy enough to be performed by anyone, given minimal training.

Because most anthropometric measurements of body composition are rather nonspecific, they are best utilized in combination with other measurements. Indeed, the combination of clinical observations with biochemical, anthropometric, and dietary indices is thought by nutritional scientists to best reflect the specific physiological "functions" of interest for nutritional research purposes. For example, functional tests of light adaptation coupled with clinical and dietary data may be used as measures of vitamin A nutrition. Whether a diet is adequate to rehabilitate a starved individual can be assessed by its ability to generate weight gain. For clinical purposes, however, these standard assessment methods are less useful than feeding evaluations to determine by observation whether individuals are able to and actually do eat unassisted. Finally, it is necessary to assess the effects on functioning that may arise from nutritional or other treatments (for example, home internal feeding by pump, which is a complex, time-consuming procedure).

PROGNOSTIC INDICATORS OF
MORBIDITY OR MORTALITY

Another approach to assessing "functional" nutritional status is to develop a battery of biochemical and clinical tests that serve as predictors of morbidity and mortality and assist clinicians in determining the appropriate course of further treatment for the patient.

In comparison to the more global indices of functioning in daily life, these indices have a more narrow focus of morbidity and function; thus, quality of life may be de-emphasized. Another limitation is that prognostic indicators tend to focus on prognoses for specific types of patients who either suffer from certain diseases or are candidates for risky or expensive procedures (e.g., surgery, chemotherapy for advanced cancers).

Several indices have shown some prognostic significance for morbidity and mortality. One such popular index is the Prognostic Nutritional Index, or PNI, developed by Mullen and colleagues.[75] The PNI consists of 16 nutritional and immunological variables that are used to predict subsequent morbidity and mortality patterns in surgical patients with various cancers and other conditions. In Mullen's original research, the 3 (of the 16) variables that correlated most closely with outcomes were serum transferrin, serum albumin, and delayed hypersensitivity reaction from skin test antigens. Patients who had poor scores on these three major factors usually had poorer prognoses than other patients; however, the association may have been due not to their poor nutritional status but to their poor general health status.

The PNI is efficient in discriminating populations at high risk of morbidity and mortality, but it is not as effective in selecting individuals who are at risk when only one of the risk factors is abnormal. In addition, the index provides no estimate of the severity of the individual's malnutrition problem. Thus, the prognostic indices are of little use for decisions about whether to proceed with a surgery immediately or to wait until a patient can be nutritionally rehabilitated. The risks of withholding surgery are usually well known, particularly when cancer has been diagnosed; there are no similar quantitative estimates of the risks posed by malnutrition (i.e., the failure to wait and rehabilitate the patient).

A second prognostic index quite similar to the PNI was developed a decade ago by another group at the New England Deaconess Hospital, also to assess risks of later morbidity and mortality in surgical patients.[42] In addition, other risk indices have been developed by other investigators as nutritional prognostic indicators in medical conditions. All have failings similar to those discussed for the PNI, however, and none are presently viewed as acceptable for all patients in all circumstances. Only recently have indices been developed that include age-related criteria.[4]

Theoretically, it should be possible to develop prognostic indicators that have a rehabilitative focus instead of concentrating solely on morbidity and mortality. The techniques for such efforts have been available for many years in the rehabilitation medicine and occupational therapy literature.[66,103] An investigator observes as many as 100 different activities, many associated with food and eating, and records whether the patient can perform the task either independently, only with adaptive devices, with supervision, with assistance, or not at all. It is from such longer inventories that the few key activities thought to be most highly associated with a lack of functional disability for independent living were originally developed. After these activities were identified, arbitrary scores were assigned and a numeric score calculated for each patient from which progress or deterioration in self-care could be determined.[103]

Many different indices are available, including the Barthel index,[72] the Kenney system,[94] and the Katz index of active life expectancy.[55] The Katz index classifies patients into one of seven groups and avoids arbitrary point systems. Class A refers to a patient who is independent in feeding, continence, transferring, toileting, dressing, and bathing. Class B patients are independent in all but one of these areas. Class C patients are independent in all but bathing and one additional function, and so on. The underlying assumption of the Katz method is that there is an order of maintenance of function, which proceeds in chronological fashion; consequently, feeding ability is maintained longer than the ability to bathe independently. When this is not true, the patient must be classified as "other." Because the ability to self-feed is lost relatively late in many cases, the index does not discriminate among nuances of function in eating and feeding, which would argue for development of more sensitive indicators. (The many problems of developing systems de novo have been well reviewed, however.[57]) Nevertheless, these indices in general are highly correlated in predicting self-care ability and are accurate in about two-thirds of all cases. Of the existing indices, the Barthel index is considered to be the most sensitive and the Katz index the least sensitive.[26,37]

NUTRITIONAL RISK SCREENING INDICES

Another approach that attempts to measure both social and biological functioning is the Nutritional Risk Index (NRI) for morbid and disabling conditions associated with nutrition. The NRI is an easily administered screening test developed by Wolinsky and colleagues[120] that attempts to tap five factors often associated with poor nutritional health: (1) existing illness in the digestive system, (2) the use of medications associated with that system, (3) the use of dentures, (4) smoking, and (5) bowel-related problems. The Wolinsky group developed a short, 16-item test to tap various aspects of these problems; items include the use of prescribed or self-prescribed medications in the past month, previous abdominal problems or operations, trouble with eating or with foods "not agreeing" with the individual, special diets, stomach pains, bowel trouble, diarrhea or constipation over the past month, anemia, presence of illness cutting down on appetite, smoking, trouble swallowing, and gain or loss of weight over the past month. The test-retest reliabilities of the instrument were .5 to .6. The investigators assessed the validity of the instrument using factor analysis and comparisons on outcome measures between those at risk and those not at risk. These analyses showed that individuals with higher risk scores had poorer health and consumed more health services than those with lower risk scores. Although there was no apparent relationship between the NRI and the informal use of health services (e.g., restricted activities, bed disability days), the NRI did predict formal health services utilization quite well.

Much work needs to be done before the NRI or any other index of nutritional risk is widely accepted. Any broad-scale use of such an index must recognize that, at any given level of nutritional status, individuals vary greatly in their functional status with respect to daily living and coping. Not only nutrient intake but the social aspects of food and eating are important to consider, and the need for assistance in food- and diet-related activities depends on both biological and social circumstances. Clearly, it is important to assess all of these aspects, and work is continuing on questionnaires to assess aspects of functional status that are associated with nutritional risk.[121,122,123] As yet, however, correlations of nutritional risk indices with clinical status or nutritional status are low or remain unproven. More thorough means of assessing the activities of daily living with special attention to nutrition are needed.[29] These assessments can supplement and augment other routinely collected information on function.[76]

NUTRITION IN A FUNCTIONAL PERSPECTIVE

In this report, *impairment* is considered to be the condition involved in causing the loss or abnormality of psychological, physiological, or anatomical structure and function. Among the impairments that may be associated with malnutrition-related diseases and that are relatively common among aging adults, visceral, skeletal, intellectual, and other psychological impairments are most prominent. The most common categories of disability associated with malnutrition are probably physical disabilities affecting the use of the hands, arms, and legs and thus movement of the individual; that is, upper body and hand function but lower body and mobility problems may be involved in some cases—for example, massive obesity or complications of cardiovascular disease. These problems (e.g., lack of cardiovascular fitness or muscle strength) can reverse themselves quickly if active lifestyles are adopted.

Handicaps in the nutritional realm consist of the disadvantages that result from an impairment or disability that limit or prevent fulfillment of an individual's normal roles. Malnutrition can lead to handicaps related to physical independence and mobility and occupational and social integration, as well as difficulties and handicaps involving economic self-sufficiency.

BURDEN

Prevalence

The prevalence of various forms of malnutrition differs depending on the type, stage, and condition being considered. Each of the dietary components to be discussed in this report are dealt with separately below or in the chapters devoted to risk factors that include a nutritional component.

Costs

There have been several attempts over the past two decades to estimate the cost of diet-related diseases. There is no consensus on these estimates, however, because of the different definitions used and uncertainties regarding the proportion of total risk for a disease or condition attributable to diet or to other aspects of diet-related health risks. Furthermore, the synergistic effects of these various risk factors on the chronic degenerative diseases that are thought to involve diet are difficult to quantify. For example, it is well known that the addition of hyperlipidemia to other cardiovascular risk factors raises morbidity and mortality considerably, but these relationships are often unclear or based only on limited data after ages 50 or 60.[35] Today, reanalyses of diet-related interventions to decrease coronary artery disease risks appear to indicate benefits in decreased medical expenditures (by decreasing morbidity), even late in life.[32] However, estimates of cost-benefit ratios and cost-effectiveness of dietary interventions after the age of 50 are not yet available.

One set of costs that are clear are the losses of time, money, and happiness associated with the nutritional remedies that carry exaggerated, unproven claims of efficacy for the ills often associated with aging. The elderly are particularly susceptible to such claims, the economic consequences of which are enormous.[110] The health consequences of nutritional quackery and fraud include the failure to seek conventional and more effective care for illnesses and the rejection of legitimate medical advice. Moreover, the practice of inappropriate self-medication may itself give rise to illness, especially as some dietary remedies are potentially toxic in and of themselves, particularly if the elderly individual is already ill.[45]

PREVENTABILITY OF BURDEN

This section reviews selected interventions in the area of nutrition, including screening and case-finding strategies that have not been previously discussed. Particular attention is given to interventions that are likely to have positive interactions with other factors singled out for attention in this report.

Table 10-1 describes various forms of malnutrition that may be secondary to other disease processes and the kinds of effects they are likely to have, particularly in terms of nutritional status with respect to function. Table 10-2 briefly summarizes possible interventions that might be considered. Some of these selected options are discussed in the following sections under the risk factor most relevant to a particular disease process.

Table 10-3 shows how diet and nutritional status may alter other risk factors among individuals over the age of 50. Much effort is being devoted to developing better evidence that dietary counseling, food programs, and related nutritional interventions can change food habits and that these altered food habits in turn decrease risk factors and thereby bring about desirable health and economic benefits.[23,24,69,92,100] Until very recently, however, the relative costs and benefits of nutritional counseling and interventions were virtually unknown. Now, as evidence is rapidly becoming available, new studies are being planned.[2,77]

High Blood Pressure

The burden imposed by high blood pressure on aging individuals is well documented in Chapter 3. In addition to its close association with mortality from stroke, high blood pressure is also a major cause of morbidity. Stroke may give rise to physical difficulties in walking, lifting, and moving the upper extremities; all of these limitations

TABLE 10-1 Malnutrition That is Secondary to Disease,
Physiological State, or Medication Use

Disease or Condition	Effects on Nutritional Status
Atherosclerosis	This condition may increase difficulties in regulating fluid balances if disease is caused by congestive heart failure. Also, if the individual is incapacitated, energy needs decrease.
Cancer	In metastatic disease, increased emaciation is common owing to lack of appetite. Secondary malnutrition is common.
Dental and oral disease	This type of disease may alter the ability to chew and thus reduce dietary intake; if severe it may give rise to digestive problems if large food boluses are swallowed. It may also increase the likelihood of choking or aspirating large food boluses.
Depression and dementia	Increased or decreased food intakes are common. In dementia there may be decreased ability to get food for oneself, or the appetite may be very small or very great. Judgment and balance in meal planning are generally absent.
Diabetes mellitus (insulin dependent)	Increased risk of undernutrition results if untreated, and there is increased risk of other diet-related risk factors such as hyperlipidemia, and decreased resistance to infections. Therapeutic diets limited in type and amount of carbohydrates and fats that are timed to coincide with insulin doses are essential to avoid ketoacidosis and losses of nutrients in urine, as well as shock and other acute and possibly longer-term complications.
Diabetes mellitus (non-insulin dependent)	This condition brings increased risk of other diet-related diseases such as hyperlipidemia. Weight loss is needed to control acute complications if obesity is present. Risk of alcohol intoxication is increased among dependent elderly at home.
End-stage kidney disease	This conditions often alters fluid and electrolyte needs. Uremia may alter appetite and increase consequent risks of malnutrition. Infections and low-grade fever may increase energy output and weight loss because appetite is often poor. Special diets low in protein and phosphorus may be needed to control symptoms.
Gastrointestinal disorders	Such disorders increase the risk of malabsorption of nutrients and consequent undernutrition, as well as other forms of malnutrition.
High blood pressure	Hyper- or hypokalemia can be increased by dietary means; weight gain may exacerbate high blood pressure.

TABLE 10-1 Continued

Disease or Condition	Effects on Nutritional Status
Osteoporosis	Osteoporosis limits the ability to purchase and prepare food if mobility is affected. If severe scoliosis is present, the appetite may be altered.
Osteoarthritis	This condition makes motion difficult, including those activities related to purchasing, serving, eating, and cleaning up after meals. It predisposes people to a sedentary lifestyle and may give rise to obesity. Drug-nutrient relationships are common.
Smoking	Smoking may alter weight status. It also alters serum levels of some nutrients such as ascorbic acid and carotenes although the health significance of such alterations is unknown. Chronic smoking gives rise to emphysema and chronic obstructive pulmonary disease (COPD), which makes it difficult to eat owing to breathing problems.
Stroke	Paralytic stroke may alter abilities in the cognitive and motor realms related to food and eating. If the individual is incapacitated, his or her energy needs decrease.

TABLE 10-2 Nutrition-related Interventions for Elderly Individuals

Domain	Intervention
Education	Educational programs involving food and nutrition education for the aging and elderly
Food	Nutrient recommendations and food guidance; food programs including commodities, food stamps, congregate meals, and others
Health	Nutritional assessment services Nutritional counseling services Short-term, intermediate, and long-term care services Help with food purchasing, preparation, eating, clean-up, and foodways Medical care and assistance for nutrition-related health problems and health problems with nutritional implications
Social welfare	Income support for elderly adults (both general and targeted support) Enhancement of community socioenvironmental and socioeconomic influences on older adults
Well elderly	Food, nutrition, and health services

TABLE 10-3 Potential Effects of Diet and Nutritional Status on Risk Factors for Disability Among the Elderly

Risk Factor	Alterations and Effect on Risk Factor
High blood pressure	Increased risk: Obesity and high levels of sodium and alcohol intake appear to increase risk. If diabetes, atherosclerosis, or kidney disease are present and uncontrolled by diet or drugs, the risk of sequelae increases. Decreased risk: Weight loss (if overweight) and decreased sodium and alcohol intake all decrease risks and may in turn lead to decreased drug dosages to control the condition.
Mental indolence	Increased risk: Undernutrition and starvation, protein calorie malnutrition, and other vitamin and mineral deficiencies decrease attention and performance if very severe. Alcohol abuse also contributes to mental indolence. Certain vitamin deficiencies (e.g., vitamin B12 deficiency) may be associated with degeneration of the spinal cord and confusion. Unwise use of unproven dietary remedies may cause otherwise preventable cases of depression and mental inactivity to go untreated. Decreased risk: Good nutritional status provides the individual with sufficient energy so that inanition is not a contributory cause to mental inactivity.
Physical inactivity	Increased risk: Extreme obesity decreases physical activity and makes falls or other movement-related injuries more difficult to treat. Extreme emaciation and most severe vitamin and mineral deficiencies also decrease physical activity. Alcohol abuse increases physical inactivity and also the likelihood of falls or movement-related injuries. Decreased risk: Normal weight status does not hinder physical activity.
Polypharmacy	Increased risk: Undernutrition, emaciation, and protein calorie malnutrition all alter the metabolism and disposition of drugs and the risk of overdoses. Alcohol abuse alters the likelihood of drug-nutrient interactions. Normal changes associated with aging such as decreased lean body mass, decreased total body water, and decreased resting metabolic rate increase the likelihood of drug-related overdoses. Decreased risk: Use of nonpharmacologic measures to control high blood pressure, hyperlipidemia, adult onset diabetes, and other conditions that respond to dietary alterations may decrease the risk of polypharmacy or the doses needed.
Poor oral health	Poor nutritional status owing to emaciation, undernutrition, vitamin and mineral deficiencies (especially ascorbic acid), and poor control of diet-related diseases such as diabetes may lead to oral lesions and failure of wounds to heal (as in scurvy or uncontrolled diabetes). Diets high in sticky, fermentable

TABLE 10-3 Continued

Risk Factor	Alterations and Effect on Risk Factor
	carbohydrates may increase the risks of root as well as crown caries in remaining teeth. Chronic alcohol abuse, especially among heavy smokers, increases the risks of oral and head and neck cancers.
	Decreased risk: Diets low in sticky, fermentable carbohydrates decrease the risk of root and crown caries, as does good oral hygiene. Diets containing adequate intakes of nutrients minimize risks to oral tissues as a result of dietary deficiency disease.
Osteoporosis	Increased risk: Inadequate intakes of calcium and vitamin D, especially early in life during the time of accretion of peak bone mass as well as in the premenopausal period, increase risks of osteoporosis, especially if estrogen replacement therapy is absent. Caffeine intake may also increase osteoporosis risks, as may highly acid diets. Malnutrition secondary to untreated gastrointestinal disease increases risks because absorption of calcium and vitamin D may be affected, especially if steatorrhea is present. Sedentary lifestyles with little physical activity increase risk, especially if there is little physical exercise involving weight bearing. Alcohol abuse or its consumption in large amounts may increase risks.
	Decreased risk: Adequate intakes of calcium throughout life with estrogen replacement therapy after menopause and exercise involving weight bearing decrease risks.
Smoking	Increased risk: Smoking plus chronic alcohol intake increases head and neck cancer risks. Low intakes of caratenoids and of other, as yet poorly characterized constituents of vegetables and fruits may increase smoking-related cancer risks.
	Decreased risk: Possible slight (but relatively insignificant) decrease could be achieved for certain forms of cancer from intakes of vegetables and fruits that are high in ascorbic acid, carotenoids, and other vitamin A precursors.
Social isolation, low socioeconomic status, and false stereotypes of aging	Increased risk: Undernutrition, emaciation, insufficiencies of vitamins and minerals, and excessive intakes of fat, salt, sugar, and energy are often associated with these in low-income groups. In fact, these nutritional problems may be due in part to lack of income. Those suffering from any form of malnutrition have increased risk of being socially isolated, and the process is likely to be self-perpetuating. Alcohol abuse may be especially important in causing social isolation. Malnutrition reinforces the stereotype that being old is being sick.
	Decreased risk: Good nutrition in all respects minimizes the above barriers.

make food getting and eating difficult. High blood pressure is also a major cause of multi-infarct dementia and may be responsible for milder and more subtle losses of intellectual capacity that occur occasionally with older people and are probably due to subclinical cerebrovascular disease.[41,46,82]

Treatment for high blood pressure has potent effects on the risk of stroke and of cardiovascular disease. It is likely that, in both middle-aged and older people, reductions in moderate or severe high blood pressure add more to life expectancy than most other interventions.[62,108,119] Indeed, because many elderly people are already taking medications for other reasons, there are distinct advantages to treating high blood pressure by nonpharmacological means. Diet and exercise constitute two such means that are given particular emphasis in this report.

The effectiveness of altering high blood pressure and subsequent mortality and morbidity from cardiovascular and renovascular disease is well documented. Among the measures for achieving such control are dietary counseling to bring about weight reduction, sodium restriction, and in some cases abstinence from alcohol.

There is good reason to think that weight control and moderation in sodium intake are reasonable health measures for all aging adults. Studies have shown that weight loss per se decreases blood pressure by about 1 to 2 mmHg systolic and 1 mmHg diastolic per pound lost.[17,44,48,102,115] Restriction of sodium also appears to be effective in some persons who are sodium sensitive, although such individuals cannot be identified in advance.[50] Data on the efficacy of increasing the intake of other nutrients (e.g., calcium and magnesium) to lower blood pressure are more controversial. These findings have been reviewed in another recent Institute of Medicine report.[17]

The costs and effectiveness of various dietary therapies to control high blood pressure have been well reviewed by Disbrow.[23] Few of these studies involved individuals over 65 years of age. At present there is too little age-specific information to determine the effectiveness of nonpharmacologic therapies for hypertension in the elderly. Theoretically, they offer three potent advantages: a low cost in comparison with the sometimes expensive antihypertensive drug therapies that are often used, decreased side effects, and avoidance of drug-drug interactions common in the elderly. Indeed, studies have shown that blood pressure control can often be maintained by dietary means even after medications are withdrawn or reduced.[65,101,102,114] Therefore, tests of the effectiveness of nonpharmacologic therapies, including but not limited to diet, should be encouraged in the elderly.

Hypercholesterolemia

Several of the modifiable risk factors for cardiovascular disease involve diet. They include high blood pressure, hypercholesterolemia, diabetes mellitus of the adult onset type, and physical inactivity.[52] Screening for these conditions may be useful for behavioral reinforcement and education. It may also allow monitoring of individuals at risk of hyperlipidemias because of other problems such as diabetes, hypothyroidism, nephrotic syndrome, or heredity. In addition, screening permits the identification and treatment of otherwise asymptomatic adults so as to improve their health and prolong their lives.

Recommendations vary with respect to cholesterol screening and dietary modifications for lowering serum cholesterol. One group of experts recently concluded that screening and treatment plans for treatment of hyperlipidemias needed to be individualized and that for the elderly (e.g., those over 70 years of age) the predictability of risk was not well defined; thus, the efficacy of cholesterol reduction remained unproven.[35] The analyses and criteria they employed in their study for assessing intervention benefits, however, focused on cost and increased mortality rather than improved function. Moreover, studies on outcomes from dietary and drug treatment among postmenopausal women at various serum cholesterol levels are only now becoming available.

Other experts take a more optimistic view and suggest that prudence dictates attempting to reduce serum cholesterol and other risk factors among aging adults as well as the middle aged.[52] Gordon and Rifkind,[39] for example, argue for an aggressive posture based on their analysis of the Multiple Risk Factor Intervention Trial (MRFIT) and Framingham longitudinal data. They argue that attenuation of the cholesterol/coronary heart disease relationship among the elderly clearly exists but that because more coronary events are likely, the number of events that might be prevented annually might be very much greater between 56 and 74 years of age than at younger ages. In addition, the effects of earlier screening efforts in the 40- to 50-year-old age group and any ensuing preventive action may not show up until later in life; consequently, these results have not yet been factored into the analysis.

Recommendations for screening from other groups vary. In 1988, the National Cholesterol Education Program Adult Treatment Panel recommended cholesterol screening once every five years. It also advocated repeated testing for high-risk persons and those whose cholesterol levels were more than 200 milligrams per decaliter (mg/dl) (5.17mmol/L).

In summary, those who appear to benefit most from screening are high-risk populations—for example, those individuals who already have marked hypercholesterolemia or who have other risk factors that place them at high risk (e.g., smokers, hypertensives, etc.). Those for whom screening offers morbidity reductions (even if mortality and life expectancy are not affected) include persons who have a family history of hypercholesterolemia, who are not being treated with lipid-altering medications, or who have secondary hyperlipoproteinemias arising from diabetes or other causes.[35]

There is little doubt that initial reductions in serum cholesterol can be accomplished by dietary means. The problem is that long-term adherence to dietary regimens is difficult to achieve, and without sustained counseling, serum cholesterol levels are likely to drift upward again.[10,25,89] It may be, however, that the elderly are more likely to comply with dietary regimens than younger adults and that the appeal of avoiding medications may further increase adherence to dietary treatment strategies by the aging.

It is important to note that the relationship between serum cholesterol levels and cardiovascular risk changes with age. Thus, in asymptomatic elderly persons, the association between serum cholesterol levels and later risk for mortality from coronary artery disease is in fact weaker than that in younger adults. Moreover, low cholesterol values in the elderly (e.g., below 150 mg/dl) appear to be associated with excess mortality, independent of cancer incidence.[31] Although there is no clear cause-and-effect relationship, the association of low cholesterol levels with mortality has raised concern in the minds of some experts about the advisability of oversensitizing aging adults to the importance of low serum cholesterol levels. Finally, the treatment of hypercholesterolemic patients in elderly age groups may not reduce mortality rates to those of untreated patients with lower cholesterol levels. All of these questions should be settled by additional research.

The reasons for the differing associations among serum cholesterol, morbidity, and mortality in aging individuals are still unknown. In part, the differences may be due to genetically high HDL cholesterol levels among some of the surviving elderly.[1,93] The menopause also leads to increases in serum cholesterol in females. Current recommendations are to screen for serum cholesterol in asymptomatic adult men at least every five years and more frequently in symptomatic men. At least one group still regards screening in such asymptomatic adults as optional for women and the elderly.[35] Others suggest that screening is warranted for all individuals on the five-year schedule. Various intervention studies have shown that, in younger individuals when serum cholesterol decreases by 2 to 13 percent, coronary artery disease mortality also decreases, whereas all-cause mortality exhibits relatively few changes.[35,70,79] However, for the very old and especially for middle-aged and older women, the effectiveness of interventions involving dietary change on serum cholesterol lowering is unknown because relatively few interventions have been instituted in these groups. Gordon and Rifkind[39] recently concluded that treatment of hypercholesterolemia in the elderly might bring about a greater reduction in absolute risk than in younger persons, even though the strength of the cardiovascular disease/cholesterol relationship decreases with age. The decreased strength of that relationship may be due to the increasing influence of age-related changes in the arterial wall, to selective survival, to faulty attribution of causes of death on death certificates (leading to underreporting of the true number of deaths from cardiovascular causes), to confounding factors causing low serum cholesterol levels that are a sign of other underlying diseases, or to some other factor. In fact, it is clear that a series of factors are involved. For example, healthy octogenarians do not all appear to have very high HDL cholesterol levels or very low LDL cholesterol levels (as those who favor a solely genetic basis for a weakened cholesterol/coronary artery disease relationship sometimes used to argue).[93] Such patterns may be present in more instances in certain families;[36] however, other influences are probably also involved in the attenuation of the relationship between serum cholesterol and heart disease in the elderly.[117]

The cost-effectiveness of lowering serum cholesterol by diet appears to be greater than by other means.[5,62,81,108] For example, Berwick and coworkers' best estimate was that the cost was about $11,000 in 1975 dollars per year of life saved.[5] Taylor and colleagues[108] used a 7 percent effect of diet on serum cholesterol lowering to estimate that, at age 60, 13 months for females and 2 months for males were added to life expectancy. Using a larger serum cholesterol-lowering effect (20 percent), 36 months for women and 5 months for men were added to life expectancy. These effects were much less than those experienced from decreasing blood pressure or from quitting smoking, but they nevertheless amounted to one or two years.[101] These results have been challenged and rebutted.[33] In summary, however, the analyses seem to favor positive effects from the lowering of serum cholesterol and suggest that underestimates of life expectancy are not large. Nevertheless, it is useful to remember that the life-prolonging effects of any intervention may be small for the individual but much greater for the population at large.

Lowering of serum cholesterol may be efficacious, but most

studies agree that it results in very few and rather small effects on medical care costs, at least in younger men.[62,81] Yet because the absolute risk of myocardial infarction rises with age (even if the cholesterol/coronary artery disease relationship is weaker in older people), the benefits from treatment could still be considerable on a population basis. Diet therapy was the least expensive option of those assessed.[62] Estimates of days of work lost, measures of health care use, and activity limitations other than those mentioned above were not available.

Hypertriglyceridemia

Screening for high serum triglycerides (and subsequent interventions to lower triglycerides if they are elevated) is more controversial than screening for serum cholesterol, even at younger ages. Serum triglycerides are not consistent, independent predictors of cardiac risk, nor does serum triglyceride lowering lead to diminished mortality among healthy individuals.[3] Therefore, triglyceride screening is not generally recommended for the healthy. Individuals at higher risk, however, including those with familial combined hyperlipidemia and those with secondary hypertriglyceridemia resulting from diabetes or obesity, may benefit.[35]

Renal Disease-related Risks

The three nutrition-related causes of kidney disease that are thought to be avoidable or at least partially treatable by diet are high blood pressure, diabetic nephropathy, and renal artery atherosclerosis. Dietary factors may hasten the progression of renal deterioration. Brenner[9] and others have postulated that modification of protein and phosphorus intake early in the course of chronic renal insufficiency can slow or stop the progression of the disease.[9,112] This theory is now being tested in a large-scale randomized clinical trial. If in fact it is found that dietary therapy can slow renal disease progression, the cost of dialysis will be much reduced. Moreover, the functional abilities of patients with renal disease might be improved if dialysis were delayed. Among individuals suffering from renal disease, including the elderly, nutritional counseling has proven helpful in decreasing hospitalizations, especially among individuals who have lost a large amount of weight.[58,71] Home hemodialysis coupled with dietary modifications has also resulted in somewhat greater freedom for patients. Other advantages over hospital dialysis include considerable cost savings, fewer clinical complications, and greater comfort for many patients.[74]

Diabetes Mellitus

Several severe disabling conditions among older individuals may arise from diabetes mellitus. For example, one of the four leading causes of blindness in those over the age of 40 is diabetic retinopathy.[61] In addition, other vascular complications of diabetes (e.g., vascular disease in the lower extremities) may inhibit walking. Diabetic vascular disease in the legs, especially when combined with smoking, is a major cause of amputation among the elderly.[64,104] Finally, the elderly with diabetes, especially uncontrolled diabetes, are also more likely than the nondiabetic to develop cognitive impairments, a probability that applies to those with Type II diabetes.[85] Yet diabetes mellitus is another common cardiovascular disease risk factor that can be controlled in part by dietary interventions. Diabetic control in adult onset diabetes (Type II, or non-insulin-dependent diabetes mellitus) can often be achieved without the use of insulin or oral hypoglycemic agents using dietary manipulation and adjustments in exercise. Patients who suffer from insulin-dependent diabetes (Type I) generally require extensive dietary counseling.

Weight loss alone can often bring satisfactory control of non-insulin-dependent diabetes. In a recent study of elderly individuals suffering from Type II diabetes, a combination of dietary counseling and peer support resulted in weight loss and improved diabetic control as measured by glycosylated hemoglobin.[118] Four months later, however, most of the elderly participants had returned to their original weight, pointing to the need for continued dietary counseling and assistance. In addition, even after weight loss, some elderly non-insulin-dependent diabetics continue to require drugs to achieve satisfactory glycemic control or to achieve better values on other risk factors that may also need modification (e.g., serum cholesterol). At present, estimates of the effectiveness of nutritional interventions are optimistic, but there are too few data to make definitive judgments.[54]

Most studies of interventions for diabetes involve young and middle-aged populations rather than the elderly. Nevertheless, some generalization is possible. The effects of diabetes education programs on subsequent hospitalization for diabetes, especially those admissions related to a lack of diabetes self-management skills, have been the subject of several studies; it appears that hospital admissions do decrease following such programs, although the programs usually involve some form of residence in a hospital for training and therefore are rather costly.[30] Other programs that have a similar goal—to help patients manage their diets and medications more completely—but that involve ambulatory care also appear to be effective and are less expensive than programs with a hospital training component.[20,105,116]

These ambulatory programs generally include several counseling visits with a registered dietitian; they too appear to decrease hospitalizations. Other positive outcomes, such as better metabolic control as measured by glycosylated hemoglobin and blood sugar levels, also appear to be moderately affected by dietary education programs.[23,49] In addition, there is some evidence that nutritional counseling services can help reduce the number of amputations resulting from diabetic vascular disease and achieve substantial cost savings.[20]

Weight Reduction

The effectiveness of interventions involving weight reduction in managing several chronic degenerative diseases is well demonstrated.[23,78] Very little information is available, however, regarding the specific benefits of weight reduction in individuals over age 50. One study, conducted in the late 1950s by the Anticoronary Club of New York City, involved middle-aged men in a weight loss program that divided participants into treatment and control groups. The program was able to achieve much lower obesity rates among those individuals who were provided with treatment and given ongoing help to maintain weight loss than among controls.[15] The problem was not the short-term efficacy of weight loss efforts but the need to include long-term maintenance as part of the therapeutic program. Quite apart from the effect of obesity on chronic degenerative diseases is the direct functional effect on activities of daily living—transferring, toileting, stooping, and climbing stairs.

The type, length, and location of weight loss programs for the elderly vary. Because many of the elderly are already taking several different drugs, there may be particular advantages to using diet and physical activity programs to bring weight into line instead of relying on anorectic or other drugs. In general, control of obesity is of particular importance among elderly persons who suffer from high blood pressure. Indeed, the positive effects of weight reduction in this group may be greater than the effects observed in younger populations.[19] Of particular salience from the functional standpoint are the benefits weight loss brings in improving mobility and decreasing pain in osteoarthritis affecting weight-bearing joints.[8] In addition, weight reduction may improve—in some cases, quite dramatically—ischemic and hypertensive cardiac disorders that decrease work performance. In many instances, when weight is brought to normal, symptomatology (including excessive urination and other annoying problems owing to poor glucose tolerance) may also come under control.[52]

Physical Activity

Disuse atrophy or marked decline in physiological function because of lack of physical activity is more common than might be supposed in persons over the age of 50, and it becomes increasingly common with advancing age. Fortunately, the condition is partially reversible with increased physical activity.[6] There is good evidence that rather large improvements can be made in muscle strength, lean body mass, and oxygen consumption,[104] as well as somewhat smaller increments in glucose tolerance, blood pressure, and blood lipid control.[12,47] If sedentary lifestyles in middle age can be avoided, the risks of obesity, high blood pressure, and eventual cardiovascular disease may also be lowered by increased physical activity after age 50.[53,84,109] Finally, flexibility and physical activity may retard osteoporosis (see Chapter 6).

Polypharmacy: Controlling Side Effects

Individuals over 50 years of age use more prescribed and over-the-counter drugs than younger people. Drug use among the elderly averages more than two drugs a day in most studies.[14] Drug- nutrient interactions are quite common. Patients on multiple drug regimens often suffer from dysgeusia and changes in salivation that may adversely affect their appetite. Diet can also affect drug metabolism.[91] Therefore, all elderly patients who receive long-term drug therapies, especially drugs that cause diarrhea, appetite change, or other symptoms that affect the gut or appetite, should be carefully monitored for drug-nutrient interactions.[14] In addition, effective nutritional therapies warrant careful consideration in aging populations, as they offer the advantage of keeping drug therapies to a minimum.

Nutrition Fraud

More than a quarter of all Americans have used questionable health care products and treatments, according to a recent survey conducted by the Food and Drug Administration.[40] Many of these individuals were elderly, and many of the products they used were dietary supplements.

Advances in nutritional science and the still poorly understood possible role of dietary factors in chemoprevention of certain disorders have increased attention and interest in nutrition. At the same time such attention has also provided new and fertile ground for false and misleading promotional efforts. The 1984 report of the Select

Committee on Aging placed health quackery costs at $10 billion.[110] Other, more recent reviews document the fact that diet-related nostrums and homeopathic remedies of unproven effectiveness account for substantial unnecessary expenditures by the elderly (total costs may exceed $40 billion or more for all forms of fraud).[2,110] Indeed, the Select Committee estimated that the elderly accounted for more than 30 percent of the fraud victims in this country, a burden particularly heavy in that such losses by older individuals are disproportionate because the elderly are slower to recover physically, financially, and mentally than younger, more affluent victims.

Common among the frauds perpetrated on the elderly are the so-called nutritional therapies for various chronic degenerative diseases and conditions. The extensive use of vitamin and mineral supplements is well documented.[63] Overreliance on such remedies often means that diseases or impairments that might otherwise be prevented or assisted by medical means (e.g., arthritis) may become both economically and medically handicapping. Elderly individuals with chronic degenerative diseases such as cancer, heart disease, arthritis, and gastrointestinal disturbances are especially at risk. Even those who do not have overt signs and symptoms of these diseases often assume themselves to be at special risk of vitamin or mineral deficiencies, although they may not necessarily be so.[28]

At the federal level, the Food and Drug Administration has major enforcement responsibilities to prevent health fraud by regulating health claims for the efficacy of nutrients and other substances in the prevention, cure, and treatment of disease. The agency is also responsible for other measures to assure that the food supply is safe. In addition, the U.S. Postal Service, the Federal Trade Commission, and other federal agencies act to ensure that the mails and communications media are not used to aid and abet fraudulent sales of products.

The education of consumers on the steps they can take to avoid nutritional and other types of fraud is crucial. By assisting individuals to avoid inefficacious or fraudulent remedies and by helping them obtain appropriate medical help, many conditions that would otherwise lead to severe losses of independent function can be identified and treated. The American Association of Retired Persons, the American Cancer Society, the American Arthritis Foundation, and other groups such as the Council on Health Fraud all have a role to play in educating consumers on these issues.

Oral Health

The oral health of aging individuals often influences their nutritional status. For example, in one study, elderly veterans with self-perceived chewing problems had lower protein and calorie intake than control subjects who did not perceive that they had such problems. Indeed, perceptions of this kind may be a useful indicator of an individual's nutritional state, even more so, in fact, than actual dental status.[38] The loss of teeth can also contribute to poor appetite and to social isolation. Finally, the dentate elderly who have retained their teeth are vulnerable to crown or root caries, and diet is a significant risk factor for the development of either. Further discussion of this issue is provided in Chapter 8.

Nutritional Support: Food Programs

Nutritional support is a term that covers a variety of different types of alimentation of patients. It includes meeting nutritional needs by the usual oral, enteral, and parenteral routes, as well as social support. It also covers instances in which social and physiological types of problems may be involved simultaneously.

The living arrangements of the elderly are such that the social aspects of eating are often ignored or are difficult to sustain, especially for those who are confined to their homes, among whom nutrient deficiencies may be present.[96] Such problems were described in the first National Health and Nutrition Examination Survey (NHANES 1). They also surfaced in NHANES 2; for example, those data showed that elderly individuals who lived alone were more likely to eat alone, to eat away from home, and to skip meals than their peers of the same age who lived with one or more persons.[21] Most of the well elderly, however, maintain a good nutritional status, although there are some differences between the younger and older well elderly, the older elderly generally being less well nourished.[11,73] Among elderly women, limited intake of some nutrients is thought to contribute to poor nutritional status, for which diet interventions may bring improvements.[73]

A number of meal programs are available to assist the elderly. In fact, those who participate in the elderly meal programs are generally in good health. As the elderly age, however, the very old, that is, those over age 80 or 90 who are living at home, are at special risk, and they may be unable to attend aging programs[18] (although the effectiveness of such programs is still unproven owing to a lack of evaluation). Some of those at special risk among the elderly who participated in meal programs, such as recipients of the Meals on Wheels programs, and who were found to be nutritionally deficient responded with weight gain. However, there was no improvement in hematologic or immunological responses from supplementing the program for several months with high-calorie nutrients.[67] Some housebound elderly who receive Meals on Wheels services exhibit negative nitrogen balances, but this deficit may be due to disease rather than diet. It is clear that as larger numbers of the very old continue to live at home, better food and nutritional support services will be needed in the community.

In addition to the actual provision of food, some elderly people need ambulatory nutritional services of other sorts, such as dietary counseling and help in meal planning. The costs and benefits of ambulatory nutrition care for senior adults have been reviewed recently by Disbrow.[23] There appear to be positive benefits of ambulatory nutritional services for the elderly, but more studies are needed. Benefits are concentrated in four areas: reduced health care costs, reduced needs for long-term care, improved health status and quality of life owing to better self-management of chronic disease, and subsequent reduction of related complications.[22] In addition, several studies indicate that there were positive associations between nutritional status and participation in the Nutritional Programs for Older Adults Congregate Meal Services.[67] The clearest benefits come as a result of screening and the referrals generated by such programs, but other benefits have also been observed as a result of diet counseling, exercise, adult education, and other classes and activities associated with the congregate meals services. Additional possible benefits from such interventions include retention of mobility, sustained quality of life through improved socialization, and positive self-perceptions of health. Ambulatory nutrition counseling may also be of benefit in helping the elderly with meal planning and food purchasing and in coping with disabilities. At present, however, these benefits are not well documented and await further study.

Home health services and food delivery for the elderly constitute another set of services in the spectrum of social interventions designed to maintain independent function among the elderly to the greatest extent possible. Although home health care for the elderly is not necessarily less costly than hospital or clinic care, it may nevertheless do a great deal to preserve an individual's independence if the alternative is the disruption that often accompanies hospitalization. Home health and nursing care costs are roughly similar.[67] Home-delivered meals, on the other hand, are usually much more expensive than the congregate meals programs. These cost differences and the stress on volume of meals served make it difficult for all those who need home meal delivery services to obtain them. Homemaker services, hospital-based home health care visits, and nutritionist visits have all been described in the literature. It is not yet clear whether the benefits of these home services exceed their costs, although clearly, for some patients who wish to avoid institutionalization and still maintain acceptable levels of quality of life and health, there is no other alternative.[43,73]

Increasing numbers of the very old are institutionalized during their final years of life, and in such settings the adequacy and appropriateness of the food served to them vary greatly. The simple fact of residence in a long-term care facility does not imply immunity from malnutrition or undernutrition. Indeed, several studies show that the nutritional status of residents of long-term care facilities leaves much to be desired.[98] It is difficult to evaluate these groups, however, because some of the supposed indicators of nutritional status among elderly patients may be altered for nonnutritional reasons (e.g., disease).[96] In addition, although biochemical tests of malnutrition are useful, they vary greatly in their specificity and sensitivity, especially in the elderly. There is as yet no generally agreed upon battery of tests that will provide accurate assessments of risk.[59]

The benefits of inpatient nutritional care have recently been reviewed.[23] Among the most cost-effective strategies are weekly nutrition rounds, made with the dietary supervisor, a consultant dietitian, and a registered nurse, to assess patient status. The results of such sessions have been generally positive and include improved dietary intake, weight status, bowel status, and skin health; the costs associated with the sessions were less than those associated with conventional procedures. Other studies have shown that the use of high-fiber (bran) diets among elderly institutionalized patients can dramatically decrease laxative abuse. Because the amount of time presently devoted to dietetic surveillance is only 10 minutes or less per patient per month, efficient means for nutritional care assessment, intake evaluations, counseling, and documentation need to be found. It is also essential that dietitians develop more services in these areas and that funding be made available to investigate the cost-effectiveness of such services.

The nutrient intake of elderly long-stay hospital patients is often inadequate; in fact, those patients whose healing is the most retarded often prove to have the poorest intake. Attention to dietary intake may be particularly helpful in some cases to stimulate healing postsurgery. For example, malnutrition adversely affects the prognosis for lower limb amputations, but it seems to have less effect on more proximal amputations.[56] Similarly, certain biochemical parameters associated with malnutrition (e.g., reduced serum albumen, transferrin, absolute lymphocyte count, energy) are associated with both morbidity and mortality. Furthermore, patients judged to be malnourished at admission had longer stays in the same DRG (diagnostic-related group) category than those judged to be well nourished.[90]

A barrier to more widespread use of nutritional support measures in the elderly involves various clinical issues surrounding the use of special nutritional support measures, such as total parenteral nutrition and enteral nutrition using nasogastric or other tube feedings and pumps. Ethical and legal questions further complicate this issue. In fact, in some cases such measures are clinically justified for use even in the very old, and they may improve quality of life as well.[16,68]

RECOMMENDATIONS

Services

1. Using current knowledge, consensus recommendations should be developed for nutritional screening and monitoring and for nonpharmacologic interventions, including diet, in asymptomatic individuals of both sexes over the age of 50. The age ranges considered should include the following: from 50 to 64, 65 to 74, and 75 and over. Nonpharmacologic intervention should be considered for persons with atherosclerosis, high blood pressure, diabetes mellitus, physical inactivity, and osteoporosis.

2. Methods should be explored for maintaining independent functioning with respect to nutrition among individuals living at home. Methods of particular interest include participation in meals programs (e.g., Meals on Wheels) and congregate dining.

3. Methods are needed to screen older populations for nutritional risk. Such methods must be reliable, valid, and predictive of later maintenance of independent function.

4. Model standards should be developed for the nutritional component of food services, including functionally oriented nutritional assessments, for use in nursing homes and long-term care facilities. The means for reimbursement of these assessments and services under Medicare should also be devised.

5. The regulatory authority of the Food and Drug Administration should be extended to deal adequately with health claims on food products and to guard against nutritional fraud.

6. Mechanisms should be developed to assess problems and assist the families of cognitively impaired elderly people, as well as other older individuals who have difficulty eating.

7. Functional assessments and nutritional care plans should be required in federally funded hospitals, nursing homes, and extended care facilities. Such plans should emphasize independent function, minimization of polypharmacy, and maximization of physical activity while maintaining good nutritional status.

Research

1. The association of serum cholesterol lowering and alterations in other risk factors for cardiovascular disease should be determined. Special attention should be paid to clarifying the associations and trade-offs among serum cholesterol lowering, the use of postmenopausal estrogen replacement therapy with progestins, physical activity, and other interactive interventions in the sixth through ninth decades of life.

2. A major research effort should be mounted to clarify the associations between nutritional requirements and function.

3. Common drug-diet interactions among the elderly should be studied, and alternative pharmacological or nonpharmacological therapies should be developed to reduce functional difficulties.

Education

1. Courses of study for students in dietetics, the nutritional sciences, nursing, dentistry, and medicine should include an emphasis on functional assessments of nutritional status and the preservation of independent functioning.

2. Mass media and other educational presentations should be developed to assist elderly individuals in self-care, especially in the area of nutrition. Advice should include attention to problems that arise when commonly coexisting diseases are present.

3. More complete, easy-to-read food labels should be developed for those who have common dietary restrictions.

4. The recommendations provided in the 1989 National Research Council report on diet and health[17] should be implemented. Although the evidence is definitive in only a few areas (e.g., coronary artery disease), there is reason to suspect that benefits will result and that risks are few.[51] There is also evidence to suggest that dietary moderation should be coupled with a physically active life to the greatest extent possible, given the disabilities of aging. There is no need for vitamin and mineral supplements if healthful diets in line with these recommendations are followed.

REFERENCES

1. Abbott, R. D., Wilson, P. F., Kannel, W. B., and Castelli, W. P. High density lipoprotein cholesterol, total cholesterol screening and myocardial infarction: The Framingham study. Arteriosclerosis 1988; 8:207-211.
2. American Dietetic Association. Costs and Benefits of Nutrition Care: Phase I. Chicago: American Dietetic Association, 1979.
3. Barrett-Connor, E., and Khaw, K. T. Borderline fasting hypertriglyceridemia: Absence of excess risk of all cause and cardiovascular disease mortality in healthy men without hypercholesterolemia. Preventive Medicine 1987; 16:1-8.
4. Bernard, M. A., and Rombeau, J. C. Nutritional support for the elderly patient. In: E.A. Yong (ed.), Nutrition, Aging and Health. New York: Alan A. Liss, 1986, pp. 229-258.
5. Berwick, D. M., Cretin, S., and Keller, E. B. Cholesterol, Children and Heart Diseases: An Analysis of Alternatives. New York: Academic Press, 1979.
6. Bortz, W. A. Disuse atrophy and aging. Journal of the American Medical Association 1982; 248:1203-1208.
7. Braun, J. V., Wykle, M. W., and Cowling, W. R. Failure to thrive in older persons: A concept derived. Gerontologist 1988; 28(6):809-812.
8. Bray, G. A. Complications of obesity. Annals of Internal Medicine 1988; 103:1056-1062.
9. Brenner, B. M., Meyer, T. W., and Hostetter, T. H. Dietary protein intake and the progressive nature of kidney disease: The role of hemodynamically mediated glomerular injury in the pathogenesis of progressive glomerular sclerosis in aging, renal ablation and intrinsic renal disease. New England Journal of Medicine 1982; 307:652.
10. Brown, H. B. The National Diet Heart Study: Implications for dietitians and nutritionists. Journal of the American Dietetic Association 1968; 52:279.
11. Burns, R., Nichols, L., Calkins, E., Blackwell, S., and Pragay, D. Nutritional assessment of community living well elderly. Journal of the American Geriatrics Society 1986; 34(11):781-786.
12. Cade, R., Mars, D., Wagemaker, H., et al. Effect of aerobic exercise training on patients with systemic arterial hypertension. American Journal of Medicine 1984; 77:785-790.
13. Casanova, C., Agarwal, N., and Cayten, C. G. Basal energy expenditures in the elderly (abstract). Journal of Parenteral and Enteral Nutrition 1987; 11:205.
14. Chan, L. H., Liu, S., Newell, M. E., and Barnes, K. Survey of drug use by the elderly and possible impact of drugs on nutrition status. Drug-Nutrient Interaction 1985; 3(2):73-86.
15. Christakis, G., Kinzler, S. H., Archer, M., and Kraus, A. Effect of the Anticoronary Club program on coronary artery disease risk factor status. Journal of the American Medical Association 1966; 198:129.
16. Clark, N. G., Rappoport, J. I., DiScala, C., et al. Nutritional support of the chronically ill elderly female at risk for elective or urgent surgery. Journal of the American College of Nutrition 1988; 7:17.
17. Committee on Diet and Health, National Research Council. Diet and Health: Implications for Reducing Chronic Disease Risk. Washington, D.C.: National Academy Press, 1989.
18. Czajka Narins, D. M., Kohrs, M. B., Tsui, J., and Nordstan, J. Nutritional and biochemical effects of nutrition programs in the elderly. Clinics in Geriatric Medicine 1987; 3:275-287.

19. Dahms, W. T., Molitch, M. E., Bray, G. A., Greenway, F. L., Atkinson, R. L., and Hamilton, K. Treatment of obesity: Cost benefit assessment of behavioral therapy, placebo and two anorectic drugs. American Journal of Clinical Nutrition 1978; 31:774.

20. Davidson, J. K., Delcher, H. K., and Englund, A. Spin off cost benefits of expanded nutritional care. Journal of the American Dietetic Association 1979; 75:250.

21. Davis, M. A., Murphy, S. P., and Neuhaus, J. M. Living arrangements and eating behaviors of older adults in the U.S. Journal of Gerontology Social Sciences 1988; 43(3):S96-S98.

22. Department of Health, Education and Welfare, Public Health Service. Healthy People: The Surgeon General's Report on Health Promotion and Disease Prevention. DHEW Publ. No. 79-55071. Washington, D.C.: Department of Health, Education and Welfare.

23. Disbrow, D. Ambulatory nutrition care: Adults weight reduction and management. Journal of the American Dietetic Association 1989; 89(4):530-534.

24. Disbrow, D., and Bertram, K. Cost-Benefit and Cost Effectiveness Analysis: A Practical Step by Step Guide for Nutritional Professionals. Modesto, Calif.: Bertram Nutrition Associates, 1984.

25. Dolecek, T. A., Milas, N. C., VanHorn, L. V., Farrand, M. E., Gorder, D. D., Dyer, J. R., and Randall, B. C. A long term nutrition intervention experience: Lipid responses and dietary adherence patterns in the MRFIT trial. Journal of the American Dietetic Association 1986; 86:752.

26. Donaldson, S. W., Wagner, C. C., and Gresham, G. E. A unified ADL evaluation form. Archives of Physical Medicine and Rehabilitation 1973; 54:175.

27. Downes, J. Association of the chronic diseases in the same person and their association with overweight. Milbank Memorial Fund Quarterly 1955; 31:124.

28. Expert Scientific Working Group. Summary of a report on assessment of the iron nutritional status of the U.S. population. American Journal of Clinical Nutrition 1985; 42:1318-1330.

29. Fillenbaum, G. G. The Wellbeing of the Elderly: Approaches to Multidimensional Assessment. World Health Organization Offset Publ. No. 84. Geneva: World Health Organization, 1980.

30. Fishbein, H. A. Precipitants of hospitalization in insulin dependent diabetic mellitus: A statewide perspective. Diabetes Care 1985; 8(Suppl.):61.

31. Forett, B., Tortrat, D., and Wolmark, Y. Cholesterol as a risk factor for mortality in elderly women. Lancet 1989; 1(8643):868-871.

32. Fries, J. Aging, illness and health policy: Implications of the compression of morbidity. Perspectives in Biology and Medicine 1988; 31:407-428.

33. Frommer, P. L., Verter, J., Witters, J., and Castelli, W. Cholesterol reduction and life expectancy. Annals of Internal Medicine 1988; 1908:313-314.

34. Gaffney, J. T., and Singer, G. R. Diet needs of patients referred to home health. Journal of the American Dietetic Association 1985; 85:198-202.

35. Garber, A. M., Sox, H. C., and Littenberg, B. Screening asymptomatic adults for cardiac risk factors: The serum cholesterol level. Annals of Internal Medicine 1989; 110:622-639.

36. Glueck, C. J., Gartside, P. S., Steiner, P. M., et al. Hyperalpha and hypobeta lipoproteinemia in octogenarian kindreds. Atherosclerosis 1977; 27:387-406.

37. Gresham, G. E., Phillips, T. E., and Labi, M. L. C. ADL status in stroke: Relative merits of 3 indices. Archives of Physical Medicine and Rehabilitation 1962; 61:355.

38. Gordon, S. R., Kelley, S. L., Sybyl, J. R., Mill, M., Kramer, A., and Jahnigen, D. W. Relationship in very elderly veterans of nutritional status, self perceived chewing ability, dental status and social isolation. Journal of the American Geriatrics Society 1985; 33(5):334-339.

39. Gordon, D. J., and Rifkind, B. M. Treating high blood cholesterol in the older patient. American Journal of Cardiology 1989; 63:48H-52H.

40. Grigg, W. Quackery: It costs more than money. FDA Consumer, July-August 1988, pp. 30-31.

41. Haccinski, V. C., Lassen, N. A., and Marshall, J. Multiinfarct dementia: A cause of mental deterioration in the elderly. Lancet 1974; 2:207-210.

42. Harvey, K. B., Ruggiero, J. A., Regan, C. S., Bistrian, B. R., and Blackburn, G. L. Hospital morbidity mortality risk factors using nutritional assessment. Clinical Research 1978; 26:581A.

43. Hatten, A. M. The nutrition consultant in home care services. Journal of the American Dietetic Association 1976; 68:250.

44. Havlik, R. J., Hubert, H. B., Fabsitz, R. R., and Manning, F. Weight and hypertension. Annals of Internal Medicine 1983; 98:855.

45. Herbert, V., and Barrett, S. Vitamins and Health Foods: The Great American Hustle. Philadelphia: Stickley, 1981.

46. Hertzog, C., Shaie, K. W., and Gribbin, K. Cardiovascular disease and changes in intellectual functioning from middle to old age. Journal of Gerontology 1978; 33:872-883.

47. Holloszy, J. O., Schultz, J., Kusnierkiewicz, J., Hagveeg, J. M., and Ehsani, A. A. Effects of exercise on glucose tolerance and insulin resistance. Acta Medica Scandinavica (Suppl.) 1986; 711:55-65.

48. Hovell, M. F. The experimental evidence for weight loss treatment of essential hypertension: A critical review. American Journal of Public Health 1982; 72:359.

49. Jacobson, J. M., O'Rourke, P. J., and Wolf, A. D. Impact of a diabetes teaching program on health care trends in an Air Force Medical Center. Military Medicine 1983; 148:46.

50. Jeffrey, R. W., Gillum, R., Gerber, W. M., Jacobs, D., Elmer, P. J., and Prineas, R. J. Weight and sodium restriction for the prevention of hypertension: A comparison of group treatment and individual counseling. American Journal of Public Health 1983; 73:691.

51. Kane, R. A., and Kane, R. L. Assessing the Elderly. Lexington, Mass.: Lexington Books, 1981, pp. 25-67.

52. Kannel, W. B. Nutritional contributions to cardiovascular disease in the elderly. Journal of the American Geriatrics Society 1986; 34(1):27-36.

53. Kannel, W. B., and Sorlie, P. Some health benefits of physical activity: The Framingham study. Archives of Internal Medicine 1979; 139:857-861.

54. Kaplan, R. M., and Davis, W. K. Evaluating the costs and benefits of outpatient diabetes education and nutrition counseling. Diabetes Care 1986; 9:81.

55. Katz, S., Branch, L., Branson, M. H., et al. Active life expectancy. New England Journal of Medicine 1983; 309:1218-1224.

56. Kay, S. P., Morland, J. R., and Schmitter, E. Nutritional status and wound healing in lower extremity amputations. Clinical Orthopedics 1987; 217:253-256.

57. Kellman, H. R., and Willner, A. Problems in measurement and evaluation of rehabilitation. Archives of Physical Medicine and Rehabilitation 1962; 43:172.

58. Kelly, M. P., Gettel, S., Gee, C., Meltzer, L., Yamaguchi, J., and Aaron, M.

Nutritional and demographic data related to the hospitalization of hemodialysis patients. CRN Quarterly 1987; 2:16.

59. Kergoat, M. J., Leclerc, B. S., Petit Clerc, C., and Imbach, A. Discriminant biochemical markers for evaluating the nutritional status of elderly patients in long term care. American Journal of Clinical Nutrition 1987; 57:376-379.

60. Kerzner, L. J., Greb, L., and Steel, K. History taking forms and the care of geriatric patients. Journal of Medical Education 1982; 57:376-379.

61. Kini, M. M., Liebowitz, H. M., Colton, T., Nickerson, R. J., Galey, J., and Dawber, T. R. Prevalence of senile cataract, diabetic retinopathy, senile macular degeneration and open angle glaucoma in the Framingham study. American Journal of Ophthalmology 1978; 895:28-34.

62. Kinosian, B. P., and Eisenberg, J. M. Cutting into cholesterol: Cost effective alternatives for treating hypercholesterolemia. Journal of the American Medical Association 1988; 259:2249-2254.

63. Krasinski, S. D., Russell, R. M., Otradovec, C. L., Sadownski, J. A., Hartz, S. C., Jacob, R. A., and McGandy, R. B. Relationship of vitamin A and vitamin E intake to fasting plasma retinol, retinyl binding protein, retinyl esters, carotene, alpha tocopherol and cholesterol among elderly people and young adults: Increased plasma retinyl esters among vitamin A supplement users. American Journal of Clinical Nutrition 1989; 49:112-120.

64. Kreines, K., Johnson, E., Albrink, M., et al. The course of peripheral vascular disease in non insulin dependent diabetes. Diabetes Care 1988; 8:235-243.

65. Langford, H. G., Blaufox, D., Oberman, A., Hawkins, C., Curb, J. D., Cutter, G. R., Wassertheil-Smoller, S., Pressel, S., Babcock, C., Abernathy, J. D., Hotchkiss, J., and Tyler, M. Dietary therapy slows the return of hypertension after stopping prolonged medication. Journal of the American Medical Association 1985; 253:657.

66. Lawton, E. B. Physical Rehabilitation for Daily Living. New York: McGraw-Hill, 1952.

67. Lipschitz, D. A., Mitchell, C. O., Steele, R. W., and Milton, K. Y. Nutritional evaluation and supplementation of elderly subjects participating in a Meals on Wheels program. Journal of Parenteral and Enteral Nutrition 1985; 9(3):343-347.

68. Maslow, K. Total parenteral nutrition and tube feeding for elderly patients: Findings of an OTA study. Journal of Parenteral and Enteral Nutrition 1988; 12(5):425-432.

69. Mason, M., Hallahan, I. A., Monsen, E., Mutch, P. B., Polobo, R., and White, H. S. Requisites of advocacy: Philosophy, research, documentation. Phase II of the costs and benefits of nutritional care. Journal of the American Dietetic Association 1982; 80:213.

70. McCormick, J. S., and Krabanek, P. Coronary heart disease is not preventable by population interventions. Lancet 1988; 2:839-841.

71. Mitch, W. E., and Sapir, D. G. Evaluation of reduced dialysis frequency using nutritional therapy. Kidney International 1980; 20:122.

72. Moheney, F. I., and Barthel, D. W. Functional evaluation: The Barthel Index. Maryland State Medical Journal 1985; 14:61.

73. Morgan, D. B., Newton, H. M., Schorah, C. J., Jewitt, M. A., Hancock, M. R., and Hullin, R. P. Abnormal indices of nutrition in the elderly: A study of different clinical groups. Age and Aging 1986; 15(2):65-76.

74. Muehrcke, R. C., Sheehan, M., Lawrence, A., Moles, J. B., and Mandel, A. K. Home hemodialysis. Medical Clinics of North America 1971; 55:1473.

75. Mullen, J. L., Buzby, G. P., Waldman, M. T., Gertner, M. H., Hobbs, C. L., and Rosato, E. F. Prediction of operative morbidity and mortality by preoperative nutritional assessment. Surgical Forum 1979; 30:80-82.

76. National Center for Health Statistics. Characteristics of nursing home residents, health status and care received: National Nursing Home Survey. PHS Publ. No. 81-11712. National Center for Health Statistics, Vital and Health Statistics, Series 13, No. 51, 1981.

77. National Center for Health Statistics (Lin, B. M., Kovar, M. G., et al). Health statistics in older people: U.S. 1986. Vital and Health Statistics, Series 3, No. 25, June 1987.

78. National Institutes of Health Consensus Conference. Lowering blood cholesterol to prevent heart disease. Journal of the American Medical Association 1985; 253:2080-2090.

79. Oliver, M. F. Reducing cholesterol does not reduce mortality. Journal of the American College of Cardiology 1988; 12:814-817.

80. Oster, G., and Epstein, A. M. The cost effectiveness of antihyperlipemic therapy in the prevention of coronary heart disease: The case of cholestyramine. Journal of the American Medical Association 1987; 258:2381-2387.

81. Oster, G., and Epstein, A. M. Primary prevention of coronary heart disease: The economic benefits of lowering serum cholesterol. American Journal of Public Health 1986; 76:647-656.

82. Ostfeld, A. M. A review of stroke epidemiology. Epidemiologic Reviews 1980; 2:136-152.

83. Owen, O. E., Holip, J. L., D'Alesso, D. A., et al. A reappraisal of the calorie requirements of men at different ages. Journal of Gerontology 1986; 21:581.

84. Paffenbarger, R. S., and Hale, W. E. Work activity and coronary heart mortality. New England Journal of Medicine 1975; 292:545-550.

85. Perlmutter, J., Hakani, M. K., Hodgson, H. C., et al. Decreased cognitive function in aging non insulin dependent diabetic patients. American Journal of Medicine 1984; 77:1043-1048.

86. Pinholt, E. M., Kroenke, K., Hanley, J. F., Kussman, M. J., Twyman, P. L., and Carpenter, J. L. Functional assessment of the elderly: A comparison of standard instruments with clinical judgment. Archives of Internal Medicine 1987; 147:484-488.

87. Posner, B. M., and Krachenfels, M. M. Nutrition services in the continuum of health care. Clinics in Geriatric Medicine 1987; 3(2):261-274.

88. Ramsdell, J. W., Swart, J. A., et al. The yield of a home visit in the assessment of geriatric patients. Journal of the American Geriatrics Society 1989; 7(1):17-24.

89. Remmell, P. S., Casey, M. P., McGrandy, R. B., and Stare, F. J. A dietary program to lower serum cholesterol. Journal of the American Dietetic Association 1969; 54:12.

90. Robinson, G., Goldstein, M., and Levine, G. M. Impact of nutritional status on DRG length of stay. Journal of Parenteral and Enteral Nutrition 1987; 11(1):49-51.

91. Roe, D. A. Drug nutrient interactions in the elderly. Geriatrics 1986; 41(3):57-59, 63-64, 74.

92. Ross Laboratories. Benefits of Marketing Services: A Costing and Marketing Approach. Report of the Seventh Annual Ross Roundtable on Medical Issues. Columbus, Ohio: Ross Laboratories, 1987.

93. Schaefer, E. J., Moussa, P. B., Wilson, P. W. F., McGee, D., Dallal, G., and Castelli, W. P. Plasma lipoproteins in healthy octogenarians: Lack of reduced

high density lipoprotein levels; results from the Framingham heart study. Metabolism 1989; 38:293-296.

94. Schoening, H. A., and Iversen, I. A. Numerical scoring of self care status: A study of the Kenney self care evaluation. Archives of Physical Medicine and Rehabilitation 1968; 49:221.

95. Scultz, Y., Bray, G., and Margen, S. Postprandial thermogenesis at rest and during exercise in elderly men ingesting two levels of protein. Journal of the American College of Nutrition 1987; 6:497.

96. Sherman, M. N., Lechich, A., Brickner, P. W., Greenbaum, D., Kellogg, F. R., Scharer, L. K., Starita, L., and Daniel, B. L. Nutritional parameters in homebound persons of greatly advanced age. Journal of Parenteral and Enteral Nutrition 1982; 7(4):165-177.

97. Simko, M. D., and Conklin, M. T. Focusing on the effectiveness side of cost effectiveness equations. Journal of the American Dietetic Association 1989; 89:485-488.

98. Smith, J. L., Wickiser, A. A., Korth, L. L., Granjean, A. C., and Schaefer, A. E. Nutritional status of an institutionalized aged population. Journal of the American College of Nutrition 1984; 3:13-20.

99. Smith, F. A., and White, H. S. Intervention in an elderly population. In: Costs and Benefits of Nutritional Care, Phase 1. Chicago: American Dietetic Association, 1979.

100. Splett, P., and Caldwell, M. Costing Nutrition Services: A Workbook. Chicago: Department of Health and Human Services Region 5, November 1985.

101. Stamler, R., Stamler, J., Grimm, R., Dyer, A., Gosch, F. L., Berwin, R., Elmer, P., Fishman, J., Van Heel, N., Civinelli, J., and Hocksma, R. Nonpharmacologic control of hypertension. Preventive Medicine 1985; 14(3):336-345.

102. Stamler, R., Stamler, J., Grimm, J. R., Gosch, F. C., Elmer, P., Dyer, A., Berwin, R., Fishman, J., Van Heel, N., Civinelli, J., and McDonald, A. Nutrition therapy for high blood pressure. Final report of a 4 year randomized controlled trial: The Hypertensions Control Program. Journal of the American Medical Association 1987; 257:1484.

103. Steinberg, F. U. Care of the Geriatric Patient, 6th ed. St. Louis: C. V. Mosby, 1983.

104. Steer, H. W., Cuckle, H. S., Frankling, P. M., and Morris, P. J. The influence of diabetes mellitus on peripheral vascular disease. Surgery, Gynecology and Obstetrics 1983; 157:64-72.

105. Strock, E., Spencer, M., Sandell, J., and Hollander, P. Reimbursement of an ambulatory insulin program. Diabetes 1987; 36:33A.

106. Suter, P. M., and Russell, R. M. Vitamin requirements of the elderly. American Journal of Clinical Nutrition 1987; 45:501-512.

107. Sydenstricker, E., and Wiehl, D. G. A study of the incidence of disabling sickness in South Carolina cotton mill villages in 1918. Public Health Reports 1924; 39:17-23.

108. Taylor, W. C., Pass, T. M., Shepard, D. S., and Komaroff, A. L. Cholesterol reduction and life expectancy: A model incorporating multiple risk factors. Annals of Internal Medicine 1987; 106:605-614.

109. Tuxworth, W., Nevill, A. M., White, C., and Jenkins, C. Health, fitness, physical activity and morbidity of middle aged male factory workers. British Journal of Industrial Medicine 1986; 43:733-753.

110. U.S. Congress. Quackery: A $10 Bullion Scandal: A report by the Chairman

of the Subcommittee on Health and Long Term Care of the Select Committee on Aging. 98th Cong., 2d sess. Committee Print No. 98-435. Washington, D.C.: U.S. Government Printing Office, 1984.

111. Vallbona, C., and Baker, S. B. Physical fitness prospects in the elderly. Archives of Physical Medicine and Rehabilitation 1984; 65:194-200.

112. Walser, M. Does dietary therapy have a role in the predialysis patient? American Journal of Clinical Nutrition 1980; 33:1629.

113. Warnold, I., Falkheden, T., Hulten, B., and Isaksson, B. Energy intake and expenditure in selected groups of hospital patients. American Journal of Clinical Nutrition 1978; 31:742.

114. Wasserthiell Smoller, S., Langford, H. G., Flaufox, M. B., Oberman, A., Hawkins, M., Levine, B., Cameron, M., Babcock, C., Presel, S., Caggiula, A., Cutter, G., Curb, D., and Wong, R. Effective dietary intervention in hypertensives: Sodium restriction and weight reduction. Journal of the American Dietetic Association 1980; 85:423.

115. Weinsier, R. L., Johnston, M. H., and Doleys, D. M. Time calorie displacement diets for weight control. Evaluation of safety and efficiency. American Journal of Clinical Nutrition 1980; 33:950.

116. Whitehouse, F. W., Whitehouse, I. J., Cox, M. S., Goldman, J., Kahkonen, D. M., Partamian, J. O., and Tamayo, R. T. C. Outpatient regulations of the insulin requiring person with diabetes (an alternative to hospitalization). Journal of Chronic Disease 1983; 36:433.

117. Wilson, P. W. F., Garrison, R. T., Castelli, W. F., et al. Prevalence of coronary heart disease in the Framingham offspring study and the role of lipoprotein cholesterols. American Journal of Cardiology 1980; 46:649-664.

118. Wilson, W., and Pratt, C. The impact of diabetes education and peer support in weight and glycemic control of elderly persons with noninsulin dependent diabetes mellitus. American Journal of Public Health 1987; 77:6234.

119. Winkelstein, W. Some ecological studies of lung cancer and ischemic heart disease mortality in the United States. International Journal of Epidemiology 1987; 14:39-57.

120. Wolinsky, F. D., Coe, R. M., Chavez, M. N., Prendergast, J. M., and Miller, J. Further assessment of reliability and validity of a nutritional risk index: Analysis of a 3 wave panel to study elderly adults. Health Services Research 1986; 20:977-990.

121. Wolinsky, F. D., Coe, R. M., Miller, D. E., et al. Measurement of global and functional dimensions of health status in the elderly. Journal of Gerontology 1984; 39:88-92.

122. Wolinsky, F. D., Prendergast, J. M., Miller, D. E., Coe, R. M., and Chavez, N. M. Preliminary validation of a nutritional risk index. American Journal of Preventive Medicine 1985; 1:53-59.

123. Wolinsky, F. D., Coe, R. M., et al. Further assessment of reliability and validity of a nutritional risk index. Health Services Research 1986; 20(6, Pt. 2):977-990.

11

Cigarette Smoking

M cKeown[17] has classified the "causes" of health and disease into four types of components: (1) genetic, (2) environmental, (3) behavioral, and (4) preventive. The 1979 Department of Health, Education, and Welfare publication *Healthy People*[12] accepted his concept and went on to estimate that, of all potentially preventable disease, about 10 percent could be forestalled by genetic counseling and prenatal diagnosis, 30 percent by means of environmental interventions, and another 10 percent by the vigorous application of preventive and other health services. The report also estimated that approximately 50 percent of all preventable illness could be avoided by modifying one or more of those health factors (e.g., diet, physical activity, cigarette smoking, alcohol consumption) that exert such profound effects on health. Although some might rank diet as first among these factors, cigarette smoking is usually ranked as the behavior that can be most efficiently modified to reduce the risk of disease and untimely death. For instance, in the United States, current estimates attribute about 21 percent of coronary heart disease, 82 percent of chronic obstructive lung disease, and more than 90 percent of cancer to cigarette smoking.[28] In addition, Abbott and coworkers, Bonita and colleagues, and Wolf and associates in three separate studies all determined that cigarette smoking was a significant risk factor for stroke,[1,3,31] although Himmelmann and colleagues failed to find such an association.[14]

One of the reasons that modifying smoking behavior is an efficient preventive intervention is that the adverse health effects of smoking can be abruptly altered by quitting. The ex-smoker's risk of coronary heart disease (CHD) 12 months following cessation is approximately that of the person who has never smoked.[7] Cessation also slows the development of chronic obstructive pulmonary disease (COPD),[11] and Wolf has observed that ex-smokers quickly shed the excess risk of stroke that can be attributed to cigarette smoking.[31] Reduction in lung cancer risk, however, is slower, and the ex-smoker will always have a risk for this disease between 1.5 and 2 times that enjoyed by those who have never smoked.[7]

PREVALENCE

The 1985 Health Interview Survey[26] reported that 30 percent of adults in the United States were current smokers. Although smoking rates were fairly uniform between the ages of 20 and 55, the rate dropped rapidly among the elderly. Those 55 to 64 years of age still maintained a smoking rate of 30.2 percent; of those 65 to 74 years of age the rate was only 21.5 percent, and over age 75 the rate dropped to 8.5 percent.

There are three possible explanations for these findings. First, the birth cohort for those currently over the age of 65 may have had a lower rate of initiating cigarette smoking during adolescence and adulthood (i.e., the ever-smoked rate is lower in these cohorts). Second, it is possible that there are increasing cessation rates among those over age 65. Finally, some of the decrease in smoking rates may be due to the decreased survivorship of smokers. What evidence there is indicates that all three factors may be operative. Secular trends certainly explain some of the lower smoking rates among older women because the habit did not become socially acceptable for women until about 40 years ago. Direct evidence indicates that cessation rates have been observed to increase with age,[29] thus confirming the intuitive concept that, because most cessation attempts are unsuccessful, the elderly who have lived longer will therefore have had more opportunities to achieve cessation of smoking. Smoking certainly shortens life expectancy for both sexes, thus selectively eliminating smokers, particularly men, from surviving into old age.

BURDEN

The answer to the question of whether the health effects of cigarette smoking are age specific is complex. There is no evidence for such effects, yet the duration of smoking is an important factor and pack-years of cigarette smoking an important variable for lung and other cancers. Therefore, one may assume that duration and rate of cigarette smoking would be more important than age, although the two obviously would be related because the elderly would have had an opportunity to smoke for more years than the members of younger birth cohorts. Evidence has shown, however, that the current rate of cigarette smoking is the most important smoking variable related to cardiovascular disease, including coronary heart disease, stroke, and peripheral arterial disease (i.e., intermittent claudication).[10] In addition, Branch reported that cigarette smoking was associated with subsequent physical disability among a cohort of elderly men.[4]

The evidence also indicates that cigarette smoking continues to shorten life expectancy beyond the age of 50 and that it continues to predict lung and other cancers.[8] Jajich and coworkers determined that, among a sample of 2,674 persons aged 65 to 74 years, the coronary heart disease death rate of current cigarette smokers was 52 percent higher than the rates for nonsmokers, ex-smokers, and those who smoked pipes and cigars.[15] Moreover, Branch and Jette determined that never smoking cigarettes was the only personal health practice that achieved a statistically significant multivariate relationship with lower mortality.[5]

Khaw and colleagues studied the predictors of stroke-associated mortality in the Rancho Bernardo study and determined that cigarette smoking was a stronger predictor of stroke mortality than blood pressure.[16] It was also a significant risk factor for stroke with relative risks ranging close to 2.0 for heavy (i.e., 40 cigarettes or more per day) smokers. The evidence regarding CHD and peripheral arterial disease among seniors, however, is much less convincing. Whereas cigarette smoking is a powerful risk factor for these diseases for individuals under the age of 65, particularly men, the effect weakens markedly for both sexes over that age. Some studies suggest that cigarette smoking predicts both mortality and recurrence in patients who have developed coronary heart disease,[29] although data from the Framingham study regarding smokers and nonsmokers following acute myocardial infarction have not confirmed these findings. Recent data from the Coronary Artery Surgery Study (CASS) on the effects of smoking cessation among 1,893 men and women over the age of 55 with documented CHD demonstrated that the six-year mortality rate was greater for those who continued to smoke than for those who had quit the year before entering the study and who had continued to abstain. Furthermore, the beneficial effect did not decrease with increasing age.[13]

Earlier data from the CASS had shown that a history of cigarette smoking was one of five variables that predicted perioperative mortality following coronary artery bypass grafting.[9] The Duke Longitudinal Study, which followed volunteers 60 to 94 years of age, found associations between exercise, maintaining moderate weight, and abstention from cigarette smoking and both lower mortality and illness rates among its sample.[22] In addition, Rundgren and Mellstrom suggest that cigarette smoking may be a cause of osteoporosis. Their studies revealed that, of 409 men and 559 women between the ages of 70 and 79, the smokers had a bone mineral content that was 10 to 30 percent lower than that of nonsmokers.[25]

In summary, the weight of the evidence indicates that cigarette smoking continues to be a risk factor for untimely death from all causes in persons over the age of 50. As people age, however, smoking becomes less predictive of certain forms of cardiovascular disease.

EVIDENCE THAT SMOKING CESSATION IS BENEFICIAL

For both practical and ethical reasons, there have been no double-blind, randomized trials of the effects of cessation of cigarette smoking. Therefore, it has been necessary to derive data regarding these effects from multiple risk factor intervention trials that have included cigarette smoking intervention or from observations of large cohorts over time (comparing quitters with never-smokers and smokers).[6] These data are limited in other respects as well: intervention trials are often restricted to men (e.g., the multiple risk factor intervention trials),[18] and analyses have rarely focused selectively on the elderly.

The available data indicate that cigarette smoking cessation increases life expectancy at all ages and that the increase for older individuals, although less in the absolute number of years than for younger subjects, is proportionally as great.[6] The benefits are most prompt for coronary and other manifestations of cardiovascular disease in which the full benefits may be realized within the first 12 months after cessation. Cancer risk reduction, on the other hand, takes place more slowly; consequently, the risk of ex-smokers remains between 1.5 and 2 times that of nonsmokers even after 10 years or more of abstention. Other benefits include an improved sense of smell and improved pulmonary function. However, quitters on average gain 5 pounds in weight during the subsequent 12 months, and the weight gain is proportional to the smoking rate prior to cessation. Although some of this increase may be due to increased caloric intake, most of the gain can be ascribed to the elimination of the metabolic effects of nicotine, which can account for as many as 500 kilocalories per day.[2] There is no evidence that these effects are any different for seniors than they are for younger individuals.

SMOKING CESSATION TECHNIQUES

Most individuals who have stopped smoking do so on their own with only informal encouragement from family, friends, and health professionals. Yet the rate of smoking cessation has slowed among certain age-sex groups, and smoking rates are actually increasing among poor women.[30] These data suggest that formal smoking cessation techniques may gain increasing importance during the next decade if a smoke-free society in the United States is to be achieved by the year 2000.

Physicians play an important role in cigarette smoking cessation. More than two-thirds of U.S. adults have a professional encounter with a physician each year. For the elderly, this figure may exceed 90 percent. Many of these visits are for symptoms of smoking-related diseases, thus increasing the likelihood that the patient will be motivated to quit.[25] Some studies, based on patient interviews, have reported that fewer than half of patients who smoke can recall their physician counseling them to stop.[21] These studies disagree with other data from physicians that indicate that as many as 85 percent counsel their patients on some health issue at the time of office visits. Far fewer physicians, however, feel competent to counsel patients regarding smoking cessation, and in one survey only 3 percent[31] were confident of their effectiveness. Some investigators have attempted to improve physicians' counseling skills. For example, Ockene and coworkers used a three-hour training program to teach family practice and internal medicine residents patient-centered counseling techniques. After completion of the program the residents demonstrated a significant increase in knowledge and a perception of themselves as having more influence on their patients who smoked.[19]

Formal smoking cessation techniques include group counseling with peer support, aversion techniques such as rapid smoking, and hypnosis. Nicotine-containing chewing gum has also been evaluated as an adjuvant to help patients stop smoking.[16,23] Its efficacy largely depends on how it is used: it has been shown to be effective if combined with behavioral programs, particularly for heavy smokers who are highly dependent on nicotine, but if prescribed alone, it is of little or no benefit. Unfortunately, few studies have attempted to evaluate the relative effectiveness of these programs among older individuals as compared with younger smokers.

PASSIVE SMOKING

The health risks of passive smoking of side-stream smoke are far less than the risks incurred by smoking of the mainstream. Nevertheless, relative risks of up to 3.3 for cancer of the lung have been reported for nonsmoking wives of smoking husbands.[22] The size of the risk indicates that passive smoking is a problem that should be addressed.

RECOMMENDATIONS

Those Over the Age of 50

1. Those older individuals who smoke cigarettes should be made aware of both the deleterious health effects of cigarette smoking and the many health and other benefits of quitting and should discuss the various cessation methods with their primary care physician.
2. Elders who are ex-smokers should advise their smoking peers of the health and other benefits they will enjoy after quitting.
3. The surgeon general's goal of a smoke-free environment by the year 2000 should be actively supported.

Services

1. Physicians and other health professionals should set a good example by not smoking cigarettes. Those who are ex-smokers should draw on their own personal experiences during smoking withdrawal in counseling their smoking patients.
2. A smoking history on all patients should always be taken.
3. Health care professionals should assess their smoking patients' motivation for quitting and improve their skill in counseling such patients in the office-practice setting.
4. Physicians and other health professionals should familiarize themselves with the formal smoking cessation programs available in patients' communities.
5. Nicotine-containing gum should be prescribed appropriately and effectively.

Public Health and Environmental Policymakers

1. The feasibility of applying the same controls for the sale of cigarettes as those now established for the sale of alcoholic beverages should be considered.

2. Policymakers should continue to develop and enforce regulations prohibiting cigarette smoking on common carriers and in other public places.

3. The establishment of a tax on cigarettes should be studied, that is, a tax sufficient to cover both the direct and indirect costs of cigarette smoking borne by local, state, and federal governments.

4. State and federal legislation should be proposed to permit the smoking-risk rating of both life and health insurance.

5. Federal subsidies to tobacco growers should be eliminated.

6. All school health education programs should be required to include curriculum on the risk of smoking.

7. Cigarette advertising should be prohibited.

8. Research should continue to focus on effective means of smoking cessation. Research should also focus on eliminating the initiation of smoking.

Advocacy Groups

1. Efforts should continue to pressure policy makers and legislatures to promote antismoking health measures.

2. Formal smoking prevention and smoking cessation programs should be developed and promoted.

3. Print, audio, and visual aids to prevent cigarette smoking initiation and promote cigarette smoking cessation should be made available to those who need them. In addition, industry should continue to develop products that can assist health professional and voluntary health agencies to prevent the initiation of cigarette smoking by those who have never smoked and encourage its cessation among those who do.

REFERENCES

1. Abbott, R. D., Reid, D. M., and Yano, K. Risk of stroke in male cigarette smokers. New England Journal of Medicine 1986; 315:717-720.
2. Benowitz, N. L. Pharmacological aspects of cigarette smoking and nicotine addiction. New England Journal of Medicine 1988; 319:1318.
3. Bonita, R., Scragg, R., Stewart, A., et al. Cigarette smoking and the risk of premature stroke in men and women. British Medical Journal of Clinical Research 1986; 295:6-9.
4. Branch, L. G. Health practices and incident disability among the elderly. American Journal of Public Health 1985; 75:1436-1439.
5. Branch, L. G., and Jette, A. M. Personal health practices and mortality among the elderly. American Journal of Public Health 1984; 74:1126-1129.
6. Castelli, W. P., Garrison, R. J., Dawber, T. R., McNamara, P., Feinleib, M., and Kannel, W. B. The filter cigarette and coronary heart disease: The Framingham study. Lancet 1981; 2(8238):109-113.

7. Fielding, J. E. Medical progress: Smoking. Health effects and control, Part I. New England Journal of Medicine 1985; 313(8):491-498.

8. Fielding, J. E. Medical progress: Smoking. Health effects and control, Part II. New England Journal of Medicine 1985; 313(9):555-561.

9. Gersh, B. J., Kronmal, R. A., Frye, R. L., Schaff, H. V., Ryan, T. J., Gosselin, A. J., Kaiser, G. C., and Killip, T. Coronary artery and coronary artery bypass surgery: Morbidity and mortality in patients ages 65 and older. A report from the Coronary Artery Surgery Study. Circulation 1983; 67:483-491.

10. Gordon, T., Kannel, W. B., Dawber, T. R., and McGee, D. Changes associated with quitting cigarette smoking: The Framingham study. American Heart Journal 1975; 90:322-328.

11. Health Consequences of Smoking. Chronic Obstructive Lung Disease: A Report of the Surgeon General. Washington, D.C.: U.S. Department of Health and Human Services, Public Health Service, 1984.

12. Healthy People: The Surgeon General's Report on Health Promotion and Disease Prevention. Publ. No. 79-55071A. Washington, D.C.: U.S. Department of Health, Education and Welfare, Public Health Service, 1979.

13. Hermanson, B., Omenn, G. S., Kronmal, R. A., and Gersh, B. J. Beneficial six-year outcome of smoking cessation in older men and women with coronary artery disease. New England Journal of Medicine 1988; 319:1365-1369.

14. Himmelmann, A., Hansson, L., Svensson, A., Harmsen, P., Holmgren, C., and Svanborg, A. Predictors of stroke in the elderly. Acta Medica Scandinavia 1988; 224:439-443.

15. Jajich, C. L., Ostfeld, A. M., and Freeman, D. H., Jr. Smoking and coronary heart disease mortality in the elderly. Journal of the American Medical Association 1984; 252:2831-2834.

16. Khaw, K. T., Barrett-Connor, E., Suarez, L., and Criqui, M. H. Predictors of stroke-associated mortality in the elderly. Stroke 1984; 15:244-248.

17. McKeown, T., and Lowe, C. R. An Introduction to Social Medicine, 2nd ed. London: Blackwell Scientific Publications, Oxford University Press, 1966.

18. Multiple risk factor intervention trial: Risk factor changes in mortality results. Journal of the American Medical Association 1982; 248:1465-1477.

19. Ockene, J. K., Quirk, M. E., Goldberg, R. J., et al. A residents' training program for the development of smoking intervention skills. Archives of Internal Medicine 1988; 148:1039-1045.

20. Orleans, C. T. Understanding and promoting smoking cessation: Overview and guidelines for physician intervention. Annual Review of Medicine 1985; 36:51-61. Shipley, R. H., and Orleans, C. S. Treatment of cigarette smoking. In: P. A. Boudewyns and F. T. Keefe (eds.), Behavioral Medicine in General Medical Practice. Menlo Park, Calif.: Addison-Wesley, 1982.

21. Palmore, E. Health practices and illness among the aged. Gerontologist 1970; 10:313-316.

22. Pershagen, G., Hrubec, Z., and Suensson, C. Passive smoking and lung cancer in Swedish women. American Journal of Epidemiology 1987; 125:17-24.

23. Raw, M. Does nicotine chewing gum work? British Medical Journal 1985; 290:1231-1232.

24. Rigotti, N. A., and Tesar, G. E. Smoking cessation in the prevention of cardiovascular disease. Cardiovascular Clinics 1985; 3:245-257.

25. Rundgren, A., and Mellstrom, D. The effect of tobacco smoking on the bone

mineral content of the aging skeleton. Mechanisms of Aging and Development 1984; 28:273-277.

26. Schoenborn, C. A., and Cohen, B. H. Trends in smoking, alcohol consumption and other health practices among U.S. adults: 1977 and 1983. National Center for Health Statistics, Advance Data No. 118, pp. 1-16, 1986.

27. Stokes, J., and Rigotti, N. A. The health consequences of cigarette smoking and the internist's role in smoking cessation. Advances in Internal Medicine 1988; 33:431-460.

28. Stokes, J., Kannel, W. B., D' Agostino, R. B., Wolf, P. A., and Cupples, L. A. Blood pressure as a risk factor for cardiovascular disease. The Framingham study: 30 years of follow-up. Hypertension 1989; 13(5, Pt. 2):113-118.

29. Stoto, M. A. Changes in adult smoking behavior in the United States: 1955-1983. Harvard University, J.F.K. School of Government, Institute for the Study of Smoking Behavior and Policy, 1986.

30. Wechsler, H., Levine, S., Idelson, R. K., et al. The physicians' role in health promotion—a survey of primary-care practitioners. New England Journal of Medicine 1983; 308:97-100.

31. Wolf, P. A., D'Agostino, R. B., Kannel, W. B., Bonita, R., and Belanger, A. J. Cigarette smoking as a risk factor for stroke. Journal of the American Medical Association 1988; 259:1025-1029.

12

Depression

———

O f all the possibilities for improving the lot of the elderly in this country, none may yield greater returns in human happiness and economic well-being than recognition and appropriate control of depression. Recent advances have made depression an eminently treatable disorder; yet only a minority of elderly depressed persons are receiving adequate treatment, in large part because of inadequate recognition of the disorder. Depression is seriously underdiagnosed and often misdiagnosed. Vast resources are expended in fruitless diagnostic searches, in medical treatment of somatic symptoms without a detectable basis, and in neglect of the underlying, treatable psychiatric disorder. This chapter addresses a broad range of medical and social factors that contribute to these difficulties and reviews the prevalence, definition, risk factors, and remediability of depression. It concludes with recommendations to improve the treatment of depression in the elderly.

DEFINITION AND PREVALENCE

Until quite recently, the prevalence and incidence of depression among the elderly have been sorely neglected topics of interest and research. Present assessments remain clouded by the difficulties of reaching a consensus on a definition of depression. "Depression" can mean many things—a mood, a symptom, or a psychiatric disorder. Although moods and symptoms may unfavorably influence the quality of life, it is depression as a psychiatric disorder that provides the greatest opportunity for the reduction of suffering and the containment of costs. Accordingly, this chapter focuses on depression as a psychiatric disorder. Table 12-1 summarizes the results of recent studies comparing the percentage of depressive symptoms with the percentage of depressive disorders. As the table shows, there is a far lower rate of disorders than of symptoms.

The most striking feature of recent studies is the very low prevalence of depression among elderly persons who do not have associated medical problems. The highest figures are lower than those for younger persons, and studies explicitly comparing the prevalence of depression across age groups have led to a growing consensus that major depressive disorders (in contrast to symptoms) are less prevalent among the elderly.[7] As noted above, in the elderly, symptoms of depression are more frequent than the psychiatric disorder, but whether they are more prevalent than among younger persons is not clear.

TABLE 12-1 Results of Recent Studies Among the Elderly Comparing Rates (percentage) of Depressive Disorders with Rates of Depressive Symptoms

Author	Year Reported	Rate of Depressive Disorders (%)	Rate of Depressive Symptoms (%)
Community surveys			
Blazer et al.[5]	1987	4.0	27
Blazer and Williams[9]	1980	3.7	4-13
Weissman et al.[67]	1985	1.9	
Nielsson and Persson[50]	1984	1.0	
Berkman et al.[4]	1986		15
Medical facilities (outpatients)			
Borson et al.[10]	1986	1.0	24
Koenig et al.[40]	1988	11.5	23
Nursing home			
Parmelee et al.[51]	1989	12.4	30.5
Goldman et al.[26]	1986		31-57
Demented			
Reifler et al.[53] (community)	1982	23.0	
Wragg and Jeste[70] (review of 30 studies of Alzheimer's disease)	1989	10.0–20.0	40–50
Ernst et al.[16] (nursing home)	1977	25.0	56

The evidence regarding the mental health of the elderly comes as something of a surprise, and the reasons for it are unclear. Perhaps it is a survival effect: those persons more prone to depression may have died. Among elderly persons with associated physical illness the prevalence of depression is much higher, perhaps by a factor of four or five. The presumption that physical illness is a causal factor in this increased prevalence is supported by research of Harwood and Turner;[33] they found that older persons were less apt to be depressed than younger persons when the influence of physical illness was controlled. The fact that physical illness and disability not only influence depression but are often inextricably intertwined with it further complicates an understanding of these problems.

High rates of depression and of depressive symptoms have been found in select populations—for example, among the elderly in nursing homes, where illness and disability are complicated by dependency and the loss of personal control. The highest rates of depression are found among the demented. Nearly a quarter of the demented suffer from major depression, and a majority are at least mildly depressed, adding to the already staggering burden of care.

Clearly, depression is common and inflicts a disproportionate burden of illness on older people. Just how great a burden is unclear because of problems in the diagnosis of depression. Depression among the elderly can appear almost as a different disorder from depression among younger persons, a difference that has found expression in such terms as "masked depression" or "somatic equivalents." A striking difference is in the significance of depressed mood. Among the elderly, just as fever may be absent in infection, so too may depressed mood be present in the absence of detectable disease.[11,19] At the same time, somatic symptoms play a far larger role in depression among the elderly than among younger persons. Somatic symptoms in the absence of physical disease present serious diagnostic difficulties to physicians and to survey researchers attempting to assess the extent of an individual's problem.

These difficulties in defining depression render critical aspects of health policy analysis more difficult. Once specific criteria for the diagnosis of depression in older persons are better defined and instruments developed for their application, far more effective studies of prevalence, incidence, and symptom severity can be carried out, both in the community and in high-risk groups. In addition, more precise estimates of the monetary as well as the psychological and emotional costs of depression will be possible, and improved cost-effectiveness estimates of treatment can be made.

RISK FACTORS

A discussion of risk factors in relation to depression encompasses two different directions of influence. The first is risk factors for depression; the second is depression as a risk factor for distress, disability, and suicide. The first of these directions has been investigated more thoroughly than the second, and a rather high degree of consensus has been reached about some of the major factors. These factors are listed in Table 12-2.

Blazer and Maddox[8] have focused on the risk factor of social stress and its interaction with social support in the onset of late life depression. Blazer describes nine potential mechanisms (for further discussion of social isolation as a risk factor, see Chapter 14):

1. Social stressors, such as stressful life events, cause major depressive illness.

2. Social stressors decrease physical health status. The individual may react to the decline in physical health with a major depressive illness.

3. Social stressors in an individual's past lead to a physical and

TABLE 12-2 Categories of Risk Factors for Depression and Depressive Symptoms

Category	Factor
Biological	Family history of depression
	Depression earlier in life
Changes in physical function	Illness and medically imposed limitation
	Limitations in strength or ambulation, or both
	Changes in cognitive function
	Sensory losses
Grief and bereavement	Loss of a child
	Loss or disability of spouse
	Death of siblings
	Death(s) of friends or extended family
Changes in network of support	Geographic isolation
	Loss of loved ones from death or illness
	Unplanned retirement
	Lack of confiding relationships

SOURCE: Adapted from G. L. Gottlieb, "Optimizing Mental Function of the Elderly" in *Practicing Prevention for the Elderly*, by R. Lavizzo-Mourey, S. C. Day, D. Diserens, and J. A. Grisso, Hanley and Bellfus, Inc., Philadelphia, 1988, pp. 153-166.

psychological condition that predisposes the individual to develop a major depressive illness at a later time.

4. Decreased social interaction causes major depressive illness.

5. Although social stressors lead to major depressive illness, this relationship is buffered by perceived social support. When perceived social support decreases, the effects of stressors are enhanced.

6. The lack of significant roles and attachments, such as the presence of a spouse, leads to major depressive illness.

7. The absence of important attachments in the social network leads to a decreased frequency of social interaction, which in turn leads to an increase in major depressive illness.

8. A decline in perceived social support directly contributes to an increase in major depressive illness.

9. The causal relationship of social stressors and major depressive illness is buffered by the frequency of social interaction. When frequency of social interaction decreases, the causal relationship between social stressors and depressive illness becomes clearer.

Constraints on sexuality have been identified by Butler and Lewis[12] as a significant risk factor for depression. Some of these constraints are social, deriving from prejudice against sexual activity on the part of older persons that limits their opportunities and impairs their confidence in themselves. Other constraints may be pharmacological, especially the wide use of antihypertensive medications, and, paradoxically, medication for the treatment of depression itself.

Although not a risk factor, sleep disorders occur with some frequency concurrently with depression in the elderly.[21,54] Physicians should be sensitive to sleep difficulties in older patients, especially early morning waking or frequent interruptions in sleep, as indications of depression.

REMEDIABILITY: OUTCOME OF TREATMENT

Treatment of depression in the elderly is one of the most rewarding activities that a health care worker can undertake. Many older people respond well to treatment. Such response is gratifying to both patients and their families who all too often may see the older person's deteriorating condition as an irreversible aspect of normal aging. Because relapse and recurrence of depression are all too frequent, continuing ready access to treatment is important.

Given the effectiveness of treatment for depression, the first and perhaps most serious problem in managing depression is the failure to recognize its presence. It appears likely that a majority of elderly depressed patients escape medical attention for their disorder. Both patients and physicians, each for their own reasons, contribute to this problem. Many older persons find it painful to acknowledge the presence of emotional difficulties, and they find it even harder to seek medical attention for them. It may seem easier to ascribe their problems to the normal aging process and to believe there is nothing to be done about them.

Physicians often share their patients' disinclination to recognize depression, in part because their medical education has left them poorly equipped to cope with the complicated psychiatric problems of the elderly. Most are far more comfortable making a physical rather than a psychiatric diagnosis. Furthermore, even physicians who are prepared to make a psychiatric diagnosis may find themselves daunted by the special features of depression in the elderly, which may appear to be quite different from depression in the young. The absence of depressed mood may be particularly confusing; in addition, depression in the elderly is not infrequently intertwined with physical illness that complicates and obscures it.

Fortunately, this problem is remediable by improvement in the teaching of psychiatry and geriatrics. Even modest educational efforts can be useful. Thus, feedback of the results of a screening test to primary care physicians significantly improved their recognition of depression.[23,25]

Primary care physicians are strategically placed to recognize the presence of depression and may be the only source of care acceptable to the patient and his or her family. Patients and their families usually seek help from primary care physicians, and these care givers supply a greater proportion of the care of depressed elderly individuals than any other group of health workers. In addition, depression is one of the most common problems seen in their practices, occurring in as many as 30 percent of their patients. Many primary care physicians are skilled at recognizing depression; many, however, do not recognize, let alone diagnose and treat, this condition.[64,65] The immediate result of this lack of recognition may be neglect of the problem or inappropriate and expensive medical workups, as well as a longer duration of illness, a risk factor for chronicity. The final result may be a significant increase in direct and indirect medical costs and in psychosocial costs.[29]

The first step in treatment, before any prescription, is a careful history and physical examination. There are several medical disorders that can lead to a depressed mood, and despite the strictures against excessive diagnostic workups, these disorders should be ruled out first. Correction of electrolyte disturbance or hypothyroidism can be a most effective and economical way of controlling depressive symptoms that arise from these sources.

The value of a review of medications should not be underestimated. A significant percentage of the disorders that afflict the elderly, including depression, are drug induced. Some of these disorders are ones in which medication toxicity is more readily recognized, such as the confusional states and dementias. Attention to medications thus can pay large dividends. There are two major approaches to the treatment of depression in the elderly: somatic and psychosocial. Both forms of treatment are often indicated.

Antidepressant medication is the mainstay of treatment for major depression, and the most widely used agents are tricyclic antidepressants. In the hands of well-trained physicians, they are quite effective. Most younger depressed patients respond to such medication—about 60 to 70 percent of patients to the first tricyclic and another 20 percent to a second.[27,41] These agents are the most widely used antidepressants among the elderly as well as among younger persons. Unfortunately, however, there is little information about their effects in the elderly. As Jarvik and Gerson[37] point out in their review, it is paradoxical that older persons, for whom such information is sorely needed, have been largely excluded from treatment outcome research. Although understandable in terms of the difficulty of conducting such trials, this omission has left serious gaps in knowledge regarding how to treat depression in the elderly. This gap is particularly serious in the area of side effects, which constitute a formidable problem in the elderly, one that may well contribute to the inadequate treatment of depression in this age group. Many physicians are sufficiently daunted by this problem to refrain from the kind of vigorous pharmacotherapy of depression that would produce results.

Prominent side effects are those involving the cardiovascular system, including increased conduction time and increased heart rate. Earlier concerns that tricyclic antidepressants might induce arrhythmias, however, were probably unwarranted; in fact, they may even reduce arrhythmias. Other side effects are anticholinergic ones such as dry mouth, blurred vision, and urinary retention, a problem of particular concern in the elderly. Constipation and delirium are other troublesome side effects because of their negative influence on elderly patients' trust in their physician. Postural hypotension is another common problem and a reason for intensive education, particularly to prevent falls.

Overdosage is a concern that affects all pharmacotherapy of the elderly. The decreased rate of drug clearance is a particular problem with the tricyclic antidepressants. Current practice is to start these medications at one-third to one-half the standard dosage and to increase it carefully thereafter.[61]

These problems warrant caution in the use of tricyclic antidepressants, but the experienced clinician can still use them to good effect.[24] Electrocardiographic monitoring during the course of treatment greatly reduces cardiovascular risks, and recognition of the various side effects permits rapid response to problems that may develop. Still, the many side effects of tricyclic antidepressants raise the question of whether there may not be other, safer medications. These concerns have led to increased attention to another family of antidepressants, the monoamine oxidase (MAO) inhibitors. Among younger patients in recent years the effectiveness of tricyclic antidepressants and various problems with the MAO inhibitors had led to a decline in their use, except for some forms of treatment-resistant depression. The minimal cardiac and anticholinergic effects of the MAO inhibitors, however, have brought about a revival of interest in their use for the treatment of depression in the elderly.[24]

Problems with traditional antidepressant medication have led to great interest in new generations of these agents. Although tests in the elderly of the new generation of antidepressants have been limited, three new agents, Trazadone, Prozac, and Wellbutrin, have few side effects and are believed to have efficacy at least as great as that of older agents. Rapid development of new and more potent antidepressants means that medication will assume increasing importance in the years ahead.

It is to be hoped that past reluctance to assess the effects of medication in older persons will be overcome in the near future and that there will be no further delay in determining the value of these agents and indications for their use in the elderly. Indeed, excellent opportunities exist for industry to target this age group for clinical trials of antidepressant medications. Such trials would be expensive, but the expense could well be repaid, even in the short term, by the recognition that would be accorded an agent that had undergone testing in the elderly.

Electroconvulsive therapy, or ECT, deserves special attention in a discussion of treatment of depression among the elderly. Its use in this population has been limited by the same kind of prejudice that affects its use in general, an unfortunate outcome because ECT appears to be significantly more effective than medication in various forms of severe depression. In one instructive series, 86 percent of patients with delusional depression responded to ECT, compared with 32 percent who responded to medication.[44] Thus, ECT may be both more effective and safer than the tricyclic antidepressants. It also has fewer side effects, but its major side effect, memory loss, although usually transient, creates special problems in a population in which memory loss is already a problem. Yet the efficacy of ECT is so marked that it might be considered the first form of treatment for some severely depressed patients, without waiting for the failure of drug therapy, as is now the case. Further research could yield rich dividends in establishing more precise indications for its use among the elderly.[17,66]

Primary care physicians are capable of treating most older depressed patients who come to them, but there are some circumstances in which physicians should seek consultation from a psychiatrist until they gain sufficient experience in managing antidepressant medications. Gottlieb[28] recommends such consultation, preferably with a geriatric psychiatrist, and in some instances referral of patients with certain specific problems: major depression with delusional or other psychotic features; suicidal or homicidal ideation or a previous history of destructive behavior; treatment-resistant depression; symptoms (medical and neurological) that are difficult to distinguish from depression; and medical conditions that are made worse by depressive symptoms or antidepressant interventions.

The discussion above has considered the treatment of depression largely in terms of pharmacotherapy delivered by primary care physicians. Psychosocial therapies for depression in the elderly are also reasonably effective—and safer. Cognitive-behavioral treatment of depression has proved to be as effective as pharmacotherapy in less severe depressions, and it avoids the troublesome side effects of medication. A major limitation of such labor-intensive treatment is its cost. Even when delivered by nonphysicians, the fact that it is not reimbursable puts it beyond the reach of most elderly persons.

The issue of costs highlights the attractiveness of community-based programs that rely on volunteer or low-cost personnel more than on professional help. The experience of recent years has suggested that these approaches have merit, although few have achieved any degree of permanence and fewer yet have been evaluated. A common feature of these programs is their anticipation of stressful events, particularly bereavement, and their provision of supportive services.[36,52,57] Controlled trials showed that one program of bereavement counseling achieved a significant decrease in morbidity,[52] whereas a television-assisted approach produced some improvement in mood in the study participants.[46] One innovative approach that deserves further exploration attempted to change negative attitudes toward aging and the aged by emphasizing Eastern philosophical traditions that associate aging with increased spiritual development.[1] The results of these various efforts are promising, and further research into this area seems warranted.

Finally, the committee notes that there is a serious discrepancy between the need for professional mental health assistance for elderly depressed people and the availability of such assistance. A survey in North Carolina revealed that no more than 8 percent of mentally impaired persons were receiving any professional mental health services, even though 20 percent of them were receiving psychotropic medication from their primary care physicians.[8] The inadequacy of professional mental health care is even more striking among minority groups. A survey of an elderly Hispanic population with a high prevalence of depressive disorders showed that not a single person had ever received any professional mental health care, or even any antidepressant medication, even though at least 75 of them were judged to be suffering from a major depression.[38]

COSTS

An understanding of the costs of mental illness in general and of depression in particular lags far behind knowledge of the treatment of these disorders. This statement is true of all age groups and is particularly true of the elderly. The importance of obtaining more accurate estimates of these costs is underscored by the disproportionate use of medical resources by the elderly: although they constitute 12 percent of the population, they utilize 30 percent of medical resources.[22] This problem of health care costs will increase with the growth of the elderly population, and particularly of the very old population with its even higher utilization of medical resources.

The special problem of underdiagnosis of depression among the elderly makes cost estimates especially difficult. Such cost estimates are important because of the very large hidden costs arising from three problems noted earlier: expensive and often fruitless diagnostic searches for physical illness; the often risky medical treatment of somatic symptoms without a physical basis; and inadequate or delayed treatment of depression leading to chronicity and disability. This triad of problems has not been addressed in any estimates of the costs of medical care of the elderly, and there is every reason to believe that it contributes significantly to such costs.

In addition to the monetary costs associated with depression, profound social and psychological costs have become apparent. These costs are described in the report of the RAND Corporation's recent

Medical Outcomes Study.[58,67] This large "treated prevalence" outpatient study utilized a 20-item general health survey to measure the functioning and well-being of patients suffering from depression and eight chronic medical conditions—angina, arthritis, back problems, coronary artery disease, diabetes, gastrointestinal problems, high blood pressure, and lung problems. The survey of 11,000 patients revealed serious underestimation of the impact of depression on such routine activities as bathing, climbing stairs, dressing, socializing with friends, walking, and working. Its disabling effects were comparable to those of a serious heart condition and greater than those of most of the seven other medical conditions.[68] Only arthritis was judged to be more painful, and only serious heart conditions resulted in more days in bed.

An important and surprising finding of the study was the extent of the disability experienced by persons with depressive symptoms who did not meet the full criteria for a depressive disorder: these patients suffered from disability as severe as that of patients who did meet the full criteria.[68] The reasons for this unexpected finding are unclear; it may have been a result of the additive effect of chronic medical conditions. Nevertheless, because so little is known about the treatment of depressive symptoms independent of major depressive disorder, this finding is a major challenge to the health care system.

There have been few reports of studies of the economic costs of depression. The study of Stoudemire and colleagues[59] placed a lower bound on the costs of depression at $16.3 billion in 1986, and these authors suggest that a full economic burden calculation might produce high estimates. Harwood and coworkers[32] estimated the total costs of mental illness in 1980 to be $54.2 billion. It now appears that these values underestimated the actual costs. More precise estimates wait on additional assessments, such as that of the Medical Outcomes Study.

The potential for cost savings from more accurate psychiatric diagnosis and more appropriate treatment is suggested by growing understanding of the so-called "offset effect." An offset effect occurs when the provision of one type of service leads to a reduction in other types of services. A review by Mumford and colleagues[47] described 58 reports of reductions of medical services in conjunction with the provision of mental health services. This review established that outpatient psychiatric treatment reduced the overall costs of medical care, primarily through reduced utilization of inpatient medical services. Of particular importance was the finding that the effect was larger for persons over the age of 55 than for younger individuals.

Subsequent research has begun to define the parameters of importance. For example, the offset effect is particularly marked in the case of alcoholism[34,43] and is considerably weaker among persons of lower socioeconomic status.[43] One striking, well-controlled study (that of Levitan and Kornfeld[42]) showed that the introduction of a part-time psychiatrist into an orthopedic ward decreased the median duration of stay from 42 to 30 days among elderly patients who underwent surgical repair of the femur. In New York City at this time (1980), hospital costs averaged $200 per day, and the authors estimated that a reduction of this magnitude in length of stay resulted in savings of $55,200 over the six-month period while the cost of the psychiatrist was only $5,000. Given the costs of underdiagnosis of psychiatric disorders and the inadequacy of psychiatric treatment, introducing psychiatric programs into medical care of the elderly should realize major cost savings.

Four studies provide convincing evidence of the value of outpatient psychiatric treatment. McCaffree[44] demonstrated that cost reductions for custodial care more than compensated for increased costs of active intervention in the Washington State mental hospital system. In addition, Cassel and colleagues[13] and Endicott and coworkers[15] found that community-based psychiatric treatment was as effective, and less expensive, than hospital-based treatment. Finally, the Hu research group[35] showed that the costs of caring for an elderly demented person at home were no more than half the costs incurred in a nursing home.

SUICIDE

One type of cost specific to depression is suicide. Stoudemire[59] has estimated a total mortality cost of suicide resulting from depression at $4.2 billion, but the costs in human suffering are more difficult to estimate. Although official statistics show that suicide claims 30,000 lives in the United States each year,[60] this figure is almost certainly larger owing to underreporting. Underreporting of suicide probably affects older persons more strongly than younger ones (R. Butler, Mount Sinai Medical Center, personal communication, June 1989) because physicians and the families of the elderly may be likely to ascribe death to causes other than suicide out of sentiment and compassion.

More than half of all suicides occur in persons suffering from depression.[2] The increased risk of suicide among depressed persons of all ages is 30 times that of the non-affectively ill population; the lifetime risk of suicide of persons suffering from depression is 15

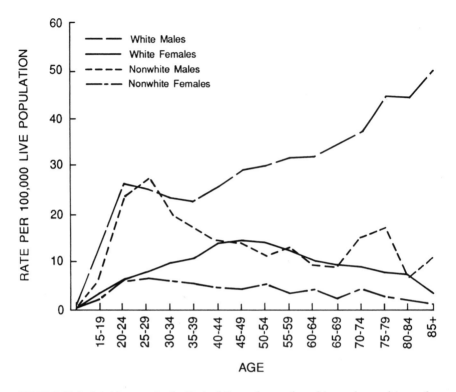

FIGURE 12-1 Suicide rates in the United States by age for white and nonwhite males and females. Source: National Center for Health Statistics, Mortality Statistics Branch, "Suicide Rates in the United States by Age, Sex, and Color, 1975."

percent.[31] Elderly depressed persons are at even higher risk than younger ones: 20 percent of all suicides occur in persons over the age of 65, and the rates are strikingly higher for elderly white men than for other groups (see Figure 12-1).[62]

These grim figures also have an optimistic side. Suicide is second only to lung cancer as a potentially preventable disorder, and there is usually considerable warning before a suicide attempt. Two-thirds of persons who take their lives have communicated their intent to at least one person, and most of them have consulted a physician hours to weeks before their suicide.[55] Consultation with suicidal patients often presents physicians with a golden intervention opportunity, as most patients will tell their physicians of their plans if they are asked. Preventing suicide, however, requires recognition of the problem, and the same factors that limit recognition of depression in the elderly (inadequate teaching and training of physicians in both psychiatry and geriatrics) also affect recognition of suicidal intent. An inexperienced physician may dismiss as perfectly understandable the depressive ruminations of elderly patients who have recently undergone losses. But, as Fawcett[17] maintains, "the presence of a reason for depression is not a good reason to ignore the presence of depression." Thus, the clinician would be well advised to follow the injunction of Robins[55] who asserts that the risk of suicide in elderly, depressed white men who express suicidal intent is so great that they should be hospitalized without delay.

The prevention of suicide requires not only better recognition of persons at risk but also improved mental health services, especially for the elderly. The benefits of improved mental health services in suicide prevention are indicated by the record of specialized centers for the treatment of affective disorders at which, even among the very high-risk populations in these centers, the suicide rate is negligible.[39]

REIMBURSEMENT

Reimbursement is a critical aspect of the management of depression, and control of depression could be greatly improved by changes in reimbursement schedules.[30] Seventy-five percent of hospital care for the elderly is provided by Medicare, with private insurance covering 8 percent of costs and 5 percent each being contributed by Medicaid, the Veterans Administration, and other governmental agencies. Nursing home care, on the other hand, is financed to a great extent (50 percent) by patients and their families. Outpatient care is financed by Medicare Part B, a voluntary individual insurance program. (The monthly premium in 1989 was $31.90, and the plan had an annual deductible of $75.)

In contrast to federal support of most medical care, federal support of psychiatric care is severely limited. Although there is no limit to the total number of days provided for surgical or medical diagnoses, coverage in psychiatric hospitals is limited to a lifetime total of 190 days. Medicare reimbursement for outpatient psychiatric treatment has been even more limited—with even more deleterious consequences. Only "acute care" can be reimbursed, and a copayment of 50 percent is required for mental health care, compared with 20 percent for other medical treatment. Medicaid provides some support for psychiatric services, but reimbursement remains far below prevailing fees in most states. Private insurance coverage of psychiatric disorders is also severely limited: only 53 percent of private policies cover inpatient mental illness expenses in the same way that they cover physical illness, and no more than 7 percent cover outpatient expenses in a manner similar to coverage of outpatient medical costs.[30] In November 1989, Congress took a large step toward removing discrimination in the treatment of psychiatric disorders by eliminating a long-standing limitation on the total annual payment for mental health services. The other limitations, however, persist.

Even attempts to improve coverage for psychiatric disorders may misfire. The Omnibus Budget Reconciliation Act (OBRA) of 1987 required that all patients applying for admission to nursing homes be screened for mental disorders. The goal of this regulation was to provide appropriate care for these patients, but the result has too often been the opposite—preventing access to nursing home care for patients found to be in need of "active psychiatric treatment."

These discriminatory reimbursement practices severely limit the use of psychiatric services in hospitals, nursing homes, and ambulatory settings. The inadequacy of psychiatric services in nursing homes is particularly egregious. Furthermore, current practices lead to a serious imbalance in the type of site at which services are rendered, with expensive inpatient treatment being favored over more economical outpatient services. The limitation of support for outpatient care of psychiatric disorders, with its potential for the cost savings conferred by avoidance of hospitalization, is particularly short-sighted. Such discrimination also reinforces the disinclination of primary care physicians to make psychiatric diagnoses and encourages their often fruitless treatment of depressive symptoms while ignoring the root disorder. Finally, inadequate reimbursement seriously limits the availability of psychiatrists skilled in geriatrics.

RESEARCH AND THE FUTURE

Research advances promise major improvements in treatment of depression in the elderly. Attempts to predict the future direction of such treatment, however, are fraught with difficulty because the most important developments in treatment are likely to occur not in targeted areas but from unanticipated consequences of basic research. The prospects of unanticipated consequences of research on depression are good, and they are getting better.

Studies of Alzheimer's disease have already established a genetic basis for some instances of that disorder and have begun to elucidate patterns of transmission. The rapid development of molecular genetics gives hope that one day the genetic basis of Alzheimer's disease will be understood and an effective therapy will be available. Another important research area is that of the newer imaging techniques, which provide extraordinary views of brain structure and function. These techniques range from computerized tomography that provides increasingly detailed pictures of brain structure to electrical assessment of brain physiology and fine-grained analyses of brain metabolism provided by positron emission tomography and magnetic resonance imaging. Finally, continuing progress in understanding the biochemistry of neurotransmitters and neuromodulators will inevitably pay dividends in improved diagnosis and treatment.

RECOMMENDATIONS

Services

Insurance Providers (Governmental and Private)

Despite the recent removal of the Medicare limitation on outpatient care, inadequate reimbursement for psychiatric care in both the public and private sectors contributes to the (mis)diagnosis of depression as physical illness and, as a consequence, inadequate treatment. *The committee's major service recommendation is the removal of discriminatory limitations of reimbursement for psychiatric care.* Removal of the Medicare cap should be accompanied by reduction of the 50 percent copayment required for "psychiatric" treatment to the 20 percent copayment now required for "medical" treatment.

Clinicians (Particularly Primary Care Physicians)

The following recommendations are directed toward clinicians whose practice includes the elderly.

1. New patients and, periodically, old patients should be screened for the presence of emotional disturbance (particularly depression), using, for example, either the Beck Depression Inventory[3] or the Geriatric Depression Scale,[71] and for the presence of related cognitive dysfunction using the Mini-Mental State Examination.[20]

2. Psychosocial and environmental stressors in the patient's life should be identified. Grief and bereavement are probably the most powerful external threats to emotional well-being but the clinician should assess all of the risk factors for depression noted earlier in this chapter.

3. The bereaved or grieving patient should be encouraged to establish at least one intimate, confiding relationship. The primary

care physician is ideally placed to assist in this effort, which may include mobilization of friends and relatives, referral to senior adult programs, and, if necessary, referral for supportive psychotherapy during the period of acute loss.

4. The person about to retire should be encouraged to plan carefully. Social workers, occupational therapists, and career counselors may be quite helpful in locating skilled volunteer work, part-time employment, and structured recreational activities.

5. The extent of loss in the functionally impaired patient should be assessed. Auditory and visual function should be evaluated and corrected to the extent possible with hearing aids and glasses; cataracts and glaucoma should be treated. Physical and occupational therapies can be helpful in compensating at least partially for disability resulting from medical, orthopedic, and neurologic disorders.

Persons Over the Age of 50

Elderly individuals should recognize that depression and cognitive dysfunction are pathological and not a normal result of the aging process. They should be encouraged to seek out and participate in activities designed to prevent withdrawal and social isolation. The essential ingredient of these activities is that they be meaningful.

Research

1. *The committee's major recommendation in this area is to increase financial support for research on depression in the elderly.* This support should be directed to two agencies: the Program on Mental Health of the Aging in the National Institute of Mental Health (its $47 million research budget on the aging currently funds only 25 percent of the grants that are approved on the basis of scientific merit) and the National Institute on Aging, which should pursue research on depression secondary to physical illness and medication.

2. Diagnostic criteria for depression in the elderly and instruments (including structured interviews) for their application should be developed and assessed. These instruments should then be used to determine the prevalence, incidence, costs, and symptom severity of depression in elderly populations, including the institutionalized, the medically ill, and community samples stratified according to socioeconomic status.

3. A practicable case-finding package (that includes depression and dysphoria) should be developed for high-risk groups. It should be used to extend prevalence and cost studies to such high-risk groups

as persons over the age of 85, elderly persons living alone, persons who have recently changed their dwelling, widows and widowers, and persons who have recently been discharged from the hospital.[65]

4. Studies should be conducted to compare treatment costs for depressed elderly persons in nursing homes with costs for matched, depressed elderly persons in the community.

5. Criteria should be developed for evaluation and treatment of older adults with psychiatric disorders to improve the quality of care and encourage third parties to assume broader coverage of these disorders.

6. Treatment strategies directed toward nonresponse, recurrence, and relapse should be pursued. Studies should include an examination of innovative, nontraditional treatments and the development of protocols for continuation of treatment and maintenance following treatment.

7. Small-scale pilot studies of intervention efficiency should be carried out, using cost-effectiveness analyses to evaluate resource utilization, economic costs, and utility (perceived value).

8. The efficacy and safety of electroconvulsive therapy should be assessed and the indications for its use in the elderly determined.

9. Studies should be conducted on innovative psychosocial measures (particularly in the community) designed to restore and preserve morale during stressful periods such as bereavement.

10. The pharmaceutical industry should conduct controlled trials of antidepressants in the elderly to determine their efficacy, safety, and indications.

Education

The committee's major recommendation regarding education is to develop programs to train physicians to detect and treat mental disorders, including depression, in the elderly. In addition, older persons should be informed that depression is an illness that can be successfully treated and that it may occur in the absence of a depressive mood. Information is best conveyed in settings such as senior centers and before the onset of symptoms.

REFERENCES

1. American Institute for Research. Senior actualization and growth explorations: A geriatric human potential program. Innovations 1977; 4:11-18.
2. Barraclough, B., Bunch, J., Nelson, B., and Sainsbury, P. A hundred cases of suicide: Clinical observations. British Journal of Psychiatry 1974; 125:355-373.

3. Beck, A. T., Ward, C. H., Mendelson, M., et al. An inventory for measuring depression. Archives of General Psychiatry 1961; C:561-571.

4. Berkman, L. F., Berkman, C. S., Casl, S., Freeman, D. H., Leo, L., et al. Depressive symptoms in relation to physical health and functioning in the elderly. American Journal of Epidemiology 1986; 124:372-388.

5. Blazer, D. G., Hughes, D., and George, L. K. The epidemiology of depression in an elderly community population. The Gerontologist 1987; 27:281-287.

6. Blazer, D. G. Depression in Late Life. St. Louis: C. V. Mosby, 1982.

7. Blazer, D. G. The epidemiology of late life depression and dementia: A comparative study. In: A. Tasman (ed.), The Annual Review of Psychiatry, vol. 9. Washington, D.C.: American Psychiatric Press, 1990, pp. 210-219.

8. Blazer, D. G., and Maddox, G. Using epidemiology survey data to plan geriatric mental health services. Hospital and Community Psychiatry 1982; 33:42-45.

9. Blazer, D. G., and Williams, C. D. Epidemiology of dysphoria and depression in an elderly population. American Journal of Psychiatry 1980; 137:439-444.

10. Borson, S., Barnes, R. A., Kukull, W. A., Okimoto, J. T., Veith, R. C., et al. Symptomatic depression in elderly medical outpatients. I. Prevalence, demography and health service utilization. Journal of the American Geriatrics Society 1986; 34:341-347.

11. Busse, E. W., and Simpson, D. Depression and antidepressants and the elderly. Journal of Clinical Psychiatry 1983; 44(5):35-39.

12. Butler, R. N., and Lewis, M. I. Love and Sex After Sixty. New York: Harper & Row, 1988.

13. Cassel, W. A., Smith, C. M., Grunberg, F., Boan, J. A., and Thomas, R. F. Comparing costs of hospital and community care. Hospital and Community Psychiatry 1972; 23:197-200.

14. Diehr, P., Williams, S. J., Martin, D. P., and Price, K. Ambulatory health services utilization in three provider plans. Medical Care 1984; 22:1-13.

15. Endicott, J., Herz, M. I., and Gibbon, M. Brief vs. standard hospitalization: The differential costs. American Journal of Psychiatry 1978; 135:707-712.

16. Ernst, P., Badash, D., Beran, B., et al. Incidence of mental illness in the aged: Unmasking the effects of diagnosis of chronic brain syndrome. Journal of the American Geriatrics Society 1977; 8:371-375.

17. Fawcett, J. Suicidal depression and physical illness. Journal of the American Medical Association 1972; 219:1303-1306.

18. Fogel, B. S. Electroconvulsive therapy in the elderly: A clinical research agenda. International Journal of Geriatric Psychiatry 1988; 3:181-190.

19. Fogel, B. S., and Fretwell, M. Reclassification of depression among the medically ill elderly. Journal of the American Geriatrics Society 1985; 33:446-448.

20. Folstein, M. F., Folstein, S. E., and McHugh, P. R. "Mini-mental state": A practical method for grading the cognitive state of patients for the clinician. Journal of Psychiatric Research 1975; 12:189-198.

21. Ford, D. E., and Kamerow, D. B. Epidemiologic study of sleep disturbances and psychiatric disorders. Journal of the American Medical Society 1989; 262:1479-1484.

22. Fowles, D. G. A Profile of Older Americans, 1987. Washington, D.C.: American Association of Retired Persons, 1988.

23. Gask, L., Goldberg, D., Lesser, A. L., and Millar, T. Improving the psychiatric skills of the general practice trainee: An evaluation of a group training course. Medical Education 1988; 22(2):732-738.

24. Georgotas, A., McCue, R. E., Hapworth, W., Friedman, E., Kim, O. M., Welkowitz, J., Chang, I., and Cooper, T. B. Comparative efficacy and safety of MAOIs versus TCAs in treating depression in the elderly. Biological Psychiatry 1986; 21:1155-1166.

25. German, P. S., Shapiro, S., Skinner, E. A., Von Korff, M., Klein, L. E., Turner, R. W., Teitelbaum, M. L., Burke, J., and Burns, B. J. Detection and management of mental health problems of older patients by primary care providers. Journal of the American Medical Association 1987; 257:489-493.

26. Goldman, H., Feder, J., and Scanlon, W. Chronic mental patients in nursing homes: Reexamining data from the National Nursing Home Study. Hospital and Community Psychiatry 1986; 37:269-272.

27. Goodwin, F. K. Drug treatment of affective disorders: General principles. In: M. E. Jarvik, (ed.), Psychopharmacology in the Practice of Medicine. New York: Appleton-Century-Crofts, 1976, pp. 241-253.

28. Gottlieb, G. L. Optimizing mental function of the elderly. In: R. Lavizzo-Mourey, S. C. Day, D. Diserens, and J. A. Grisso, Practicing Prevention for the Elderly. Philadelphia: Hanley and Bellfus, Inc., 1988, pp. 153-166.

29. Gottlieb, G. L. Cost implications of depression in older adults. International Journal of Geriatric Psychiatry 1988; 3:191-200.

30. Gottlieb, G. L. Financial issues affecting geriatric psychiatric care. In: L. Lazarus, L. Jarvik, et al. (eds.), Essentials of Geriatric Psychiatry. New York: Springer, 1988, pp. 230-248.

31. Guze, S., and Robins, E. Suicide and primary affective disorders. British Journal of Psychiatry 1970; 117:437-438.

32. Harwood, H. J., Napolitano, D. M., Kristiansen, P. L., and Collins, J. J. Economic costs to society of alcohol and drug abuse and mental illness: 1980. Research Triangle Park, N.C.: Research Triangle Institute, 1984.

33. Harwood, H. J., and Turner, H. B. Social dimensions of mental illness among rural elderly populations. International Journal of Aging and Human Development 1988; 26(3):169-190.

34. Holder, H. D. Alcoholism treatment and potential cost saving. Medical Care 1987; 25:52-71.

35. Hu, T., Huang, L., and Cartwright, W. S. Evaluation of the costs of caring for senile demented elderly: A pilot study. Gerontologist 1986; 26:158-163.

36. Jacobson, A. Melancholy in the 20th century: Causes and prevention. Journal of Psychiatric Nursing and Mental Health Services 1980; 18:11-21.

37. Jarvik, L. F., and Gerson, S. Outcome of drug treatment in depressed patients over the age of 50. In: C. A. Shamoian (ed.), Treatment of Affective Disorders in the Elderly. Washington, D.C.: American Psychiatric Press, Inc., 1985, pp. 29-36.

38. Kemp, B. J., Staples, F., and Lopez-Acqueres, W. Epidemiology of depression and dysphoria in an elderly Hispanic population. Journal of the American Geriatrics Society 1987; 35:920-926.

39. Khuri, K., and Akiskal, H. S. Suicide prevention: The necessity of treating contributing psychiatric disorders. Psychiatric Clinics of North America 1983; 6:193-207.

40. Koenig, H. G., Meador, K. G., Cohen, H. J., and Blazer, D. G. Depression in elderly hospitalized patients with medical illness. Archives of Gerontological Medicine 1988; 148:1929-1936.

41. Lehman, H. E. Affective disorders in the aged. Psychiatric Clinics of North America 1982; 5:27-44.

42. Levitan, S. J., and Kornfeld, D. S. Clinical and cost benefits of liaison psychiatry. American Journal of Psychiatry 1981; 138(6):790-793.

43. Luckey, J. W. Cost savings of alcohol treatment. Alcohol, Health and Research World 1987; 12(1):8-15.
44. McCaffree, K. M. The cost of mental health care under changing treatment methods. American Journal of Public Health 1966; 556:1013-1025.
45. Meyers, B. S., Greenberg, R., and Mei-Tal, V. Delusional depression in the elderly. In: C. A. Shamoian (ed.), Treatment of Affective Disorders in the Elderly. Washington, D.C.: American Psychiatric Press, 1985, pp. 17-28.
46. Munoz, R. F., Glish, M., Soo-Hoo, T., and Robertson, J. The San Francisco mood survey project: Preliminary work toward the prevention of depression. American Journal of Community Psychology 1982; 10:317-329.
47. Mumford, E., Schlesinger, H. J., Glass, G. V., et al. A new look at evidence about reduced cost of medical utilization following mental health treatment. American Journal of Psychiatry 1984; 141:1145-1158.
48. Murrell, S. A., Himmelfarb, S., and Wright, K. Prevalence of depression and its correlates in older adults. American Journal of Epidemiology 1983; 2(117):173.
49. Myers, J. K., Weissman, M. M., Tischler, G. L., et al. Six month prevalence of psychiatric disorders in three communities. Archives of General Psychiatry 1984; 41:959-967.
50. Nielsson, L. V., and Persson, G. Prevalence of mental disorders in an urban sample examined at 70, 75 and 79 years of age. Acta Psychiatrica Scandinavica 1984; 69:519-527.
51. Parmelee, P. A., Katz, I. R., and Lawton, M. P. Depression among institutionalized aged. Assessment and prevalence estimation. Journal of Gerontology: Medical Sciences 1989; 44:1722-1729.
52. Raphael, B. Preventive intervention with the recently bereaved. Archives of General Psychiatry 1977; 34:1450-1454.
53. Reifler, B. V., Larson, E., and Hanley, R. Coexistence of cognitive impairment and depression in geriatric outpatients. American Journal of Psychiatry 1982; 139:623-626.
54. Reynolds, C. F., Kupfer, D. J., Taska, L. S., Hoch, C. C., et al. EEG sleep in elderly depressed, demented, and healthy subjects. Society of Biological Psychiatry 1985: 20:431-442.
55. Robins, E. Suicide. In: H. Kaplan and B. J. Sadock (eds.), Comprehensive Textbook of Psychiatry, 4th ed., vol. 2. Baltimore, Md.: Williams & Wilkins, 1985, p. 1313.
56. Robins, E., Gasner, S., Kayes, J., et al. The communication of suicidal intent: A study of 134 consecutive cases of successful (completed) suicide. American Journal of Psychiatry 1959; 115:724-733.
57. Smyer, M. A., Davies, B. W., and Cohn, M. A prevention approach to critical life events of the elderly. Journal of Primary Prevention 1982; 2:195-204.
58. Stewart, A. L., Greenfield, S., Hays, R. D., Wells, K., Rogers, W. H., Berry, S. D., McGlynn, E. A., and Ware, J. E., Jr. Functional status and well-being of patients with chronic conditions: Results from the Medical Outcomes Study. Journal of the American Medical Association 1989; 262:907-913.
59. Stoudemire, A., Frank, R., Hedemark, N., Kamlet, M., and Blazer, D. The economic burden of depression. General Hospital Psychiatry 1986; 8:387-394.
60. U.S. Bureau of the Census. Statistical Abstract of the United States, 1989 (109th ed.). Deaths and Death Rates, by Selected Causes: 1970-1986 (Table No. 117). Washington, D.C., 1989.
61. Veith, R. C. Cardiovascular effects of the antidepressants: Treating the elderly patient. In: C. A. Shamoian (ed.), Treatment of Affective Disorders

in the Elderly. Washington, D.C.: American Psychiatric Press, 1985, pp. 37-50.

62. Vital Statistics of the United States. Suicide rates in the United States by age, sex and color, 1975. Washington, D.C.: Mortality Statistics Branch, National Center for Health Statistics.

63. Wasylenki, D. Depression in the elderly. Canadian Medical Association Journal 1980; 122:525-532.

64. Waxman, H. M., and Carner, E. A. Physicians' recognition, diagnosis and treatment of mental disorder in elderly medical patients. Gerontologist 1984; 24:593-597.

65. Waxman, H. M., Carner, E. A., and Klein, M. Underutilization of mental health professionals by community elderly. Gerontologist 1984; 24:23-30.

66. Weiner, R. D. Does electroconvulsive therapy cause brain damage? Behavioral and Brain Sciences 1984; 7:1-53.

67. Weissman, M. M., Meyers, J. K., Tischler, G. L., Holzer, C. E., Leaf, P. J., et al. Psychiatric disorders (DSM-III) and cognitive impairment among the elderly in a U.S. urban community. Acta Psychiatrica Scandinavica 1985; 71:366-379.

68. Wells, K. S., Stewart, A. L., Hays, R. D., Burman, M. A., Rogers, W. H., Daniels, M., Berry, A. D., Greenfield, S., and Ware, J. E., Jr. The functioning and well-being of depressed patients: Results from the Medical Outcomes Study. Journal of the American Medical Association 1989; 262:914-919.

69. Williamson, J. Screening, surveillance and case-finding. In: T. Arie (ed.), Health Care of the Elderly. London: Croom Helm, 1981.

70. Wragg, R. E., and Jeste, D. V. Overview of depression and psychosis in Alzheimer's disease. American Journal of Psychiatry 1989; 146:577-587.

71. Yesavage, J. A., Brink, T. L., Rose, T. L., et al. Development and validation of a geriatric depression screening scale: A preliminary report. Journal of Psychiatric Research 1983; 17:37-49.

13
Physical Inactivity

───

The problem of physical inactivity, especially among the elderly, needs greater attention from the service and research communities. Recognition of the importance of addressing this issue is apparent in the work of several government agencies. For example, the Public Health Service's (PHS) health objectives for the nation for 1990 called for 60 percent of adults to participate in regular, vigorous exercise;[12] the health objectives for the year 2000 identify the need to understand the determinants of physical activity and exercise. A workshop conducted by the Centers for Disease Control in 1984 on the epidemiology and public health aspects of physical activity and exercise underscored the importance of physical activity and pointed out the difficulties involved in its measurement.[28]

The term *physical activity*, defined as "any bodily movement produced by skeletal muscles that results in energy expenditure," has been used interchangeably with *exercise* and *physical fitness*.[9] However, exercise is a subcategory of physical activity in that exercise is planned, structured, repetitive, and purposive (i.e., designed to move individuals toward physical fitness). Physical fitness on the other hand, is "a set of attributes that people have or achieve."[9] The three terms can be conceived as a hierarchy with fitness dependent on exercise and exercise requiring physical activity or the ability to move. The quantitative requirements of motion and exercise necessary to promote health and prevent disability as people age are the focus of this chapter.

Physical inactivity, which has generally been studied as a precursor or an outcome of disease and disability, is the central focus of this review. The general perspective of this chapter is informed by two fundamental assumptions. First, for most persons 50 years of age and older, increasing age is not a cause of physical inactivity.[13] As noted by Berger,[1] current research, especially by Smith,[40] suggests that 50 percent of the decline frequently attributed to physiological aging is, in reality, disuse atrophy resulting from inactivity in an industrialized world. Second, the ability to remain physically active underpins the ability to perform the activities of daily living.

This chapter considers physical activity separately from disease and disability. Research on the activities of daily living has been most closely associated with measuring detriments to the performance of specific, essential physical activities, caused by disease and disability; consequently, a discussion of such research falls outside the focus of this chapter. Therapeutic exercise prescribed for a specific disability or injury also will not be addressed in this chapter. Rather, what is known of the benefits of physical activity in general and how such activity can be encouraged and maintained during the "second 50" will guide the discussion that follows.

BURDEN

Prevalence

One measure of physical inactivity is sedentariness, which is defined as either no physical activity or physical activity less than three times per week and/or physical activity of less than 20 minutes per occasion.[27] The Centers for Disease Control reported the prevalence of a sedentary lifestyle in selected states using data from its Behavioral Risk Factor Surveillance System. The results of a 1985 telephone survey of 25,221 respondents were analyzed, and approximately 55 percent of the respondents were classified as sedentary. Being sedentary was more common among women than men and increased with age (Figure 13-1).

To estimate the percentage of individuals in the United States who maintained appropriate levels of physical activity as specified by the 1990 PHS objectives, Caspersen and colleagues analyzed data from the National Health Interview Survey conducted in 1985. They developed detailed scoring procedures using intensity codes for each activity and determined that almost one-third of the population between the ages of 45 and 64 and close to half of the over-65 age group, were sedentary. Table 13-1 shows their data for leisure-time

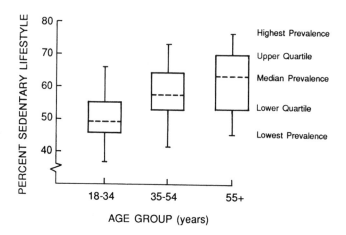

FIGURE 13-1 Box-plot summaries of the age-specific distribution of sedentary lifestyle prevalence from 22 states participating in the 1985 Behavioral Risk Factor Surveillance System. Source: "Leads from the MMWR: Sex-, Age-, and Region-specific Prevalence of Sedentary Lifestyle in Selected States in 1985—The Behavioral Risk Factor Surveillance System," *Journal of the American Medical Association*, Vol. 257, p. 2271, 1987.

TABLE 13-1 Leisure-time Physical Activity (percentage) by Sex and Age as Reported in the 1985 National Health Interview Survey

Characteristic	Sedentary	Irregularly Active	Regularly Active But Inappropriate Activity	Appropriate Activity
Sex				
Men	24.8	30.9	36.2	8.1
Women	30.2	31.3	31.5	7.0
Age (years)				
18–29	18.3	30.1	41.5	10.1
30–44	24.2	34.5	33.7	7.7
45–64	32.7	31.9	30.8	4.7
65 +	42.6	25.0	24.9	7.5

SOURCE: Adapted from C. J. Caspersen, G. M. Christenson, and R. A. Pollard, "Status of the 1990 Physical Fitness and Exercise Objectives—Evidence from NHIS," *Public Health Reports*, Vol. 101, pp. 587-592, 1986.

physical activity by sex and age. In his review of physical activity, Blair[2] points out that there has been a decline in the prevalence of sedentariness from approximately 40 percent in the early 1970s to 27 percent in 1985 (Figure 13-2); however, unclear definitions of physical activity and a variety of measurement techniques make it difficult to quantify changes in physical activity habits.

Yet despite the apparent decrease in sedentariness over the years, the majority of the U.S. adult population are not vigorously active. In fact, less than half of the adult population engage in regular physical activity. Four studies show the decline in physical activity that occurs as people age from 20 or 30 to 80 years of age.[2]

1. Activity limitations owing to chronic health problems were reported in the 1982 National Health Interview Survey. The data indicate that the number of reported activity limitations begins to increase markedly some time after age 44. Activity limitations were reported by 23.9 percent of the population aged 45 to 64 years of age and 45.7 percent of the population over age 65.[44]

2. In data drawn from two national probability samples of blacks (the National Survey of Black Americans and the Three-Generation Black Family Study), almost 50 percent of those aged 65 to 74 (N = 472) reported limitations in physical functioning. The percentage exceeds 50 percent in the 80 and older group (Table 13-2).[18]

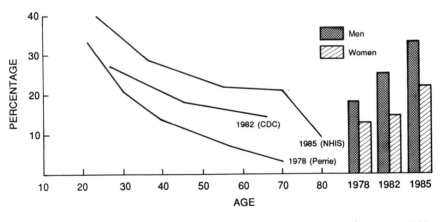

FIGURE 13-2 Percentage of U.S. adult population who are vigorously active, 1978-1985 (>12.6kJ [(3 kcal)] · kg⁻¹ · day⁻¹ of leisure-time activity). Source: T. Stephans, "Secular Trends in Physical Activity: Fitness Boom or Bust?" *Research Quarterly for Exercise Sport*, Vol. 58, pp. 94-105, 1987. Reprinted by permission of the American Alliance for Health, Physical Education, Recreation, and Dance, 1990 Association Drive, Reston, Virginia 22091.

TABLE 13-2 Physical Health and Functioning of the Black Elderly
(percentage) Comparing the Young, Middle-aged, and Very Old
(N = 734)

Physical Functioning	Age Groups		
	65–74 (N = 472)	75–79 (N = 142)	80 and older (N = 130)
Number of problems with activities of daily living (ADL)			
None[a]	42.2	38.8	23.8
1-2[b]	36.6	35.0	40.0
3-7[c]	21.1	26.3	36.3
Extent of physical or functional limitation			
Not limited at all or limited very little	50.9	53.5	40.8
Limited some	23.2	21.8	24.6
Limited "a great deal"	26.0	24.6	34.6

[a]Three-generation telephone respondents were excluded from the percentage base.
[b]Sources on the Overall Health Status Index from 1–13 (high scores = worse health).
[c]Cross-section respondents excluded from percentage base.

SOURCE: Adapted from R. C. Gibson and J. Jackson, "The Health, Physical
Functioning, and Informal Supports of the Black Elderly," Vol. 65, Suppl., p. 2,
Milbank Quarterly, 1987.

3. In the Harvard Alumni Study,[31] the most active men in the
two oldest age groups (60 to 69 and 70 to 84) had about one-half the
risk of dying prematurely as that for the least active men. (Figure 13-
3 shows the age-specific death rates over a 16-year follow-up period.)
4. Numerous reports from the Alameda County Study[24] show all-
cause mortality to be significantly and positively associated with
smoking, poor sleep habits, physical inactivity, relative overweight,
immoderate alcohol intake, not eating breakfast, and regular snack-
ing. The data also show a relative risk of 1.38 for all-cause mortality
in sedentary versus physically active individuals in the 60 to 69 age
group and a risk of 1.37 in the 70 and older group.

Impairment, Disability, and Handicap

Most of the literature concerned with the elderly does not use
the World Health Organization's (WHO) classification for the consequences of disease[46] (see Chapter 2) to describe the various burdens
experienced by individuals who are physically inactive. The obser-

vations of a number of authors, however, are roughly analogous to the three descriptive categories (i.e., impairments, disabilities, and handicaps) used in that classification system. Therefore, the discussion below is organized around these categories.

The ability of skeletal muscle to perform aerobically for sustained periods of time is influenced by two primary factors: the delivery of oxygen by the cardiovascular system and oxygen consumption by mitochondria in the tissue. Reductions in the oxidative capacity of tissue and reduced oxygen delivery, which often accompany the aging process, support the proposal that aging muscle has impaired ability.[7] Yet the precise causes of muscle impairment in the elderly are uncertain.[7] Muscle power and strength increase until the third decade; they then plateau and begin to decline in the middle years. With advanced age and senescence, further reductions have been observed. Cross-sectional research using muscle biopsies of healthy older adults indicates that impairments can be attributed to reduced muscle mass as a result, primarily, of a loss of muscle fiber. There are, however, other factors that need further study, including muscle fiber area and changes with age in the ratio of Type I and Type II muscle. Longitudinal studies and more comprehensive

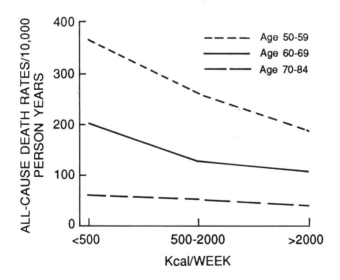

FIGURE 13-3 Age-specific death rates from all causes in Harvard Alumni Study over 16 years of follow-up, according to physical activity levels in kilocalories per week. Source: Adapted from R. S. Paffenberger, R. T. Hyde, A. L. Wing, and C. C. Hsieh, "Physical Activity, All-Cause Mortality and Longevity of College Alumni," *New England Journal of Medicine*, Vol. 314, pp. 605-613, 1986.

biopsy techniques (with and among muscles) are needed. Decrements in physical performance are also accounted for by structural and metabolic changes in aging muscle, as well as decreased impulse conduction velocity in the aging nervous system.

The causal link between physical work capacity and physical activity is much stronger.[3] Physical work capacity (PWC) is important for functional capability as it relates to routine household, occupational, and recreational tasks. The best single indicator of physical work capacity is the maximal oxygen uptake (VO_2max).[40] Determinants of the VO_2max are the cardiac output (itself determined by heart rate, which decreases with age, and stroke volume, which may or may not decrease with age), which is a central adjustment of the body to exercise; arteriovenous oxygen difference, which is a peripheral adjustment to exercise; and pulmonary function, which is measured by the maximum ventilation in the lungs.

The prevention of disability and handicaps through physical fitness can be crucial in the elderly. For the general population, the loss of functional capacity that accompanies low levels of physical fitness can be disabling: it is at the least an inconvenience and may diminish an individual's quality of life. The consequences for the elderly may be even more serious, however; in addition to the general disabilities experienced by the sedentary, the physically unfit elderly may lose the capacity for independent living.[2]

Impaired muscle becomes tired sooner than healthy muscle. Therefore, a given work rate will require a greater percentage of maximal aerobic power in sedentary older persons. This, in turn, contributes to a greater rate of fatigue.[7] As Blair[2] points out, persons with very low maximal aerobic power may have difficulty providing the energy expenditure necessary for required activities; they may be able to meet day-to-day demands but become exhausted if additional exertion is needed. Shephard[36] has postulated that the minimal level of aerobic power necessary for independent living is a VO_2max of 15 to 16 mL of oxygen per kilogram of body weight per minute, and Blair[2] has claimed that individuals who have power levels lower than this threshold cannot care for themselves and may have to be institutionalized. Under the World Health Organization (WHO) classification system, this level of difficulty is considered a handicap.[46]

Physical inactivity has also been linked to increased risk for several diseases. In a study of 2,950 men with colon cancer listed in a population-based registry in Los Angeles, Garabrant and coworkers[16] rated the occupational physical activity of the participants. Men in sedentary jobs (e.g., accountants, social workers, bus drivers) had a colon cancer risk that was 1.6 times higher than those with highly active jobs (e.g., gardeners, mail carriers). A similar finding resulted from a 19-year follow-up study of 1.1 million men in Sweden.[17] The Swedish men in sedentary jobs had a colon cancer risk that was 1 to 3 times that of their active peers. Coronary artery disease has also been linked to physical inactivity.[33]

If inactivity can increase the risk for disease, then intuitively, physical activity should reduce those risks. However, the evidence for such benefits is preliminary. It has been suggested that physical activity lowers the risk for some cancers, although much work remains to be done before this benefit is established.[2]

There are 5.8 million known diabetics among the civilian noninstitutionalized population of the United States,[29] and diabetes is known to cause significant disability. Approximately half of all diabetics report some activity limitation.[2] Although the value of exercise in metabolic control in insulin-dependent diabetics is not established, several studies conclude that regular exercise increases peripheral insulin sensitivity.[2] In one study a lower prevalence of diabetes was found in female athletes compared with nonathletic classmates.[15] The age-adjusted relative risk for diabetes in that study was 2.24 for the nonathletes.

PREVENTABILITY OF BURDEN: AVAILABILITY AND EFFECTIVENESS OF INTERVENTIONS

If physical inactivity in aging can be termed the "problem" or diagnosis with which this chapter is concerned, then "activation" must become the goal of "treatment." Rather than focusing on the prevention of specific diseases or disabilities, the "prescription" is aimed at increasing active life expectancy and the maintenance of independence.[25] To achieve this goal the means of initiating and maintaining physical activities for the elderly must be explored. There is great potential for increased physical activity among the elderly. Studies indicate that no more than 20 percent, and possibly less than 10 percent, of adult North Americans get optimal amounts of physical activity, and 40 to 50 percent are nearly totally sedentary. Unfortunately, the determinants of exercise in the elderly remain largely unexplored by empirical research,[13] despite the myriad studies and articles about the positive effects of physical activity on both physical and mental health. Scientific knowledge of physical activity determinants is almost exclusively restricted to persons aged 18 to 64.[13] This information is certainly useful, but research to inform efforts to initiate exercise programs among the elderly is necessary.

It is possible, however, to set intelligent general exercise program goals based on accumulated experience. The following programs, organized by target, provide basic guidelines from which to determine specific goals in a wide range of settings.

Individuals

Exercise programs recommended for older individuals have been based on programs designed for the general adult population. Healthy adults have been advised by the American College of Sports Medicine (as reported by Pollock[32]) to train three to five days a week, with an intensity of 50 to 80 percent VO_2max or maximum heart rate (HRmax) reserve. Training should be from 20 to 60 minutes (the lower the intensity, the greater the duration); longer lasting, lower intensity programs are recommended for nonathletic adults. Exercise should use large muscle groups in continuous motion (as in jogging and rhythmic aerobics) and should include resistance training of moderate intensity that is nevertheless sufficient to develop and maintain fat-free weight and bone integrity.

The great variations in fitness levels among the elderly, however, make certain precautions necessary before exercise programs are initiated: programs often need to be modified to suit the particular needs and abilities of the participants. Writing for the American College of Sports Medicine, Heath recommends that individuals who participate in supervised exercise programs complete a brief medical history and risk factor questionnaire.[22] Diagnostic tolerance testing is recommended for participants with diabetes mellitus or coronary heart disease and for individuals known to be at risk for these diseases. For vigorous programs, the college advises exercise leaders to ensure that program applicants have had a physical examination by a physician within the two years previous to program initiation.[22]

Adaptations of exercise programs may vary considerably. In the old-old population (usually 75 years of age and older), emphasis often is placed on maintaining flexibility, strength, coordination, and balance rather than on aerobic training. However, moderate aerobic training may be included in programs for the young-old.[45] Programs for the elderly are likely to require exercises of lower intensity and impact and to approach their most strenuous moments more gradually than programs designed for the general adult population.[32] As a result, the diminished intensity of these exercises may call for increased frequency. The American College of Sports Medicine's recommended adaptations for older persons include exercising between five and seven days a week for periods of 20 to 40 minutes.[22] Given the vast differences among elderly individuals and the dearth of research on exercises for the elderly, however, the recommendation to individualize programs remains prudent.

Physicians should recommend exercise training for their elderly patients and should provide information regarding the physiologic and psychological benefits of exercise.[24] The committee's message to physicians echoes the advice to program designers: individualize the program prescribed. Physicians should make recommendations to their patients with regard to intensity, duration, frequency, and type of exercise. They may also need to emphasize the importance of non-weight-bearing activities, such as cycling, swimming, and chair and floor exercises, for frail individuals. In addition, because intense stretching exercises and calisthenics may present difficulties for patients with knee and hip mobility problems or for those with degenerative joint changes,[22] these activities should not be part of an exercise program for patients with such problems. Finally, because women and individuals from lower socioeconomic classes and minorities are less inclined to adopt rigorous exercise programs,[2] physicians and policymakers should take steps to encourage their participation.

Although interventions to increase physical activity among persons 65 or older have received study,[13] supervised exercise has been shown to increase peak VO_2[11,35] and physical activity interventions offer the promise of increasing active life expectancy.[6] However, the actual activity is dependent on the individual to carry it out. Variables that affect whether individuals engage in exercise (either supervised or spontaneous) were summarized by Dishman and colleagues[14] (Table 13-3). The table summarizes both cross-sectional and correlational, as well as experimental, findings, but the authors warn that there is "little standardization in defining and assessing determinants and physical activity." When planning supervised activities, it is important to consider individual behavioral differences. Unfortunately, those who may benefit the most from an exercise regimen seem most resistant to adopting or maintaining one. Interventions aimed at personal change, therefore, may be more effective if they help improve an individual's self-image than if they focus exclusively on knowledge of the health benefits of physical activity and exercise.[14]

At present, research needs for studies of the determinants of exercise in the elderly can only be stated as abstract goals. It therefore follows that the ability to perform detailed analytic evaluations of the effectiveness of these interventions cannot compare with other fields in which there is greater confidence in definitions and standards. Nevertheless, the abstract and perhaps subjective goals that are currently available provide an initial direction necessary for development.

TABLE 13-3 Summary of Variables that May Determine the
Probability of Exercise

Determinant	Changes in Probability	
	Supervised program	Spontaneous program
Personal characteristics		
Past program participation	++	
Past extra-program activity	+	
School athletics, 1 sport	+	0
School athletics, > 1 sport		+
Blue-collar occupation	—	*
Smoking	—	
Overweight	—	
Type A behavior	*	
High risk for coronary heart disease	++	
Health, exercise knowledge	*	0
Attitudes	0	+
Enjoyment of activity	+	
Perceived health	++	
Mood disturbance	—	—
Education	+	++
Age	00	*
Expectation of personal health benefit	+	
Self-efficacy for exercise		+
Intention to adhere	0	0
Perceived physical competence	00	
Self-motivation	++	0
Evaluating costs and benefits	+	
Behavioral skills	++	
Environmental characteristics		
Spouse support	++	+
Perceived available time	++	+
Access to facilities	++	0
Disruptions in routine	—	
Social reinforcement (staff, exercise partner)	+	
Family influences		++
Peer influence		++
Physical influences		+
Cost		0
Medical screening	*	
Climate	*	
Incentives	+	
Activity characteristics		
Activity intensity	00	*
Perceived discomfort	—	*

Note: ++ = repeatedly documented increased probability; + = weak or mixed
documentation of increased probability; 00 = repeatedly documented that there is no
change in probability; 0 = weak or mixed documentation of no change in probability;
* = weak or mixed documentation of decreased probability; — = repeatedly documented
decreased probability. Blank indicates no data.

SOURCE: R. K. Dishman, J. F. Sallis, and D. R. Orenstein, "The Determinants of
Physical Activity and Exercise," *Public Health Reports*, Vol. 100, No. 2, p. 161, 1985.

Researchers have only begun to probe the factors that contribute to an individual's maintenance of physical activity. Those most likely to engage in regular exercise tend to be well-educated and self-motivated, with "the behavioral skills to plan an exercise program and prepare for relapses."[14] Beyond this, little is known, although Dishman and colleagues[14] have postulated that successful programs address behavioral and environmental factors affecting exercise maintenance. These programs encourage self-regulation of exercise as well as preparation for relapse, and they include tangible reinforcements of activity. Simply encouraging elderly persons to exercise because the evidence suggests it will be to their benefit is not sufficient in most cases. Programs should prompt, reinforce, and remove the barriers to maintaining physical activity.[13]

The Community

There have been relatively few attempts to promote physical activity at the community level. Early community intervention studies in California and Finland did not give major emphasis to physical activity and did not report improvements in physical activity participation. The second generation of community studies appears to place more emphasis on a reduction in sedentary living habits.

One study evaluated the effectiveness of a public health intervention for increasing stair use at a commuter train station (Figure 13-4). The investigators found overall diminution in the targeted behavior following withdrawal of the intervention.[6] Those planning community-based programs are advised to strongly encourage senior participants to consult with a physician before starting such a program, and to provide options to accommodate the physical and behavioral difficulties elderly individuals sometimes experience.

Worksite

The promotion of physical activity at the worksite has become extremely popular. One program that follows the community health model, Johnson and Johnson's Live for Life project, demonstrated striking changes in population physical activity. Blair reports that, by the end of two years, 20 percent of the initially sedentary women and 30 percent of the initially sedentary men were exercising regularly at or above the optimal level.[2] Economic analyses of the Live for Life program show reduced hospitalization costs.[4] Other benefits of employee participation in a worksite exercise program include decreased absenteeism, turnover, and medical care costs.[38]

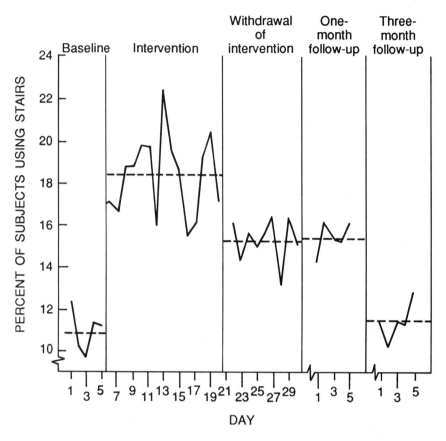

FIGURE 13-4 Percentage of subjects using stairs before, during, and after a public health intervention for increasing stair use at a commuter train station in Philadelphia (N = 24,603). Source: K. D. Brownell, A. J. Stunkard, and J. M. Albaum, "Evaluation and Modification of Exercise Patterns in the Natural Environment," *American Journal of Psychiatry*, Vol. 137, p. 1542, 1980.

COST-EFFECTIVENESS OF INTERVENTIONS

Questions regarding the effects of exercise on the health of elderly persons have prompted great speculation. Many have wondered if the benefits of physical fitness would have significant implications for the reduction of dependency; others have seen increased physical fitness as a way to reduce health care costs. Shephard has suggested that participation by the elderly in three one-hour exercise classes per week may reduce health care costs from acute and chronic treatment, mental health treatment, and extended residential care by more than $600 for each senior citizen per year.[38]

If true, these findings would indicate that exercise is a great economy. Systematic research to determine how often exercise can make a difference, how much of a difference, and whether it can postpone or reduce dependency of the elderly has yet to be performed.[44] Therefore, the potential economic benefits of physical activity in the elderly have yet to be quantified.

RECOMMENDATIONS

Services

1. The heterogeneity of the over-50 population in terms of physical capability and maintenance of function must be recognized. The research of Harris and coworkers[20] indicates that a substantial proportion of persons aged 80 and older have no functional impairment and maintain that status at least over a short-term follow-up period. Continued physical ability at baseline was associated with lack of cardiovascular disease or arthritis and moderate body weight.

2. Interventions to modify physical inactivity should be accompanied by an explanation of the benefits of exercise.

3. Practitioners need to apply behavioral research to encourage physical activity in persons over the age of 50. Good examples of such studies include the work of Berger[1] and Owen and Lee.[30] In fact, the committee has abstracted the following recommendations from selected guidelines developed by Owen and Lee[30] and endorses their principles.

• Exercise programs should accommodate the participants. Programs should be inexpensive and convenient, provide a wide variety of clear, specific, entertaining alternatives, and use existing social networks, although there may be alternatives that can be performed alone that will also encourage maintenance of function.

• The stages of the behavioral change process must be understood and used. To facilitate the adoption of a new behavior, a person must be made aware of the problem created by the old behavior, motivated to adopt a new one, taught how to change, and encouraged to adopt and then maintain the new behavior. Program planners must determine where an individual is in this process and intervene accordingly. At the community level, this precept requires programs in which all stages are addressed.

• The program must respect the diversity of participant health statuses. Specifically, realistic targets must be set, and interventions should be available at several levels.

4. The above recommendations apply generally to all adults; however, there are several specific recommendations for the elderly developed by Berger.[1]

• New activities such as walking, swimming, and aerobics classes should be adopted to replace working roles.
• An explicit association should be established with one's age group (e.g., community organizations, sports organization, or senior citizens center).
• Work responsibilities should be replaced by enjoyable activities that are not dependent on a work environment.
• Satisfactory physical living arrangements should be developed including easy access to shopping, medical care, friends, and recreational activities.

Research

Dishman and colleagues have produced a long, detailed list of research priorities from a review of the literature.[14] The following areas have been identified by the committee as prime research areas for determining the factors that lead to exercise or the decision to begin exercise.

1. The relevance of an individual's cognitive, behavioral, and physical abilities should be investigated—for example, the kind of interactions necessary for initiation of exercise, the perception of barriers, and the relationship of other health risks to physical inactivity interventions.
2. The relevance of the individual's occupational background, history of physical activity, lifestyle, and age should be explored.
3. Environmental factors are also worthy of investigation. These include, specifically, the kind of activities participants are requested to perform, whether there is supervision, and whether various activities reinforce or negate each other.
4. Longitudinal (three to four years) and other studies that trace the determinants of exercise maintenance at particular stages should be performed. Some studies should isolate particular groups.
5. The use of methodological ground rules could greatly assist research efforts. Researchers should attempt to reach a consensus over study questions, variables, and measurement methods. Moreover, the concerns of current studies suggest a need to bridge applied questions with theory if physical activity, exercise, and fitness are to be examined in relation to other health behaviors and outcomes.

Education

As Berger[1] points out, "Organized exercise programs, individualized for the needs of specific subpopulations, are greatly needed to combat the ageism stereotypes that are rampant in American society. Diminished self-expectancies coupled with social expectancies that one should act his or her age greatly reduce the amount of exercise most older individuals pursue. Supervised exercise programs that encourage the elderly to explore, develop, and extend their physical capabilities are urgently needed" (p. 54).

1. Health care professionals need to provide recommended protocols for individualizing exercise programs. This information should include specific assessment criteria, types of exercises and their effects, and how to monitor and evaluate exercise programs.

2. The expertise of other related professions that may not always be consulted in the care of the elderly (e.g., physical educators and specialists in human kinetics, physical and occupational therapists) would enhance any activity program. Physical and occupational therapists in particular possess specialized knowledge of the use of movement and exercise for treatment of injury and disability. Their knowledge can add greatly to the prevention of injury and disability as well.

3. Unsafe environments (e.g., lack of sidewalks, poorly lighted streets, inaccessible or hidden bus stops far from populated areas) should be eliminated. In addition, city planners, architects, councilpersons, mayors, and others who make decisions regarding aspects of the physical environment should take into account the effect of these decisions on the elderly person's use of resources.

Policymakers

General recommendations for policy regarding exercise programs for the overall population have already been developed.[30] Although these recommendations are not specifically aimed at exercise for the "second 50," several are applicable.

1. Guidelines should be developed for selecting a particular population group or subgroup for attention, and efforts should be focused specifically on these individuals (thus avoiding a "scattergun" approach).

2. Incentives and facilities for exercise programs should be provided in occupational and institutional settings. Adequate facili-

ties (e.g., showers, changing rooms) as well as flexible exercise times are essential. Management and employee groups need to cooperate to enhance opportunities for exercise in the workplace.

3. Training programs and further education for health practitioners in exercise counseling, instruction, and promotion should be developed.

4. Explicit policy directives should be formulated to encourage liaison among different government units that are currently or potentially will be involved with exercise.

5. Better use should be made of existing community facilities (e.g., the use of churches during the week or schools on weekends). The promotion of mall walking, with inexpensive, convenient transportation provided to and from the mall, might go a long way toward helping elderly people become less sedentary.

REFERENCES

1. Berger, B. G. The role of physical activity in the life quality of older adults. In: W. W. Spirduso and H. M. Eckert (eds.), Physical Activity and Aging. American Academy of Physical Education Paper No. 22. Champaign, Ill.: Human Kinetics Books, 1989, pp. 42-58.
2. Blair, S. N. Exercise, health, and longevity. In: D. R. Lamb and R. Murray (eds.), Perspectives in Exercise Science and Sports Medicine. Vol. 1, Prolonged Exercise. Indianapolis: Benchmark Press, 1988, pp. 443-488.
3. Blair, S. N., Brill, P. A., and Kohl, H. W. Physical activity patterns in older individuals. In: W. W. Spirduso and H. M. Eckert (eds.), Physical Activity and Aging. American Academy of Physical Education Paper No. 22. Champaign, Ill.: Human Kinetics Books, 1989, pp. 120-139.
4. Bly, J. L., Jones, R. C., and Richardson, J. E. Impact of worksite health promotion on health care costs and utilization: Evaluation of Johnson & Johnson's Live for Life Program. Journal of the American Medical Association 1986; 256:3235-3240.
5. Brody, J. A. Prospects for an aging population. Nature 1985; 315:463-466.
6. Brownell, K. D., Stunkard, A. J., and Albaum, J. M. Evaluation and modification of exercise patterns in the natural environment. American Journal of Psychiatry 1980; 137:1542.
7. Buskirk, E. R., and Segal, S. S. The aging motor system: Skeletal muscle weakness. In: W. W. Spirduso and H. M. Eckert (eds.), Physical Activity and Aging. American Academy of Physical Education Paper No. 22. Champaign, Ill.: Human Kinetics Books, 1989, pp. 19-36.
8. Caspersen, C. J., Christenson, G. M., and Pollard, R. A. Status of the 1990 physical fitness and exercise objectives—evidence from NHIS 1985. Public Health Reports 1986; 101:587-592.
9. Caspersen, C. J., Powell, K. E., and Christenson, G. M. Physical activity, exercise, and physical fitness: Definitions and distinctions for health-related research. Public Health Reports 1985; 101(2):126-131.
10. Cornoni-Huntley, J., Brock, D. B., Ostfeld, A. M., Taylor, J. O., and Wallace, R. B. (eds.) Established Populations for Epidemiologic Studies of the Elderly:

Resource Data Book. NIH Publ. No. 86-2443. Bethesda, Md.: National Institute on Aging, Public Health Service, 1986, p. 428.

11. Cunningham, D. A., Rechnitzer, P. A., Howard, J. H., and Donner, A. P. Exercise training of men at retirement: A clinical trial. Journal of Gerontology 1987; 42(1):17-23.

12. Department of Health and Human Services. Promoting Health/Preventing Disease: Objectives for the Nation. Washington, D.C.: U.S. Government Printing Office, 1980.

13. Dishman, R. K. Determinants of physical activity and exercise for persons 65 years of age or older. In: W. W. Spirduso and H. M. Eckert (eds.), Physical Activity and Aging. American Academy of Physical Education Paper No. 22. Champaign, Ill.: Human Kinetics Books, 1989, pp. 140-162.

14. Dishman, R. K., Sallis, J. F., and Orenstein, D. R. The determinants of physical activity and exercise. Public Health Reports 1985; 100(2):158-171.

15. Frisch, R. E., Wyshak, G., Albright, N. L., et al. Lower prevalence of breast cancer and cancers of the reproductive system among former college athletes compared to non-athletes. British Journal of Cancer 1985; 52:885-891.

16. Garabrant, D. H., Peters, J. M., Mack, T. M., and Bernstein, L. Job activity and colon cancer risk. American Journal of Epidemiology 1984; 119:1005-1014.

17. Gerhardsson, M., Norell, S. E., Kiviranta, H., Pedersen, N. L., and Ahlbom, A. Sedentary jobs and colon cancer. American Journal of Epidemiology 1986; 123:775-780.

18. Gibson, R. C., and Jackson, J. S. The health, physical functioning, and informal supports of the black elderly. Milbank Quarterly 1987; 65(Suppl. 2):421-454.

19. Guralnik, J. M., and Kaplan, G. A. Predictors of healthy aging: Prospective evidence from the Alameda County study. American Journal of Public Health 1989; 79(6):703-708.

20. Harris, T., Kovar, M. G., Suzman, R., Kleniman, J. C., and Feldman, J. J. Longitudinal study of physical ability in the oldest-old. American Journal of Public Health 1989; 79(6):698-702.

21. Haskell, W. L., Montoye, H. J., and Orenstein, D. Physical activity and exercise to achieve health-related physical fitness components. Public Health Reports 1985; 100:206.

22. Heath, G. W. Exercise programming for the older adult. In: S. N. Blair, P. Painter, R. R. Pate, L. K. Smith, and C. B. Taylor (eds.), American College of Sports Medicine Resource Manual for Guidelines for Exercise Testing and Prescription. Philadelphia: Lea and Febiger, 1988.

23. Idiculla, A. A., and Goldberg, G. Physical fitness for the mature woman. Medical Clinics of North America 1987; 71:135-149.

24. Kaplan, G. A., Seeman, T. E., Cohen, R. D., Knudsen, L. D., and Guralnick, J. Mortality among the elderly in the Alameda County Study: Behavioral and demographic risk factors. American Journal of Public Health 1987; 77:309.

25. Lampman, R. M. Evaluating and prescribing exercise for elderly patients. Geriatrics 1987; 42:63-76.

26. Larson, E. B., and Bruce, R. A. Health benefits of exercise in an aging society. Archives of Internal Medicine 1987; 147:353-356.

27. Leads from the MMWR. Sex-, age-, and region-specific prevalence of sedentary lifestyle in selected states in 1985—the behavioral risk factor surveillance system. Journal of the American Medical Association 1987; 257:2270-2272.

28. Mason, J. O., and Powell, K. E. Physical activity, behavioral epidemiology, and public health (editorial). Public Health Reports 1985; 100(2):113-115.
29. National Center for Health Statistics (Drury, T. F., and Powell, A. L.). Prevalence, impact and demography of known diabetes in the United States. DHHS Publ. No. (PHS) 86-1250. Advance Data from Vital and Health Statistics, No. 114, 1986.
30. Owen, N., and Lee, C. Development of behaviorally-based policy guidelines for the promotion of exercise. Journal of Public Health Policy 1989; 10:(1):43-61.
31. Paffenbarger, R. S., Hyde, R. T., Wing, A. L., and Hsieh, C. C. Physical activity, all-cause mortality and longevity of college alumni. New England Journal of Medicine 1986; 314:605-613.
32. Pollock, M. L. Exercise prescriptions for the elderly. In: W. W. Spirduso and H. M. Eckert (eds.), Physical Activity and Aging. American Academy of Physical Education Paper No. 22. Champaign, Ill.: Human Kinetics Books, 1989, pp. 163-174.
33. Powell, K. E., Thompson, P. D., Caspersen, C. J., and Kendrick, J. S. Physical activity and the incidence of coronary heart disease. Annual Review of Public Health 1987; 8:253-257.
34. Russell, L. B. Is Prevention Better than Cure? Washington, D.C.: The Brookings Institute, 1986.
35. Seals, D. R., Hagberg, J. M., Hurley, B. F., Ehsani, A. A., and Holloszy, J. O. Endurance training in older men and women. I. Cardiovascular responses to exercise. Journal of Applied Physiology 1984; 57:1024-1029.
36. Shephard, R. J. Exercise and aging. In: R. S. Hutton (ed.), Exercise and Sports Sciences Reviews. Philadelphia: Franklin Institute Press, 1979, pp. 1-57.
37. Shephard, R. J. The impact of exercise upon medical costs. Sports Medicine 1985; 2:133-143.
38. Shephard, R. J. Physical Activity and Aging, 2nd ed. London: Croom Helm, 1987.
39. Somers, A. R. Preventive health services for the elderly. In: R. Andres, E. L. Bierman, and W. R. Hazzard (eds.), Principles of Geriatric Medicine. New York: McGraw-Hill, 1985.
40. Smith, E. L. Age: The interaction of nature and nurture. In: E. L. Smith and R. C. Serfass (eds.), Exercise and Aging: The Scientific Basis. Hillside, N.J.: Enslow, 1981, pp. 11-17.
41. Stamford, B. A. Exercise and the elderly. In: K. B. Pandolf (ed.), Sports Sciences Review. New York: Macmillan, 1988, pp. 341-379.
42. Stelmach, G. E., and Goggin, N. L. Psychomotor decline with age. In: W. W. Spirduso and H. M. Eckert (eds.), Physical Activity and Aging. American Academy of Physical Education Paper No. 22. Champaign, Ill.: Human Kinetics Books, 1989, pp. 6-18.
43. Stephens, T. Secular trends in physical activity: Fitness boom or bust? Research Quarterly for Exercise Sport 1987; 58:94-105.
44. U.S. Department of Health and Human Services (Bloom, B.). Current Estimates from the National Health Interview Survey; United States, 1981. National Center for Health Statistics, Public Health Service. DHHS Publ. No. (PHS) 82-1569. Washington, D.C.: U.S. Government Printing Office, 1982.
45. Wheat, M. E. Exercise in the elderly. Western Journal of Medicine 1987; 147:477-480.
46. World Health Organization. International Classification of Impairments, Disabilities, and Handicaps. Geneva: World Health Organization, 1980.

14

Social Isolation Among Older Individuals
The Relationship to Mortality and Morbidity

Social isolation is considered a risk factor in the development of disease and in the disability that can occur in the course of existing disease. It has been included as well in the measure of quality of life and thus is an outcome as well as a risk factor. A consideration of social isolation almost always occurs in the context of social support, and the two in most cases are used interchangeably. Both concepts have been defined inexactly over the past few decades, and this lack of a standard definition has become more apparent with the increase in the body of work analyzing social isolation as a risk factor for the general well-being of the older population. For this reason, a brief explication and history of these concepts may clarify the definition of this important but sometimes elusive area of interest.

DEFINITION

Social isolation can be defined structurally as the absence of social interactions, contacts, and relationships with family and friends, with neighbors on an individual level, and with "society at large" on a broader level. The most parsimonious definition of social support is "the resources provided by other persons."[11] These resources, which may include emotional, social, physical, financial, and other types of care, cover a broad array of individuals and institutions as the source of this care. Social isolation is defined and then measured by the strength of the older person's existing social network and the characteristics of the individuals and institutions providing support to him or her through this network. The absence or weakness of the social support network forms the basis for identifying individuals who are socially isolated. This definition is thus a qualitative one denoting the absence of meaningful relationships. Social support has been used as and continues to be an indicator of the degree of social isolation, and it can serve as the major independent variable in studies of the effect of social isolation as a risk factor of disease or dysfunction. Although the level of social support can serve as well as an outcome variable of quality of life, the discussion here will be limited to its function as a risk factor for health and quality of life.

There is agreement on the overall concept of social support in the body of theoretical work, but an examination of the research reveals inconsistency in both its definition and measurement. An early study[32] used a subjective definition, allowing each individual to decide what constituted an intimate relationship. Kahn and Antonucci[24] include three aspects of social support in their definition: instrumental or tangible support, emotional support, and agreement with the statements or acts of others. They add an important concept of the "convoy of support," which is intended to capture the dynamic nature of social support as it changes throughout life.

The problems of measurement follow from the problems of definition. A major issue is whether social support is a concept to be enumerated by the quantitative dimensions of the network of formal and informal helpers or whether the focus should be on the quality of the relationships making up this network. A footnote to this dilemma involves the competing concepts of social support as a specific set of observable phenomena that can be identified and replicated or social support as nonobservable and subjective—and therefore different for each individual.

Bruhn and Phillips[8] list several factors to consider in measuring the concept:

1. Environmental and physical factors should be included in addition to social, interpersonal, and cultural factors.

2. Quantitative aspects should be measured despite the greater ease of focusing on the qualitative aspects of social support.

3. Social support and health status are more robust indicators when measured together. There is some evidence from prospective studies that baseline assessments of either health status or social support are of little value in predicting subsequent measurements of either variable. If social support and health status result together in

a more robust indicator, it is a moot point to debate how they might be measured separately.

4. Social support does not have the same importance or the same components in all cultures.

5. Social support may vary according to the age and life situation of the individual.

6. Social support is present in normal as well as in crisis situations.

7. The reciprocity of social support needs further study.

8. Community support systems and networks operate and change over time, and more needs to be learned about how they differ according to cultural setting and how members of the community are linked to those systems. Although some of these issues are debatable, particularly in their relevance to studies of risk factors for disease and disability, they reflect the common concerns of researchers in this area.

Bruhn and Phillips[8] also list 14 major scales that have been used by researchers to measure social support, categorizing them as including feelings and perceptions, individual functioning, social integration, social participation, emotion, tangible and informational functions, the number of social ties, and the relative importance of these ties. One of the first of these scales to be developed that has had wide use is the Social Readjustment Rating Scale,[21] which weights events according to the degree of adjustment each event may require. This approach was used to understand the impact of social support by identifying and quantifying universal occurrences hypothesized as stressors. The sum of the weights for the events experienced by a person for a given period of time constituted the risk for that individual.

Kasl and Berkman[27] list several types of indicators of health status that have been used in studies of social support. These include general and specific mortality rates, expectation of life at a specific age, rates of specific morbidity, levels of impairment, indices of disability, and contacts with the health care system. The problems with the measures emerging from this review are several. The data do not reveal which end of the disease spectrum is most influenced by the psychosocial variable in question (e.g, levels of risk factors, onset of clinical disease, gap between onset and diagnosis and treatment, case fatality). In addition, the health consequences of some behaviors may become manifest 20 or 30 years after the individual engages in the behavior. Moreover, the cumulative effect of lifelong practices is rarely explored in studies, and dose-responses or length of exposure relationships generally have not been identified. These investigators believe an overriding fault in the field is the assumption of differences among the elderly population and younger populations that have not been documented. Kasl and Berkman consider this belief to be an obstacle to a "dispassionate" examination of the evidence. Consequently, further work must be done to increase standardization of definitions and strengthen measurement.

BURDEN

Prevalence

The few existing studies of the prevalence of social isolation indicate that a total absence of relationships is relatively rare for the elderly.[23] Furthermore, when social isolation is identified as a condition of older individuals, the phenomenon is generally accepted as the continuation of a lifelong pattern rather than a development of late life. However, elderly individuals, perceiving themselves to be frail and dependent, may isolate themselves to disguise their loss of autonomy. The limited empirical evidence available on the prevalence of social isolation[1,46] seems to corroborate a low prevalence of true social isolation. Theoretical as well as empirical work on the effect of social isolation makes use of social support as an indicator of the degree of social isolation.

Although evidence of total isolation among older individuals may not exist, there has been work suggestive of the existence of relatively low levels of social support for some elderly. In a follow-up study of research involving a community population, 35 percent of the older individuals surveyed reported that they had no confidant (a confidant being defined as someone with whom to discuss serious problems, who was easily available, and with whom there was at least monthly contact).[17]

Costs

The very early, almost primitive level of definition, measurement, and hence attribution of specific risk to this factor in disease and its outcome is undoubtedly the basis for the lack of estimates of the cost of social isolation, although related areas have been studied. There have been rough estimates made of the cost to families and other care givers for specific diseases, notably Alzheimer's disease;[16] in addition, there have been efforts made to analyze the cost-effectiveness of prevention programs for older individuals. The general conclusion regarding most of this work is that the methods have not been rigorous and that this area requires the attention of carefully designed and scientifically managed research.[2]

Impairment, Disability, and Handicap

The theoretical base as well as empirical work on social isolation and disease has not been consistent in differentiating prevention of occurrence (primary prevention) and the various levels of morbidity and mortality (secondary and tertiary prevention). One seminal theory, linking social isolation and resultant stress to weakened host resistance, suggests a nonspecific effect. This tendency is confirmed in the studies reported below on all-cause mortality rates. The studies suggest effects at all stages, pre- and post- impairment, disability, and handicap.

Although specific investigations do not always fit neatly in the various stages of prevention, the work on lack of social support and its effects is a singularly apt illustration of this broader scope in prevention. There have been both empirical investigations and the building of theoretical constructs centering on the strength of social supports in preventing the occurrence of disease, that is, primary prevention. However, much attention has also been focused, particularly for the older population, on secondary or tertiary prevention when the population of interest includes a large percentage of individuals with existing disease. Often, this means a chronic condition that will be a characteristic of the individual to the end of his or her life; therefore, the focus on impairment, disability, and handicap is an appropriate model. In this way a broader, more inclusive strategy can be developed to analyze the effect of social supports (or of any risk factor). The paradigm-like proposition derived from the World Health Organization's (WHO) efforts to achieve standard definitions of disability was used by one of the working groups of the Public Health Service's Health Objectives for the Nation: Year 2000.[33] The framework suggested by the group was that of a hierarchy at the disease end of the spectrum of health status, beginning with the development of disease and leading to impairment, disability, and finally handicap, in that order. The positive end of this spectrum begins with independence, leads to productivity, and ends with life satisfaction. This framework is the background against which impairment, disability, and handicap are considered.

The mechanism by which social isolation, one strong source of stress, contributes to morbidity and mortality affords insights into specific outcomes in the course of disease. Much research on social isolation points toward a nonspecific effect of this factor on health status. Rahe,[35] for example, notes similarities between the non-specificity of recent life change risk factors and coronary heart disease risk factors, which can come from a variety of sources. Early theorizing regarding causal pathways that link stress to biological changes was pioneered by Cassel.[9] He described stress in epidemiologic terms as affecting host resistance and thereby increasing susceptibility to disease. Cassel did not specify the constituents of stress nor identify specific diseases as a result. Rather, he hypothesized a generalized weakening of the host that makes the individual susceptible to insults. Commenting on Cassel's hypothesis, Reed and coworkers[37] assert that it is unlikely that specific social processes are inherently stressful to most people in most places and that it is more likely that the individual reacts differently to the situation depending on perception of the situation, personality, prior experience, and means of coping. However, this type of approach would still have consequences for the occurrence of disease and for subsequent impairment, disability, and handicap.

Kasl[26] describes the stages of disease subsequent to stress using as a framework the epidemiologic schema that describe the spectrum of health through the natural history of disease development. These stages are as follows: (1) asymptomatic status, risk factor absent; (2) asymptomatic status, risk factor present; (3) subclinical disease susceptible to detection; (4) initial symptom experience; (5) initial event (diagnostic criteria for a disease are met); (6) course of disease; (7) institutionalization; and (8) mortality. He observes that the very broad concepts and general theoretical formulations about underlying processes make it more difficult to identify optimal points in the overall causal matrix at which to consider prevention and intervention.

The state of the art in measurement of social supports has not reached the point where there can be differentiation of the stage of disease at which a lack of social supports has the greatest impact.

Several salient questions illustrate these limitations:

1. Are the factors that relate to the initial onset of disease the same as those that affect the course and outcome of disease?

2. How are existing biological risk factors and the structure of social supports representing psychological risk factors related in the overall disease etiology?

3. Will social isolation or other psychosocial stressors occurring early in life affect outcome in the same manner as they would if they occurred later in life?

The preceding discussion reflects the early state of the art regarding the role of social isolation in disease. Because of this limited understanding, a precise assessment of the burden occasioned by this risk factor and the potential for prevention is, of necessity, tenuous. An examination of theoretical and empirical work is essential to begin increasing the accuracy of burden assessment. This approach will serve as well as a background for the discussion of preventability that follows.

The role in health of such phenomena as social support and social isolation has its roots in early consideration and theoretical formulation of the mind/body controversy. Despite the hazy and at times unscientific approaches to this area of human functioning, the role of psychosocial concepts in disease and health demands attention. Eastwood described the beginnings of "psychosomatic medicine," which addressed the mind/body paradox, as an attempt to identify psychological variables that promote diseases.[15] This early "psychosomatics" movement was reflected in a 1964 WHO report,[49] which concluded that the relationship of mind and body was a dynamic one and that the human system can be affected by either psychological or physiological insult and stress. Over the years, and particularly during the 1960s and 1970s, a significant corpus of work emerged in this area.[13,20,44]

This early, pioneering approach evolved into later large-scale studies to test the role of social supports in mortality and morbidity. This trend began in the mid-1970s and is typified by the studies of House and colleagues,[22] Berkman and Syme,[3] and Blazer.[4] Later research examined prevention strategies designed to delay the onset of disease, affect the early detection of disease, contain the course of functional impairment in the presence of disease, and maintain the highest quality of life in the face of impairments and disability as the result of disease. (This approach clearly addresses all of the stages of the WHO classification and the framework of the Health Objectives for the Nation working group.) The three prospective cohort studies noted above[3,4,22] showed higher rates of mortality from all causes for socially deprived older persons. These studies used different measures of social support and varying time intervals over which the effect took place. Yet the analysis in each is convincing in linking the absence of social support to higher mortality rates.

Berkman and Syme[3] reported on a nine-year follow-up study of a random sample of 6,928 adults in Alameda County, California. They found that people who lacked social and community ties were more likely to die in the follow-up period than those with more extensive contacts. Their findings also indicated that the "association between social ties and mortality was . . . independent of the self-reported physical health status at the time of the 1965 survey, year of death, socioeconomic status, and health practices such as smoking, alcoholic beverage consumption, obesity, physical activity, and utilization of prevention health services as well as a cumulative index of health practices" (p. 186). Social support in this study was defined as the presence of a spouse, contact with friends, or church and community group membership.

Seventeen-year mortality data from the Alameda County Study were used to examine the relative importance of social ties as predictors of survival at different ages.[43] Comparisons of the relative importance of four types of social ties reveal an interesting shift across the age groups. Marital status assumes primary importance for those aged less than 60 years at baseline. However, ties with close friends or relatives assume greater importance for those aged 60 and older.

A study reported by Blazer[4] of 331 persons aged 65 and older has a similar finding of a higher death rate among persons who were socially deprived. This effect on mortality occurred over a shorter period—30 months. The measurement of social isolation was based on three factors: roles and available attachments, perceived social support, and frequency of social interactions.

A similar finding of decreased mortality risk associated with higher levels of social relationships was reported by House and coworkers, [22] but the finding in this instance was limited to men. The study, the Tecumseh County Health Survey, followed a cohort of 2,754 adults for 9 to 12 years. Trends were similar for women but generally nonsignificant. The measure of social support comprised intimate social relationships, formal organizational involvement outside of work, active and relatively social leisure, and passive and relatively solitary leisure. The findings of these large studies appear to have relevance for each stage of prevention.

There have been other major studies that looked at the relationship of social networks to specific diseases. Haynes,[19] for example, examined coronary heart disease using cross-sectional data from the Framingham study. He showed that, for men and women over the age of 65, marital dissatisfaction or disagreements were significantly related to the prevalence of coronary heart disease. This association occurred only for the older age group (aged 65 and older), suggesting that risk factors may change at different ages.[27]

Reed and colleagues[36] reported that prevalence rates for myocardial infarction, angina, and all coronary heart disease were associated with a lack of social network (the study controlled for 12 other

known risk factors). The associations, however, were with prevalence of disease rather than mortality and thus draw attention to
primary prevention. The study population comprised 4,653 men of
Japanese ancestry in northern California and a cohort in Honolulu
who were taking part in the Honolulu Heart Program. The measure
of social support consisted of structural questions regarding the
individual's social network: marital status, closeness of parents,
number of living children, number of persons in the household,
frequency of social activities, frequency of discussing serious personal
problems with coworkers, frequency of attendance of religious services,
and number of social organizations attended regularly.

Wortman and Conway[50] reviewed the literature on social support
and recovery from illness, the majority of which constitutes studies
of recovery from disease in the hospital. In general, Wortman and
Conway found that the effect of social support in recovery from
disease is less clear than in longitudinal studies over a long period of
time with all-cause disease outcome measures. They note that
spurious results can be obtained because of the inability to disentangle
socially competent and nonneurotic individuals who may have easier
access to social support than less socially able persons and who may
be more effective in negotiating the health care system. In spite of
these dangers, they believe the majority of interventions provide
clear evidence that social support facilitates recovery.

Wallston and coworkers[47] believe research evidence supporting a
direct link between social support and physical health is more
modest than other reviewers have claimed. They categorized studies
in terms of the effect of social support on illness onset, the use of
health services, adherence to medical regimens, recovery, rehabilitation,
and adaptation to illness. (This effort is the most direct parallel to
the WHO stages of disability and to various stages and types of
prevention.) Wallston and colleagues maintain that these studies
fail to distinguish between psychosocial assets as a buffer against the
negative health effects of stressful situations and social support as a
buffer against illness occurrence. There have been attempts to
identify a relationship between social network characteristics and
patterns of utilization of health care, but these authors feel the
findings from this research are equivocal. In addition, they believe
there is evidence for a relationship between social support and
adherence to medical regimens. They conclude that there is consistent evidence for positive effects on recovery, rehabilitation, adaptation,
and mortality but that it is unclear whether this outcome is due to
one type of support or to combinations of support.

PREVENTABILITY OF BURDEN

Available Interventions

The limitations discussed above addressing specificity of burden and the early developmental stage of research have a direct bearing on an assessment of the range of possibilities for prevention of disease, impairment, disability, and handicap through interventions aimed at the risk factor of social isolation. The literature suggests different pathways between social supports and continuing good health and social supports and the various levels of the outcome of disease once it has been diagnosed. The observations that emerge from past work reflect this dichotomy.

Broadhead and colleagues,[7] in their extensive review of social support research, identified concepts inherent in the link between social support and health as well as characteristics of social supports.

1. Temporality: Poor social support precedes adverse psychological outcomes and mortality.
2. Consistency: There is a similarity in the direction and magnitude of effect across all major study designs and across a wide variety of age, sex, race, ethnic, and health status groups. However, the effect of social support is greater for women than for men in most studies.
3. Biological gradient: There is an apparent increase in the numbers of physical and psychological symptoms and mortality with incremental decreases in number and frequency of social contacts. The relationship is less clear for perceived qualitative measures of social support.
4. Biological plausibility: Experimental evidence (animal and human) suggests neuroendocrine mechanisms, possibly mediated by B endorphin, that might explain both the proposed direct and stress-modifying effects of social support.
5. Coherence: Social support theory is bolstered by studies in ethology and existing psychosocial theory. Biological evidence can be used to explain the effect of social support in the proposed causal chain between exposure and disease.
6. Specificity of outcome: The generalized effects on the body of neuroendocrine mechanisms are consistent with the wide number of physical and psychological outcomes associated with variations in social support.
7. Measurement of exposure: A wide range of definitions of

social support have been used, many inappropriately, and thus length or depth of exposure is dubiously documented.

8. Determinants of social support: A large number of environmental and individual characteristics interact to produce a person's social support system at any one point in time.

There are two conclusions that relate directly to intervention:

1. Experiment/intervention: Social support intervention has improved psychological outcomes of chronically ill children and pregnancy outcomes of women in labor. Otherwise there is a dearth of research adequately evaluating the effect of intervention.

2. Dynamics of social support: The nature of all these determinants change with sequential role changes and other life events as an individual proceeds through the life cycle.

The evidence thus suggests that lack of social support can play a role in disease and disability and that the existence of strong social support can play a role in sustaining good health as well. Behavioral scientists postulate that the force of social support can be manifested through perceived support inherent in close relationships and through the structure or network of relationships with others. Most researchers[12,48] in this area believe social support acts indirectly as a buffer, intervening to protect rather than building up a stronger host. The action of making the host stronger is referred to as "direct effect hypothesis" by Cohen and Syme[11] and postulates that support enhances health and well-being irrespective of the stress level. Langlie[31] suggests the effect derives from preventive health practices or the buffer or indirect effect. People with strong social networks will be encouraged and actively assisted in following better health practices, thereby achieving better health and increased longevity.

Bruhn and Phillips[8] suggest a paradigm of social support in which a hypothetical dose-response-type curve is postulated under conditions of high or low social support. The ratio of the intensity of stress to duration is plotted against the ratio of the number of illness episodes to a specified period of time. Krause,[30] however, found that increases in social support tended to increase feelings of control but only up to a certain threshold. Beyond this threshold, additional support tended to decrease feelings of personal control.

The biological link with social support has attracted a great deal of attention. Recent work by Stein and colleagues[45] develops the theoretical basis for the biological link between stress related to social isolation and the immune system. In another study, Keller and colleagues[28] showed the effect of stress on lymphocyte stimulation in rats and later demonstrated this response in men in the first two months of bereavement.[40] The immune system is one of the major integrative networks involved in biological adaptation, and there is evidence that a variety of psychosocial factors influence the central nervous system so that suppression or enhancement of immune functions may result. Braveman[6] contends that, in the study of older people, the immune system should be viewed as part of an interactive network of systems whose job is to maintain homeostasis.

Clarification of the difference between intervention to prevent disease occurrence and intervention to reduce the inexorability of impairment from disease leading to disability and handicap is important to help target groups for preventive services. Kaplan and coworkers[25] point out a useful distinction at an operational level. Prevention against social isolation relating to primary prevention can be said to involve education and training in coping to teach a person to use social resources to maintain health. Intervention involves training professionals to identify high-risk families and individuals to teach them to manipulate the environment so as to acquire social support. Although this strategy points to different approaches for two target groups, the elderly and the professionals serving them, such intervention can be applied at all levels of prevention—primary, secondary, and tertiary.

Rook[39] delineates three levels at which intervention against social isolation may occur: to prevent loneliness, to help the already lonely person establish satisfying interpersonal ties, and to prevent loneliness from evolving into or contributing to more serious problems. Interventions can seek to restructure existing opportunities for social contact or create new opportunities for social contact through network building, thereby bolstering an individual's ability to cope with social loss. One caveat in all intervention studies is that difficult ethical issues may be part of the consideration. For example, when volunteer visits in a Friendly Visitor Program are withdrawn, it may cause stress to the recipient. Schultz and Hanusa[42] carried out studies in which residents of a retirement home were given control over the frequency and duration of visits by volunteers. Although these residents showed an initial gain in well-being, after the program was concluded they declined and had poorer adjustment than persons who had not been visited at all.

There are other guides to the nature of intervention for social isolation. Cobb[10] organizes categories of support into the instrumental support of counseling, guidance toward better coping, active support or nurturing, and material support. Schoenbach[41] observes that social support mechanisms are more likely to be strengthened than social stress decreased. If the hypothesized positive impact of social support is upheld, however, a greater lapse of time may be required to observe a true outcome.

Finally, Rodin and coworkers[38] propose the following taxonomy of intervention categories based on qualitative differences: (1) cognitive domain (memory, language, and intellectual abilities); (2) social interaction to bolster social support and increase the social interactions of older people; and (3) motivational interventions (changing thoughts and feelings, looking at motivational states). These authors contend that prevention is not merely the alleviation of undesirable states but enrichment in an attempt to optimize function. (This type of approach addresses the upper end of the WHO health scale—away from disease—and presents social support as an outcome indicating life satisfaction.) For the elderly, this enrichment implies malleability of function even as the body ages. Rodin notes four themes that appear repeatedly in intervention studies: plasticity (or the ability to change) within the aging process; between-subject variability in response as well as in status, a phenomenon that appears to increase with age; the concept of control or efficacy or the degree of direction over one's life; and the nature of the intervention and its perceived efficacy.

Effectiveness of Each Intervention

Bloom[5] summarized the literature on recent prevention programs in a monograph for the National Institute of Mental Health that was written for the purpose of disseminating and exchanging information on prevention activities. He notes the difficulty of evaluating such programs, especially primary prevention in mental morbidity, and underscores the nonspecific nature of the causal link between concepts of social isolation and social support and disease. Evidence of the effectiveness of prevention programs should be sought by assessing all of the health outcomes that may be affected. This review notes the additional problem of identifying experimental and control groups who have undergone the same stressful life events or set of events and who do not differ significantly on demographic characteristics that are thought to be associated with outcome.

RECOMMENDATIONS

Services

The dearth of hard data on the most effective and efficient methods for decreasing social isolation and increasing positive social supports has been emphasized. There is, however, a good deal of knowledge on the older population, particularly regarding their use of services, that can serve as a guide when considering strategies for decreasing the risk factor of social isolation. For one thing, it is known that networks of services for the elderly exist in most communities. It is also known that this population makes ongoing, extensive use of medical care[34] and that attitudes of the elderly to their physicians have been held to be positive and strong.[18]   From this combination of "conventional wisdom" and certain established facts, tentative recommendations can be made regarding the role of services in approaches to social isolation.

1. At-risk individuals must be identified. This process should take place in service delivery sites and should include clinicians as well as other providers. There are indications that the first opportunity for such an identification of needs is at the source of medical care, usually the older person's primary care giver. Other sites include adult protection agencies, home health agencies, senior centers, nutritional settings in churches or schools, and other such locations.
2. Sources for referral should be identified. Once an individual in need has been identified, a knowledge of sources for referrals is essential. The dissemination of resource information generally is necessary so that family and friends, unattached to formal service-giving, will be in a position to direct attention appropriately to the needy elderly person.
3. Age-restricted elderly housing developments and retirement communities should begin experimenting with a variety of mechanisms to increase social supports. There are no guides to approaches to isolated individuals because the most successful programs tend to be used by those least in need of aggressive outreach. Very select groups of individuals are found in successful socializing programs in the community,[14] which support and enhance the functioning of older people. However, the individuals using such services must be able to attend programs at senior centers and to participate and interact. Thus, they are not necessarily the group for whom services should be a high priority. Whether the methods used in the centers now serving a group of functioning and motivated individuals could

be adapted to other target groups is an unanswered question. Certainly these services represent a point of departure for planning ways to identify and help socially isolated older people.

Research

The knowledge base for social isolation as a risk factor for disease, for functional incapacity in general, and for disability and handicap as a result of that incapacity is in an early, even primitive stage when compared with knowledge regarding the risk of smoking, the importance of dietary control, and other more directly observable and more thoroughly researched areas. However, the work to date provides sufficient evidence of the serious consideration commanded by social isolation as a risk factor. Much depends on continuing delineation of research questions and intervention evaluations. Crucial questions have been raised earlier that shape priorities in research. The basic questions on age differences for this risk factor, for example, and the designation of the point at which preventive services can be of greatest benefit to an older population are two of the unanswered questions that are most important in clearly identifying appropriate target groups as well as appropriate interventions. The question of "directionality" must also be addressed; that is, do ties and support diminish, remain constant, or increase when older individuals become ill, and under what circumstances? Basic issues of definition, measurement, and causal relationships are generic types of research that parallel these more specific issues.

The committee recommends that the following questions, posed by Kiesler,[29] be addressed as high-priority research areas:

1. Does social support reduce stress in ways that can be objectively measured and that are socially desirable?

2. Is the effect causal?

3. Which type of support is most effective: self-help groups, professional intervention, or the strengthening of relationships of family and friends?

4. If most effective support sources are identified, what are the ways to increase such support to large populations?

5. What are the characteristics associated with differences in the amount and type of social supports that are available and used?

6. Does the current style of service facilitate or interfere with increasing social support?

7. Does social support have similar effects on physical and mental health?

The answers to these questions constitute designs for a variety of research projects, which require careful construction to parallel each of the areas that have been identified (definition, measurement, relationship to health and disease). This research should be integrated into experimental, targeted intervention studies for reducing the risk factor of social isolation and for examining the effects of doing so.

Education

Education as part of an overall strategy in reducing social isolation, to be most effective, must be aimed at three populations: providers of care, including clinicians; other care givers such as families, friends, and neighbors of older individuals who may be isolated or poorly supported; and the elderly themselves.

Providers

1. All health care providers should be educated in the importance of strong social supports.
2. Providers should be trained in methods of identifying those at high risk.

For providers of care, methods of identifying at-risk individuals and information on existing resources are probably the most efficacious means of attacking this problem. Unless the support falls within the particular purview of the specific service being rendered, education in providing direct support may be inefficient in the case of physicians. Rather, clinician education should focus on the importance of social supports and methods of identifying those at high risk. Following identification, it will be necessary to find appropriate services and transmit knowledge of how to use such services.

Families

1. Strategies should be developed to provide information about the social needs of elderly family members.
2. Strategies should be developed to provide information about available resources and access to their use.

For families, information about the problem, wide dissemination of information regarding available services, and the motivation to make use of such services constitute a strong educational approach to reduce this risk factor. The problem in this case may be circular in that those most in need of such services are the least likely to have families, friends, and neighbors, or others with sufficient concern to take action. A general campaign to provide information about social needs and resources with easy access to meet those needs is one possible approach to this problem.

The Elderly

The majority of elderly persons know the importance of a social network. The committee recommends that educational resources be developed to attract and then inform them of available resources.

Education of the elderly themselves parallels comments on educational efforts for the first two groups. It would be disingenuous to presume that people are isolated because they do not know that it is important to have a support network. How the elderly are educated in this matter requires careful investigation using various strategies to attract and then educate a group in need. There have been investigations and demonstrations with older individuals along a broad spectrum of psychosocial needs and activities. This past work requires consideration, plus specific recommendations and trials to establish the best way to proceed.

REFERENCES

1. Atchley, R. C. The process of retirement: Comparing women and men. In: M. Szinovacz (ed.), Women's Retirement. Beverly Hills, Calif.: Sage Publications, 1982, pp. 153-168.
2. Banta, H. C., and Luce, B. R. Assessing the cost-effectiveness of prevention. Journal of Community Health 1983; 9(2):145-165.
3. Berkman, L. F., and Syme, S. L. Social networks, host resistance and mortality: A nine-year follow-up study of Alameda County residents. American Journal of Epidemiology 1979; 109:186-204.
4. Blazer, D. G. Social support and mortality in an elderly community population. American Journal of Epidemiology 1982; 115:684-694.
5. Bloom, B. L. Stressful Life Event Theory and Research: Implications for Primary Prevention. Rockville, Md.: Alcohol, Drug Abuse and Mental Health Administration, National Institute of Mental Health, 1985.
6. Braveman, N. S. Immunity and aging: Immunologic and behavioral perspectives. In: M. W. Riley, J. D. Matarazzo, and A. Baum, (eds.), The Aging Dimension. Hillsdale, N.J.: Lawrence Erlbaum Associates, Inc., 1987, pp. 93-124.
7. Broadhead, W. E., Kaplan, B. H., James, S. A., et al. The epidemiologic evidence for a relationship between social support and health. American Journal of Epidemiology 1983; 117:521-537.

8. Bruhn, J. G., and Phillips, B. V. Measuring social support: A synthesis of current approaches. Journal of Behavioral Medicine 1984; 7(2):151-169.

9. Cassel, J. C. The contribution of the social environment to host resistance. American Journal of Epidemiology 1976; 104:107-123.

10. Cobb, S. Social support and health through the life course. In: M. W. Riley (ed.), Aging from Birth to Death. Boulder, Colo.: Westview Press, 1979, pp. 93-106.

11. Cohen, S., and Syme, S. L. (eds.) Social Support and Health. New York: Academic Press, 1985.

12. Dohrenwend, B. S., and Dohrenwend, B. P. Life stress and illness: Formulation of the issues. In: B. S. Dohrenwend and B. P. Dohrenwend (eds.), Stressful Life Events and Their Contexts (part of the Monographs in Psychosocial Epidemiology series). New York: Prodist, 1981, pp. 1-27.

13. Dohrenwend, B. S., and Dohrenwend, B. P. Some issues in research on stressful life events. Journal of Nervous Disorders 1978; 166:7-15.

14. Dychtwald, K. Wellness and Health Promotion for the Elderly. Rockville, Md.: Aspen Publications, 1986.

15. Eastwood, M. R. The Relation Between Physicians and Mental Illness. Toronto: University of Toronto Press, 1975.

16. Frank, R., German, P. S., et al. Use of services by cognitively impaired elderly persons residing in the community. Hospital and Community Psychiatry 1988; 38(5):555-557.

17. German, P., and Burton, L. Factors affecting decline in function among older persons. Johns Hopkins University, School of Hygiene and Public Health, 1989.

18. Haug, M. R. Elderly Patients and Their Doctors. New York: Springer Publishing Co., 1981.

19. Haynes, S. G., Feinleib, M., Devine, S., Scotch, N., and Kannel, W. E. The relationship of psychosocial factors to coronary heart disease in the Framingham study. American Journal of Epidemiology 1978; 107:384-402.

20. Hinkle, L. E., and Wolff, H. G. The nature of man's adaptation to his total environment and the relation of this to illness. Archives of Internal Medicine 1975; 99:441-460.

21. Holmes, T. H., and Rahe, R. H. The social readjustment rating scale. Journal of Psychosomatic Research 1967; 11:213-218.

22. House, J. S., Robbins, C., and Metzner, H. L. The association of social relationships with mortality: Prospective evidence from the Tecumseh Community Health Study. American Journal of Epidemiology 1982; 116:123-140.

23. Kahana, B. Social isolation. In: The Encyclopedia of Aging. New York: Springer Publishing Co., 1987, pp. 369-370.

24. Kahn, R. L., and Antonucci, T. C. Convoys of social support: A life-course approach. In: S. B. Kiesler, J. N. Morgan, and V. K. Oppenheimer (eds.), Aging: Social Change. New York: Academic Press, 1981, pp. 383-405.

25. Kaplan, B. H., Cassel, J. C., and Gore, S. Social support and health. Medical Care (Suppl.) 1977; 15(5):47-58.

26. Kasl, S. V. The detection and modification of psychosocial and behavioral risk factors. In: L. A. Aiken and D. H. Mechanic (eds.), Applications of Social Science to Clinical Medicine and Health Policy. New Brunswick, N.J.: Rutgers University Press, 1986, pp. 359-391.

27. Kasl, S. V., and Berkman, L. F. Some psychosocial influences on the health status of the elderly: The perspective of social epidemiology. In: J. L.

McGaugh and S. B. Kiesler (eds.), Aging: Biology and Behavior. New York: Academic Press, 1981, pp. 345-386.

28. Keller, S., Weiss, J., and Schleifer, S. Suppression of immunity by stress: Effect of a graded series of stressors on lymphocyte stimulation in the rat. Science 1981; 213:1387-1400.

29. Kiesler, C. A. Policy implications of research on social support and health, In: S. Cohen and S. L. Syme (eds.), Social Support and Health. New York: Academic Press, 1985, pp. 347-363.

30. Krause, N. Understanding the stress process: Linking social support with locus of control beliefs. Journal of Gerontology 1987; 41(6):589-593.

31. Langlie, J. D. Social networks, health beliefs and preventive behavior. Journal of Health and Social Behavior, 1977; 18(3):244-260.

32. Lowenthal, M. F., and Boler, D. Voluntary vs. involuntary social withdrawal. Journal of Gerontology 1965; 29:363-371.

33. Mortimer, J. A. Health Objectives for the Nation: Year 2000. Maintenance of Health and Quality of Life of Older People: Notes from the Working Group. Bethesda, Md.: Public Health Service, August 1988.

34. National Center for Health Statistics. Health statistics on older persons, United States, 1986. Vital and Health Statistics, Series 3, No. 25. Washington, D.C.: U.S. Government Printing Office, 1987.

35. Rahe, R. H. Developments in life change measurement: Subjective life change unit scaling. In: B. S. Dohrenwend and B. P. Dohrenwend (eds.), Stressful Life Events and Their Contexts (part of the Monographs in Psychosocial Epidemiology series). New York: Prodist, 1981, pp. 48-62.

36. Reed, D., McGee, D., Yano, K., et al. Social networks and coronary heart disease among Japanese men in Hawaii. American Journal of Epidemiology 1983; 117:384-386.

37. Reed, D., McGee, D., and Yano, K. Psychosocial processes and general susceptibility to chronic disease. American Journal of Epidemiology 1984; 119:356-370.

38. Rodin, J., Cashman, C., and Desiderato, L. Intervention and aging. In: M. W. Riley, J. D. Matarazzo, and A. Baum (eds.), The Aging Dimension. Hillsdale, N.J.: Lawrence Erlbaum Associates, Inc., 1987, pp. 93-124.

39. Rook, K. S. Promoting social bonding: Strategies for helping the lonely and socially isolated. American Psychologist 1984; 38:1389-1407.

40. Schleifer, S. J., Keller, S. E., Camerino, M., Thornton, J. C., and Stein, M. Suppression of lymphocyte stimulation following bereavement. Journal of the American Medical Association 1983; 249:374-377.

41. Schoenbach, V. J. Behavior and life style as determinants of health and well-being in the elderly. In: H. T. Phillips and S. A. Gaylord (eds.), Aging and Public Health. New York: Springer Publications Co., 1985, pp. 183-216.

42. Schultz, R., and Hanusa, B. H. Long-term effects of control and predictability-enhancing interventions: Findings and ethical issues. Journal of Personality and Social Psychology 1978; 36:1194-1201.

43. Seeman, T. E., Kaplan, G. A., Knudsen, L., Cohen, R., and Guralnik, J. Social network ties and mortality among the elderly in the Alameda County Study. American Journal of Epidemiology 1987; 126(4):714-723.

44. Srole, L., Langner, S., Opler, M., and Rennie, T. Mental Health in the Metropolis: The Midtown Manhattan Study. New York: Blakiston Division, McGraw-Hill, 1962.

45. Stein, M., Schleifer, S. J., and Keller, S. E. Immunity and aging: Experimental and clinical studies. In: M. W. Riley, J. D. Matarazzo, and A. Baum

(eds.), The Aging Dimension. Hillsdale, N.J.: Lawrence Erlbaum Associates, Inc., 1987, pp. 125-141.

46. Townsend, P. Isolation, desolation and loneliness. In: Shanas, E., Townsend, P., Wedderburn, D., Friis, H., Mihog, P., and Stehouwer, J. (eds.), Old People in Three Industrial Societies. New York: Arno Press, 1980.

47. Wallston, B. S., Alagna, S. W., DeVellis, B. M., and DeVellis, R. D. Social support and physical health. Health Psychology 1983; 2:367-381.

48. Wan, T. T. H. Stressful Life Events, Social Support Networks and Gerontological Health. Lexington, Mass.: D.C. Heath, 1982.

49. World Health Organization. Psychosomatic Disorders. World Health Organization Technical Report No. 775. Geneva: World Health Organization, 1964.

50. Wortman, C. B., and Conway, T. L. The role of social support in adaptation and recovery from physical illness. In: S. Cohen and S. L. Syme, Social Support and Health. New York: Academic Press, 1985, pp. 281-298.

15

Falls in Older Persons
Risk Factors and Prevention

———

Falls are a marker of frailty, immobility, and acute and chronic health impairment in older persons. Falls in turn diminish function by causing injury, activity limitations, fear of falling, and loss of mobility. Most injuries in the elderly are the result of falls; fractures of the hip, forearm, humerus, and pelvis usually result from the combined effect of falls and osteoporosis.

Prevention of falls must span the spectrum of ages and health states within the older population and address the diversity of causes of falls without unnecessarily compromising quality of life and independence. Intrinsic risk factors for falls have been found in controlled studies, which allow the identification of those at risk and suggest potential preventive interventions. Elderly individuals with multiple health impairments are at greatest risk, but many healthy older persons also fall each year. Current understanding of the etiology of postural instability and falling is limited, and there is little information about the effectiveness of interventions to prevent falls.

A fall is an unintentional event that results in the person coming to rest on the ground or another lower level.[56] Falls can be described in terms of three phases. The first phase is an initiating event that displaces the body's center of mass beyond its base of support. Initiating events involve extrinsic factors such as environmental hazards; intrinsic factors such as unstable joints, muscle weakness, and unreliable postural reflexes; and physical activities in progress at

263

the time of the fall. The second phase of a fall involves a failure of the systems for maintaining upright posture to detect and correct this displacement in time to avoid a fall. This failure is generally due to factors intrinsic to the individual, such as loss of sensory function, impaired central processing, and muscle weakness. The third phase is an impact of the body on environmental surfaces, usually the floor or ground, which results in the transmission of forces to body tissue and organs. The potential for injury is a function of the magnitude and direction of the forces and the susceptibility of tissues and organs to damage. A fourth phase, although not part of a fall, concerns the medical, psychological, and health care sequelae of the fall and attendant injuries. These sequelae affect the degree of damage and disability resulting from the fall. Approaches to preventing falls and their consequences should focus on factors related to each of these phases.

Falls with certain initiating characteristics (e.g., loss of consciousness, stroke, overwhelming external force from a motor vehicle accident, or violence) are often excluded from the definition of falls in older persons.[56] The causes of these falls are different from the typical fall associated with neuromuscular and sensory impairment in an older person and are therefore a distinct topic. The committee concurs in this exclusion; consequently, such falls will not be covered in this chapter.

THE HEALTH BURDEN OF FALLS AND FALL-RELATED INJURIES IN OLDER PERSONS

Mortality

In 1986, there were 8,313 deaths from falls reported in the United States for persons aged 65 and older, making falls the leading cause of death from injury in the elderly.[94] This number, derived from death certificates, may underestimate the number of deaths in which falls are a contributing factor.[27,49] The rate of fall-related deaths rises rapidly with age for whites aged 70 and older; it rises less dramatically for nonwhites 75 and older (Figure 15-1). By age 85, approximately two-thirds of all reported injury-related deaths are due to falls.[6] Older men are more likely than older women to die from a fall; the highest mortality rate occurs in white men aged 85 and over (171 per 100,000), followed by white women aged 85 and over (127 per 100,000). The rate of mortality from falls has declined in recent decades[77] (Figure 15-2), which may reflect increased survival of hip fracture patients[92] and improved trauma care.[95] Some studies suggest

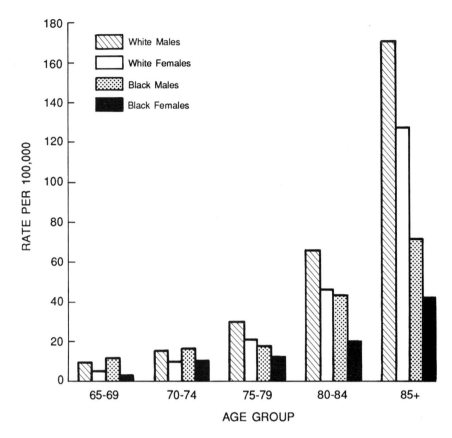

FIGURE 15-1 Death rates from falls per 100,000 persons by age, sex, and race: United States 1986. Source: National Center for Health Statistics annual mortality data tapes reporting external underlying cause of death.

that falls in the frail elderly, especially falls with a "long lie" (a long waiting time on the ground after a fall before help arrives), are associated with increased mortality independent of injury severity;[36,112] this finding, however, is still uncertain.[16]

Fall-related Injuries

In general, fractures are the most common serious injury resulting from falls in older persons. Specifically, fractures of the hip, wrist, humerus, and pelvis in this age group result from the combined effects of falls, osteoporosis, and other factors that increase susceptibility to injury.[21,65] Each year in the United States there are approximately

220,000 each of hip and wrist fractures in persons over the age of 65[73] (see Chapter 6). Although precise estimates are not available, there are several times as many fractures of other bones in persons aged 65 and older as there are hip and wrist fractures.[29,33,81] The proportions of some frequently occurring fractures (e.g., those of the rib, hand, foot, and ankle) that result from falls versus other types of trauma are also uncertain. The epidemiology of fracture is reviewed in greater detail in Chapter 6.

Other serious injuries resulting from falls include hematoma, joint dislocation, severe laceration, sprain, and other disabling soft tissue injury. There are few data on fall-related injuries other than fracture in the U.S. population. In a regional study in northeastern Ohio, the rate of emergency room treatment of fall-related injuries in persons aged 75 and older approached 80 per 1,000 per year in women and 60 per 1,000 per year in men.[29] Another recent study in Dade County, Florida, found an exponential increase with age in the rate of fall injuries that received hospital and emergency room treatment among persons aged 65 and older. These rates were higher in women than men at all ages.[95] Among those over age 75, fall injury rates in women exceeded 100 per 1,000 per year; in men they exceeded 80 per

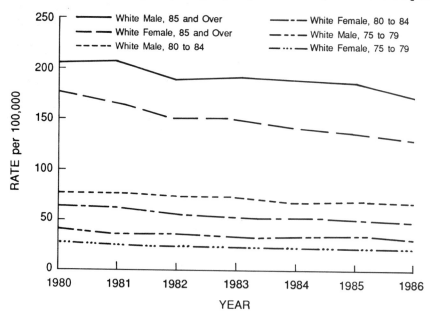

FIGURE 15-2 Death rates from falls per 100,000 persons by age, sex, and year: United States. Source: National Center for Health Statistics annual mortality data tapes reporting external underlying cause of death.

1,000 per year. About 40 percent of treated fall injuries were fractures.

Most falls, however, do not cause sufficient injury to receive medical attention. Only 3 to 5 percent of falls in elderly persons who reside in the community and in nursing homes result in fractures, with fewer than 1 percent of falls causing hip fractures.[36,75,93,103] Only about 5 to 10 percent of falls cause other serious injuries requiring medical care.[36,102] Between 30 and 50 percent of falls result in a variety of minor soft tissue injuries that do not receive medical attention; the remainder cause no injury or only trivial damage.[36,75,82]

Frequency of Falls

The few large community surveys of falls in this country and elsewhere have been retrospective, asking respondents about falls in the past year. This focus probably results in significant underreporting and misclassification.[22,75] Nevertheless, these studies find that about one-quarter of persons aged 65 to 74 and a third or more of those aged 75 and older report a fall in the previous year,[17,84,92] figures that are roughly consistent with 12-month recall data from the National Health Interview Survey (Figure 15-3). About half of those elderly persons (of all ages) who report falling in the previous year fall two or

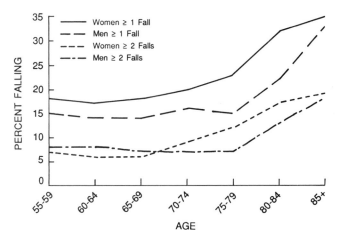

FIGURE 15-3 Percentage of older individuals reporting falls in the previous 12 months by age and sex: United States. Source: National Health Interview Survey's 1984 Supplement on Aging.

more times, a finding consistent with recent prospective studies.[75,103] The rate of falls is even higher in health care institutions, with an annual average incidence of about 1,600 per 1,000 nursing home patients.[93]

Disability

Estimates from the National Health Interview Survey indicate that, among persons aged 65 and older in 1986, there were 5.8 million acute injuries of all types associated with 58.9 million days of restricted activity and 18.8 million bed days.[74] Falls probably account for a large part of this total injury burden. About one-quarter of falls in the community result in an activity limitation owing to injury or fear of falling.[75,103] Disabilities resulting from hip, wrist, and other fractures in the elderly are substantial (see Chapter 6), but there are few data on disability-associated fall injuries other than fracture. One study found that about half of those persons aged 65 and older living at home who are hospitalized for a fall injury are not discharged to their home;[95] this group also includes one-third of those with injuries other than a hip fracture.

The psychological and functional consequences of falls can be severe whether or not an injury occurs, but such consequences have received insufficient attention and study. Postural instability or a fall can lead to fear of falling and anxiety about normal activities on the part of the older person at risk, as well as among family members and care givers. The result may be a reduction in activity, decreased mobility, and increased dependence, often self-imposed but sometimes originating from others (e.g., family members, care givers). Fear of falling, or "postfall syndrome," may contribute to nursing home admissions[109] and loss of independence.[56]

Costs

Meaningful estimates of the medical and other economic costs of falls in the elderly are not possible. Fall-related fractures, however, constitute the major portion of the costs of osteoporosis, which have recently been estimated at $7 to 10 billion annually.[81] For example, about 90 percent of the estimated $5.2 billion in direct medical costs for osteoporosis in 1986 were attributable to hospital and nursing home care; 66 percent of hospitalizations and 82 percent of nursing home care admissions for osteoporosis involve fractures in which a fall is usually the source of trauma in an elderly person.[83] Studies are needed of the costs of fall injuries other than fractures, of fall injuries treated on an outpatient basis, of nursing home admissions triggered by fear of falling, and of activity limitations and disability owing to falls.

DETERMINANTS OF FALLS: RISK FACTORS AND CAUSES

Current prospects for the prevention of falls are uncertain, although several intrinsic and pharmacologic factors that are associated with an increased risk of falls have been identified. Many falls in the elderly are probably multifactorial, resulting from the convergence of several intrinsic, pharmacologic, environmental, behavioral, and activity-related factors. However, knowledge regarding the etiologic mechanisms of these risk factors and how they combine to produce falls remains limited. Perhaps even more limited is an understanding of situational and environmental factors that precipitate a fall in persons with predisposing characteristics. Situational and environmental factors may be among the most important determinants of risk in healthy older persons. Finally, a better understanding is needed of factors that affect the risk of injury and other adverse outcomes of a fall.

Intrinsic Risk Factors

Falls are a recognized marker of frailty and mobility impairment in the elderly. The presence and severity of functional disability is a useful indicator of the risk of falling in individuals and populations (Table 15-1). Data from the National Health Interview Survey's 1984 Supplement on Aging indicate that persons aged 75 to 84 who require help with activities of daily living are 14 times more likely, and those with limitations in walking, transfer, and balance activities are 10 times more likely, to report having two or more falls in the previous 12 months compared with persons with no limitations.[43] The association of falls with frailty and functional disabilities in the elderly is also evident in the high rates of falls reported in nursing homes.[93] The design of effective preventive measures, however, requires knowledge of treatable impairments and conditions that contribute to functional disability, frailty, and falls in older populations.

Normal gait and postural stability depend on the proper functioning of sensory, neuromuscular, and musculoskeletal systems. Limb proprioceptive and tactile input, visual input, and vestibular input are critical for maintaining the body's center of gravity within

TABLE 15-1 Selected Intrinsic Risk Factors for Falls

Type of Risk Factor	Measure (Studies)	Strength of Evidence[a]
Demographic	Age ≥ 80 Men (7,15,75,103)	Strong
	Female (9,75,103)	Inconsistent
General health and functioning	ADL, IADL, mobility impairment (17,31,62,75,90,103,105,111)	Strong
	Reduced physical activity/exercise (15,75,103)	Weak
	Past history of falls (15,55,75,103, 105,112)	Strong
Medical conditions	Arthritis (9,14,32,75,90,103,105)	Moderate
	Stroke (15,62,75,84)	Moderate
	Parkinson's disease (15,32,75)	Strong
	Dementia (13,14,32,68)	Strong
	Incontinence (55,62,75,90,103,105)	Strong
	Postural hypotension (15,17,75,90, 103,105)	Inconsistent
Musculosketal and neuromuscular	Reduced knee, hip, or ankle strength (14,15,75,90,104,105,110,112)	Strong
	Reduced grip strength (9,15,75,110)	Strong
	Hip or knee pain/arthritis	Moderate
	Foot problems (9,31,75,82,103)	Inconsistent
	Impaired knee/plantar reflexes (31,75,90)	Weak
	Slowed reaction time (1,31,75)	Weak
Sensory	Impaired visual acuity (11,15,17,75, 82,90,103,105)	Strong
	Reduced depth perception (75)	Weak
	Visual perceptual error (15,89,106)	Weak
	Impaired lower extremity sensory function (11,14,75,90,97,103,105)	Inconsistent
Other neurologic signs	Frontal cortex/release (90,105)	Weak
	Cerebellar, pyramidal, extrapyramidal (75,90)	Weak
Gait, balance, physical performance	Gait "abnormalities" (37,75,90,103, 105,112)	Strong
	Reduced walking speed (15,37,52,75)	Strong
	Postural sway (11,15,75,89)	Moderate
	Impaired dynamic balance (75,89,90, 103,105, 112,113)	Strong
	Impaired tandem gait, one leg balance (14,75, 103)	Moderate
	Difficulty arising from chair (15,75, 103,104)	Strong
Cognitive, psychological	Reduced mental status test score (13,15,17,55, 69,75,84,90,103, 105,112)	Strong
	Depression (17,32,69,75,103,105)	Strong

TABLE 15-1 Continued

Type of Risk Factor	Measure (Studies)	Strength of Evidence<i>a</i>
Medication use	Sedatives, hypnotics, anxiolytics (9,15,17,32, 55,62,75,84,86,90, 97,103,105,111,112)	Strong
	Antidepressants (9,17,62,75,86)	Moderate
	Cardiovascular (9,15,17,32,75,84, 90,103,105)	Inconsistent
	NSAIDS* (15,32)	Weak
	Number of medications (9,14,15,32, 90,105)	Strong

Note: ADL = Activities of Daily Living; IADL = Instrumental Activities of Daily Living. Numbers in parentheses indicate references.

aStrong = association in multiple studies; at least two of which are prospective; moderate = association in multiple studies, only one of which is prospective—some studies are negative; Weak = association in only a few studies, none of which are prospective—some studies are negative; Inconsistent = generally conflicting and inconsistent findings in multiple studies.

*NSAIDS = National Health Interview Survey Supplement on Aging, 1984.

its base of support, and these sensory pathways may be compromised by age and disease.[114] In addition, age-related disturbances in the organization and central neurological integration of sensory and motor functions may impair the speed, effectiveness, and reliability of postural reflexes, leading to falls.[99,115] Age-related slowing of postural reflexes may increase the muscular force required for an effective response to postural disturbances,[99] but the strength of skeletal muscles involved in postural control and walking declines with increasing age.[12,35,117] Weak muscles and unstable or painful joints may also initiate postural disturbances during voluntary movement.

Several studies have found that impaired vision, lower extremity sensory impairment, reduced lower extremity strength, and reduced grip strength are associated with the risk of falls (see Table 15-1). Arthritis in lower extremity joints and foot disorders contribute to gait and balance problems and are also associated with falls in several studies (Table 15-1). Other sensory problems that may contribute to falls, including cervical mechanoreceptor[116] and vestibular disorders,[72] and the role of impaired central processing in postural instability and falls,[53] need more investigation. A few studies have assessed the association of falls with slowed reaction time, impaired reflexes, and other neurologic signs, with inconclusive results (Table 15-1).

Performance-based measures of gait, balance, and neuromuscular function are strong predictors of falls (Table 15-1), probably because they reflect the combined effect of sensory, neurological, and musculoskeletal impairments on postural stability during the activities in which falls commonly occur.[38,103] Impaired cognitive function and depression are associated with an increased risk of falls in several studies. Whether the association of cognitive impairment and falls reflects neurological and psychomotor causes of falls, or behavioral factors related to mental and psychological states, is uncertain.[70]

It is suspected that psychotropic, diuretic, antihypertensive, and antiparkinsonian medications, especially when inappropriately dosed, may contribute to falls in the elderly by decreasing alertness, depressing psychomotor function, or causing fatigue, dizziness, and postural hypotension.[60] Evidence is strongest for an association of falls with the use of hypnotic-anxiolytic drugs, particularly benzodiazepines[85] (Table 15-1). The role of diuretic and antihypertensive medications in increasing the risk of postural hypotension and falls needs further investigation.[85] Several studies have found an association of falls with the number of medications being taken. Research is needed to determine possible synergistic effects among drugs that might increase postural instability.[10]

Several common chronic medical conditions, including arthritis, dementia of the Alzheimer's type, stroke, cataracts, and urinary incontinence, as well as such uncommon conditions as Parkinson's disease, are associated with falls in one or more studies (Table 15-1). Although most studies have not found an association of falls with chronic cardiovascular conditions, including postural hypotension, their role as risk factors remains uncertain. Falls may also be a nonspecific manifestation of a variety of chronic and acute conditions.[102]

In sum, many impairments, disabilities, and conditions repeatedly have been found to be associated with the risk of falls in the elderly. This risk appears to increase with the number of risk factors a person has,[76,103] so that those persons most likely to fall can be identified. Additional research is needed, however, including controlled trials, to determine which treatable risk factors are causal.

Situational and Extrinsic Risk Factors

The risk of falls in apparently healthy older persons is substantial,[76,103] suggesting that behavioral, psychosocial, activity-related, and environmental factors are important in the etiology of falls and may combine with intrinsic risk factors to increase risk. For example, minor environmental hazards that are easily negotiated by a healthy individual can become major obstacles to mobility and safety for a person with gait or balance impairments. More generally, the physical demands of certain activities or tasks may exceed the competence of the individual, resulting in a fall.[47] Although potentially an important area of inquiry, current understanding of this type of fall risk factor is quite limited.

In healthy, active older persons, situational and extrinsic factors may be the predominant determinants of risk. Compared with frail and impaired elderly persons, falls among the individuals in this group are thought more often to involve overt environmental hazards, risk-taking activities like climbing ladders, hurrying, or running; in addition, they are more often likely to occur away from home.[56] Exposure to fall risks is spread over a wide range of physical environments and activities. In contrast, falls in health-impaired older persons are thought to occur during routine ambulation and transfer maneuvers, usually without an overt environmental hazard, and to occur at home. Among the functionally impaired elderly, fall risks are focused on activities required for basic mobility within a familiar environment.

If these contrasting patterns of fall risk are valid, then preventive efforts may need to be tailored to the health level of the population.[54] In addition, the two contrasting patterns of risk define a continuum along which many people move with advancing age and declining function. Behavioral, cognitive, and psychological factors that influence how an individual perceives and adapts to the dynamic and changing fit between his or her capabilities and environmental and task demands are a potentially important focus for fall prevention.[47,50,106] Additional research in this area is needed to guide the design of behavior-oriented prevention efforts.

Individual adaptations to increasing fall risks range from avoidance of specific high-risk activities and removal of environmental hazards, to enhancement of personal and environmental resources to maintain desired activities, to general curtailment of mobility and activities. Modification of activities and behaviors aimed at reducing risk is often appropriate; however, a delicate balance must always be struck between reduction in risk and maintenance of quality of life and independence. Although drastic reductions in activity may decrease falls in the short term by reducing exposure, over the long term, reduced self-confidence and physical deconditioning may only increase risk.

Environmental Factors

Environmental hazards potentially include poor stairway design and disrepair, inadequate lighting, clutter, slippery floors, unsecured mats and rugs, and lack of nonskid surfaces in bathtubs, among many others. Environmental factors are implicated by self-report as contributing to one-third to one-half of falls,[56,76,93,103] but most studies do not compare exposure to environmental hazards in those who fall with a control group. Only a few prospective studies have assessed hazards in the home as risk factors, with inconclusive results.[76,103] No studies have assessed hazards outside the home or quantified exposure to hazards (in terms of frequency, duration, and intensity) to develop a true estimate of risk; the usual approach is simply to note the presence of hazards in the homes of subjects. In addition, definitions of environmental hazards and methods for assessing them are difficult to standardize.[91]

The contribution of environmental factors to falls depends on both intrinsic risk factors and other situational variables, but these interactions are poorly understood. Persons with functional disabilities may be especially susceptible to a cluttered, poorly designed, or poorly illuminated environment. In addition, postural stability in an older person may be affected by subtle environmental cues such as lighting and visual and spatial design.[80,99,107,115] Although previous experience or familiarity with a particular environmental obstacle may reduce the risk per exposure,[102] factors that suddenly precipitate a misstep or trip in these familiar contexts are poorly understood, and methods to study such questions are needed.

Determinants of Injury and Other Outcomes of Falls

For injuries resulting from mechanical energy, such as a fall, the severity of impact, the resistance of the body through inertial forces, the elastic capacity of tissue, and the viscous tolerance of the body organs play an important role in the risk of injury.[18] Because of declines in the strength and resiliency of muscle, bone, and other tissues, older persons have an increased risk of injury compared with a younger person subjected to similar impact forces.[94] For example, bone mineral density is highly correlated with bone strength; after age 50, bone density declines about 1 percent per year at key sites such as the proximal femur.[65] The risk of fractures of the hip, forearm, and other sites increases with decreasing bone density independently of age.[20,51,63] Other factors that contribute to the risk of fracture owing to a fall include the orientation of the fall, the speed and effectiveness of protective responses, the ability of skin, fat, muscle, and environmental surfaces to absorb and distribute mechanical energy, and the architecture of bone.[20,64] A better understanding of biomechanical and other factors affecting the risk of fall injuries is needed.

Older people often have a worse outcome than younger people from the same injury because of impaired tissue regeneration, decreased functional reserves, and poorer immunologic function.[18,48] The psychosocial sequelae of falls are a poorly understood but potentially important outcome because they may influence functional recovery from fall injuries as well as the risk of further falls. Very little is known about factors that precipitate a "postfall syndrome" of extreme fear and anxiety.

PREVENTABILITY OF BURDEN

Research on risk factors for falls and the causes of postural instability suggests many preventive interventions, although at present there is almost no direct evidence of the effectiveness of any approach to preventing falls.[46] This situation will soon change as a result of studies now in progress. For the moment, however, one can only speculate about which approaches are most promising. In a few instances, evidence regarding modifications of intermediate variables that are risk factors for falls provides a limited basis for speculation.

Exercise and Physical Activity

Skeletal muscle strength and mass decline with age[57,58,71] and immobility.[12] Impaired strength is a strong predictor of falls in most studies (Table 15-1) and may also increase the risk of injury from a fall. Exercise might prevent falls and injury by strengthening muscles and increasing endurance; maintaining and improving posture, joint motion, and postural reflexes; stimulating cardiorespiratory function; and improving alertness.[41] A growing body of evidence indicates that the elderly respond to exercise training and that this response (which may include increased muscle strength and mass and increased aerobic capacity[24]) continues at very old ages and extremes of frailty.[3,25] Weight-bearing exercise may also help preserve bone mass, although this benefit is uncertain.[43,81] Exercise and physical activity are positively associated with physical and mental function in cross-sectional studies, but whether exercise training in the elderly can improve physical function, postural reflexes, mental function, or general health and well-being is uncertain.[43]

The type, level, intensity, and duration of exercise required to achieve a given health objective are controversial.[42] In particular, the effects of low-level exercise and physical activity, such as walking, on muscle strength, bone mass, postural reflexes and other factors affecting fall injuries are uncertain.[12] Because low-level exercises are popular, conducive to increased compliance, especially in frail subjects, and less likely to cause adverse effects,[41] they should be considered for inclusion in prevention trials along with high-intensity, focused training regimes. Nutritional causes of skeletal muscle weakness should also be considered as targets for intervention.[93]

There are no controlled studies specifically of exercise to prevent falls, though exercise has been included as a component of a few undifferentiated multiple risk factor interventions.[50,78] Exercise, and strength training regimes in particular, will be a key feature of future trials of fall prevention. These studies must address important issues of content, cost, safety, acceptability, and compliance, particularly as these apply to a frail older population with multiple chronic conditions. Techniques for minimizing the risk of exercise-induced injury are needed. Methods are also needed to control for possible increased exposure to situational and environmental fall risks resulting from exercise and physical activity programs, and to differentiate the psychosocial and the physiological effects of exercise interventions.

Rehabilitative Therapies: Balance and Gait Training

Balance and gait abnormalities are associated with falls (Table 15-1) and may be modified through focused rehabilitative interventions.[106] Rehabilitative strategies include strength training targeted to impaired muscle groups, habituation exercises for persons with vestibular problems, motor coordination and proprioception exercises for persons with balance problems, and gait training for individuals with gait abnormalities.[37,96,106] A few studies suggest it may be possible to improve balance with focused exercise or repetition of specific voluntary movements associated with instability.[8,45,106] Additional controlled studies are needed to test the effect of rehabilitative therapies on balance, gait, and falls.

Medications

More than 70 percent of persons 65 and older living at home currently have at least one prescribed medication,[44] and the percentage is even higher among nursing home residents.[7] Randomized trials to determine whether adherence to conservative guidelines for use of psychotropic medications prevents falls are clearly warranted. Such guidelines include "a) careful assessment of the need for a psycho-tropic drug with consideration of nonpharmacologic therapy, b) use of drugs with fewer potential side effects, c) use of the lowest effective dose, d) use of drug for the shortest possible duration,"[85] and reduction of other drugs when initiating treatment with psycho-tropic medications.[10] The efficacy of such an approach is unknown. However, there is evidence that the prescribing habits of physicians can be modified.[40,87] Educational efforts emphasizing the dangers of self-medication and tinkering with prescribed doses may also be of value[5,34] and should be tested. More research is needed to determine the contribution of cardiovascular medications to the risk of falling.

Environmental and Behavioral Interventions

Although there is little epidemiologic evidence linking environ-mental hazards to the risk of falling, environmental factors remain a promising focus for intervention. Common sense suggests many modifiable factors that affect the safety of both the home and community environments, ranging from sidewalks and stairways in disrepair, to grossly inadequate lighting, to unsafe footwear, to safety measures like grab bars and nonskid surfaces in bathrooms.[56,100] More subtle environmental factors (e.g., the shape and positioning of handrails, the design of furniture, storage space, and bathrooms) may also be important.[2] Environmental assessment and modification appears feasible as a component of clinic, community-based, and institutional programs.[50,93] However, there is a large range of diffi-culties and costs of environmental and design modifications; in addition, methods for overcoming psychological and economic barriers to implementation must be considered.

Because falls tend to occur where people spend the most time, a home-oriented prevention strategy is important. Numerous check-lists are available to help identify environmental hazards in the home,[56,100] but there is little information to help prioritize remediation of the many hazards that may be found. Studies are needed to identify where falls occur in the home and the prevalence of various home hazards. Studies of the risk attributable to each of these home hazards, especially in relation to the person's time at risk and their functional disabilities, are critical to the design of prevention strate-gies. An approach that combines medical and physical therapy evaluation with a home environment assessment may be particularly effective owing to the fact that physical disabilities and environmental factors interact to cause many falls.[93,102]

Education is an essential element of the prevention of falls because the perception of health risk supports health action. Educating patients and the public to recognize potential hazards in the home and to distinguish safe from risk-taking behavior may have benefits in terms of the perception of risk and the adoption of safety practices. Some hazards can be addressed by behavioral changes alone—for example, avoiding darkened stairways or such risky activities as standing on chairs. In one study a majority of older persons who had suffered falls felt that their falls were preventable by changes in their own or another's behavior.[50] Involving the older person at risk in any assessment of the home environment is an important educational tool that will support compliance with the expert's recommendations. A better understanding of how psychological and cognitive factors affect the success of behavioral and environmental interventions to reduce fall risks would help focus supportive education and counseling.[106] Mechanisms for developing community resources and delivering them to elderly persons in need of help in making environmental or behavioral changes should be designed and tested.

Finally, physical restraints are sometimes used with institutionalized patients to prevent falls,[23] but no studies have determined whether this approach is successful or whether alternative strategies of managing fall-prone patients would be equally or more effective.

Frameworks for Multiple Risk Factor Interventions

Because of the multifactorial nature of falls and the wide range of factors involved, it is possible that the most effective clinic or community-based interventions will address several types of risk factors and involve diverse disciplines.[56,93,102] Intensive clinical evaluation of elderly individuals with instability problems often finds multiple conditions that could contribute to falls and that may be treatable.[30,93,102] To prevent falls, however, medical evaluation and treatment may need to target those impairments that are most likely to cause falls and include pharmacologic, rehabilitative, psychosocial, and environmental components in a treatment plan.

Multidisciplinary geriatric assessment and treatment programs suggest one model for multiple risk factor interventions: "Comprehensive geriatric assessment generally includes evaluation of the patient in several domains. . . physical, mental, social, economic, functional and environmental" with the goal of guiding the selection of interventions to restore or preserve health.[19] Geriatric assessment in rehabilitation and inpatient settings has demonstrated effectiveness in prolonging survival and reducing hospital and nursing home admissions; there is also some evidence it may improve functional status.[19] Preliminary results from one study suggest that a modest reduction in falls is also possible (Lawrence Rubenstein, VA Medical Center, Sepulveda, California, personal communication, 1989). Performance-oriented assessment and intervention may also be a useful model for fall prevention in medical care settings. In this approach, physical performance and mobility are evaluated in the context of the usual activities of daily living, preferably in the residential setting; those impairments that contribute to functional and mobility problems are targeted for medical, rehabilitative, or environmental remediation.[61,101,102]

Whether falls can be prevented by aggressive diagnosis, treatment, and rehabilitation of multiple risk factors, either in traditional medical settings or in settings guided by principles of geriatric medicine, remains to be tested. The cost-effectiveness of such an approach and the willingness and ability of third-party payers to finance it must also be carefully evaluated.

Although intrinsic risk factors may be most effectively addressed through clinical interventions, environmental, educational, behavioral, and low-level exercise and physical activity interventions can be implemented through community-based programs. Educational programs may encourage changes on the individual level, as well as on the level of governmental action and public awareness. For example, an increased awareness of the importance of safe access by the elderly and disabled to the broader physical environment is important for increased mobility and may be a factor in the prevention of falls. The effectiveness of community-based fall prevention programs may depend as much on social, political, and psychological factors as on the inherent value of the intervention. Therefore, trials of such programs should include in-depth process as well as outcome evaluation.

Targeting Interventions

There is substantial heterogeneity in the health and functional status of elderly populations, and the diverse causes of falls reflect this heterogeneity. The success of preventive efforts may depend on the ability to target interventions toward those risk factors that are most important in subgroups of the population. Medical and rehabilitative approaches may be most beneficial in the very impaired elderly and those living in nursing homes, whereas environmental and behavioral interventions may have most value among healthy older persons living in the community. Nevertheless, these contrasting approaches may only imply different emphases on a common set of factors, with intrinsic, environmental, and situational factors combining to cause most falls in both healthy and impaired persons. For example, slowed postural reflexes may increase the risk of falls owing to slips and trips in otherwise healthy persons, and it is possible that postural reflexes can be improved by training and exercise.

The goal of prevention should be not only to reduce falls but to reduce injury and other sequelae of falls. The risk of injury from a fall is the product of a sequence of risks, including the probability of falling, the effectiveness of protective responses, protection by local shock absorbers, including environmental surfaces, and the strength and resiliency of tissue and organs.[64] Thus, preventive efforts should address each of the phases in the injury sequence.[18] Approaches to decreasing susceptibility to fall injuries are currently limited to therapy to prevent bone loss (see Chapter 6). Environmental surfaces that cushion the impact of a fall, as well as learned protective responses, should also be explored. Finally, improved approaches to treatment and rehabilitation of injuries in the elderly should be emphasized.[18]

RECOMMENDATIONS

Research

1. Randomized trials of fall prevention interventions are a high priority. Agencies of the National Institutes of Health are currently sponsoring a program of such research, and consideration should be given to increasing funding to support a greater number of trials. Interventions that should be given a high priority for randomized trials include the following:

- focused exercise and strength training regimes;
- physical therapy, rehabilitation, and training for specific balance and gait impairments;
- comprehensive medical diagnosis and treatment focused on neuromuscular, musculoskeletal, and sensory impairments thought to cause falls;
- adherence to conservative guidelines for use of hypnotic-anxiolytic drugs;
- improved vision care and updated lens prescriptions;
- modification of environmental risks in the home;
- behavioral/educational interventions focusing on risk awareness and risk-taking behaviors; and
- multiple risk factor interventions.

Intervention trials should provide information on the effectiveness of distinct treatment components, either by focusing on a single component or, when multifactor interventions are used, through a "crossed" or "matrix" design. Where appropriate, investigators should also provide data on the costs and benefits of the program. Trials should be undertaken in both community-dwelling and institutionalized populations.

2. Support should be provided for observational studies of falls that will expand the knowledge base for future intervention designs by increasing understanding of the etiologic mechanisms of falls and of interactions among risk factors. High priority should be given to the following:

- better understanding of situational risk factors (behavioral, psychosocial, activity-related, and environmental variables) and how these interact with gait, balance, and other impairments in causing falls;
- better understanding of the pathophysiology of postural control abnormalities in the elderly to identify new leads for therapy;
- studies of the effect of psychosocial factors on adaptation and on the coping strategies of older persons adjusting to physical impairments, postural instability, and falls;
- greater understanding of the effects of injury on the psychological function and quality of life of older persons;
- studies of where falls occur in the home and of the location and prevalence of various home hazards;
- studies of the risk attributable to specific home hazards, especially in relation to the person's time at risk to these exposures and their functional disabilities;
- in cognitively impaired and demented patients, an increased understanding of the respective roles of neurological and behavioral factors in causing falls;
- studies of diuretic and antihypertensive therapy and falls that examine specific drug types, underlying cardiovascular conditions, and new versus established use, and that have the power to detect moderate increases in risk;
- studies of the distribution and determinants of risk factors for falls in populations, especially neuromuscular, sensory, gait, and balance impairments; and
- monitoring of new drugs and postmarketing surveillance in elderly patients for side effects that cause postural instability and falls.

3. Support should be provided for studies that address methodological issues in research on falls, including the following:

- use of intermediate outcome variables, such as balance and strength measures, to estimate the effectiveness of interventions in preventing falls and injuries;
- reliable methods of self-report ascertainment and description of falls in community-dwelling populations;
- development of reliable falls surveillance mechanisms for institutionalized and cognitively impaired populations, including accelerometers and other technological approaches;
- methods for quantifying exposure to fall risk, especially environmental and activity-related risk factors, which are important in assessing the efficacy of interventions that increase exposure by increasing physical activity and mobility; and
- methods for describing and classifying the full range of fall injuries and other adverse sequelae, including fear of falling and activity limitations.

4. The recommendation made in the National Research Council/Institute of Medicine report *Injury in America* for the use of E-codes (from the World Health Organization's *International Classification of Diseases*, "External Causes of Injury") in medical records, including hospital discharge records, should be implemented. This practice would allow better tracking of national health objectives, the performance of analytic studies, and evaluation of the effectiveness of proposed preventive measures. Indeed, implementation of this objective would benefit a broad range of injury research and prevention activities.

5. Studies of the biomechanical and other determinants of fall injuries, particularly the understanding of impact responses and tolerances, should be emphasized as a potential means of preventing fall injuries through the environmental control of mechanical energy. Increased research in this area might lead to the design of energy-absorbing surfaces or unobtrusive protective clothing for high-risk older persons.

6. Support should be provided for studies of the economic costs of fall-related injuries other than fractures, of outpatient treatment of fall injuries, and of nursing home admissions related to falls.

Education and Services

1. Support should be allocated for community-based demonstration projects in injury prevention in general and in prevention of

falls in particular, stressing education, reduction of environmental risks, and changes in risk-taking behavior. As part of these projects, methods for coordinating existing public- and private-sector organizations and mobilizing new community injury control resources (e.g., retired firemen, building trades workers) should be developed and evaluated.

2. State-of-the-art fall prevention techniques should be integrated into existing national/local injury control programs.

3. Public education aimed at both the older population and society at large should provide information on risk factors for falls and injuries, ways to modify risks, and sources of assistance in risk reduction. These activities should make aggressive use of several media, including television, radio, and the health care delivery system.

4. Treatment and rehabilitation programs addressing the psychological ("post-fall syndrome") and disability outcomes of falls should be developed and tested.

5. The general topic of injury prevention for the older person should be a required part of the core curriculum of training and continuing education of health professionals. Curriculum areas should include the significance of injury (and falls in particular) as a public health problem, risk factors for injury, and presumptive and demonstrated injury control strategies.

6. Professional training in architecture, city planning, product design, and human factors engineering should include information on the range of capabilities and limitations of the older population so that these factors can be incorporated into designs, standards, and plans.

7. Agencies that set and enforce architectural, building, and safety standards affecting the environments of older persons should take into account the range of capabilities in the elderly population. Applied multidisciplinary studies that address the intersection of standards for the built environment, human factors, and aging should be supported.

8. Adequate reimbursement for injury prevention efforts should be sought, including reimbursement for clinical evaluation and interventions to decrease the risk of falling.

Other Areas

In addition to implementation of the recommendations for prevention of osteoporosis outlined in Chapter 6, the recommendations of the surgeon general's 1988 Workshop on Health Promotion and Aging regarding injury control, medications, and physical activity should also be implemented, with particular emphasis on the following:

• research and evaluation of promising approaches to improving the understanding and effective use of medications in the elderly, including medication profiles and diaries, color-coding, special packaging, large print, pictographs, and messages adapted to social, cultural, and educational differences;
• education of patients, family members, and health care providers in proper use, monitoring of side effects, and management of multiple medications for the older individual;
• continued research on the full spectrum of physiological, functional, and psychosocial effects of exercise regimes and regular physical activity, including strength, endurance, bone mass, agility, coordination, flexibility, and well-being; and
• research to determine the appropriate type, intensity, frequency, and duration of exercise necessary to achieve the potential benefits in health and functional capacity across a wide age span and range of health status and abilities.

REFERENCES

1. Adelsberg, S., Pitman, M., and Alexander, H. Lower extremity fractures: Relationship to reaction time and coordination time. Archives of Physical Medicine and Rehabilitation 1970; 70:737-739.
2. American Institute of Architects Foundation. Design for Aging: An Architect's Guide. Washington, D.C.: American Institute of Architects Press, 1986.
3. Aniansson, A., Ljungberg, P., Rundgren, A., and Wettereqvist, H. Effect of a training programme for pensioners on condition and muscular strength. Archives of Gerontology and Geriatrics 1984; 3:229-241.
4. Aniansson, A., and Gustafsson, E. Physical training in elderly men with special reference to quadriceps muscle strength and morphology. Clinical Physiology 1981; 1:87-98.
5. Ascione, F. J., and Shrimp, L. A. The effectiveness of four education strategies in the elderly. Drug Intelligence and Clinical Pharmacy 1984; 18:126-131.
6. Baker, S., O'Neill, B., and Karpf, R. S. The Injury Fact Book. Cambridge, Mass.: Lexington Books, 1984.
7. Beers, M., Avorn, J., Soumerai, S. B., Everitt, D. E., Sherman, D. S., and Salem, S. Psychoactive medication use in intermediate-care facility residents. Journal of the American Medical Association 1988; 260:3016-3020.
8. Black, F. O., Wall, C. III, Rockette, H. E., Jr., and Kitch, R. Normal subject postural sway during the Romberg test. American Journal of Otolaryngology 1982; 3:309-318.
9. Blake, A. J., Morgan, K., Bendall, M. J., Dallosso, H., Ebrahim, S. B. J., Arie, T. H. D., Fentem, P. H., and Bassey, E. J. Falls by elderly people at home: Prevalence and associated factors. Age and Ageing 1988; 17:365-372.

10. Blumenthal, M. D., and Davie, J. W. Dizziness and falling in elderly psychiatric outpatients. American Journal of Psychiatry 1980; 173(2):173-203.

11. Brocklehurst, J., Robertson, D., and Groom, J. Clinical correlates of sway in old age. Age and Ageing 1982; 11:1-10.

12. Buchner, D. M. Strategies to improve functional status in older adults by increasing skeletal muscle strength: Rationale and design. In: R. Weindruch and M. Ory (eds.), Frailty Reconsidered: Reducing Frailty and Fall-related Injuries in the Elderly. Springfield, Ill.: Charles C Thomas, in press.

13. Buchner, D. M., and Larson, E. B. Transfer bias and the association of cognitive impairment with falls. Journal of General Internal Medicine 1988; 3:254-259.

14. Buchner, D. M., and Larson, E. B. Falls and fractures in patients with Alzheimer's type dementia. Journal of the American Medical Association 1987; 257(11):1492-1495.

15. Campbell, A., Borrie, M. J., and Spears, G. F. Risk factors for falls in a community-based prospective study of people 70 years and older. Journal of Gerontology 1989; 44(4):112-117.

16. Campbell, A. J., Diep, C., Reinken, J., and McCosh, L. Factors predicting mortality in a total population sample of the elderly. Journal of Epidemiology and Community Health 1985; 39:337-342.

17. Campbell, A., Reinken, J., Allan, B., et al. Falls in old age: A study of frequency and related clinical factors. Age and Ageing 1981; 10:264-270.

18. Committee on Trauma Research, Commission on Life Sciences, National Research Council/ Institute of Medicine. Injury in America. Washington, D.C.: National Academy Press, 1985.

19. Consensus Development Panel. National Institutes of Health Consensus Development Conference statement: Geriatric assessment methods for clinical decision-making. Journal of the American Geriatrics Society 1988; 36:342-347.

20. Cummings, S. R., Black, D. M., Nevitt, M. C., et al. Appendicular bone density and age predict hip fracture in women. Journal of the American Medical Association, in press.

21. Cummings, S. R., and Nevitt, M. C. A hypothesis: The causes of hip fractures. Journal of Gerontology 1989; 44(4):107-111.

22. Cummings, S. R., Nevitt, M. C. and Kidd, S. Forgetting falls: The limited accuracy of recall of falls in the elderly. Journal of the American Geriatrics Society 1988; 36:613-616.

23. Evans, L. K., and Strumpf, N. E. Tying down the elderly: A review of the literature on physical restraint. Journal of the American Geriatrics Society 1989; 37:65-74.

24. Evans, W. J. Exercise and muscle function in the frail elderly. In: R. Weindruch and M. Ory (eds.), Frailty Reconsidered: Reducing Frailty and Fall-related Injuries in the Elderly. Springfield, Ill.: Charles C Thomas, in press.

25. Evans, W. J. Exercise and muscle metabolism in the elderly. In: M. L. Hutchinson and H. N. Munro (eds.), Nutrition and Aging. New York: Academic Press, 1986, pp. 179-191.

26. Fernie, G., Gryfe, C., Holliday, P., et al. The relationship of postural sway in standing to the incidence of falls in geriatric subjects. Age and Ageing 1981; 11:11-16.

27. Fife, D. Injuries and deaths among elderly persons. American Journal of Epidemiology 1987; 126(5):936-941.

28. Fife, D., and Barancik, J. I. Northeastern Ohio trauma study. III. Incidence of fractures. Annals of Emergency Medicine 1985; 14(3):244-248.

29. Fife, D., Barancik, J. I., and Chatterjee, M. S. Northeastern Ohio trauma study. II. Injury rates by age, sex and cause. American Journal of Public Health 1984; 74(5):473-478.

30. Foley, C. J., and Wolf-Klein, G. P. Prevention of falls in the geriatric patient with osteoporosis. In: Clinical Rheumatology in Practice. New York: LeJacq, 1986, pp. 136-143.

31. Gabell, A., Simons, M. A., and Nayak, U. S. L. Falls in the healthy elderly: Predisposing causes. Ergonomics 1985; 28(7):965-975.

32. Granek, E., Baker, S. P., Abbey, H., et al. Medications and diagnoses in relation to falls in a long-term care facility. Journal of the American Geriatrics Society 1987; 35:503-511.

33. Grazier, K. L., Holbrook, T. L., Kelsey, J. L., et al. The Frequency of Occurrence, Impact, and Cost of Musculoskeletal Conditions in the United States. Chicago: American Academy of Orthopedic Surgeons, 1984.

34. Green, L. W., Mullen, P. D., and Stainbrook, G. L. Programs to reduce drug errors in the elderly: Direct and indirect evidence from patient education. Journal of Geriatric Drug Therapy 1986; 1:3-18.

35. Grimby, G., and Saltin, B. Mini-review: The aging muscle. Clinical Physiology 1983; 3:209-218.

36. Gryfe, C., Amies, A., and Ashley, M. A longitudinal study of falls in an elderly population. I. Incidence and morbidity. Age and Ageing 1977; 6:201-210.

37. Guimaraes, R. M., and Isaacs, B. Characteristics of the gait in old people who fall. International Rehabilitation Medicine 1980; 2:177-180.

38. Guralnik, J. M., Branch, L. G., Cummings, S. R., and Curb, J. D. Physical performance measures in aging research. Journal on Gerontology 1989; 44(5):141-146.

39. Haddon, W., and Baker, S. Injury control. In: D. Clark and B. MacMahon (eds.), Preventive and Community Medicine. New York: Little, Brown and Co., 1981, pp. 109-140.

40. Hanlon, J. T., Andolsek, K. M., Clapp-Channing, N. E., et al. Drug prescribing in a family medicine residency program with a pharmacotherapeutics curriculum. Journal of Medical Education 1986; 61:64-67.

41. Harris, R. Fitness and the aging process. In: R. Harris (ed.), Guide to Fitness After Fifty. New York: Plenum Press, 1977.

42. Harris, S. S., Caspersen, C. J., DeFriese, G. H., and Estes, H., Jr. Physical activity counseling for healthy adults as a primary preventive intervention in the clinical setting. Journal of the American Medical Association 1989; 261(24):3590-3598.

43. Harris, T., and Kovar, M. G. National statistics on the functional status of older persons. In: R. Weindruch and M. Ory (eds.), Frailty Reconsidered: Reducing Frailty and Fall-related Injuries in the Elderly. Springfield, Ill.: Charles C Thomas, in press.

44. Havlik, R. J., Liu, B. M., Kovar, M. G., Suzman, R., Feldman, J. J., Harris, T., and Van Nostrand, J. Health Statistics on Older Persons, United States, 1986. DHHS Publ. No. (PHS) 87-1409. Hyattsville, Md.: National Center for Health Statistics, 1987.

45. Hecker, H. C., Haug, C. O., and Herndon, J. W. Treatment of vertiginous patients using Cawthorne's vestibular exercises. Laryngoscope 1974; 84:2065.

46. Hindmarsh, J. J., and Estes, E. H., Jr. Falls in older persons: Causes and interventions. Archives of Internal Medicine 1989; 149:2217-2222.
47. Hogue, C. Falls risk: The importance of psychosocial factors. In: R. Weindruch and M. Ory (eds.), Frailty Reconsidered: Reducing Frailty and Fall-related Injuries in the Elderly. Springfield, Ill.: Charles C Thomas, in press.
48. Hogue, C. Injury in late life. Part I. Epidemiology. Journal of the American Geriatrics Society 1982; 30(3):183-190.
49. Hongladarom, G. C., Miller, W. F., Jones, J. M., et al. Analysis of the Cause and Prevention of Injuries Attributed to Falls. Olympia, Wash.: Office of Environmental Health Programs, Department of Social and Health Services, 1977.
50. Hornbrook, M. C., Wingfield, D. J., Stevens, V. J., Hollis, J. F., and Greenlick, M. R. Behavioral and environmental antecedents of falls among the community dwelling elderly: What can we learn from self-report data? In: R. Weindruch and M. Ory (eds.), Frailty Reconsidered: Reducing Frailty and Fall-related Injuries in the Elderly. Springfield, Ill.: Charles C Thomas, in press.
51. Hui, S. L., Slemeda, C. W., and Johnston, C. C. Baseline measurement of bone mass predicts fracture in white women. Annals of Internal Medicine 1989; 111:355-361.
52. Imms, F., and Edholm, O. Studies of gait and mobility in the elderly. Age and Ageing 1981; 10:147-156.
53. Isaacs, B. Clinical and laboratory studies of falls in old people: Prospects for prevention. Clinics in Geriatric Medicine 1985; 1(3):513-524.
54. Isaacs, B. Are falls a manifestation of brain failure? Age and Ageing 1978; 7(Suppl.):97-111.
55. Janken, J. K., Reynolds, B. A., and Swiech, K. Patient falls in the acute care setting: Identifying risk factors. Nursing Research 1986; 35(4):215-219.
56. Kellogg International Work Group on the Prevention of Falls by the Elderly. The prevention of falls in later life. Danish Medical Bulletin 1987; 34(4):1-24.
57. Larsson, L., Grimby, G., and Karlsson, J. Muscle strength and speed of movement in relation to age and muscle morphology. Applied Physiology 1979; 46:451-456.
58. Larsson, L., and Karlsson, J. Isometric and dynamic endurance as a function of age and skeletal muscle characteristics. Acta Physiologica Scandinavica 1978; 104:129-136.
59. Lipsitz, L. A. Orthostatic hypotension in the elderly. New England Journal of Medicine 1989; 321:952-957.
60. Macdonald, J. B. The role of drugs in falls in the elderly. Clinics in Geriatric Medicine 1985; 1(3):621-636.
61. Mathias, S., Nayak, U. S. L., and Isaacs, B. Balance in elderly patients: The "get-up and go" test. Archives of Physical Medicine and Rehabilitation 1986; 67:387-389.
62. Mayo, N. E., Korner-Bitensky, N., Becker, R., and Georges, P. Predicting falls among patients in a rehabilitation hospital. Archives of Physical Medicine and Rehabilitation 1989; 68(3):139-146.
63. Melton, L. J. III, Kan, S. H., Wahner, H. W., and Riggs, B. L. Lifetime fracture risk: An approach to hip fracture risk assessment based on bone mineral density and age. Journal of Clinical Epidemiology 1988; 41(10):985-994.

64. Melton, L. J. III, and Cummings, S. R. Heterogeneity of age-related fractures: Implications for epidemiology. Bone and Mineral 1987; 2:321-331.
65. Melton, L. J. III, Wahner, H. W., Richelson, L. S., O'Fallon, W. M., and Riggs, B. L. Osteoporosis and the risk of hip fractures. American Journal of Epidemiology 1986; 124:254-261.
66. Melton, L. J. III, and Riggs, B. L. Risk factors for injury after a fall. Clinics in Geriatric Medicine 1985; 1(3):525-530.
67. Mion, L. C., Gregor, S., Buettner, M., Chwirchak, D., Lee, O., and Paras, W. Falls in the rehabilitation setting: Incidence and characteristics. Rehabilitation Nursing 1989; 14(1):17-22.
68. Morris, J. C., Rubin, E. H., Morris, E. J., and Mandel, S. A. Senile dementia of the Alzheimer's type: An important risk factor for serious falls. Journal of Gerontology 1987; 42:412-417.
69. Morse, J. M., Tylko, S. J., and Dixon, H. A. Characteristics of the fall-prone patient. Gerontologist 1987; 27(4):516-522.
70. Mossey, J. M. Social and psychologic factors related to falls among the elderly. Clinics in Geriatric Medicine 1985; 1(3):541-554.
71. Murray, M. P., Duthie, E. F., Jr., Gambert, S. R., et al. Age-related decline in knee muscle strength in normal women. Journal of Gerontology 1985; 40:275-280.
72. Nashner, L. M., Black, F. O., and Wall, C. Adaptation to altered support and visual conditions during stance: Patients with vestibular deficits. Journal of the Neurological Sciences 1982; 2:536-544.
73. National Center for Health Statistics. 1987 Summary: National Hospital Discharge Survey. Vital and Health Statistics, No. 159 (Rev.). Washington, D.C.: U.S. Government Printing Office, 1988.
74. National Center for Health Statistics. Current estimates from the National Health Interview Survey, United States, 1986. Vital and Health Statistics, Series 10, No. 164, pp. 16-52. Washington, D.C.: U.S. Government Printing Office, 1987.
75. Nevitt, M. C., Cummings, S. R., Kidd, S., and Black, D. Risk factors for recurrent nonsyncopal falls: A prospective study. Journal of the American Medical Association 1989; 261(18):2663-2668.
76. Nevitt, M. C. Ascertainment and description of falls. In: R. Weindruch and M. Ory (eds.), Frailty Reconsidered: Reducing Frailty and Fall-related Injuries in the Elderly. Springfield, Ill.: Charles C Thomas, in press.
77. Nickens, H. W. A review of factors affecting the occurrence and outcome of hip fracture, with special reference to psychosocial issues. Journal of the American Geriatric Society 1983; 31(3):166-170.
78. Obonyo, T., Drummond, M., and Isaacs, B. Domiciliary physiotherapy for old people who have fallen. International Rehabilitation Medicine 1984; 5:157-160.
79. Overstall, P., Exton-Smith, A., Imms, F., et al. Falls in the elderly related to postural imbalance. British Medicine Journal 1977; 1:261-264.
80. Owen, D. H. Maintaining posture and avoid tripping. Clinics in Geriatric Medicine 1985; 1(3):581-600.
81. Peck, W. A., Riggs, B. L., Bell, N. H., et al. Research directions in osteoporosis. American Journal of Medicine 1988; 84:275-282.
82. Perry, B. Falls among the elderly living in high-rise apartments. Journal of Family Practice 1982; 14(6):1069-1073.
83. Phillips, S., Fox, N., Jacobs, J., and Wright, W. E. The direct medical costs of

osteoporosis for American women aged 45 and older, 1986. Bone 1988; 9:271-279.

84. Prudham, D., and Evans, J. Factors associated with falls in the elderly: A community study. Age and Ageing 1981; 10:141-146.

85. Ray, W. A., and Griffin, M. R. Prescribed medications, falling, and fall-related injuries. In: R. Weindruch and M. Ory (eds.), Frailty Reconsidered: Reducing Frailty and Fall-related Injuries in the Elderly. Springfield, Ill.: Charles C Thomas, in press.

86. Ray, W. A., Griffin, M. R., Schaffner, W., et al. Psychotropic drug use and the risk of hip fracture. New England Journal of Medicine 1987; 316(7):363-369.

87. Ray, W. A., Blazer, D. G., Schaffner, W., et al. Reducing long-term diazepam prescribing in office practice: A controlled trial of educational visits. Journal of the American Medical Association 1986; 256:2536-2539.

88. Reinsch, S., and Tobis, J. S. Intervention strategies to optimize health behaviors and environment: A cognitive-behavioral approach. In: R. Weindruch and M. Ory (eds.), Frailty Reconsidered: Reducing Frailty and Fall-related Injuries in the Elderly. Springfield, Ill.: Charles C Thomas, in press.

89. Ring, C., Nayak, U. S. L., and Isaacs, B. Balance function in elderly people who have and who have not fallen. Archives of Physical Medicine and Rehabilitation 1988; 69:261-264.

90. Robbins, A. S., Rubenstein, L. Z., Josephson, K. R., Schulman, B. L., Osterweil, D., and Fine, G. Predictors of falls among elderly people: Results of two population-based studies. Archives of Internal Medicine 1989; 194:1628-1633.

91. Rodriguez, J. G., Sattin, R. W., DeVito, C. A., and Wingo, P. A. Developing an environmental hazards assessment instrument for falls among the elderly. In: R. Weindruch and M. Ory (eds.), Frailty Reconsidered: Reducing Frailty and Fall-related Injuries in the Elderly. Springfield, Ill.: Charles C Thomas, in press.

92. Rodriguez, J. G., Sattin, R. W., and Waxweiler, R. J. Incidence of hip fractures, United States, 1970-83. American Journal of Preventive Medicine 1989; 5(3)175-181.

93. Rubenstein, L. Z., Robbins, A. S., Schulman, B. L., Rosado, J., Osterweil, D., and Josephson, K. R. Falls and instability in the elderly. Journal of the American Geriatric Society 1988; 36(3):266-278.

94. Sattin, R. W., and Nevitt, M. C. Injuries in later life: Epidemiology and environmental aspects. In: Oxford Textbook of Geriatric Medicine. New York: Oxford University Press, in press.

95. Sattin, R. W., Rodriguez, J. G., DeVito, C. A., Lambert, D. A., and Stevens, J. A. The epidemiology of fall-related injuries among older persons. In: R. Weindruch and M. Ory (eds.), Frailty Reconsidered: Reducing Frailty and Fall-related Injuries in the Elderly. Springfield, Ill.: Charles C Thomas, in press.

96. Shumway-Cook, A., and Horak, F. B. Vestibular rehabilitation: An exercise approach to managing symptoms of vestibular dysfunction. Seminars in Hearing 1989; 10(2):196-209.

97. Sorock, G. S., and Shimkin, E. E. Benzodiazepine sedatives and the risk of falling in a community-dwelling elderly cohort. Archives of Internal Medicine 1988; 148:2411-2444.

98. Stelmach, C. E., Phillips, J., DiFabio, R. P., and Teasdale, N. Age, functional

postural reflexes, and voluntary sway. Journal of Gerontology 1989; 44(4):B100-B106.

99. Stelmach, C. E., and Worringham, C. J. Sensorimotor deficits related to postural stability: Implications for falling in the elderly. Clinics in Geriatric Medicine 1985; 1(3):679-694.

100. Tideiksaar, R. Preventing falls: Home hazard checklists to help older patients protect themselves. Geriatrics 1986; 41(5):26-28.

101. Tideiksaar, R., and Kay, A. D. What causes falls? A logical diagnostic procedure. Geriatrics 1986; 41(12):32-50.

102. Tinetti, M. E., and M. Speechley. Prevention of falls among the elderly. New England Journal of Medicine 1989; 320(16):1055-1059.

103. Tinetti, M. E., Speechley, M., and Ginter, S. F. Risk factors for falls among elderly persons living in the community. New England Journal of Medicine 1988; 319(26):1701-1707.

104. Tinetti, M. E. Performance-oriented assessment of mobility problems in the elderly. Journal of the American Geriatrics Society 1986; 34(2):119-126.

105. Tinetti, M. E., Williams, F. T., and Mayewski, R. A fall risk index for elderly patients based on number of chronic disabilities. American Journal of Medicine 1986; 80:429-434.

106. Tobis, J. S., and Reinsch, S. Postural instability in the elderly: Contributing factors and suggestions for rehabilitation. Critical Reviews in Physical Rehabilitation Medicine 1989; 1(2):59-65.

107. Tobis, J. S., Reinsch, S., Swanson, J. M., Byrd, M., and Scharf, T. Visual perception dominance of fallers among community-dwelling older adults. Journal of the American Geriatrics Society 1985; 33(5):330-333.

108. U.S. Preventive Services Task Force. Recommendations for physical exercise in primary prevention. Journal of the American Medical Association 1989; 261(24):3588-3589.

109. Vellas, B., Cayla, F., Bocquet, H., dePemille, F., and Albarede, J. L. Prospective study of restriction of activity in old people after falls. Age and Ageing 1987; 16:189-193.

110. Whipple, R. H., Wolfson, L. I., and Amerman, P. M. The relationship of knee and ankle weakness to falls in nursing home residents: An isokinetic study. Journal of the American Geriatrics Society 1987; 35:13-20.

111. Wickham, C., Cooper, C., Margetts, B. M., and Barker, D. J. P. Muscle strength, activity, housing and the risk of falls in elderly people. Age and Ageing 1989; 18:47-51.

112. Wild, D., Nayak, U., and Isaacs, B. How dangerous are falls in old people at home? British Medical Journal 1981; 282:266-268.

113. Wolfson, L. I., Whipple, R., and Amerman, P. Stressing the postural response: A quantitative method for resting balance. Journal of the American Geriatrics Society, 1986; 335:845-850.

114. Wolfson, L. I., Whipple, R., and Amerman, P. Gait and balance in the elderly: Two functional capacities that link sensory and motor ability to falls. Clinics in Geriatric Medicine 1985; 1(3):649-660.

115. Woollacott, M. H., Shumway-Cook, A., and Nashner, L. Postural reflexes and aging. In: J. A. Mortimer, F. J. Pirozzolo, and G. J. Maletta (eds.), The Aging Motor System. New York: Praeger Publishers, 1982.

116. Wyke, B. Cervical articular contributions to posture and gait: Their relations to senile disequilibrium. Age and Ageing 1979; 8:251-257.

117. Young, A., Stokes, M., and Crowe, M. Size and strength of the quadriceps muscles of old and young women. European Journal of Clinical Investigation 1984; 14:282-287.

A

Can Philosophy Cure
What Ails the Medical Model?

Arthur Caplan

CAN THE AMERICAN HEALTH CARE SYSTEM
COPE WITH SUCCESS?

It is often said that Americans enjoy the finest health care system in the world. The capacity of American hospitals to deliver the best emergency and acute medical care is impressive. The world turns to America for the latest breakthroughs in drugs, devices, surgical techniques, and diagnostic technologies.

Yet there is a great deal of ferment evident in current discussions of the future of health care in the United States. Third-party payers, both public and private, who find themselves buffeted by high prices and rapidly escalating costs are demanding some form of relief.[5] Providers who see their autonomy restricted by a growing torrent of regulations, paperwork, and bureaucratic demands are complaining vociferously about the red tape that is an all too familiar feature of health care in the United States.[17,39] Some estimates maintain that 30 cents out of every dollar spent on health care in the United States goes to administrative costs.

Despite the high cost of health care, many Americans still lack adequate access to necessary services. At least 30 million Americans have no health insurance. Tens of millions of Americans, knowing they lack adequate medical insurance, dread the prospect of prolonged hospitalization or extended stay in a nursing home. Many elderly Americans are forced to impoverish themselves to gain access to long-term care. The United States has a marvelous system for the treatment of life-threatening medical problems, but it is also spending far more on health care than any other comparable nation while obtaining less access for its citizens.

America is an aging society. More Americans, owing in part to medical and public health advances, live longer lives. Others who would have died as a consequence of injuries or devastating illnesses have been rescued by the remarkable power of health care technology. This success, however, has a large price tag. When the subject turns to how to pay for the costs of success, the elderly are often described not as beneficiaries but as problems. Treating the morbidity associated with old age or paying the price to add years of life are viewed by many public policymakers as the primary causes for the current high cost of health care and as major reasons for concern about the future costs of care. Others worry that, whatever the benefits, the elderly are consuming a disproportionate amount of social resources relative to the needs of other segments of our society.[32]

The costs associated with the medical care of the elderly have led many commentators to advocate public policies that would explicitly ration access to life-extending medical services on the basis of age.[1,6,15,27] They argue that the only way to cope with the price of success is to limit the access to services of those who are old. Those who argue for a public policy that legitimates the intentional denial of medical care to older Americans cement their case by noting that Americans are not willing to pay the bill for medical care. And the evolution of health care in the United States during the past few decades would, at least at first glance, seem to provide strong support for the position that controlling the cost of success requires the drawing of clear lines of ineligibility concerning access to health care somewhere in the second half of the human lifespan.

Despite the glaring inadequacies in existing public and private insurance programs, and despite consistent public opinion poll findings that Americans are willing to pay more to remedy gaps in their health insurance coverage, Americans have shown little inclination to reach into their wallets when actually asked to ante up funds in the form of taxes of one sort or another. Congress and the President decided in the fall of 1989 to retrench the Catastrophic Health Care Program, a package of benefits that include additional hospital days for acute illness and prescription drug coverage that had been added to Medicare with the strong support of then-President Ronald Reagan and the Congress in 1988. The cutbacks in the program resulted from strident protests on the part of some older Americans about the unfairness of the surtax that had been levied on high-income Medicare beneficiaries to pay for the program. The debacle of the Catastrophic Health Care Program illustrates that, where health care benefits are concerned, Americans are very sensitive to considerations of equity and fairness in evaluating the distribution of fiscal burdens. Moreover, although Americans say in response to opinion polls and surveys that they are willing to pay more for health care, in reality they may not do so, especially if the higher costs mean extending already widely held benefits only to those who lack them.

The problem of how to afford success where medicine is concerned threatens to become worse. New technologies, both diagnostic and therapeutic, continue to pour out of the medical research cornucopia at a rapid rate.[1,37] Success in the discovery and dissemination of acute care medical technology, progress funded in large measure by public monies administered through the National Institutes of Health since the end of the World War II, has brought in its wake all manner of burdensome fiscal consequences. Health policymakers in the United States must struggle to solve an ironic problem: how to ensure equitable, affordable access to the fruits of the many already or soon to be achieved successes that have resulted from the massive public investment in biomedical research.

One answer for coping with the problem of medical success is simply to pay the price. Yet the United States' experience with an effort to make the benefits of technology available to all in need has not been salutary. In 1972 the End Stage Renal Disease (ESRD) Program was added to Medicare. The program was explicitly created to obviate the need for doctors to make hard choices about who to dialyze when faced with the prospect of more persons dying from renal failure than could be treated, given the available limited supply of dialysis machines. Initially, the program's goal was to help 20,000 Americans with renal failure overcome the hurdles of money and a shortage of machines to gain access to a life-extending treatment. Expected costs were in the neighborhood of $220 million. Today, it costs the federal government well over $2.2 billion to provide various forms of renal substitution therapy to approximately 100,000 Americans.

This early experience with solving the problem of technological success by lowering the "green screen" to allow universal access to a necessary health care service has occupied a central place in the consciousness of U.S. health policymakers. The explosive cost of the ESRD Program for those with a relatively rare form of life-threatening organ failure bred a generation of cynics regarding the public financing of health care in the United States. The costly ESRD attempt to avoid the need to ration access to care by providing universal access to all who needed a "high-tech" solution to a chronic medical problem cast an exceedingly long shadow across subsequent efforts to extend federally subsidized access to other therapies.

Americans have and continue to believe in the power of technology to solve various kinds of social and medical problems. Nevertheless, without some form of public financing or cost-shifting format from the wealthy to the poor, the high cost of many technological interventions distorts the pattern of access of many Americans to the benefits of technologies. Access to various forms of organ and tissue transplantation, for example, is closely tied to the ability to pay for these procedures.[11] This link exists despite the fact that provision of the transplanted organs and tissues depends on a system of procurement that is deeply rooted in a public policy of voluntary generosity and altruism.[7,12,26] Moreover, the ability to pay determines access to most forms of organ and tissue transplantation, although in fact it is the public that has supported the proliferation of transplant centers throughout the United States through a variety of direct and indirect subsidies for organ and tissue procurement agencies, hospitals, pharmaceutical companies, and medical education.[26]

The problems generated by success seem intractable. Costs have escalated and are likely to grow in the immediate future as more technology is added to the already bulging confines of American hospitals. The society shows no inclination to foot the bill for providing ready access to expensive technology for all who might benefit from it. In addition, the demand for medical services will grow as American society ages. There would appear to be no other option but to begin the process of denying access to medical care to those who will incur the greatest costs—those in the second 50 years of the human lifespan.

But is rationing medical care for the elderly the only public policy response that is practical and plausible? Perhaps not, if those responsible for planning health policy are willing to critically examine the philosophical premises that generate this apparently intractable dilemma: how to pay for the growing demand for more acute care medical technology when those who might benefit from this care do not want to pay for it.

CAN PHILOSOPHY CURE OUR AILING HEALTH CARE SYSTEM?

The fact that the flow of new inventions and innovations shows no sign of abating whereas the percentage of older Americans continues to grow has led to a cacophony of Cassandra-like warnings about the inevitability of rationing access to health care.[1,14,25,27] Proposals concerning how to implement rationing range from suggestions that the elderly be deliberately shut out of the health care system at some point in their lifespan,[6] to calls for rationing by excluding those who are perceived as responsible for or causing their own medical problems[3,28,35] through the choice of unhealthy lifestyles, dangerous occupations, or imprudent conduct with respect to drugs, sex, or the operation of motor vehicles. As former Surgeon General C. Everett Koop has warned, there is a grave danger that our health care system will "replace forgiveness with retribution" when confronted with health problems that are seen as arising from self-inflicted harms of one sort or another.

Still others have called for the grudging recognition that the ability to pay must be allowed to determine who does and does not have access to health care.[24,25] Proponents of the efficiency of the marketplace argue that health care will and should be distributed, as are most other goods in the United States, by price. Indeed, the moral commitment to ensuring equal care for all regardless of the ability of the individual to pay, exhibited in the development of Medicaid and Medicare in the United States and in the creation of various sorts of national health insurance schemes in such other nations as Great Britain, Canada, the Federal Republic of Germany, Norway, and Sweden, is weakening in the face of rising costs on both sides of the Atlantic. Politicians and some health care leaders now regularly aver their allegiance to public policies that would permit variations in access to health care services on the basis of the ability to pay. Some even go so far as to advocate the exclusion of some groups (e.g., the poor, the elderly, the comatose, those responsible for their poor health through self-injury) from access to certain expensive services as the only option available to national, state, and local government.[23,24,25] The volume of calls for the deliberate and public rationing of health care is likely to increase in the years to come. The American population is "greying." Improvements throughout this century in sanitation, housing, the safety of the workplace, in making food, air, and water safer along with breakthroughs in the prevention and treatment of infectious diseases have permitted more Americans to live longer. Changes in health habits and advances in the treatment of serious injury and illness mean that the demand for health care services is likely to increase for the foreseeable future. One in nine Americans in 1980 was over the age of 65. By 2030 that number will have grown to one in five.[34] The fastest growing segment of American society is the group that has the greatest risk of needing public support for health care services as a result of chronic illness, disability, functional impairment, and the loss of the ability to live independently.[34]   It is likely that, as improvements in acute care technologies lead to declines in mortality, the number of Americans who have disabilities or restrictions of some sort in their cognitive or functional abilities will increase.

The ranks of those with chronic disability and impairment will grow, not only because Americans are living longer but also because acute care technologies can be used to rescue persons who once would have died from acute disease or trauma. For example, extremely premature babies who survive as a result of neonatal intensive care units, adults who survive traumatic injuries to the brain or spinal cord as a result of advances in neurosurgery and emergency and intensive care, or those who have been severely burned and maimed as a result of accidents may be rescued from the fatal consequences of their disease or impairment only to survive with chronic, irremediable conditions.[20] Their care will add to the already burgeoning health care bill and increase the already heated debate concerning how best to contain the costs of health care in the United States.

The incessant calls for cost containment that characterize health policy debates in the United States and most other technologically advanced societies have brought in their wake a highly fractious set of debates about the aims and goals that ought to be pursued by those who provide care. Some argue that we ought to focus more of our shrinking health care dollar on children and the young as the most prudent way to utilize scarce funds.[15,32]   Others argue that we need to place much more of an emphasis within the provision of health care on the prevention of disease, injury, and disability and far less on the treatment of acute medical problems.[19] Still others maintain that what is needed is a demedicalization of health care problems in favor of more "social" approaches to the difficulties that face those who are impaired or ill.[16,41] The volume of debate about where the emphasis should lie in setting the aims and goals of health care has increased in direct proportion to the perception that rationing is and will continue to be the only plausible response to the high costs of biomedical success.

What, it is reasonable to ask, can philosophical or ethical analysis possibly contribute to this bubbling maelstrom of health policy debate? If anything is true, it would appear that the time for abstract, ethereal philosophizing is long since past in the context of America's debate about health care. Most observers of the current and future health care scene see only crisis and recommend bold action as the only plausible response.[5,27,37] The quintessential American response to crisis is to stop talking and start acting. Philosophical rumination seems a luxury that cannot be tolerated, much less afforded, in both the figurative and literal sense of the term. What is required, the experts say, are bold policy initiatives, dynamic leadership, and decisive action.

Moreover, philosophy is relatively helpless in comparison with other voices who purvey fast solutions or quick fixes for the crisis in American health care. Philosophical analysis is rarely grounded in anything that even vaguely resembles quantification, and in matters in which budgets and values conflict, victory almost always goes to those who can adduce algorithms, mathematical models, and formulae.[2]

But the attitude that the time for careful reflection is past is wrong on any number of counts. Advances in the ability of the health care system to rescue lives that would once have been lost to acute injury and disease highlight the fact that we have had relatively little discussion, much less systematic efforts to obtain societal consensus, about the aims and goals appropriate to health care when life might be prolonged but with severe impairments. Both quantity and quality of life need to be examined where the cost of medical care is concerned.

Progress in the treatment of acute disease and success in affording longer lives to more Americans open the door to key philosophical questions about the response, both in terms of health care and public policy, that is appropriate in the face of a likely rise in the incidence of chronic illness, disability, and impairment.[20] The investment of public dollars both directly and indirectly in the health care system in the decades since World War II surely ought to give legitimacy to calls for public debate about the best public policy response to the crisis of cost currently besetting our health care system. Philosophizing about the goals appropriate to health care is not so much a luxury as a necessity forced on us by our society's success in preventing or treating a wide range of what were once lethal diseases such as polio, smallpox, tuberculosis, meningitis, diphtheria, typhoid, pneumonia, renal failure, and traumatic brain injuries.

There is a grave danger that the discussion of the enormous costs of health care and the need to do something—anything—to rein them in will lead our nation to enact policies that are at best indifferent to the norms and values that historically have been viewed as necessary to guide the provision of health care and to underpin the formulation of health policy.[33] Moreover, the stakes are so high where policy options such as publicly legitimized rationing by age or some other standard are concerned that it is hardly luxurious to try and subject the health care system to philosophical examination (in terms of its aims, goals, and purposes) before prescribing such bitter policy medicine. Those who insist that economics is the only voice worth listening to in a time of crisis must reckon with the fact that economists and cost-benefit analysts have had the ear of those in positions of power with respect to the American health care system for the past 25 years and have gotten just about nowhere in terms of either containing costs or broadening access to affordable health services. Abstruse philosophy may be just what the doctor ordered for a health care system desperately in need of cures.

Odd as it may seem, some of the debates about whether and how to reorient the health care system of the United States do hinge on the definitions that are given to the fundamental concepts of biomedicine. Our view of what to do in the face of disease, impairment, and illness is very much a function of what we take these concepts to mean. Philosophers are often accused of being entranced by the meaning of words. That may be so, but in disputes over the future direction of health care, words and their meanings matter because the means for reaching our goals in this area are inevitably determined by what we take those goals to be.

IF YOU ARE NOT SICK, ARE YOU HEALTHY?

It is odd that very few medical, nursing, or pharmacy textbooks spend very much time discussing the aims or goals of professionals in these fields. The relative silence over these matters in most texts and courses is a result of the fact that the aims of medicine or nursing may seem patently obvious and thus not in need of much explication or examination.

Doctors and nurses fight disease and repair injury. That is what people who go into a health profession expect to do. Someone with a fractured tibia, emphysema, or claustrophobia does not need to converse with a philosopher to discover what they want their health care provider to do. People who are injured or sick want help, and most Americans believe that workers in the health professions have, through their training, skills, and technological equipment, the best chance of providing it.

Nevertheless, although combating disease and injury surely occupy center stage among the universally acknowledged aims of health care, there are other goals that may be served as well. For example, are those in health care fields responsible for promoting or preserving health? If so, are they then responsible for treating any and all factors that may cause injury or disease including poverty, lack of housing, illiteracy, and poor sanitation? H. Jack Geiger, a physician at the Sophie Davis Medical Center of the City University of New York, often tells of the time he and other physicians who were working in the South in the early 1960s took it upon themselves to write prescriptions for food for poor people suffering from the effects of malnutrition. The constitution that created the World Health Organization speaks of health as a "state of complete physical, mental and social well-being."[40] If that is what health is, then it will be exceedingly difficult to define any boundaries, to set any limits as to the scope and responsibilities of health professions and the health care system if they are the social institutions responsible for the advancement and preservation of health.

Even if one presumes that it is clear what health care professionals ought to do to fight illness and repair injury, what does it mean to say that those who provide health care ought to preserve or promote health? Not only is the link tenuous between health and the various interventions that health care providers offer[28] (although only slightly less so in many cases than the links between health care interventions and the repair of illness and injury), it is not at all clear what health is. If someone is not sick or injured, are they then healthy? Or is health a state of physical or mental functioning that goes beyond the absence of illness, injury, and defect?[40] To put the point another way, is health merely the absence of disease, or is it a state with its own defining properties and characteristics?

Some health care providers—psychoanalysts, cosmetic surgeons, massage therapists, sports medicine specialists, electrologists, dieticians, physical therapists, and dermatologists among others—sometimes engage in activities that have as their goal a substantive conception of health that goes beyond the absence of disease. Optimal functioning or structure is the goal of at least some of the interventions carried out in our health care system.

Moreover, it is surely possible to detect differences in the health of those who are not diseased or sick. Marathon runners and philosophy professors rarely possess the same degree of aerobic health unless they are both runners and professors. Pediatricians and endocrinologists try to decide that children are short enough to merit the administration of growth hormone now suddenly available through biotechnological engineering. The use of drugs to enhance stature is another example of a case in which disease amelioration overlaps health promotion.

It seems reasonable to view health and disease not so much as opposites but as complementary concepts. Health has as its conceptual opposite "unhealthy" whereas the conceptual opposites of impairment and disease are not healthy but "unimpaired" and "not diseased." If these distinctions are embraced, it becomes possible to ask a very basic question that is not asked often enough in current arguments about the future direction of American health policy: Who is responsible for health, and who is responsible for disease? If health and disease are not conceptual opposites, then it may be appropriate for some parts of the health care system to pursue one or the other of these outcomes but not both; alternatively, it may be appropriate to assign the goal of the pursuit of health to persons who work outside the arena of treating disease and injury. If health and disease are understood to be conceptually distinct, it is an open question for public policymakers as to which is more worthy of social resources. Finally, if health and disease are seen as complementary although parallel concepts, it is reasonable to raise the question as to which groups, institutions, and professions are best suited to meet the aims of promoting health or combating disease.

The answer to the nature of the relationship that exists between health and disease requires an examination of the ways in which disease is defined. Although such an examination is without question a philosophical task, it is an inquiry with high stakes. Not only do answers to what ought to be done to promote and preserve health hinge on what we think the relationship is between health and disease; basic questions about who ought to be involved in the treatment of disease and what sorts of skills and training they should have also revolve around the answer that is given.

THE DEFINITION OF DISEASE AND IMPAIRMENT: NORMATIVISM VERSUS NONNORMATIVISM

The stakes involving definition of disease are, as many commentators have noted, quite high.[22,29] To label a state or condition a disease is to permit intervention by medical personnel, to grant access to various forms of social benefits, to confer a degree of exculpation from social roles and moral expectations, and to provide a framework for prophylactic, ameliorative, curative, and rehabilitative strategies. This fact has hardly been lost on members of certain groups whose physical condition or behavioral propensities leave them hovering near the borders of disease. Homosexuals, alcoholics, compulsive gamblers, drug addicts, the obese, hyperactive children, and many other such subpopulations have fought long and often heated battles either to gain entry into the realm of disease or to be demitted from the rolls of its subjects.

Debates about what is or is not a disease and the evolution of professional medical opinion as to whether a particular state or behavior is or is not an instance of disease appear to provide support for one prominent line of thought concerning the definition of disease: that it is an inherently value-laden concept. Those who subscribe to the view that definitions of disease must necessarily invoke references to norms or values are sometimes referred to as normativists. Normativists believe that mere descriptions of the status of the body or mind or the functional output of an organ system say nothing about whether someone is sick, impaired, or diseased. The only way to transform a biological fact into a disease ascription is by assessing the biological fact in the light of functions, capacities, abilities, and powers that are considered desirable or undesirable, useful or useless, good or bad.

Diseases, in the normativist view, do not wear their identities on their sleeves. What is a disease in one context or social setting may not be so in another. The only way to know whether a particular state or behavior is an instance of disease is to know what it is that an individual or group values and disvalues.[13,38]

If values are truly inextricable elements of any definition of disease, there would seem to be a number of direct implications for contemporary debates concerning the future direction of health policy. The identification of disease states as targets for either therapy or prevention will depend on the degree to which societal consensus exists about whether or not a particular state or condition is good or bad. The treatment of disease might involve the provision of therapy or rehabilitation to restore function or ameliorate impairment, but it could also involve an effort to shift social views as to the evaluation that lies behind labeling a particular condition as a disease. The cure for disease or impairment in the normativist model may be changing social attitudes rather than readjusting physiological variables.

The recognition that values play determinative roles in the classification of states and behaviors as diseases indicates that the locus of intervention in responding to or coping with disease can be quite broad, including social, economic, and even moral interventions as well as pharmacological, nursing, or surgical responses. Normativists see the determination of disease or impairment as subject to the analysis of both professionals and individuals because the values that determine well-being, unhappiness, or handicap are in the eye of the beholder and the professional.

There is, however, significant opposition to the view that disease is an inextricably value-laden concept. Some view disease either as a statistical concept that indicates only abnormality or deviation from a widely recognized paradigm of what is normal or as any state that is far removed from what is the general average for the population. Others argue that disease can be defined without reference to values because disease refers to those states or behaviors that place an organism at a biological disadvantage in terms of survival or reproduction.

The foremost exponent of nonnormativism in recent times is philosopher Christopher Boorse, who argues that disease is a value-free concept whose meaning is rooted in the notion of biological disadvantage. Boorse maintains that because evolution has designed organisms, including human beings, to perform certain functions in certain specific environments, disease exists whenever there is a deviation from what is normal, species-typical functioning.[4,13] Boorse believes that values play no role in the determination of disease and injury. Other nonnormativists believe that, although value judgments may enter into the definition of disease, they need not do so when a sufficient understanding of the functional design of particular attributes of the human mind and body is available.[36]

Nonnormativism, if valid, also has direct and important repercussions for health policy and health planning. The scope and range of health care would be limited to those aspects of human life about which sufficient knowledge exists concerning the functions of the human body or mind to form a baseline for the assessment of disease. Ignorance of the design of the human mind or body or about whether a particular behavior or trait is advantageous to survival or reproduction would make it impossible to say whether something is disease or an impairment. The locus of health care interventions would be skewed toward the individual rather than toward efforts to change the environment, culture, or social values, as would be possible under a normativist view, given that linking disease to dysfunction encourages efforts to restore function directly rather than indirectly. Biology and organic functioning are the centerpieces of intervention with a nonnormativist view of disease.

Authority over disease would lie mainly in the hands of those able to make functional analyses relative to their understanding of the ideal functional design of human beings. Judgments of illness, disease, and impairment would fall to professionals because it is quite possible under the nonnormativist view of disease for persons to be sick but to feel quite well. High blood pressure or incipient diabetes are examples of diseases in which only a functional analysis can reveal the presence of a problem that would otherwise not be recognized by someone without the appropriate education and training.

Before turning to the question of whether normativism or nonnormativism is a more defensible view of disease and the implications of the answer to that question for understanding the interconnections between the concepts of disease, injury, and health, it must be said that, rightly or wrongly, nonnormativism is the view that has dominated within health care and, indeed, among health policymakers during the latter half of the twentieth century. When doctors treat disease they do so in the belief that their goal is to restore dysfunction. The emphasis on the normal and the abnormal in medical diagnosis and rehabilitation is a reflection of the prominence of nonnormativism as the dominant philosophy of medicine. And the belief that the goal of medical research is to find cures for diseases, a goal that dominates much of the funding for health care in the United States, reflects an implicit nonnormativism concerning the nature of disease. Yet despite the importance of nonnormativism in health care and health policy, the term is not often used by those interested in analyzing the philosophical presumptions of modern health care. Instead, "medical model" or "biomedical model" is used to describe what is seen as the dominant paradigm or research strategy of medicine.[9,16,41]

The medical model is usually defined in sociological terms. In fact, the classic analysis of Talcott Parsons[30] provides the identifying criteria of the medical model: exculpation from responsibility, eligibility for benefits, assumption of the "sick role," and yielding of decision-making authority to medical professionals.

Nonnormativism is a key, albeit neglected, element of the medical model. The assumption of decision-making authority by medical professionals is directly linked to the presumption that doctors can objectively assess dysfunction and disorder and then act to restore proper functioning, whether it be mental or physical. Although critics of the medical model sometimes chafe at the paternalism that is an omnipresent aspect of institutionally based health care, they fail to see that paternalism is a direct result of the presumption of nonnormativism. If doctors do not need to make value judgments in diagnosing and treating illness and disease, and if they are able to detect facts about disease or impairment that are not and cannot be known to those who seek their care, then there is little to fear on the part of patients who cede authority to professionals as part of taking on the "sick role." The medical model is social, but it is also epistemological, and in large measure the social acceptance of the medical model rests on the acceptance of the value-neutrality inherent in the epistemology of nonnormativism, which dominates medicine.

OBJECTIVITY AND VALUES IN THE DEFINITION OF HEALTH AND DISEASE

The primary benefit associated with the elimination of values from the language of disease is that it would seem to insure objectivity for medical assessments of both disease and health. If disease is nothing more than the presence of dysfunction and if dysfunction can be understood solely in terms of the biological advantages or disadvantages conferred by various physical, emotional, or psychological states, then health care providers should be able to ascertain the presence of disease regardless of variations in the culture, setting, class, or values of those who seek their care. Moreover, if health is seen as the absence of disease, then to achieve health, medicine and the entire health care system should orient themselves toward the war against disease. This war, if fought in a value-free, nonnormativist framework, will have objective targets and objective criteria by which success or failure can be assessed.

The desire to keep the foundation of medicine objective does not issue solely from the desire to minimize the issue of relativism. It also serves to keep medicine in the domain of science. For if values are omnipresent in the diagnoses, treatments, and outcome evaluations that health care providers undertake, it would seem that the claims made by medicine, nursing, public health, pharmacy, and other health professions of being scientific might collapse. Objectivity of the sort required by the norms and methods of science would not be possible in the domain of health care.

Or would it? If the driving force to ban values from the realm of health care is to secure objectivity for the provision of services, then this may not be a sufficient reason for advocating nonnormativism.

The tacit assumption behind nonnormativism is that values and objectivity are not compatible, but this presumption is by no means self-evident. If values and objectivity are compatible, then the desire to defend the objectivity of medical interventions against the charges of cultural imperialism or professional hegemony and the desire to allow for the application of scientific methods and techniques in health care may be possible under a normativist view of health and disease. Those who believe that health and disease are unavoidably value-laden concepts can acknowledge the role played by values but defend the objectivity of the concepts through the pursuit of consensus and agreement regarding the nature and role of values in defining health and disease.

As argued above, a strong case can be made that health and disease are not conceptual opposites but, rather, parallel concepts. If that is true, then the values that enter into the definition of health may not and need not be the same as those that enter into the definition of disease. Moreover, it will not be necessary to secure universal assent to the validity of particular values in defining either health or disease to secure a measure of objectivity for these concepts. What will be needed is an open, frank admission that values are at play in defining both of these concepts and then a sincere effort to examine, analyze, and defend the legitimacy of certain values for both providers and recipients of health care.

If normativism is not prima facie incompatible with objectivity in health care, the road to understanding the proper aims and goals of health care and health policy lies in the open examination of the values that providers, clients, patients, and payers bring to the health care arena. Concretely, those who say that health care cannot be afforded in our society must be willing to ask whether the care that is being provided is really the care that is sought. Providers must be willing to ask whether the care they provide is the kind of care their patients or clients want. Do the goals of those providing services adequately overlap with those who receive the services?

There are many reasons to suspect that they do not. The medical system of the United States is strongly oriented toward acute medical care with the goals of saving life and extending life. The value of the sanctity of life plays a driving role in how health care services are organized, delivered, and reimbursed. Yet other values might and probably do dominate the beliefs of many Americans who receive care. Americans talk not only about the quantity of life that medicine permits them to enjoy but also the quality of life they can have. There are well-known dangers in invoking the language of quality of life in health policy discussions because such talk carries the connotation that some lives are more worthy than others. But quality of life language need not have any connection to moral or value judgments about the worthiness of an individual or to misguided efforts to rank the comparable worth of individual lives.[7]

Quality of life connotes a set of values that make life worthwhile. Although the values held by different Americans will not all be the same, there can be little doubt that many Americans assign great importance to the quality of life they can enjoy in evaluating the aims and worth of health care interventions. Americans want to know if they will be able to think, feel, interact with others, work, enjoy recreational activities, engage in sexual behaviors, have the ability to move about, evince their religious beliefs, enjoy a degree of independence in daily living, and make choices for themselves about the course of their own lives. Although there is no consensus about the priority that ought to be given these values and there is even less consensus about whether all or only some of these values constitute what it is that is referred to in expressions such as "quality of life," there should be little doubt that wide consensus exists as to the objective importance of quality of life in making normative evaluations of both health and disease.

THE DEMEDICALIZATION OF CHRONIC ILLNESS AND DISABILITY

If values play a·key role in the definitions of both health and disease in our society, then it is clear that our society has not made a sufficient effort to engage in a discussion regarding which values are important and how they should shape and inform the provision of health care in the United States. Arguments about the inability of society to afford the benefits of acute care medicine presume that the American people are only concerned with the benefits associated with acute care—primarily the preservation and extension of life. But if Americans expect more from their health care system than the extension of life, it becomes critically important to ask what values ought to guide the health care system in serving this broader view of the goal of health care.   Just as important, when medicine is not faced with the challenge of extending or preserving life but instead must confront the reality of chronic illness or impairment, there is a crucial need for the health care system to orient itself toward a goal other than that of extending life because there is no threat to life inherent in many chronic ailments and problems.

Norms and values are ineluctable elements of health care, and the driving value of health care in the American setting is the sanctity of life as exemplified in the efforts of acute care medicine to rescue lives imperiled by injury or disease. Yet chronic illness and impairment do not sit well with this view of health care. Whatever the goals of health care ought to be in confronting chronic illness and impairment, they cannot be only the extension or preservation of life.

Chronic illness and impairment, whether in the old or the young, require fresh thinking on the part of health care professionals. An acute care model is simply inadequate. A nonnormative interpretation of what the aims and goals of chronic care should be is simply impossible. In fact, an acute care model of health or disease is entirely inappropriate for responding to the problems of chronic illness and disease. The professional norms of acute care medicine[33] are simply out of touch with the needs and wants of those who must face impairment and disability along with their families and friends. The settings for delivering care, the training of those who provide it, and the modes of paying for it in the acute care model are based on a nonnormativist view of health and disease that is conceptually misleading and inimical to the interests of those whose problems stand outside this model of disease and health.

A concrete illustration of the clash between a medicalized view of disease and health and the reality of chronic illness and impairment among the elderly emerges if one examines long-term care institutions such as nursing homes. In a recent study conducted during the past year, an interdisciplinary team at the University of Minnesota surveyed the residents and health care providers of nursing homes in five states to ascertain what they believed were the major impediments to their autonomy raised by residency in a nursing home.[21] Only competent residents were included in the survey.

The presumption of those doing the survey was that both residents and staff would be keenly concerned with their ability to maintain individual control over their medical care in the nursing home. Surprisingly, very few residents and relatively few professional staff mentioned medical care as an area of much concern. The primary focus of residents was on the quality of life permitted by control over their diet, sleep patterns, visitor rights, mobility, access to a telephone, ability to keep personal possessions, and right to leave the nursing home grounds. Professional staff were concerned with the need to maintain order and protect the safety of those in their care.[21] One of the most surprising findings to emerge from the study was that the competent residents of nursing homes viewed their environment as their home. The professional staff, nurses, nurses' aides, and medical directors were much more likely to view the nursing home as a medical facility. Granted, there are many sick and demented persons who reside in nursing homes, but the fact remains that there appears to be a fundamental disagreement about the very nature of the nursing home that revolves around the relevance or irrelevance of the acute care model of disease and health for responding to the needs of competent nursing home residents.

There is a tendency to use the model of disease that has proven successful in ameliorating so many medical problems and extend it to other challenges confronting the health care system. But to simply adopt the norms and values of nonnormativism and promulgate them as the guiding principles for responding to disability, impairment, and the chronic ailments associated with aging is a mistake. Moreover, it is a costly mistake in that the extension of the acute care, nonnormativist model will require the expenditure of far more monies than may be necessary if consensus can be achieved on the norms that ought to guide the delivery of care and services for chronic illness and impairment.

THE DEMEDICALIZATION OF HEALTH

Nowhere are the limitations of a nonnormativist conception of disease more in evidence than in the domain of health. For if health is not merely the absence of disease, then it is necessary to ask what sorts of values should guide the attempt to ensure and maintain health. If health is really well-being or a state of personal satisfaction, health promotion will have relatively little in common with disease prevention.

To promote health among the elderly, a two-pronged strategy is required. Morbidity and impairment must be prevented, but it will also be necessary to enhance health. To achieve the latter, it will be necessary to have a better sense of what it is that those who have entered the second 50 years of their lifespan believe is important to their well-being and personal satisfaction.

We know relatively little about what it means to be healthy and old. We presume that it means to be free of sickness and physical maladies. Surely, these are important goals, but health promotion requires more than disease prevention. Health promotion may be a task that also requires more than medical efforts. Indeed, it would be both unfair and unwise to ask medicine to take on the task of making people healthy. In all likelihood, promoting health is a task that will require much broader social commitment and accountability.

REFERENCES

1. Aaron, H., and Schwartz, W. B. The Painful Prescription. Washington, D.C.: Brookings Institution, 1984.
2. Avorn, J. Medicine, health and the geriatric transformation. Daedalus 1986; 115:211-226.
3. Blank, R. Rationing Medicine. New York: Columbia University Press, 1987.
4. Boorse, C. What a theory of mental health should be. Philosophy of Science 1976; 44:542-573.
5. Califano, J. America's Health Care Revolution. New York: Random House, 1986.
6. Callahan, D. Setting Limits: Medical Goals in an Aging Society. New York: Simon and Schuster, 1987.
7. Caplan, A. Requests, gifts and obligations. Transplantation Proceedings 1986; 18(3):49-56.
8. Caplan, A. Imperiled newborns. Hastings Center Report 1987; 17:5-32.
9. Caplan, A. Is medical care the right prescription for chronic illness? In: S.

Sullivan and M. Lewin (eds.), Economics and Ethics of Long-Term Care and Disability. Washington, D.C.: American Enterprise Institute, 1988.

10. Caplan, A. The concepts of health and disease. In: R. Veatch (ed.), Medical Ethics. Boston: Jones and Bartlett, 1988.

11. Caplan, A. Problems in the policies and criteria used to allocate organs for transplantation in the United States. Transplantation Proceedings 1989; 21:3381-3387.

12. Caplan, A., and Bayer, R. Ethical, Legal and Policy Issues Pertaining to Solid Organ Procurement. Hastings-on-Hudson, N.Y.: Hastings Center/ Empire Blue Cross, 1985.

13. Caplan, A., Engelhardt, H. T., Jr., and McCartney, J. (eds.), Concepts of Health and Disease. Reading, Mass.: Addison-Wesley, 1981.

14. Churchill, L. R. Rationing Health Care in America. Notre Dame, Ind.: University of Notre Dame Press, 1987.

15. Daniels, N. Am I My Parent's Keeper? New York: Oxford, 1988.

16. Estes, C. L., and Binney, E. The biomedicalization of aging: Dangers and dilemmas. The Gerontologist 1989; 29:587-596.

17. Grument, G. W. Health care rationing through inconvenience. New England Journal of Medicine 1989; 321(9):607-611.

18. Himmelstein, D., and Woolhandler, S. Cost without benefit: Administrative waste in the U.S. health care. New England Journal of Medicine 1986; 314:441-445.

19. Jennett, B. High Technology Medicine: Benefits and Burdens. Oxford: Oxford University Press, 1986.

20. Jennings, B., Callahan, D., and Caplan, A. Ethical challenges of chronic illness. Hastings Center Report 1988; 18:1-16.

21. Kane, R., and Caplan, A. (eds.) Everyday Ethics: Resolving Dilemmas in Nursing Home Life. New York: Springer, 1989.

22. Kass, L. Regarding the end of medicine and the pursuit of health. The Public Interest 1975; 40:11-42.

23. Kears, D. J. Rationing Health Care: A Rational Approach. Oakland, Calif.: Alameda County HCSA, 1989.

24. Kirp, D. Ethical Triage. Working Paper No. 169. University of California, Berkeley, August 1989.

25. Kitzhaber, J. Discussion Paper—Oregon State Senate Bill 27. May 24:1-7.

26. Kluge, E. Designated organ donation: Private choice in social context. Hastings Center Report 1989; 19:10-16.

27. Lamm, R. Megatraumas. New York: Houghton Mifflin, 1985.

28. Menzel, P. Medical Costs, Moral Choices. New Haven, Conn.: Yale University Press, 1983.

29. Nagi, S. Appendix: Disability concepts revisited. In: Disability in America: A National Agenda for Prevention. Washington, D.C.: National Academy Press, in press.

30. Parsons, T. The definitions of health and illness in the light of American values and social structures. In: E. Jaco (ed.), Patients, Physicians and Illness. New York: Free Press, 1958, pp. 165-187.

31. Payer, L. Medicine and Culture. New York: Henry Holt, 1988.

32. Preston, S. Children and the elderly in the U.S. Scientific American 1984; 251:44-49.

33. Priester, R. Rethinking Medical Morality. Minneapolis, Minn.: Center for Biomedical Ethics, 1989.

34. Rice, D. P., and LaPlante, M. P. Chronic illness, disability, and increasing

longevity. In: S. Sullivan and M. E. Lewin (eds.), The Economics and Ethics of Long-Term Care and Disability. Washington, D.C.: American Enterprise Institute, 1988, pp. 9-55.

35. Rodmill, S., and Watt, A. The Politics of Health Education: Raising the Issues. London: Routledge and Kegan Paul, 1986.

36. Scadding, J. Health and disease: What can medicine do for philosophy? Journal of Medical Ethics 1988; 14:118-124.

37. Schwartz, W. B. Rationing health care. New York Times, October 17, 1989, p. 12.

38. Sedgwick, P. Illness—mental and otherwise. Hastings Center Report 1973; 1:19-40.

39. Woolhandler, S., and Himmelstein, D. A national health program: Northern light at the end of the tunnel. Journal of the American Medical Association 1989; 262:2136-2137.

40. World Health Organization. Constitution. Geneva: World Health Organization, 1946, Vol. 2, p. 100.

41. Zola, I. The medicalization of aging and disability. In: C. Mahoney, C. Estes, and J. Heumann (eds.), Toward a Unified Agenda. San Francisco: Institute for Health and Aging, University of California, 1986.

B

Looking for Order
Health Promotion, Disability Prevention, and the Disability Classification System of the World Health Organization

———————

Ted Miller

The field of health promotion and disability prevention (HPDP) is said to lack a conceptual base. Health policymakers complain that rational policy choices cannot be made until there is a widely accepted vocabulary of concepts that will define the conditions to be addressed and inform the development of methods for their modification. Yet a considerable dispute remains over how the conceptual base should be defined. The expectations that inform this dispute are linked to two interwoven sources: the politics between competing modes of health care inside HPDP and the desire to underpin our reasoning with foundational concepts and scientific method. The former topic is briefly discussed here and in Appendix A; the latter forms the core of this discussion, which will explore the philosophical tenets that run through the goals of the World Health Organization's (WHO) *International Classification of Impairments, Disabilities, and Handicaps*. The place to begin, however, is with the relationship between the difficulties of writing an authoritative synopsis and a classic dilemma associated with the act of generalization.

Reports that intend to summarize the state of knowledge and make policy recommendations in immature fields perform a delicate balancing act. A report that leans too heavily toward a definitive description or recommendations that favor a single method risk stifling future, productive approaches. In an effort to arrive at a definitive description of a disorganized field, the report may implicitly suggest that methods currently under development, which could be valuable in the future, are no longer worth pursuing. A report that goes too far in the opposite direction risks giving its readers the impression that problems requiring immediate attention admit of no policy solutions. Definitive results are seldom produced by an immature field, but the interim findings available may suggest approaches that are, at least, better than doing nothing.

This problem is not simply applicable to summaries of the knowledge of health care. All levels of generalization, from the most catholic conceptions to detailed assertions of scientific research, experience this difficulty. This discussion is concerned with the generalizations of a system for the classification of the consequences of disease. Exploring the expected and unexpected results of system building will illustrate the way generalizations create imbalances that are sometimes redressed.

From the seventeenth century onward, Western thinkers have had an ongoing preoccupation with the creation of systems—systems designed to define, refine, and reform philosophy, science, theology, manufacturing, and so forth. The impetus behind most systems is to find fundamental principles of order, simplicity, or efficiency where there seemed to be overwhelming disorder, complexity, or inefficiency. In short, the immediate goal of making things more systematic, with the ultimate goal of making them easier, has motivated many rigorous inquiries in the West.

Yet the rigor of such inquiry owes as much to provocation as it does to the desire for ease.[7] Systems, especially complex conceptual systems, can be understood as subtle but powerful forms of intellectual provocation. Our standards for accepting systems are generally low. They are, in fact, much lower than the standards most system designers set for themselves—and often much lower than the claims made by the system designer. With the expectation of being more reasonable, straightforward, and efficient in understanding, predicting, and controlling the systematized subject, Western man has been willing to accept the fundamental principles of systems. Such popular acceptance, however, can be a source of frustration for individuals who disagree with the principles of a given system and may eventually provoke a loud and forceful dissent, even as the system is perceived as a source of convenience by the majority of the public. When these dissents unmask discrepancies between the system's performance and its creator's claims, inquiries to judge the principles at the foundation of the system may be set in motion. Systems therefore may unintentionally balance the force of their generalizations by provoking their detractors to expose their deficiencies.

As noted earlier in the report the committee has chosen to use WHO's *International Classification of Impairment, Disability, and Handicaps*[16] system for classifying the consequences of disease. The WHO system embraces two unrealized goals: to ease the flow of information about the consequences of disease through a widely acceptable set of standard terms and to guide clinical decision makers to interventions that go beyond the cognizance of the traditional clinical search for causes, signs, symptoms, and cures. Why haven't these goals been realized before? Disability, after all, has been the subject of health and public policy for years. One reason is the dissonance between different factions within the health care communities over the purposes of health care.

THE GOAL OF HEALTH CARE

The difficulties of arriving at an acceptable conceptual base are in part due to a lack of consensus over the goals of HPDP. Disagreements within the health care community can be traced roughly to the philosophies of two groups: advocates of an acute care model and those who follow more social modes of health care. The latter comprises several subgroups that find their goals in the traditions of the American public health movement, preventive medicine, rehabilitation, and long-term care. Which of the various health care communities that stake their claim in this field have the most influence in laying its foundations, and what might these foundations look like?

The ends of acute and social modes of health care overlap at many points, however they diverge in their broader goals. The boundaries that define the goals of acute care traditionally expand very slowly and cautiously. The boundaries that enclose the ends and means of social modes of care have gone well beyond acute care into social ills and broader notions of prevention and rehabilitation. The differences among these groups can be gauged by contrasting their criteria for successful care. Acute care givers are oriented toward curing their patients, where "curing" has often meant attacks on hidden, yet physically determined causes of disease.[3,4,15] The social groups succeed when their patients have been assisted or have learned to cope with their difficulties, or when society takes action to accommodate their needs.

To understand the dynamics of the disagreement between these groups, it is also necessary to know the status of the groups relative to each other. Acute care medicine has most heavily influenced the orientation and goals of American health care. A sign of its great weight is the common and automatic association between health care in general and acute care. Indeed, the public's image of health care begins with acute care medicine. The majority of services covered by Medicare are acute care interventions.[11] In a new journal that focuses exclusively on aging and health—and not, implicitly, aging and disease—an article complains of the prevalence of acute care thinking in health care for older patients.[9]

The automatic association also exists in theories of health care. The majority of bioethical questions begin with the assumption of acute care situations.[5] This assumption is also reflected in the ongoing debate over how to define and care for the mentally ill. For example, Siegler and Osmond argued for an approach to mental illness that follows a "medical model" in which acute care is taken as the heuristic ideal. (Since that time, "medical model" has become much broader and less determinate owing both to critics of Siegler and Osmond's philosophy of psychiatry and to other authors who have chosen to define the model in their own terms.)

Today, however, health care policymakers are now being asked to develop a world view that will suit the needs of an aging population, and there is a growing belief that the acute care understanding is not sufficient.[16] Health care analysts are convinced that the increased longevity and growing proportions of the elderly will be accompanied by significantly greater demands for health care for the chronically ill and disabled.[10] It is in the face of these quantitative changes in the population and the qualitative changes in their health service needs that alternatives to the acute care framework are being proposed. Health promotion and disability prevention must be counted among these alternatives, and the WHO system provides a conceptual structure that informs its goals, but each is still upstaged by acute care thinking.

THE PHILOSOPHY OF HEALTH CARE

Our notions of how health care research ought to behave as a body of inquiry are influenced by a great and muddled conceptual complex. Within this complex, which philosophic traditions inform our expectations for a system designed to classify the consequences of disease?

The professed motive behind WHO's *International Classification of Impairments, Disabilities, and Handicaps* is the desire to bridge the "ability-capability gap, the discrepancy between what health care systems can do and what they might do." The classification system is designed to serve this end by improving the quality of our conceptions of the consequences of disease. This goal, and the means of achieving it, show signs of the influence of Descartes.

The first principle of Cartesian inquiry is to be skeptical. The root of this skepticism is a very rigid dualism between the thinking mind and the physical world outside. How then are we aware of things outside the mind? The outside world is presented to the mind through our senses. The world outside the thinking mind cannot penetrate the barrier between mind and the corporeal but is *represented* to it—as if making retinal images on the "eye of the mind." Descartes' argument can be seen as reasoning with the assumption of two different worlds, one inside the mind and a world outside that makes images supplied by the senses on the internal eye.[14]

The senses, however, are unreliable, and this is why Cartesian dualism gives rise to a persistent skepticism. The knower can never be sure of the existence or accuracy of the images of the outside world. The senses are doubted because the images they present of the outside world can also be presented by the mind to itself, as in dreams. This capacity of the mind raises the possibility that representations of the outside world by the senses are distorted or fictitious. The goal of Cartesian inquiry is to ensure that this sort of self-deception will not occur. Put another way, the Cartesian intellect begins with the assumption that all representations of the outside world are dubious until proven to be true.

These assumptions prompt a search for criteria with which to identify truths. According to Descartes, the truth about the outside world is represented before the mind's eye when it is clear and distinct or when it is indubitable. As examples, Descartes provides the a priori knowledge of the existence of a supreme being, of ourselves, and of the most basic elements of matter. According to Descartes, then, the means of obtaining knowledge lie in the recognition of clear, distinct, and indubitable representations. The new task for inquiry is thus to discover the universally true qualities of the representations of the outside world by searching out the clear, the distinct, and the indubitable.

The implications of Cartesian dualism are faintly echoed in the goals of the classification of impairments, disabilities, and handicaps. One of WHO's purposes in creating these categories was to provide more relevant information about the consequences of disease (and the health care systems that deliver care for people suffering from these consequences). Yet this statement may lead us to ask, "relevant to what?" Ultimately, the answer is "relevant to the way these things really are." Implicit in this notion is the Cartesian suspicion that things as they are represented to the mind of the policymaker are perhaps a distorted or fictitious version of the truth.

The fear is that a policymaker's decisions, lacking a clear and distinct picture of the consequences of disease, will be made subjectively. That is, the decisions might have been made differently had another person—with his or her own self-deceptive perceptions—been charged with the task of deciding. The Cartesian intellect seeks objective decisions—that is, decisions that do not depend on untrustworthy perceptions but on qualities of the object agreed upon by all to be truthful.

Other important goals of Cartesian inquiry also inform the WHO system. It is not simply skepticism that is embraced but the need to coherently frame and organize the phenomena of disability. The second and third principles of Cartesian inquiry are to "divide each problem into as many parts as is feasible, and was requisite for a better solution," and "to direct thoughts in an orderly way; beginning with the simplest objects, those most apt to be known, and ascending little by little, in steps as it were, to the knowledge of the complex." This procedure for attaining knowledge carries with it the notion that the complexities of nature must be broken down into their separate elements before clear and distinct images of the world can be represented to the mind. Once this elemental level has been reached, the third step instructs one to reconstruct the subject into a coherent order.

It is clear that the order of the WHO system is not a fresh reconstruction of physical, psychological, and social domains. Rather, the system's creators have deliberately attempted to accommodate the framework of the system to long-standing methods for disease classification.[16] Through the system, they have borrowed their terminology from established health care sciences. Thus, the WHO system cannot be said to be completely Cartesian in its approach, although it shows signs of the Cartesian spirit of organization. The consequences of disease are divided into very small components; impairment, disability, and handicap are only the beginning of the organizational structure. Each of these major divisions is further divided into subcategories and, in the case of disabilities and impairments, multiple categories beneath these.

Because the study of the consequences of disease is only beginning to attempt a systematic, Cartesian approach to this problem, the philosophical influences involved are difficult to characterize. However, these influences have been operating for years in the neighboring effort to define the concept of disease. Perhaps the development of concepts of the consequences of disease will follow a similar path.

Most analysts agree that the Cartesian influence has been instrumental in developing systematic means of discovering, explaining, predicting, and controlling somatic illness. Among those who view medicine from philosophical perspectives, however, there is a consensus that the Cartesian influence has brought a reductionist spirit to medicine and psychology.[6,12,13] Indeed, it is tempting to compare Descartes' own attempt to reduce man to medical-mechanical theory with attempts to ground all human behavior in the laws of chemical reactions. The preoccupation with diagnosis over cure has been a sign of some of the dangers of the Cartesian influence; others have complained that medicine has demonstrated a preoccupation with pursuing single and elemental causes.[13] In the introduction to the WHO classification system manual,[16] its authors indicate their sensitivity to the reductionist problems of the acute care framework and emphasize the incompatibility of the inherent goals of the conceptual order of WHO's *International Classification of Disease* and the goals of the health care delivery systems designed to address the consequences of disease. It would have been strange if the creators of the WHO system had not applied a similar skepticism toward their own project, but is it possible to specify the conditions under which the consequences of disease have been adequately covered?

Thomas Kuhn's *The Structure of Scientific Revolutions*[8] provides useful preliminary insights that may be directed toward answering this question. The paradigmatic theory of scientific revolution is an interpretation of the history of mature sciences, for example, physics, chemistry, or optics. These fields are said to operate under an overarching theory that provides a coherent framework for explaining a previously muddled set of facts. Once such a theory, or paradigm, is established, the activity of mature sciences—what Kuhn calls "normal science"—consists of "mopping up" facts into the paradigm's framework.

Mopping up in normal science is Kuhn's metaphor for analytically fitting the details accounted for by the paradigm into theoretical constructs that are a part of the overall theory or that are at least compatible with the paradigmatic world view. Another way of expressing this relationship is through the notion of articulation. The paradigm is said to supply the scientific field with a stock of partially *unarticulated* theories and phenomena. The mopping up— or the practice of fitting details to theory—can be understood as the articulation of the paradigm on the level of minutiae.

Health care is an art, but it is an art that borrows from and that frequently strives to emulate science. It is when health care borrows scientific theory and method to achieve its ends or when these means are subordinated to the ends[3,15] (or vice versa) that Kuhn's analysis is most helpful. The various theories of health, disease, assessment, and disability—the majority of which are hidden in the implicit assumptions of journal articles and medical textbooks— begin with overarching concepts that attempt to coherently frame health phenomena. The following Kuhnian description of normal science applies equally well to these specialized health care research projects: "we shall want finally to describe that research as a strenuous and devoted attempt to force nature into conceptual boxes."

Thus, it would seem that the consequences of disease have been adequately covered when there is a coherent and widely accepted system to describe them. Yet we must ask if there is not a price to be paid in employing reductive thinking and conceptually rigid paradigms. Do our efforts to systematically organize information concerning disabilities force us to conceptualize disabilities in a way that is suited to the epistomological standards of health care science but inimical to the needs of people with disabilities?

This discussion does not end with a true conclusion; rather, it is a kind of prelude to a question that should be taken seriously by those health professionals who now express interest in disability. To the extent that disability classification systems attempt to organize scientific knowledge, there will be an inevitable squeezing and twisting of subjects to suit the order of a system struggling to represent nature clearly and distinctly. Yet disability is a concept that makes sense only in the context of ability, and ability has an endless capacity for defying coherent description. No sooner do we attempt to determine the essence of an individual's abilities than they escape the confines of our determination. Ability makes us unique. Thus, the question that must be asked is this: What is lost when we struggle to force the long-term disabilities and abilities of individuals into conceptual boxes?

REFERENCES

1. Caplan, A. Is medical care the right prescription for chronic illness? In: S. Sullivan and M. E. Lewin (eds.), The Economics and Ethics of Long-Term Care and Disability. Lanham, Md.: University Press of America, 1988, pp. 73-89.

2. Descartes, R. Descartes: Philosophical Writings, trans. E. Anscombe and P. T. Geach. Indianapolis: Bobbs-Merrill, 1971.

3. Engelhardt, T. Causal accounts in medicine: A commentary on Stephan Toulmin. In: E. Cassell and M. Siegler (eds.), Changing Values in Medicine: Papers Delivered at the Conference on Changing Values in Medicine, USA. Lanham, Md.: University Publications of America, Inc., 1979.

4. Engelhardt, T. The concepts of health and disease. In: A. L. Caplan, T. H. Engelhardt, and J. J. McCartney (eds.), Concepts of Health and Disease: Interdisciplinary Perspectives. Reading, Mass.: Addison-Wesley, 1981.

5. Jennings, B., Callahan, D., and A. Caplan. Ethical challenges of chronic illness. The Hastings Center Report 1988; 18(1):1-16.

6. Kass, L. Towards a More Natural Kind of Science. New York: MacMillan, 1985.

7. Kierkegaard, S. Concluding Unscientific Postscript, trans. D. Swenson and W. Lowrie. Princeton: Princeton University Press, 1971.

8. Kuhn, T. The Structure of Scientific Revolutions. Chicago: University of Chicago Press, 1970.

9. Levkoff, S., and Wetle, T. Clinical decision making in the care of the aged. Journal of Aging and Health 1989; 1(1):83-101.

10. Manton, K. Epidemiological, demographic, and social correlates of disability among the elderly. Milbank Quarterly 1989, 67(Suppl. 2, No. 1):13-58.

11. Medicare Coverage Issues Manual. Health Care Financing Administration Publ. 6 through Rev. 33 (PB89-955099). Washington, D.C.: U.S. Department of Health and Human Services, 1988.

12. Pellegrino, E. Humanism and the Physician. Knoxville: University of Tennessee Press, 1979.

13. Pellegrino, E., and D. C. Thomasma. A Philosophical Basis of Medical Practice: Towards a Philosophy and Ethic of the Healing Professions. Oxford: Oxford University Press, 1981.

14. Rorty, R. Philosophy and the Mirror of Nature. Princeton: Princeton University Press, 1979.

15. Toulmin, S. Causation and the locus of medical intervention. In: E. Cassell and M. Siegler (eds.), Changing Values in Medicine: Papers Delivered at the Conference on Changing Values in Medicine, USA. Lanham, Md.: University Publications of America, Inc., 1979.

16. World Health Organization. International Classification of Impairments, Disabilities, and Handicaps. Geneva: World Health Organization, 1985.

Index